# THE INVINCIBLE IRON MAN
## THE FIVE NIGHTMARES

WRITER: **MATT FRACTION** · ARTIST: **SALVADOR LARROCA**
COLORS: **FRANK D'ARMATA & STEPHANE PERU**
LETTERS: **CHRIS ELIOPOULOS**
ASSISTANT EDITOR: **ALEJANDRO ARBONA**
EDITOR: **WARREN SIMONS**

### DEDICATED TO STEPHANE PERU (1981-2008)

COLLECTION EDITOR: **JENNIFER GRÜNWALD**
EDITORIAL ASSISTANT: **ALEX STARBUCK**
ASSISTANT EDITORS: **CORY LEVINE & JOHN DENNING**
EDITOR, SPECIAL PROJECTS: **MARK D. BEAZLEY**
SENIOR EDITOR, SPECIAL PROJECTS: **JEFF YOUNGQUIST**
SENIOR VICE PRESIDENT OF SALES: **DAVID GABRIEL**
BOOK DESIGNER: **RODOLFO MURAGUCHI**

EDITOR IN CHIEF: **JOE QUESADA**
PUBLISHER: **DAN BUCKLEY**

**INVINCIBLE IRON MAN VOL. 1: THE FIVE NIGHTMARES.** Contains material originally published in magazine form as INVINCIBLE IRON MAN #1-7. First printing 2008. ISBN# 978-0-7851-3460-2. Published by MARVEL PUBLISHING, INC., a subsidiary of MARVEL ENTERTAINMENT, INC. OFFICE OF PUBLICATION: 417 5th Avenue, New York, NY 10016. Copyright © 2008 Marvel Characters, Inc. All rights reserved. $24.99 per copy in the U.S. and $26.50 in Canada (GST #R127032852); Canadian Agreement #40668537. All characters featured in this issue and the distinctive names and likenesses thereof, and all related indicia are trademarks of Marvel Characters, Inc. No similarity between any of the names, characters, persons, and/or institutions in this magazine with those of any living or dead person or institution is intended, and any such similarity which may exist is purely coincidental. **Printed in the U.S.A.** ALAN FINE, CEO Marvel Toys & Publishing Divisions and CMO Marvel Characters, Inc.; DAVID GABRIEL, SVP of Publishing Sales & Circulation; DAVID BOGART, SVP of Business Affairs & Talent Management; MICHAEL PASCIULLO, VP of Merchandising & Communications; JIM O'KEEFE, VP of Operations & Logistics; DAN CARR, Executive Director of Publishing Technology; JUSTIN F. GABRIE, Director of Editorial Operations; SUSAN CRESPI, Editorial Operations Manager; OMAR OTIEKU, Production Manager; STAN LEE, Chairman Emeritus. For information regarding advertising in Marvel Comics or on Marvel.com, please contact Mitch Dane, Advertising Director, at mdane@marvel.com. For Marvel subscription inquiries, please call 800-217-9158.

10 9 8 7 6 5 4 3 2 1

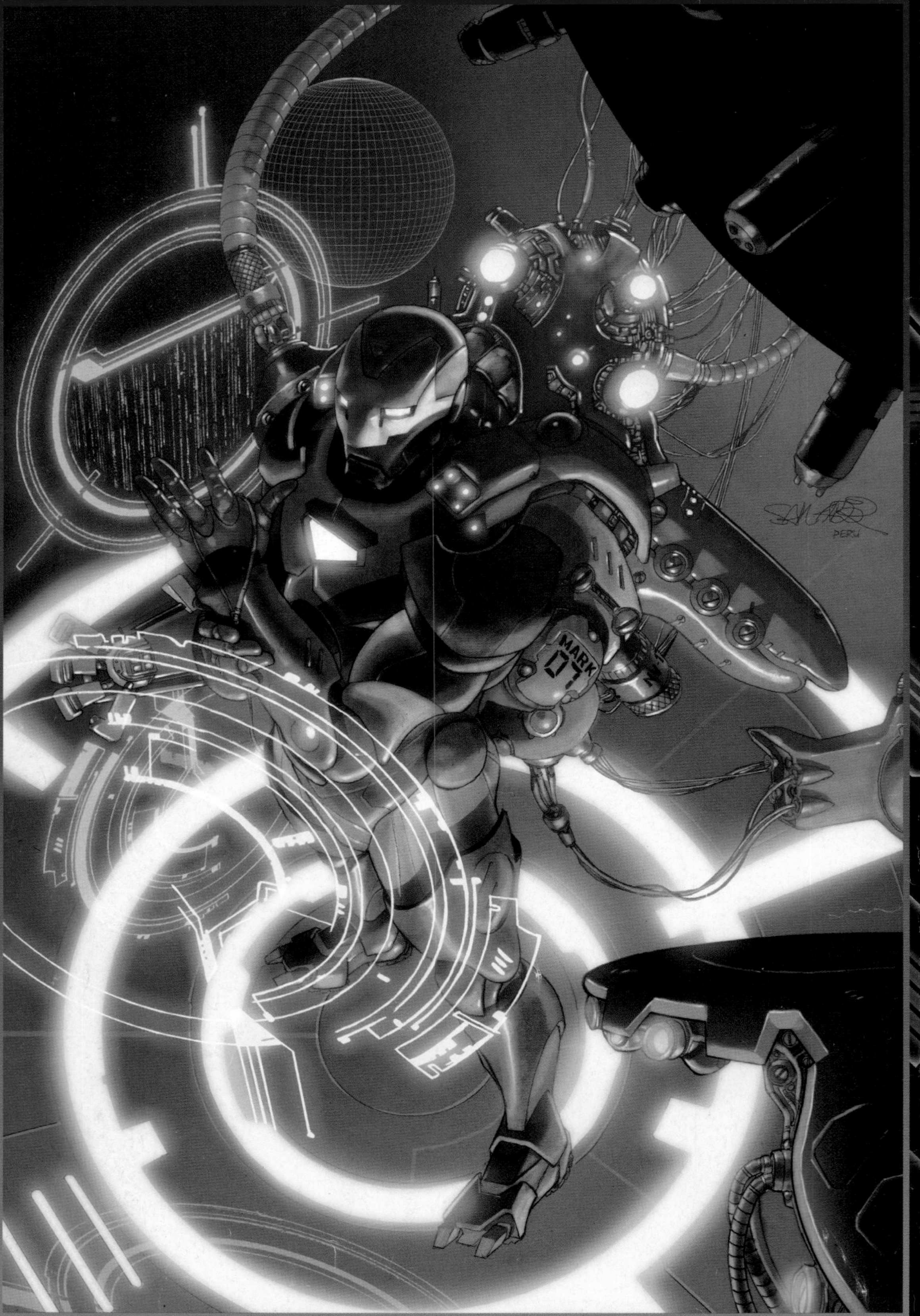
MARK
07

# 1

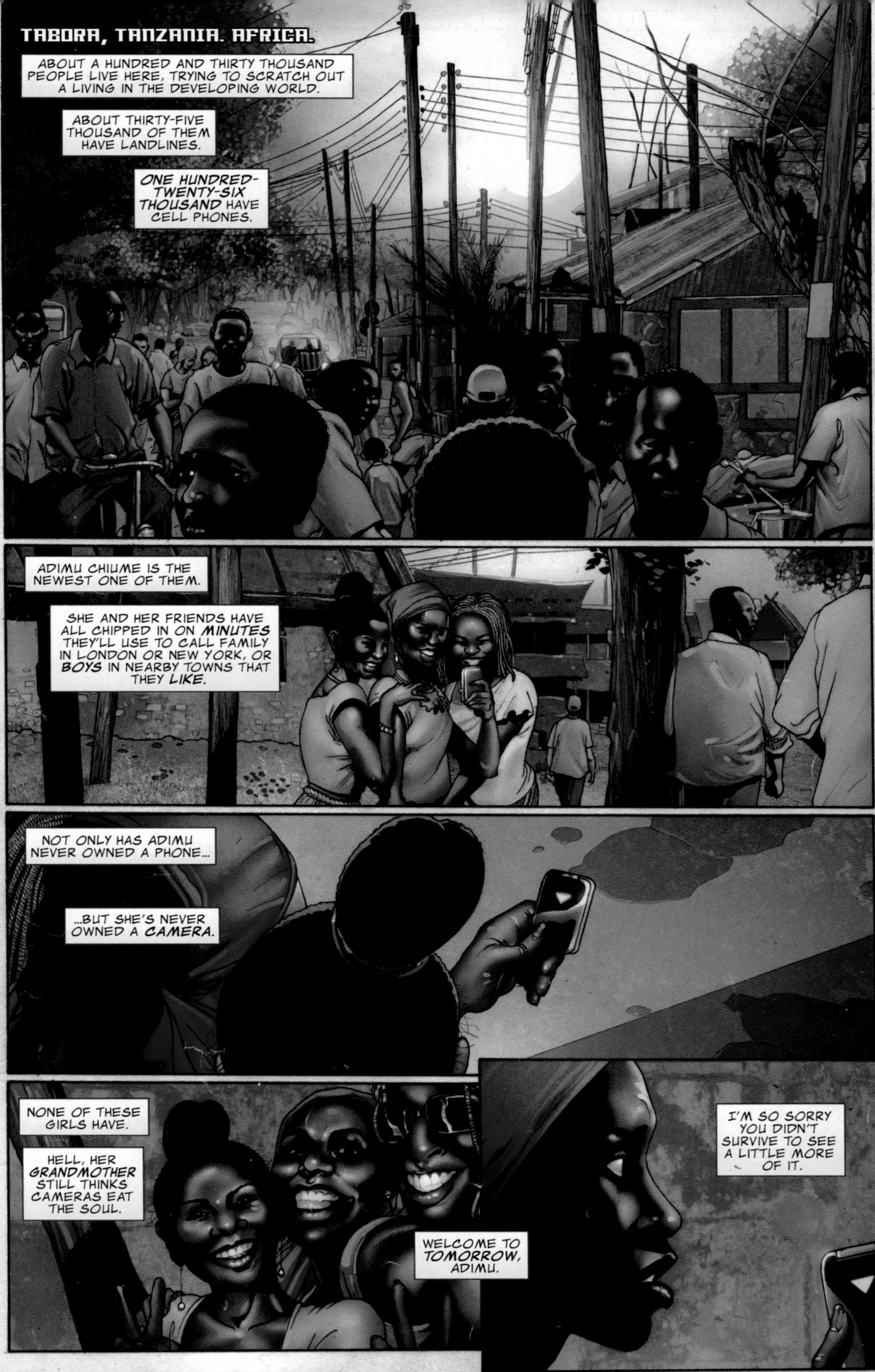
TABORA, TANZANIA. AFRICA.
ABOUT A HUNDRED AND THIRTY THOUSAND PEOPLE LIVE HERE, TRYING TO SCRATCH OUT A LIVING IN THE DEVELOPING WORLD.
ABOUT THIRTY-FIVE THOUSAND OF THEM HAVE LANDLINES.
ONE HUNDRED-TWENTY-SIX THOUSAND HAVE CELL PHONES.
ADIMU CHIUME IS THE NEWEST ONE OF THEM.
SHE AND HER FRIENDS HAVE ALL CHIPPED IN ON MINUTES THEY'LL USE TO CALL FAMILY IN LONDON OR NEW YORK, OR BOYS IN NEARBY TOWNS THAT THEY LIKE.
NOT ONLY HAS ADIMU NEVER OWNED A PHONE...
...BUT SHE'S NEVER OWNED A CAMERA.
NONE OF THESE GIRLS HAVE.
HELL, HER GRANDMOTHER STILL THINKS CAMERAS EAT THE SOUL.
WELCOME TO TOMORROW, ADIMU.
I'M SO SORRY YOU DIDN'T SURVIVE TO SEE A LITTLE MORE OF IT.

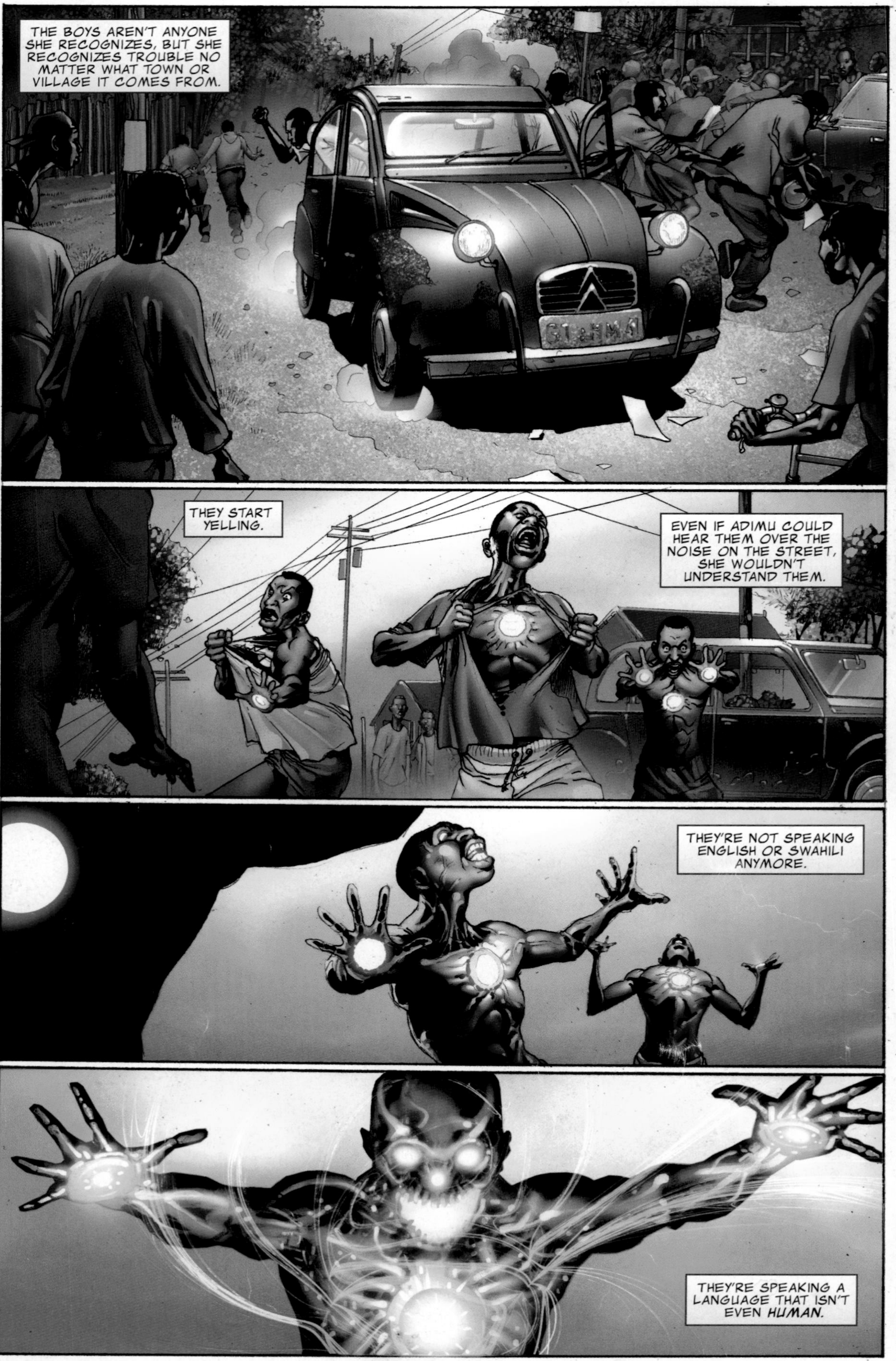
THE BOYS AREN'T ANYONE SHE RECOGNIZES, BUT SHE RECOGNIZES TROUBLE NO MATTER WHAT TOWN OR VILLAGE IT COMES FROM.
THEY START YELLING.
EVEN IF ADIMU COULD HEAR THEM OVER THE NOISE ON THE STREET, SHE WOULDN'T UNDERSTAND THEM.
THEY'RE NOT SPEAKING ENGLISH OR SWAHILI ANYMORE.
THEY'RE SPEAKING A LANGUAGE THAT ISN'T EVEN *HUMAN.*

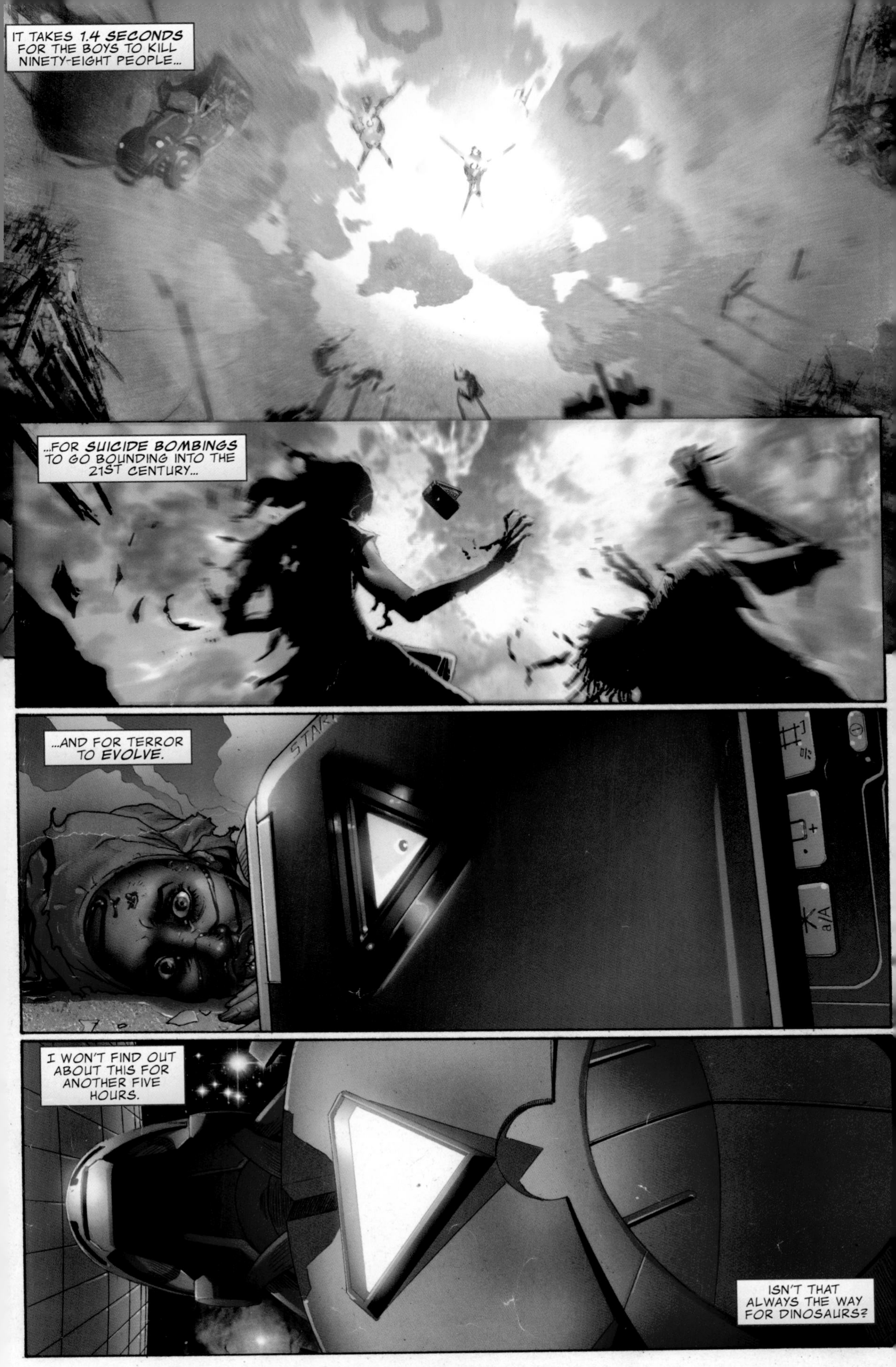
IT TAKES 1.4 SECONDS FOR THE BOYS TO KILL NINETY-EIGHT PEOPLE...
...FOR SUICIDE BOMBINGS TO GO BOUNDING INTO THE 21ST CENTURY...
...AND FOR TERROR TO EVOLVE.
I WON'T FIND OUT ABOUT THIS FOR ANOTHER FIVE HOURS.
ISN'T THAT ALWAYS THE WAY FOR DINOSAURS?

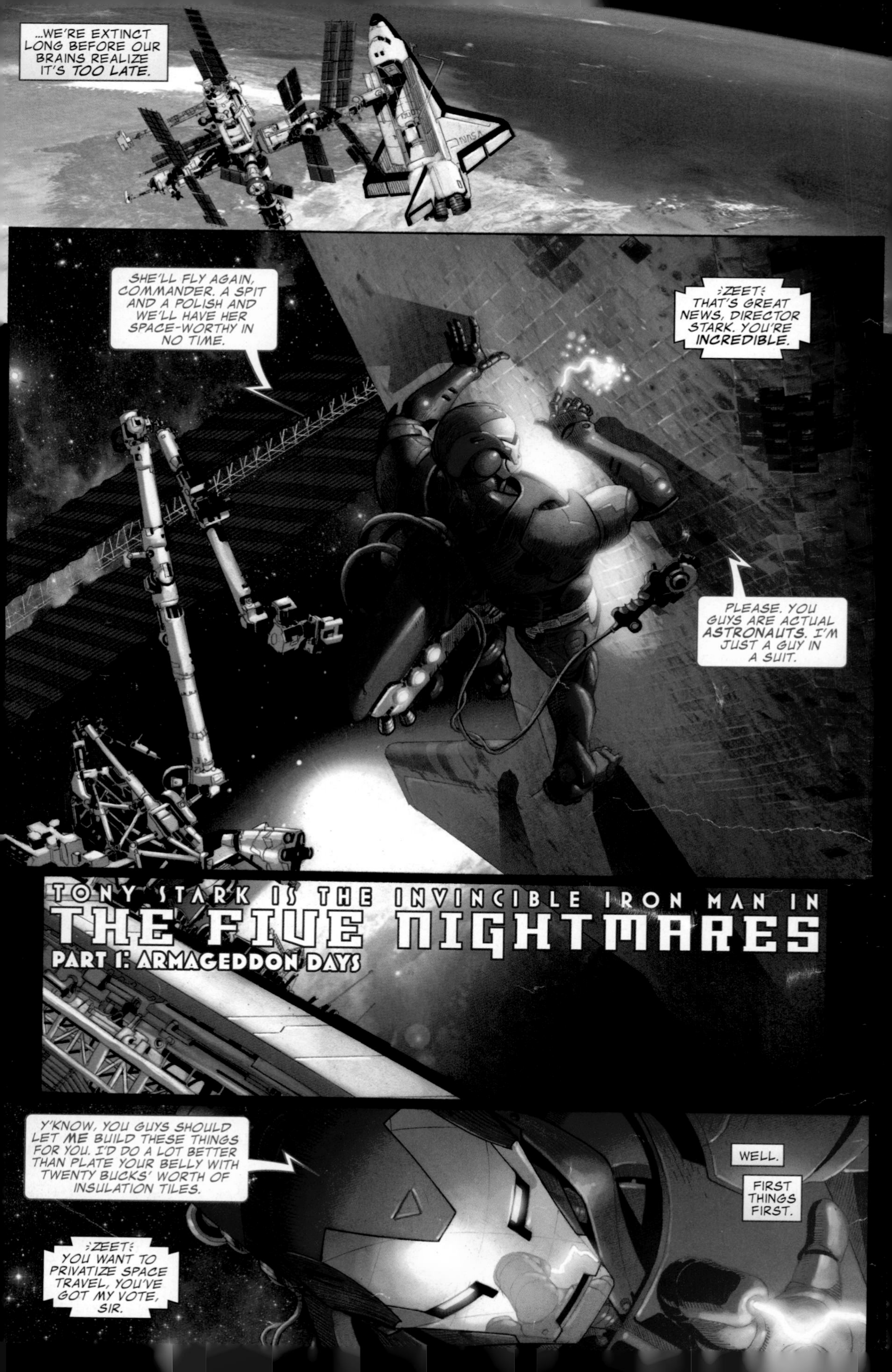
...WE'RE EXTINCT LONG BEFORE OUR BRAINS REALIZE IT'S TOO LATE.
NASA
SHE'LL FLY AGAIN, COMMANDER. A SPIT AND A POLISH AND WE'LL HAVE HER SPACE-WORTHY IN NO TIME.
ZEET THAT'S GREAT NEWS, DIRECTOR STARK. YOU'RE INCREDIBLE.
PLEASE. YOU GUYS ARE ACTUAL ASTRONAUTS. I'M JUST A GUY IN A SUIT.
TONY STARK IS THE INVINCIBLE IRON MAN IN
THE FIVE NIGHTMARES
PART 1: ARMAGEDDON DAYS
Y'KNOW, YOU GUYS SHOULD LET ME BUILD THESE THINGS FOR YOU. I'D DO A LOT BETTER THAN PLATE YOUR BELLY WITH TWENTY BUCKS' WORTH OF INSULATION TILES.
ZEET YOU WANT TO PRIVATIZE SPACE TRAVEL, YOU'VE GOT MY VOTE, SIR.
WELL.
FIRST THINGS FIRST.

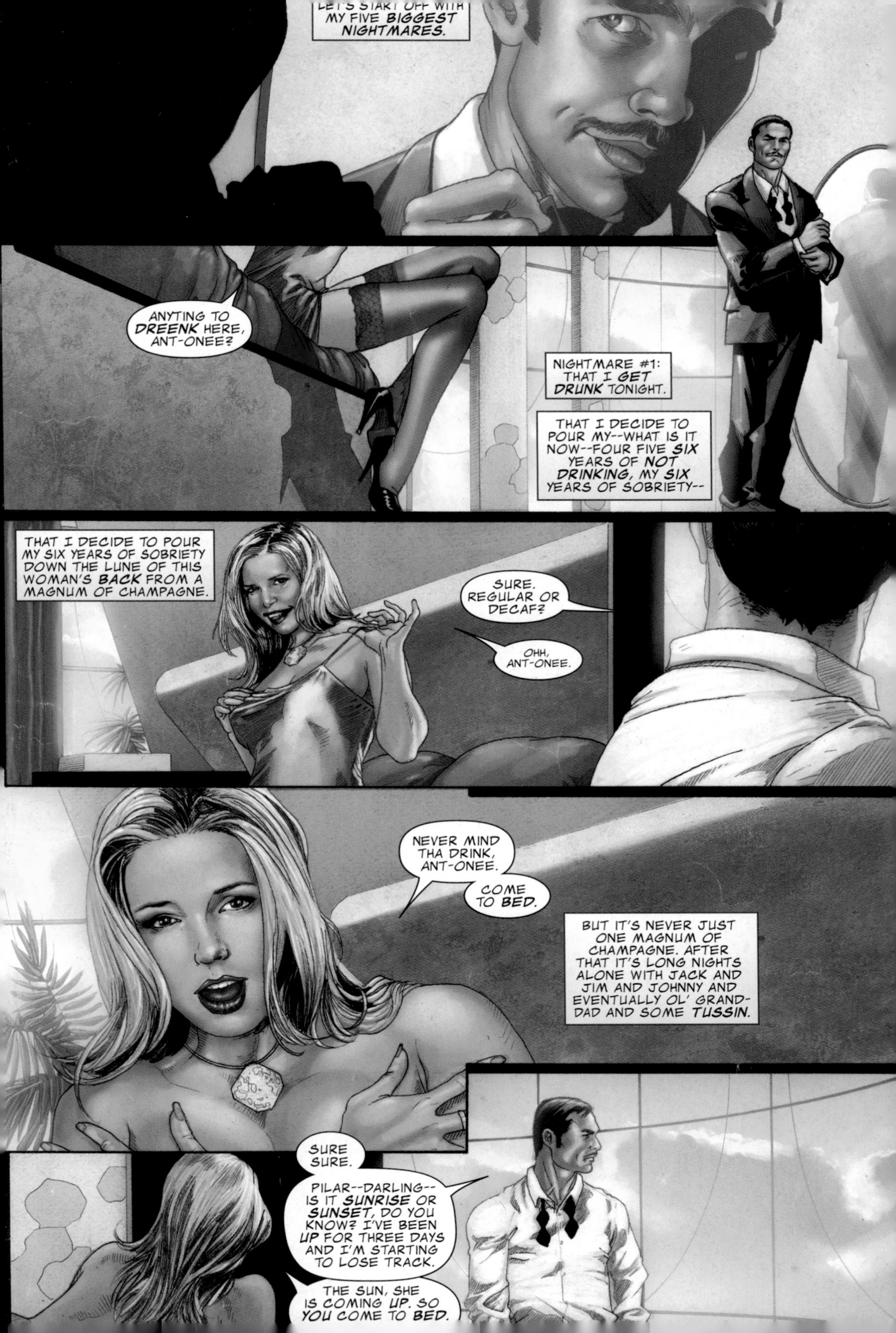
LET'S START OFF WITH MY FIVE BIGGEST NIGHTMARES.
ANYTING TO DREENK HERE, ANT-ONEE?
NIGHTMARE #1: THAT I GET DRUNK TONIGHT.
THAT I DECIDE TO POUR MY--WHAT IS IT NOW--FOUR FIVE SIX YEARS OF NOT DRINKING, MY SIX YEARS OF SOBRIETY--
THAT I DECIDE TO POUR MY SIX YEARS OF SOBRIETY DOWN THE LUNE OF THIS WOMAN'S BACK FROM A MAGNUM OF CHAMPAGNE.
SURE. REGULAR OR DECAF?
OHH, ANT-ONEE.
NEVER MIND THA DRINK, ANT-ONEE.
COME TO BED.
BUT IT'S NEVER JUST ONE MAGNUM OF CHAMPAGNE. AFTER THAT IT'S LONG NIGHTS ALONE WITH JACK AND JIM AND JOHNNY AND EVENTUALLY OL' GRAND-DAD AND SOME TUSSIN.
SURE SURE.
PILAR--DARLING--IS IT SUNRISE OR SUNSET, DO YOU KNOW? I'VE BEEN UP FOR THREE DAYS AND I'M STARTING TO LOSE TRACK.
THE SUN, SHE IS COMING UP. SO YOU COME TO BED.

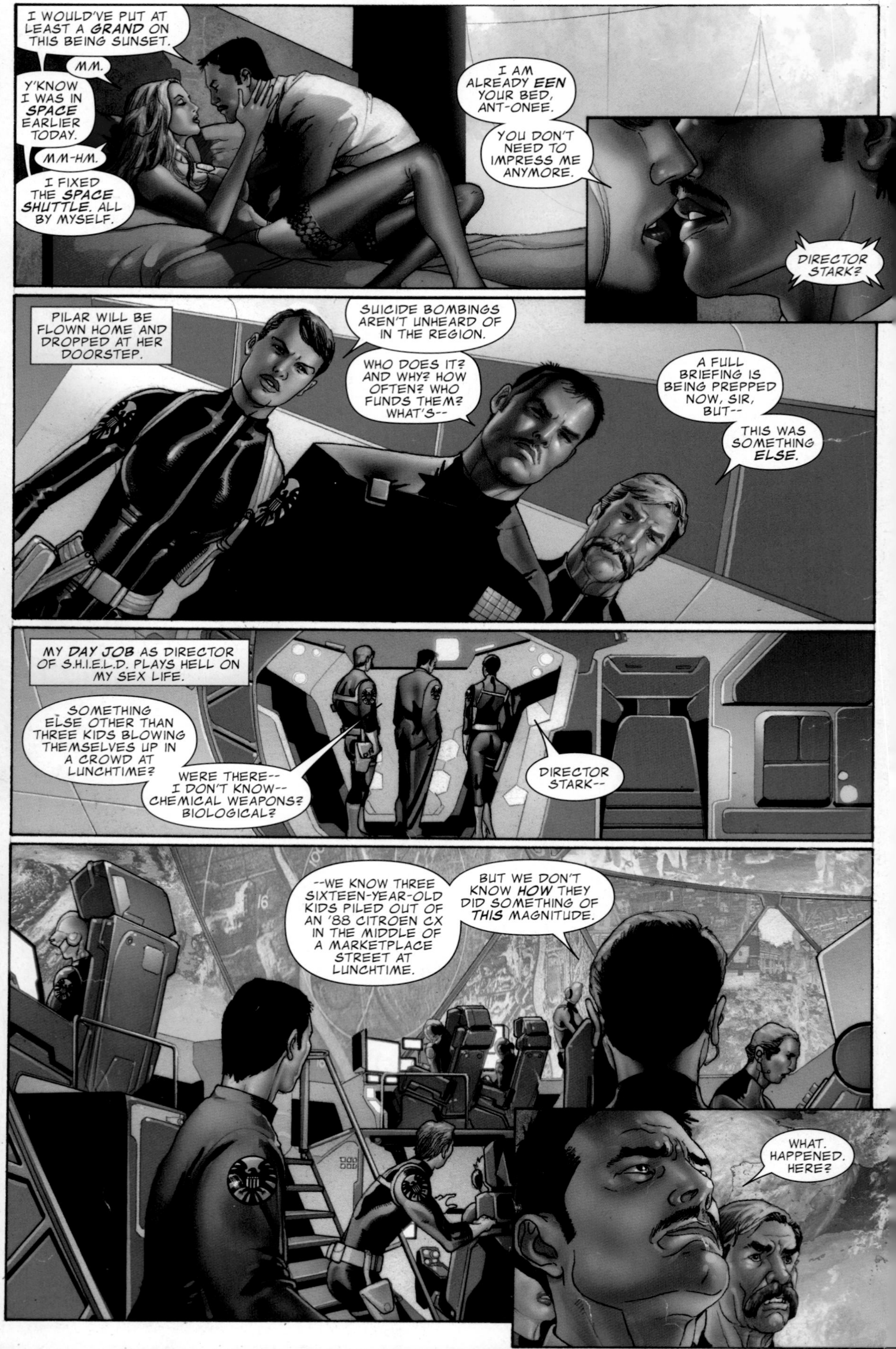
I WOULD'VE PUT AT LEAST A GRAND ON THIS BEING SUNSET.
MM.
Y'KNOW I WAS IN SPACE EARLIER TODAY.
MM-HM.
I FIXED THE SPACE SHUTTLE. ALL BY MYSELF.
I AM ALREADY EEN YOUR BED, ANT-ONEE.
YOU DON'T NEED TO IMPRESS ME ANYMORE.
DIRECTOR STARK?
PILAR WILL BE FLOWN HOME AND DROPPED AT HER DOORSTEP.
SUICIDE BOMBINGS AREN'T UNHEARD OF IN THE REGION.
WHO DOES IT? AND WHY? HOW OFTEN? WHO FUNDS THEM? WHAT'S--
A FULL BRIEFING IS BEING PREPPED NOW, SIR, BUT--
THIS WAS SOMETHING ELSE.
MY DAY JOB AS DIRECTOR OF S.H.I.E.L.D. PLAYS HELL ON MY SEX LIFE.
SOMETHING ELSE OTHER THAN THREE KIDS BLOWING THEMSELVES UP IN A CROWD AT LUNCHTIME?
WERE THERE-- I DON'T KNOW-- CHEMICAL WEAPONS? BIOLOGICAL?
DIRECTOR STARK--
--WE KNOW THREE SIXTEEN-YEAR-OLD KIDS PILED OUT OF AN '88 CITROEN CX IN THE MIDDLE OF A MARKETPLACE STREET AT LUNCHTIME.
BUT WE DON'T KNOW HOW THEY DID SOMETHING OF THIS MAGNITUDE.
WHAT. HAPPENED. HERE?

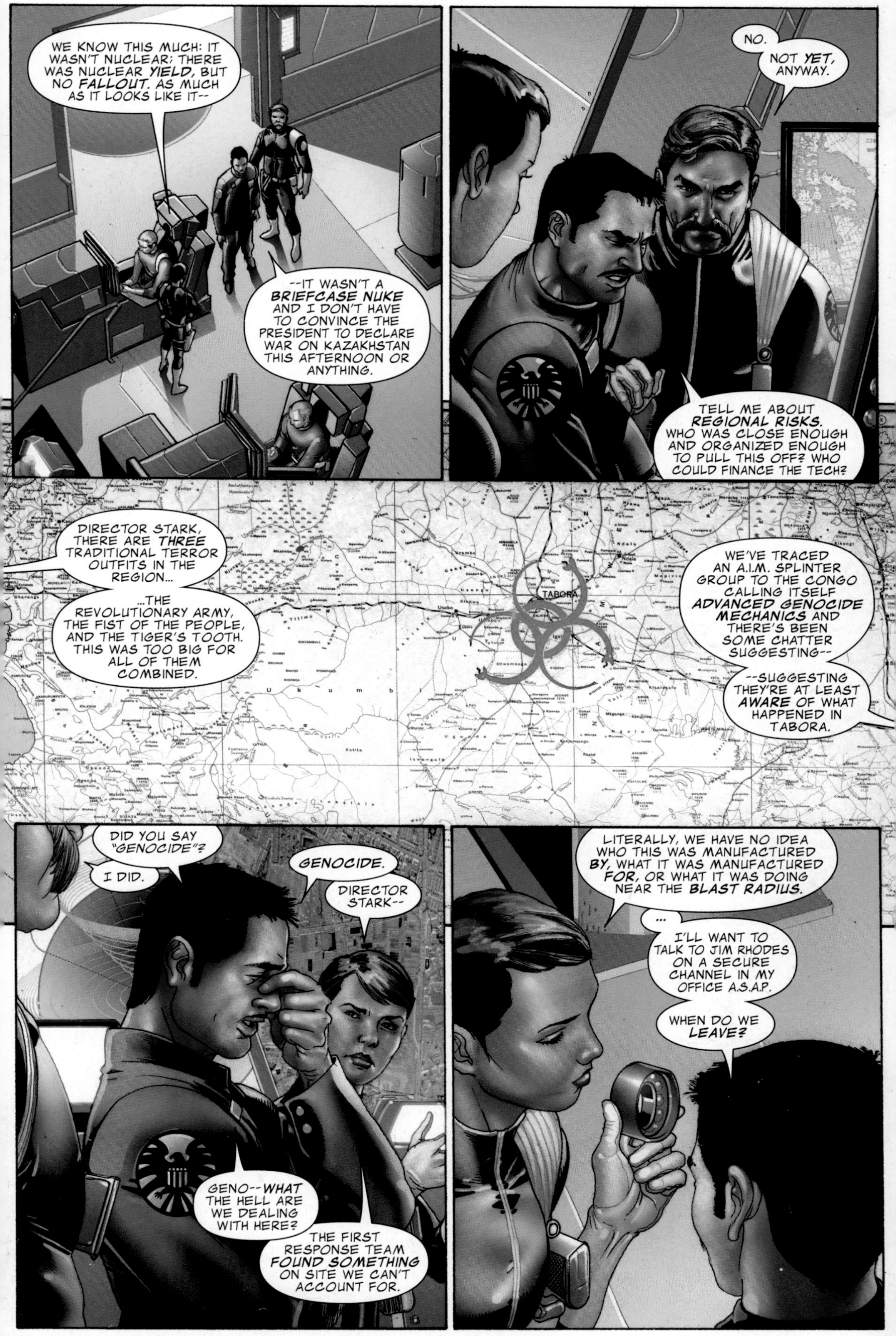
WE KNOW THIS MUCH: IT WASN'T NUCLEAR; THERE WAS NUCLEAR YIELD, BUT NO FALLOUT. AS MUCH AS IT LOOKS LIKE IT--
--IT WASN'T A BRIEFCASE NUKE AND I DON'T HAVE TO CONVINCE THE PRESIDENT TO DECLARE WAR ON KAZAKHSTAN THIS AFTERNOON OR ANYTHING.
NO.
NOT YET, ANYWAY.
TELL ME ABOUT REGIONAL RISKS. WHO WAS CLOSE ENOUGH AND ORGANIZED ENOUGH TO PULL THIS OFF? WHO COULD FINANCE THE TECH?
DIRECTOR STARK, THERE ARE THREE TRADITIONAL TERROR OUTFITS IN THE REGION...
...THE REVOLUTIONARY ARMY, THE FIST OF THE PEOPLE, AND THE TIGER'S TOOTH. THIS WAS TOO BIG FOR ALL OF THEM COMBINED.
TABORA
WE'VE TRACED AN A.I.M. SPLINTER GROUP TO THE CONGO CALLING ITSELF ADVANCED GENOCIDE MECHANICS AND THERE'S BEEN SOME CHATTER SUGGESTING--
--SUGGESTING THEY'RE AT LEAST AWARE OF WHAT HAPPENED IN TABORA.
DID YOU SAY "GENOCIDE"?
I DID.
GENOCIDE.
DIRECTOR STARK--
GENO--WHAT THE HELL ARE WE DEALING WITH HERE?
THE FIRST RESPONSE TEAM FOUND SOMETHING ON SITE WE CAN'T ACCOUNT FOR.
LITERALLY, WE HAVE NO IDEA WHO THIS WAS MANUFACTURED BY, WHAT IT WAS MANUFACTURED FOR, OR WHAT IT WAS DOING NEAR THE BLAST RADIUS.
...
I'LL WANT TO TALK TO JIM RHODES ON A SECURE CHANNEL IN MY OFFICE A.S.A.P.
WHEN DO WE LEAVE?

UH...WHEN DOES WHO LEAVE FOR WHAT, SIR?

THE RAID ON A.G.M. I'M LEADING IT. WHEN DO WE LEAVE?

SIR, I KNOW YOU'VE TAKEN A HIGHLY ACTIVE PRESENCE IN THE FIELD BEFORE BUT, WITH ALL DUE RESPECT...

WE DON'T ENTIRELY KNOW WHAT A.G.M. IS CAPABLE OF AND THE IDEA OF PUTTING YOU IN THE MIX--

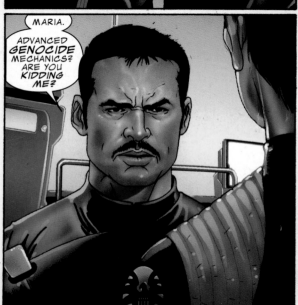

MARIA.

ADVANCED GENOCIDE MECHANICS? ARE YOU KIDDING ME?

SOMEONE'S FIGURED OUT HOW TO EARN A NEAR-NUCLEAR YIELD WITHOUT FISSION IN A DAMN STREET MARKET.

I'M NOT ASKING FOR YOUR PERMISSION TO GRIND THEM INTO THE DIRT.

WHEN. DO WE. LEAVE?

WE'RE...T-MINUS FIFTY-FOUR MINUTES, DIRECTOR STARK.

...OKAY.

DO WE NEED TO RE-SKED, SIR?

WE'VE ALREADY GOT THE MISSION CLOCK RUNNING, IF WE STOPPED--

NO, DON'T STOP IT. I'LL HAVE THE IRON MAN UP AND ACTIVATED IN TIME.

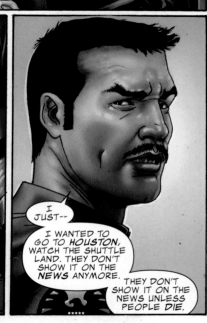

I JUST--

I WANTED TO GO TO HOUSTON, WATCH THE SHUTTLE LAND. THEY DON'T SHOW IT ON THE NEWS ANYMORE.

THEY DON'T SHOW IT ON THE NEWS UNLESS PEOPLE DIE.

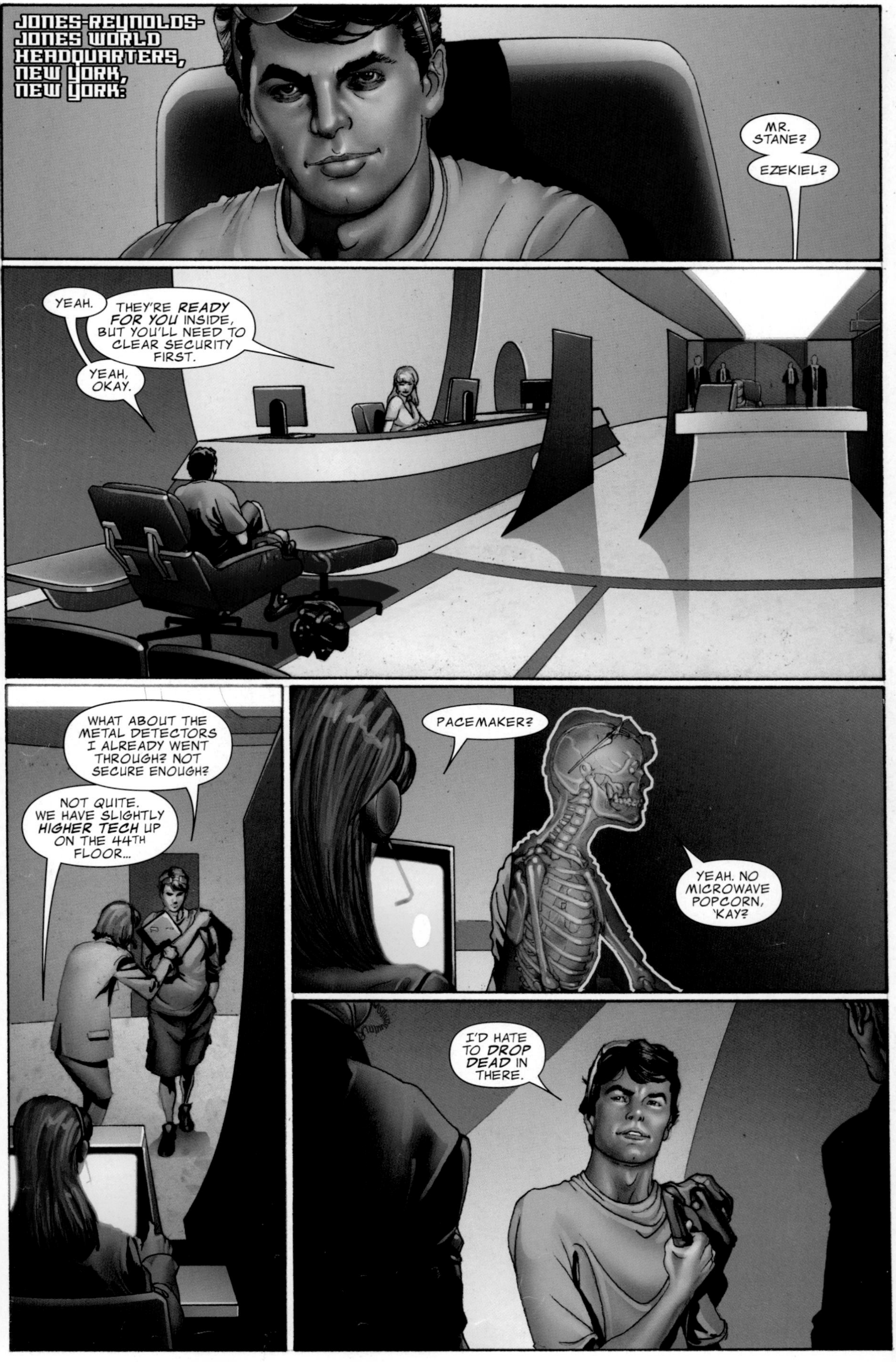
JONES-REYNOLDS-JONES WORLD HEADQUARTERS, NEW YORK, NEW YORK:
MR. STANE?
EZEKIEL?
YEAH.
THEY'RE READY FOR YOU INSIDE, BUT YOU'LL NEED TO CLEAR SECURITY FIRST.
YEAH, OKAY.
WHAT ABOUT THE METAL DETECTORS I ALREADY WENT THROUGH? NOT SECURE ENOUGH?
NOT QUITE. WE HAVE SLIGHTLY HIGHER TECH UP ON THE 44TH FLOOR...
PACEMAKER?
YEAH. NO MICROWAVE POPCORN, 'KAY?
I'D HATE TO DROP DEAD IN THERE.

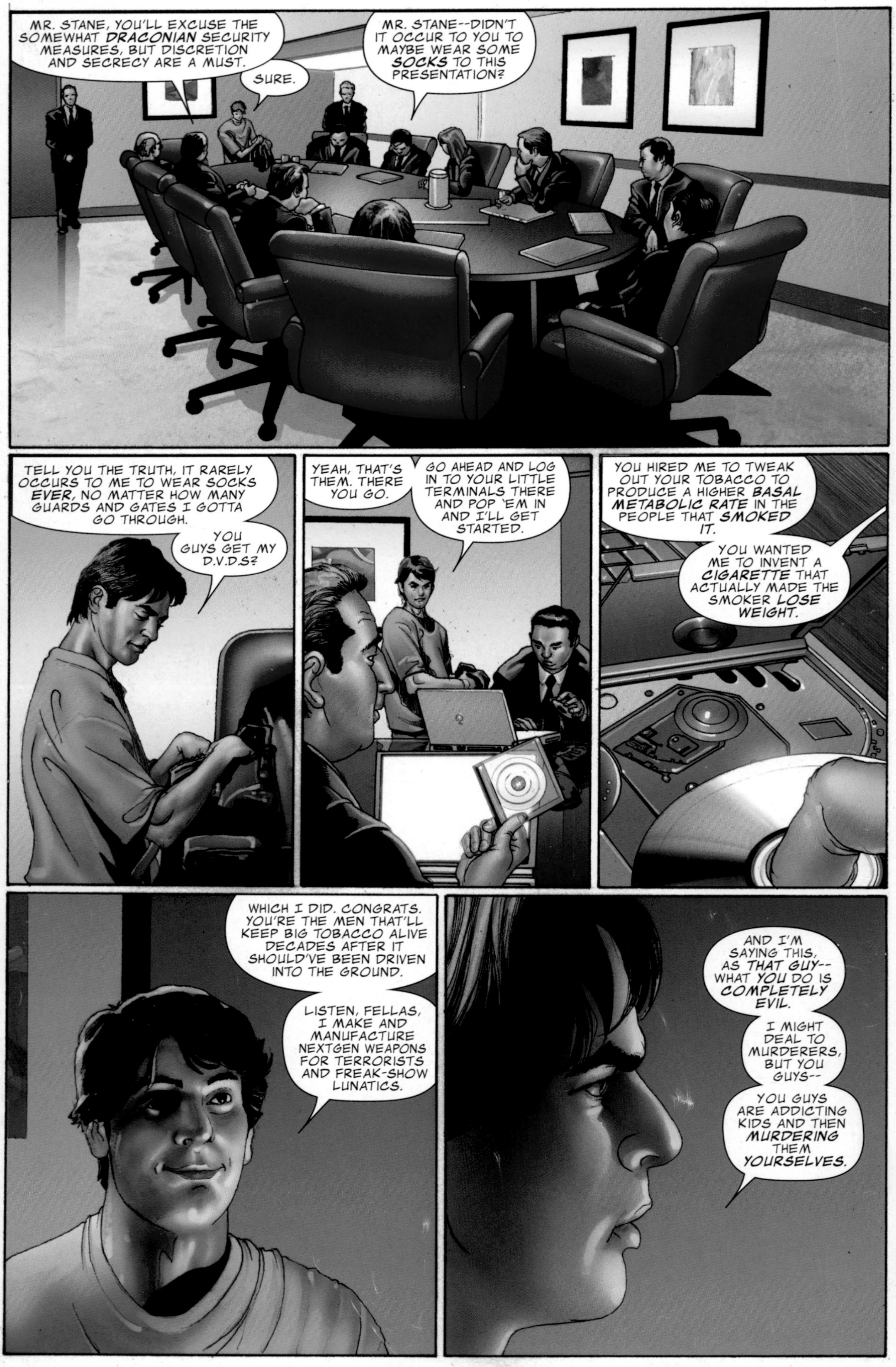
MR. STANE, YOU'LL EXCUSE THE SOMEWHAT DRACONIAN SECURITY MEASURES, BUT DISCRETION AND SECRECY ARE A MUST.
SURE.
MR. STANE--DIDN'T IT OCCUR TO YOU TO MAYBE WEAR SOME SOCKS TO THIS PRESENTATION?
TELL YOU THE TRUTH, IT RARELY OCCURS TO ME TO WEAR SOCKS EVER, NO MATTER HOW MANY GUARDS AND GATES I GOTTA GO THROUGH.
YOU GUYS GET MY D.V.D.S?
YEAH, THAT'S THEM. THERE YOU GO.
GO AHEAD AND LOG IN TO YOUR LITTLE TERMINALS THERE AND POP 'EM IN AND I'LL GET STARTED.
YOU HIRED ME TO TWEAK OUT YOUR TOBACCO TO PRODUCE A HIGHER BASAL METABOLIC RATE IN THE PEOPLE THAT SMOKED IT.
YOU WANTED ME TO INVENT A CIGARETTE THAT ACTUALLY MADE THE SMOKER LOSE WEIGHT.
WHICH I DID. CONGRATS. YOU'RE THE MEN THAT'LL KEEP BIG TOBACCO ALIVE DECADES AFTER IT SHOULD'VE BEEN DRIVEN INTO THE GROUND.
LISTEN, FELLAS, I MAKE AND MANUFACTURE NEXTGEN WEAPONS FOR TERRORISTS AND FREAK-SHOW LUNATICS.
AND I'M SAYING THIS, AS THAT GUY-- WHAT YOU DO IS COMPLETELY EVIL.
I MIGHT DEAL TO MURDERERS, BUT YOU GUYS--
YOU GUYS ARE ADDICTING KIDS AND THEN MURDERING THEM YOURSELVES.

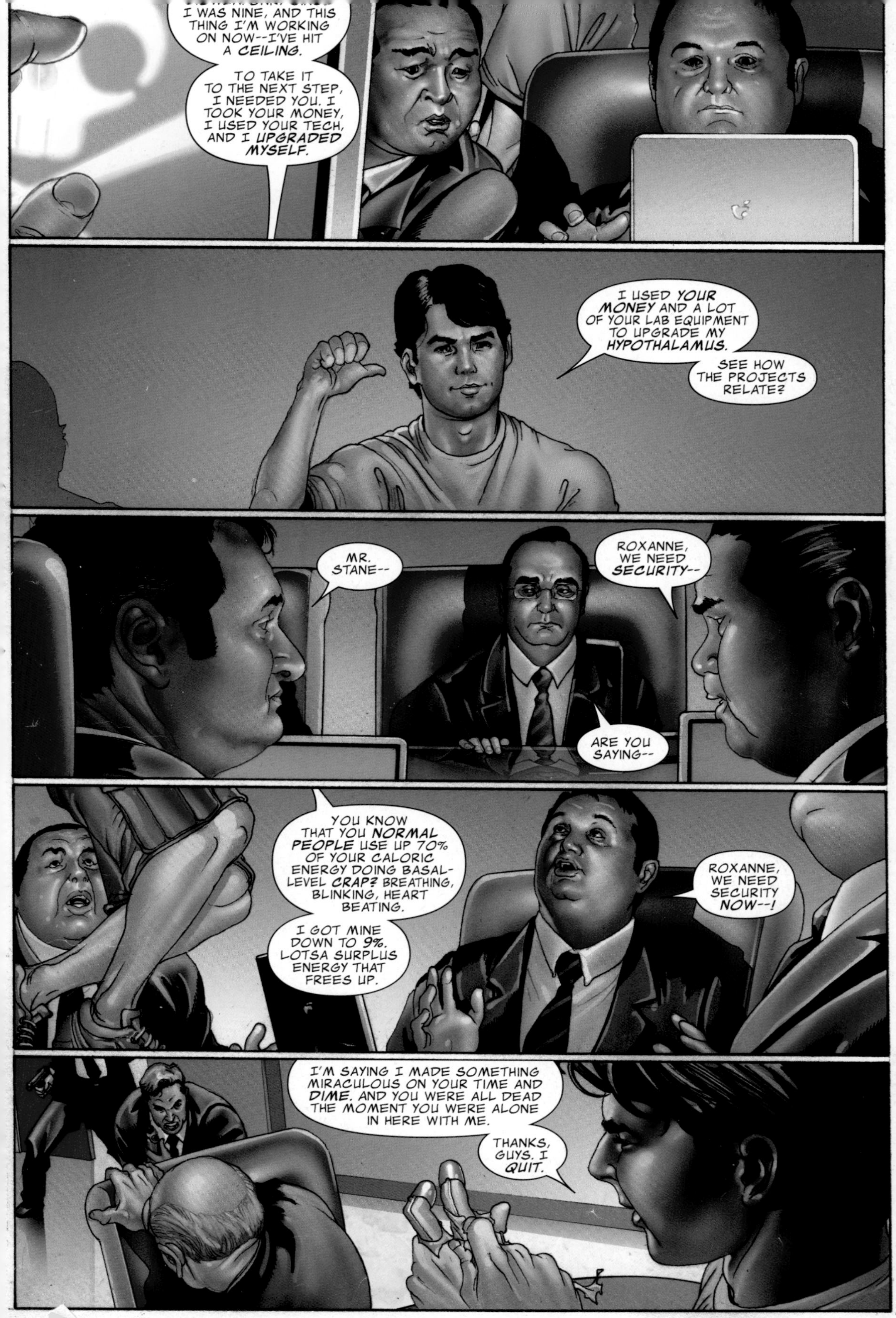
I WAS NINE, AND THIS THING I'M WORKING ON NOW--I'VE HIT A CEILING.
TO TAKE IT TO THE NEXT STEP, I NEEDED YOU. I TOOK YOUR MONEY, I USED YOUR TECH, AND I UPGRADED MYSELF.
I USED YOUR MONEY AND A LOT OF YOUR LAB EQUIPMENT TO UPGRADE MY HYPOTHALAMUS.
SEE HOW THE PROJECTS RELATE?
MR. STANE--
ROXANNE, WE NEED SECURITY--
ARE YOU SAYING--
YOU KNOW THAT YOU NORMAL PEOPLE USE UP 70% OF YOUR CALORIC ENERGY DOING BASAL-LEVEL CRAP? BREATHING, BLINKING, HEART BEATING.
I GOT MINE DOWN TO 9%. LOTSA SURPLUS ENERGY THAT FREES UP.
ROXANNE, WE NEED SECURITY NOW--!
I'M SAYING I MADE SOMETHING MIRACULOUS ON YOUR TIME AND DIME. AND YOU WERE ALL DEAD THE MOMENT YOU WERE ALONE IN HERE WITH ME.
THANKS, GUYS. I QUIT.

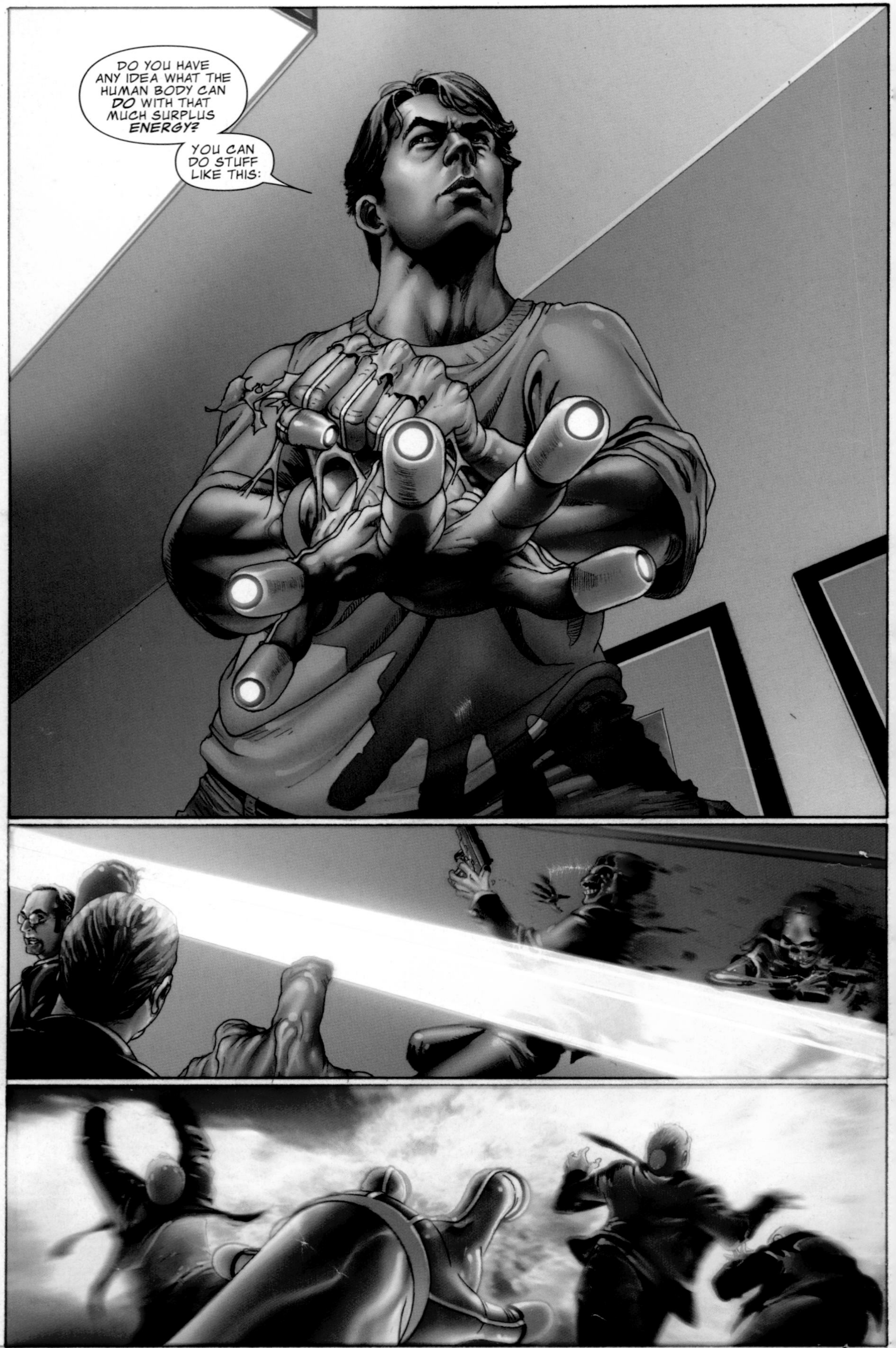
DO YOU HAVE ANY IDEA WHAT THE HUMAN BODY CAN *DO* WITH THAT MUCH SURPLUS *ENERGY?*
YOU CAN DO STUFF LIKE THIS:

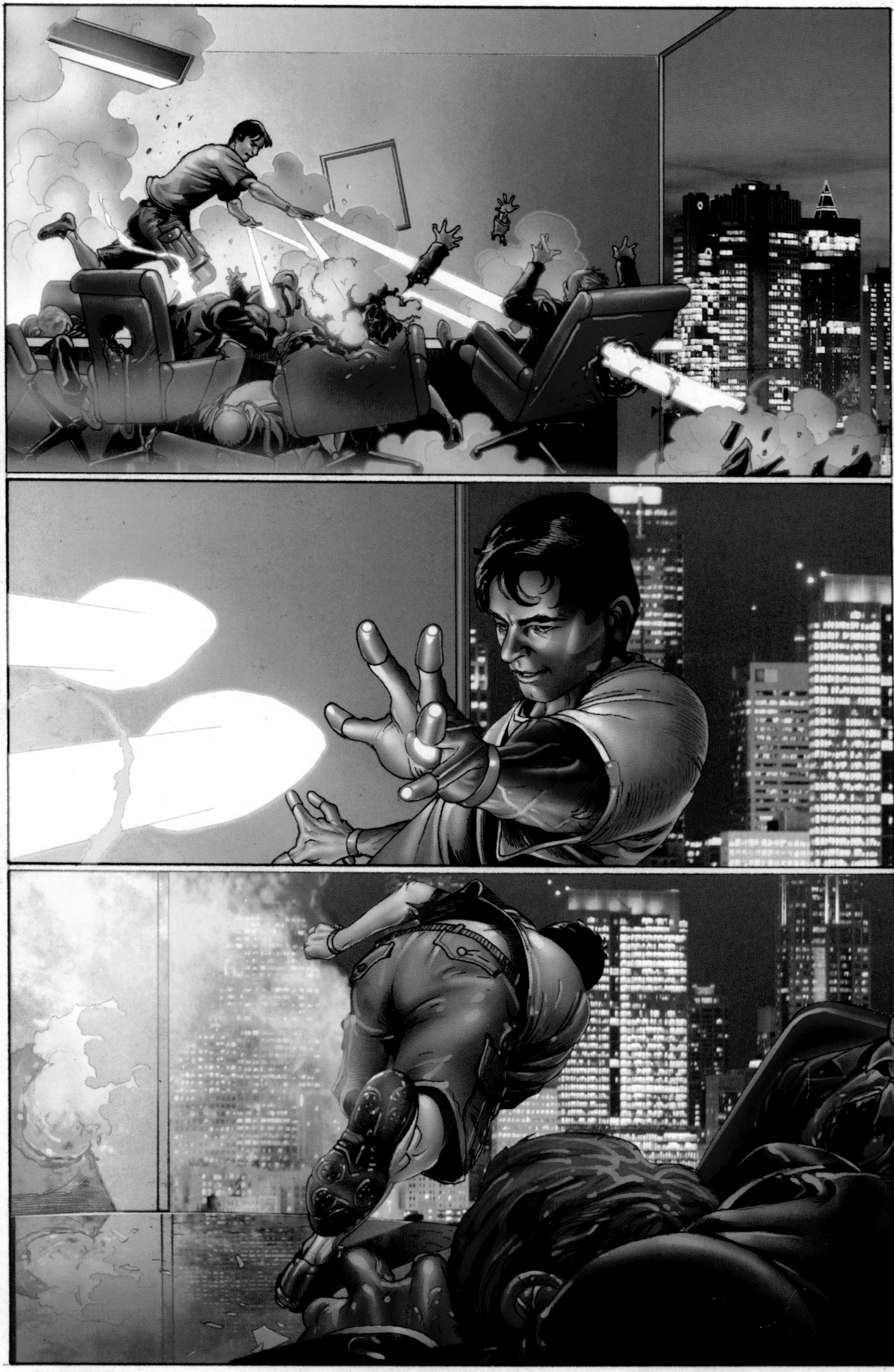

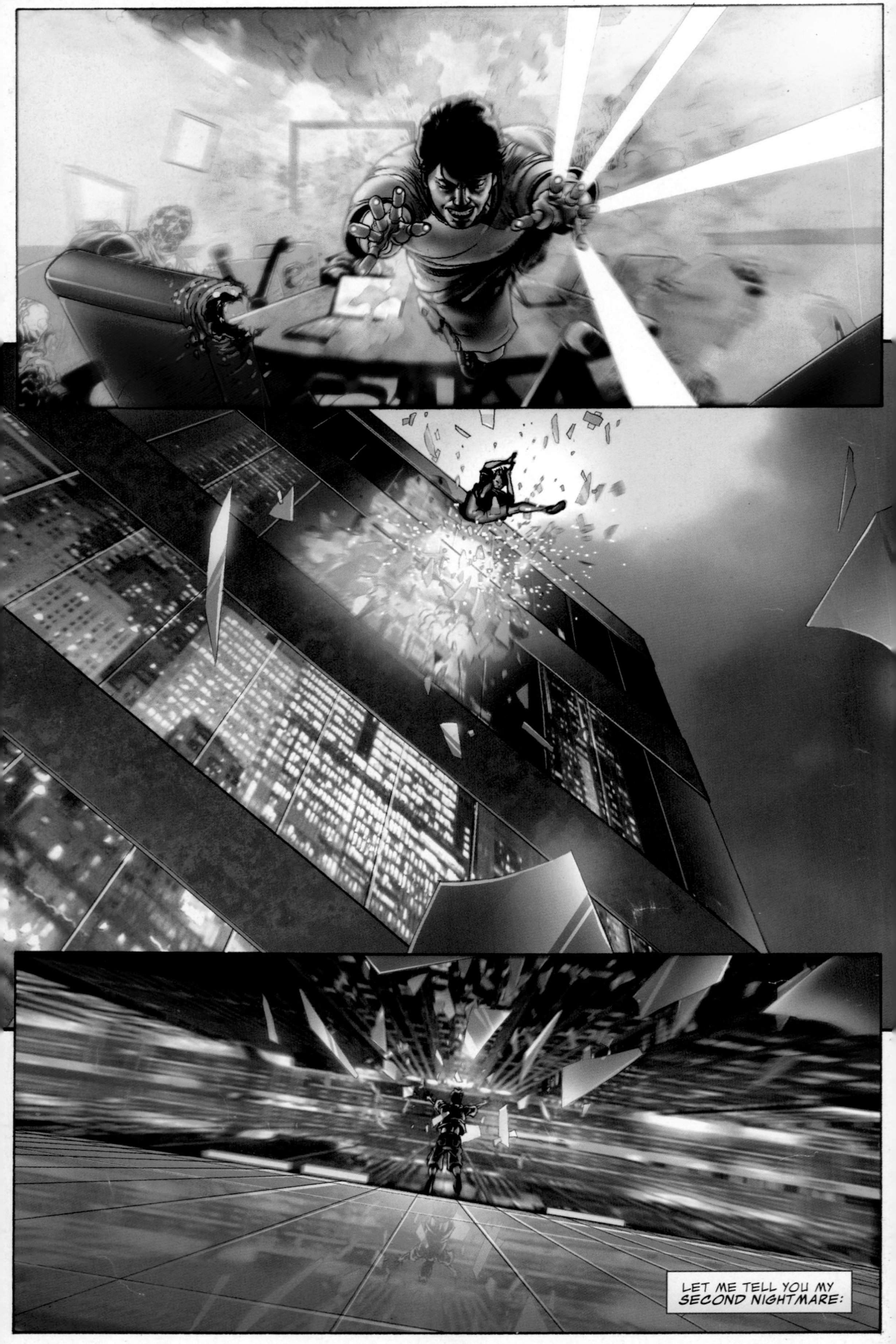
LET ME TELL YOU MY
SECOND NIGHTMARE:

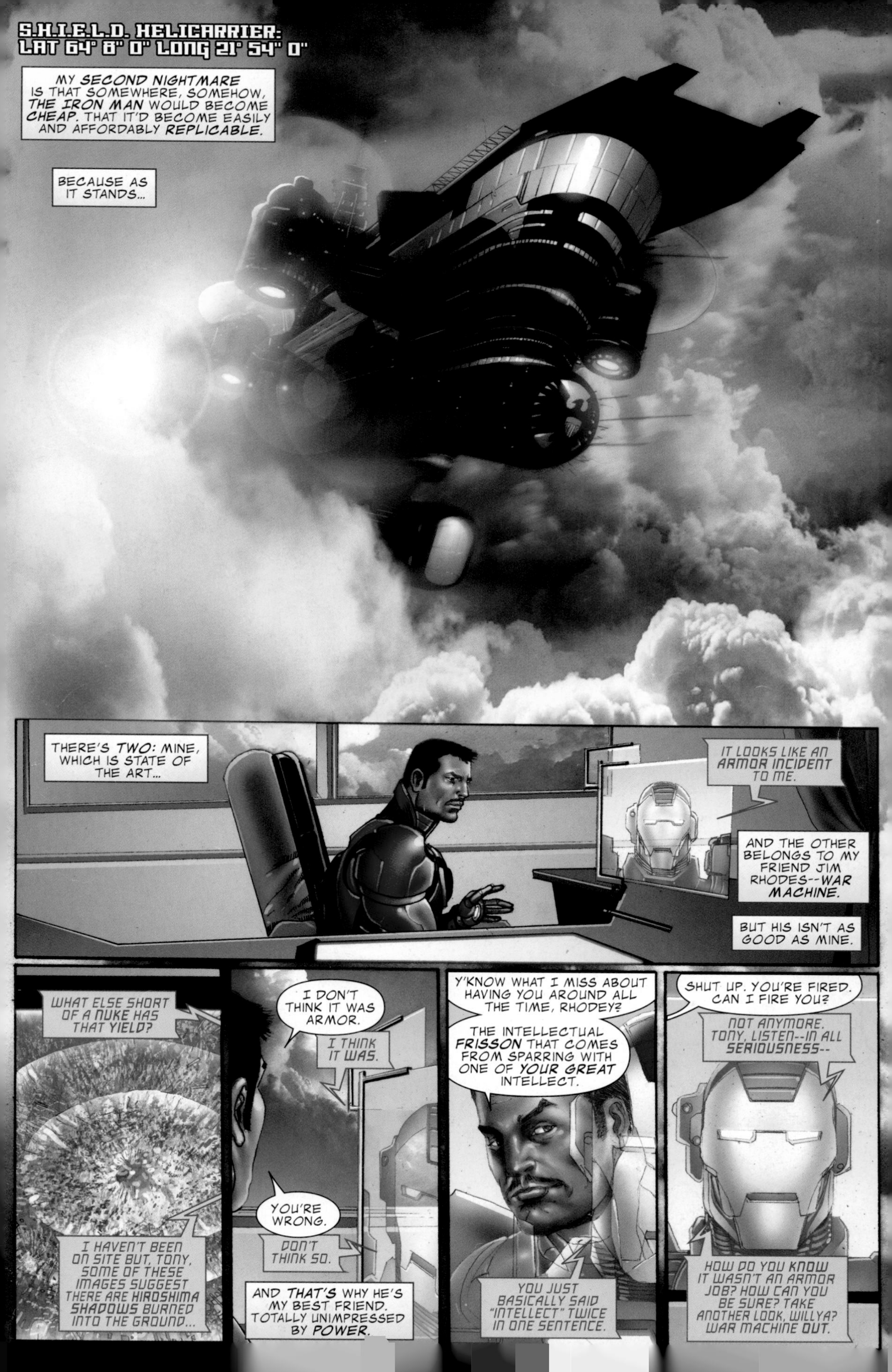
S.H.I.E.L.D. HELICARRIER:
LAT 64° 8" 0" LONG 21° 54" 0"
MY SECOND NIGHTMARE IS THAT SOMEWHERE, SOMEHOW, THE IRON MAN WOULD BECOME CHEAP. THAT IT'D BECOME EASILY AND AFFORDABLY REPLICABLE.
BECAUSE AS IT STANDS...
THERE'S TWO: MINE, WHICH IS STATE OF THE ART...
IT LOOKS LIKE AN ARMOR INCIDENT TO ME.
AND THE OTHER BELONGS TO MY FRIEND JIM RHODES--WAR MACHINE.
BUT HIS ISN'T AS GOOD AS MINE.
WHAT ELSE SHORT OF A NUKE HAS THAT YIELD?
I HAVEN'T BEEN ON SITE BUT, TONY, SOME OF THESE IMAGES SUGGEST THERE ARE HIROSHIMA SHADOWS BURNED INTO THE GROUND...
I DON'T THINK IT WAS ARMOR.
I THINK IT WAS.
YOU'RE WRONG.
DON'T THINK SO.
AND THAT'S WHY HE'S MY BEST FRIEND. TOTALLY UNIMPRESSED BY POWER.
Y'KNOW WHAT I MISS ABOUT HAVING YOU AROUND ALL THE TIME, RHODEY?
THE INTELLECTUAL FRISSON THAT COMES FROM SPARRING WITH ONE OF YOUR GREAT INTELLECT.
YOU JUST BASICALLY SAID "INTELLECT" TWICE IN ONE SENTENCE.
SHUT UP. YOU'RE FIRED. CAN I FIRE YOU?
NOT ANYMORE. TONY, LISTEN--IN ALL SERIOUSNESS--
HOW DO YOU KNOW IT WASN'T AN ARMOR JOB? HOW CAN YOU BE SURE? TAKE ANOTHER LOOK, WILLYA? WAR MACHINE OUT.

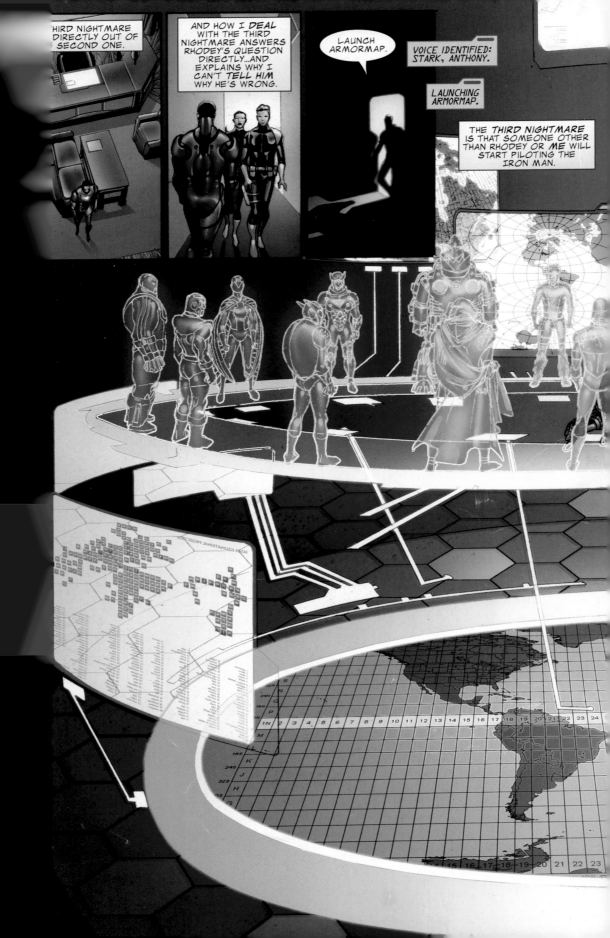

THIRD NIGHTMARE DIRECTLY OUT OF [?] SECOND ONE.

AND HOW I *DEAL* WITH THE THIRD NIGHTMARE ANSWERS RHODEY'S QUESTION DIRECTLY...AND EXPLAINS WHY I CAN'T *TELL* HIM WHY HE'S WRONG.

LAUNCH ARMORMAP.

VOICE IDENTIFIED: STARK, ANTHONY.

LAUNCHING ARMORMAP.

THE *THIRD NIGHTMARE* IS THAT SOMEONE OTHER THAN RHODEY OR ME WILL START PILOTING THE IRON MAN.

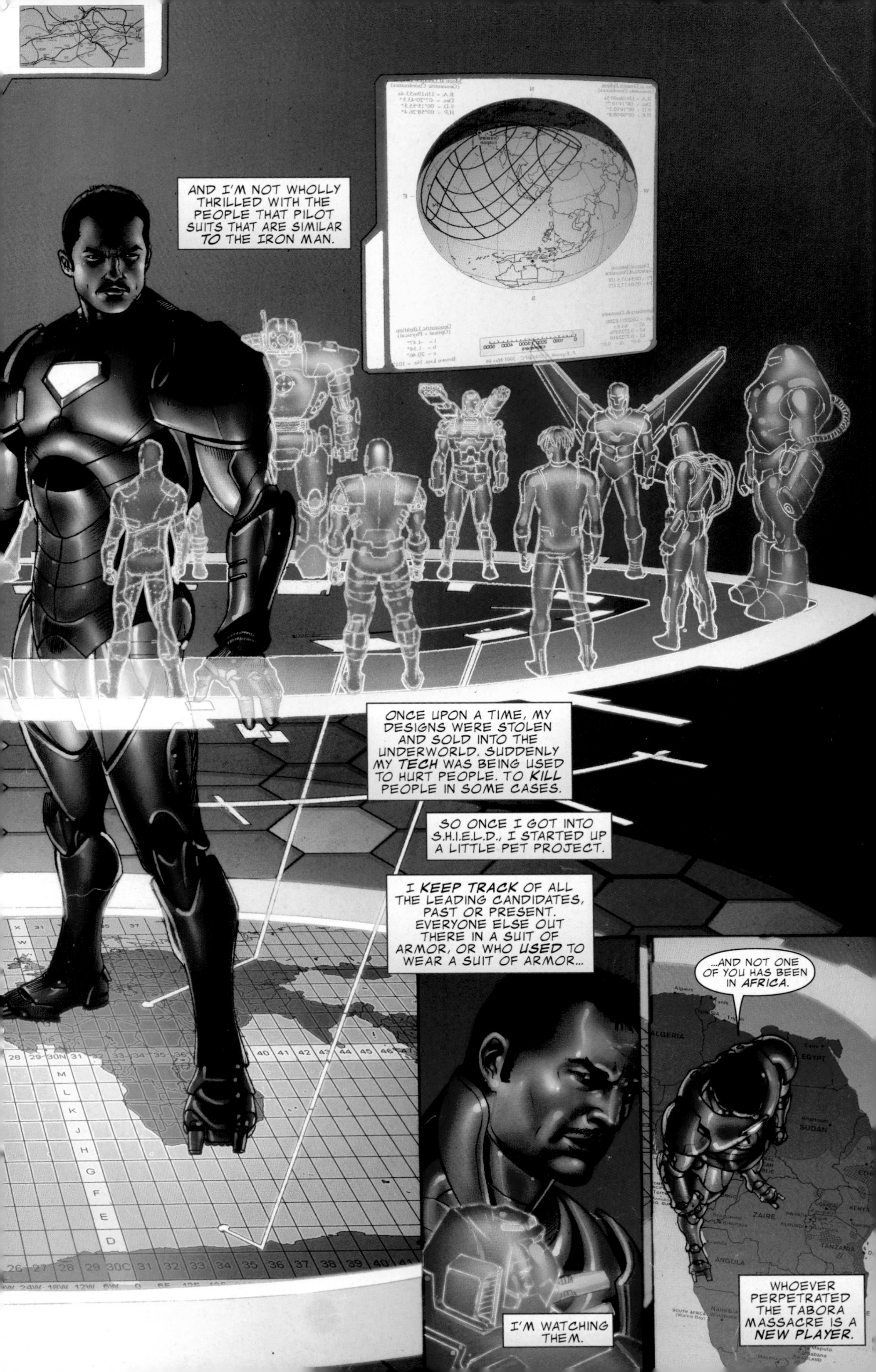
AND I'M NOT WHOLLY THRILLED WITH THE PEOPLE THAT PILOT SUITS THAT ARE SIMILAR TO THE IRON MAN.
ONCE UPON A TIME, MY DESIGNS WERE STOLEN AND SOLD INTO THE UNDERWORLD. SUDDENLY MY TECH WAS BEING USED TO HURT PEOPLE. TO KILL PEOPLE IN SOME CASES.
SO ONCE I GOT INTO S.H.I.E.L.D., I STARTED UP A LITTLE PET PROJECT.
I KEEP TRACK OF ALL THE LEADING CANDIDATES, PAST OR PRESENT. EVERYONE ELSE OUT THERE IN A SUIT OF ARMOR, OR WHO USED TO WEAR A SUIT OF ARMOR...
I'M WATCHING THEM.
...AND NOT ONE OF YOU HAS BEEN IN AFRICA.
WHOEVER PERPETRATED THE TABORA MASSACRE IS A NEW PLAYER.

I CAN'T BELIEVE YOU SURVIVED THAT.

I CAN.

WELL, YOU *SHOULDN'T HAVE.* HOW ARE YOU FEELING?

HOW AM I FEELING?

I'M FEELING LIKE I JUST SURVIVED A JUMP OUT OF A 44-STORY BUILDING AND I'M PRETTY SURE THESE ARE SECOND DEGREE--

≥KAFF≤

SECOND-DEGREE *BURNS.* HOW DO YOU *THINK* I FEEL, SASHA?

DON'T GET *SNIPPY* WITH ME, ZEKE-- THERE WERE NINETEEN KINDS OF EXIT STRATEGIES AND NOT ONE OF THEM INVOLVED *JUMPING OUT* THE DAMN WINDOW.

YOU WANTED TO PUSH YOUR *UPGRADES* TO THE *PERFORMANCE BENCHMARKS* TO SEE WHAT HAPPENED AND YOU *KNOW* IT.

HEH. YOU'RE RIGHT, BABY--YOU'RE RIGHT. I'M SORRY. I--

≥KAFF≤

I'M A LITTLE *CRANKY,* TOO-- BLOOD SUGAR AND SUCH HAVE ABSOLUTELY ZEROED OUT WHILE THESE REPAIRS ARE BEING MADE. HAND ME SOME *GOO?*

HERE.

HERE COMES 20,000 CALORIES JUST LIKE *MOM* USED TO MAKE.

MM-MM GOOD.

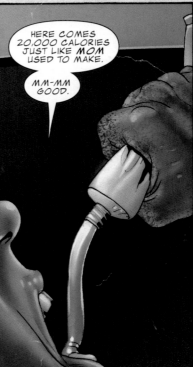

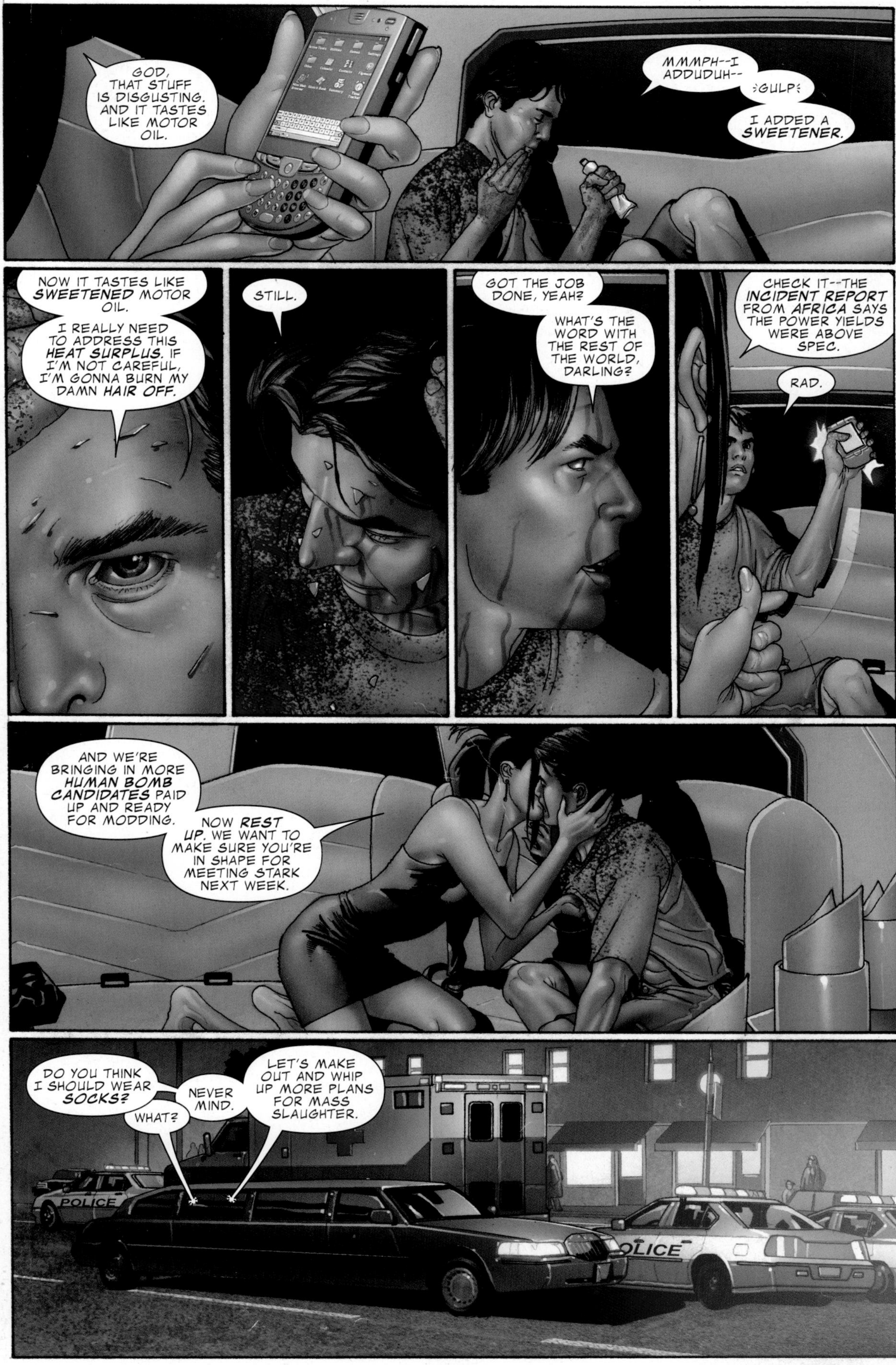
GOD, THAT STUFF IS DISGUSTING. AND IT TASTES LIKE MOTOR OIL.
MMMPH--I ADDUDUH--
GULP
I ADDED A SWEETENER.
NOW IT TASTES LIKE SWEETENED MOTOR OIL.
I REALLY NEED TO ADDRESS THIS HEAT SURPLUS. IF I'M NOT CAREFUL, I'M GONNA BURN MY DAMN HAIR OFF.
STILL.
GOT THE JOB DONE, YEAH?
WHAT'S THE WORD WITH THE REST OF THE WORLD, DARLING?
CHECK IT--THE INCIDENT REPORT FROM AFRICA SAYS THE POWER YIELDS WERE ABOVE SPEC.
RAD.
AND WE'RE BRINGING IN MORE HUMAN BOMB CANDIDATES PAID UP AND READY FOR MODDING.
NOW REST UP. WE WANT TO MAKE SURE YOU'RE IN SHAPE FOR MEETING STARK NEXT WEEK.
DO YOU THINK I SHOULD WEAR SOCKS?
WHAT?
NEVER MIND.
LET'S MAKE OUT AND WHIP UP MORE PLANS FOR MASS SLAUGHTER.
POLICE
POLICE

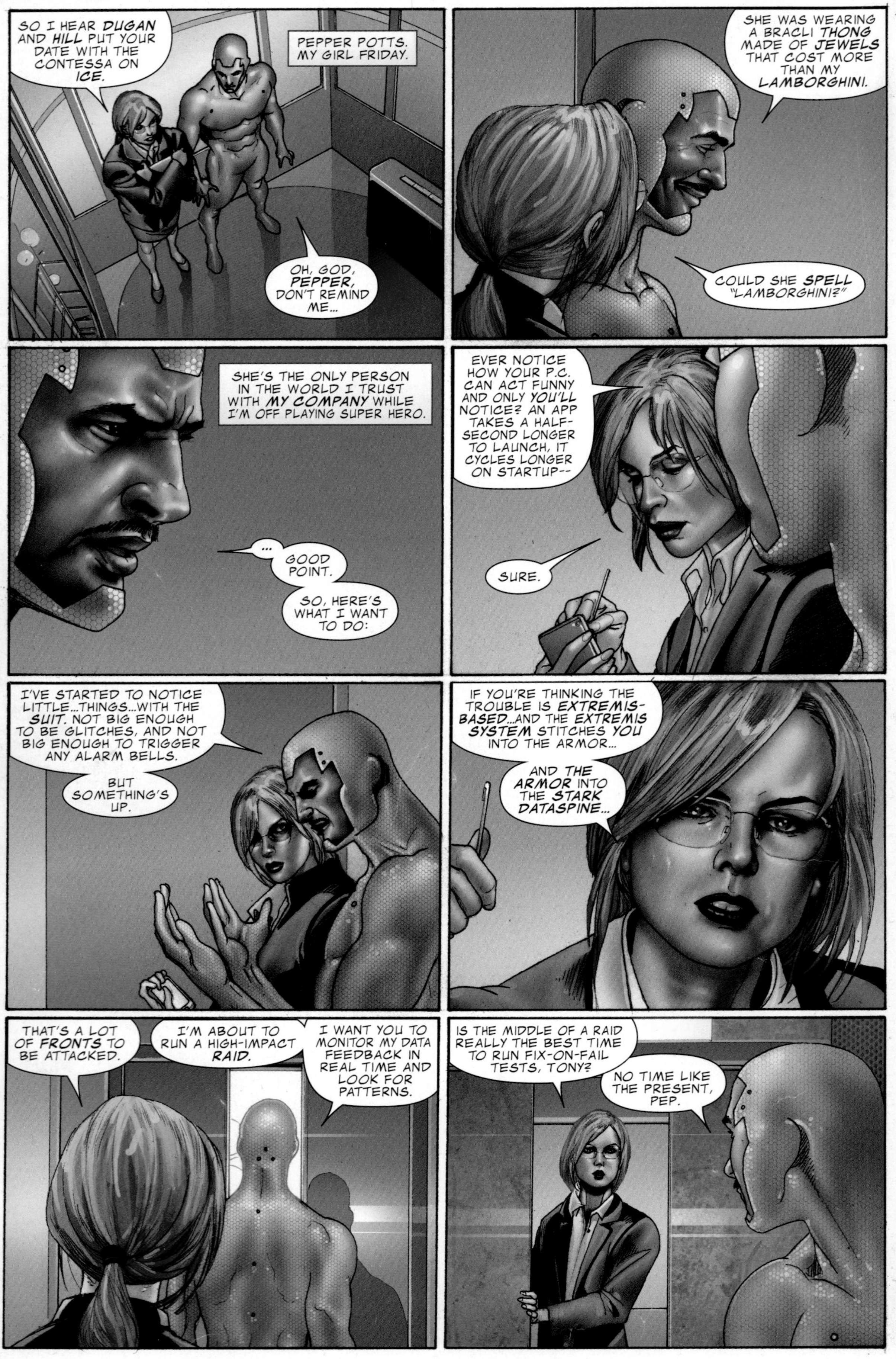
SO I HEAR DUGAN AND HILL PUT YOUR DATE WITH THE CONTESSA ON ICE.
PEPPER POTTS. MY GIRL FRIDAY.
OH, GOD, PEPPER, DON'T REMIND ME...
SHE WAS WEARING A BRACLI THONG MADE OF JEWELS THAT COST MORE THAN MY LAMBORGHINI.
COULD SHE SPELL "LAMBORGHINI?"
SHE'S THE ONLY PERSON IN THE WORLD I TRUST WITH MY COMPANY WHILE I'M OFF PLAYING SUPER HERO.
...GOOD POINT.
SO, HERE'S WHAT I WANT TO DO:
EVER NOTICE HOW YOUR P.C. CAN ACT FUNNY AND ONLY YOU'LL NOTICE? AN APP TAKES A HALF-SECOND LONGER TO LAUNCH, IT CYCLES LONGER ON STARTUP--
SURE.
I'VE STARTED TO NOTICE LITTLE...THINGS...WITH THE SUIT. NOT BIG ENOUGH TO BE GLITCHES, AND NOT BIG ENOUGH TO TRIGGER ANY ALARM BELLS.
BUT SOMETHING'S UP.
IF YOU'RE THINKING THE TROUBLE IS EXTREMIS-BASED...AND THE EXTREMIS SYSTEM STITCHES YOU INTO THE ARMOR...
AND THE ARMOR INTO THE STARK DATASPINE...
THAT'S A LOT OF FRONTS TO BE ATTACKED.
I'M ABOUT TO RUN A HIGH-IMPACT RAID.
I WANT YOU TO MONITOR MY DATA FEEDBACK IN REAL TIME AND LOOK FOR PATTERNS.
IS THE MIDDLE OF A RAID REALLY THE BEST TIME TO RUN FIX-ON-FAIL TESTS, TONY?
NO TIME LIKE THE PRESENT, PEP.

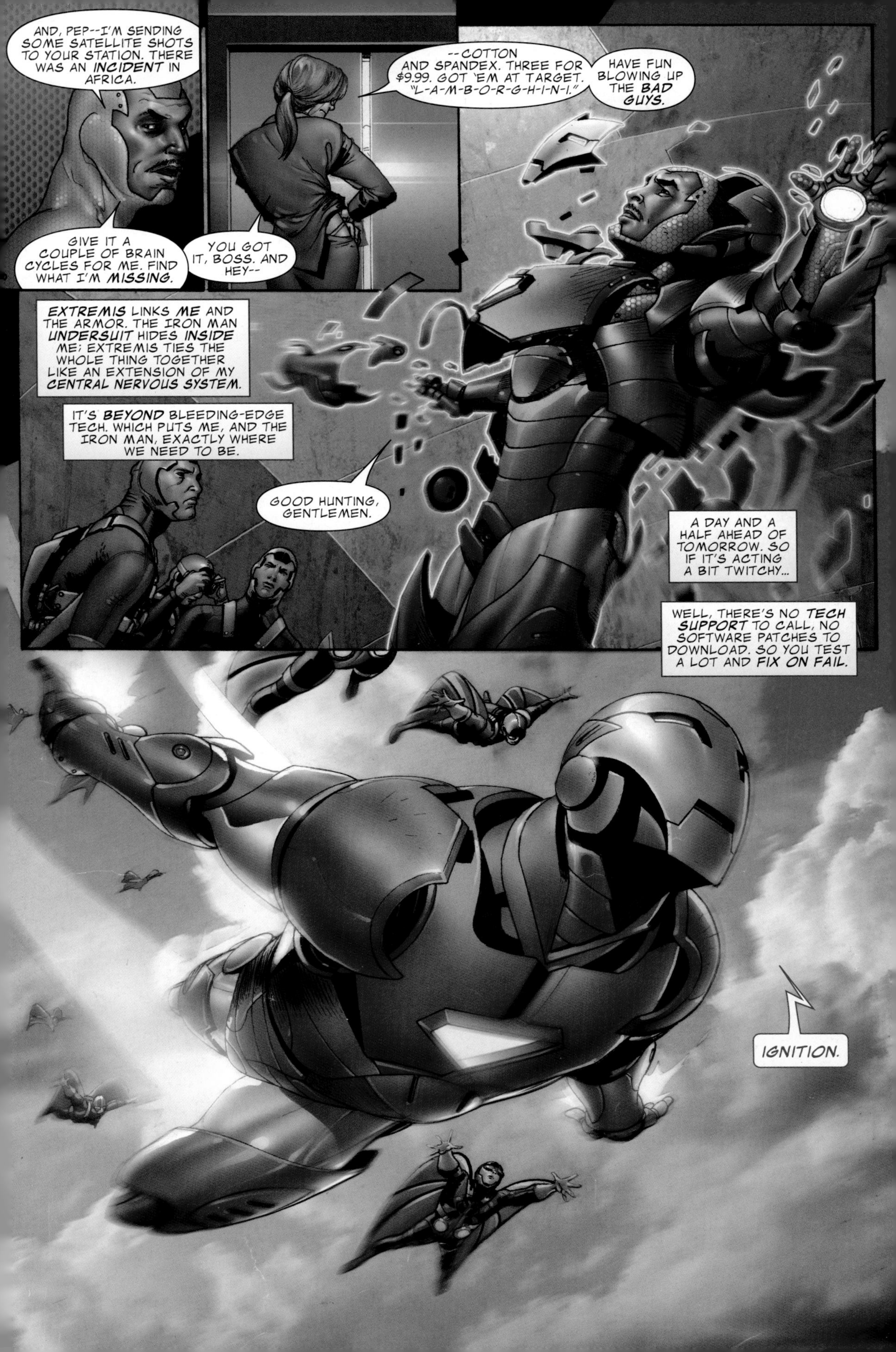
AND, PEP--I'M SENDING SOME SATELLITE SHOTS TO YOUR STATION. THERE WAS AN INCIDENT IN AFRICA.
GIVE IT A COUPLE OF BRAIN CYCLES FOR ME. FIND WHAT I'M MISSING.
YOU GOT IT, BOSS. AND HEY--
--COTTON AND SPANDEX. THREE FOR $9.99. GOT 'EM AT TARGET. "L-A-M-B-O-R-G-H-I-N-I."
HAVE FUN BLOWING UP THE BAD GUYS.
EXTREMIS LINKS ME AND THE ARMOR. THE IRON MAN UNDERSUIT HIDES INSIDE ME; EXTREMIS TIES THE WHOLE THING TOGETHER LIKE AN EXTENSION OF MY CENTRAL NERVOUS SYSTEM.
IT'S BEYOND BLEEDING-EDGE TECH. WHICH PUTS ME, AND THE IRON MAN, EXACTLY WHERE WE NEED TO BE.
GOOD HUNTING, GENTLEMEN.
A DAY AND A HALF AHEAD OF TOMORROW. SO IF IT'S ACTING A BIT TWITCHY...
WELL, THERE'S NO TECH SUPPORT TO CALL, NO SOFTWARE PATCHES TO DOWNLOAD. SO YOU TEST A LOT AND FIX ON FAIL.
IGNITION.

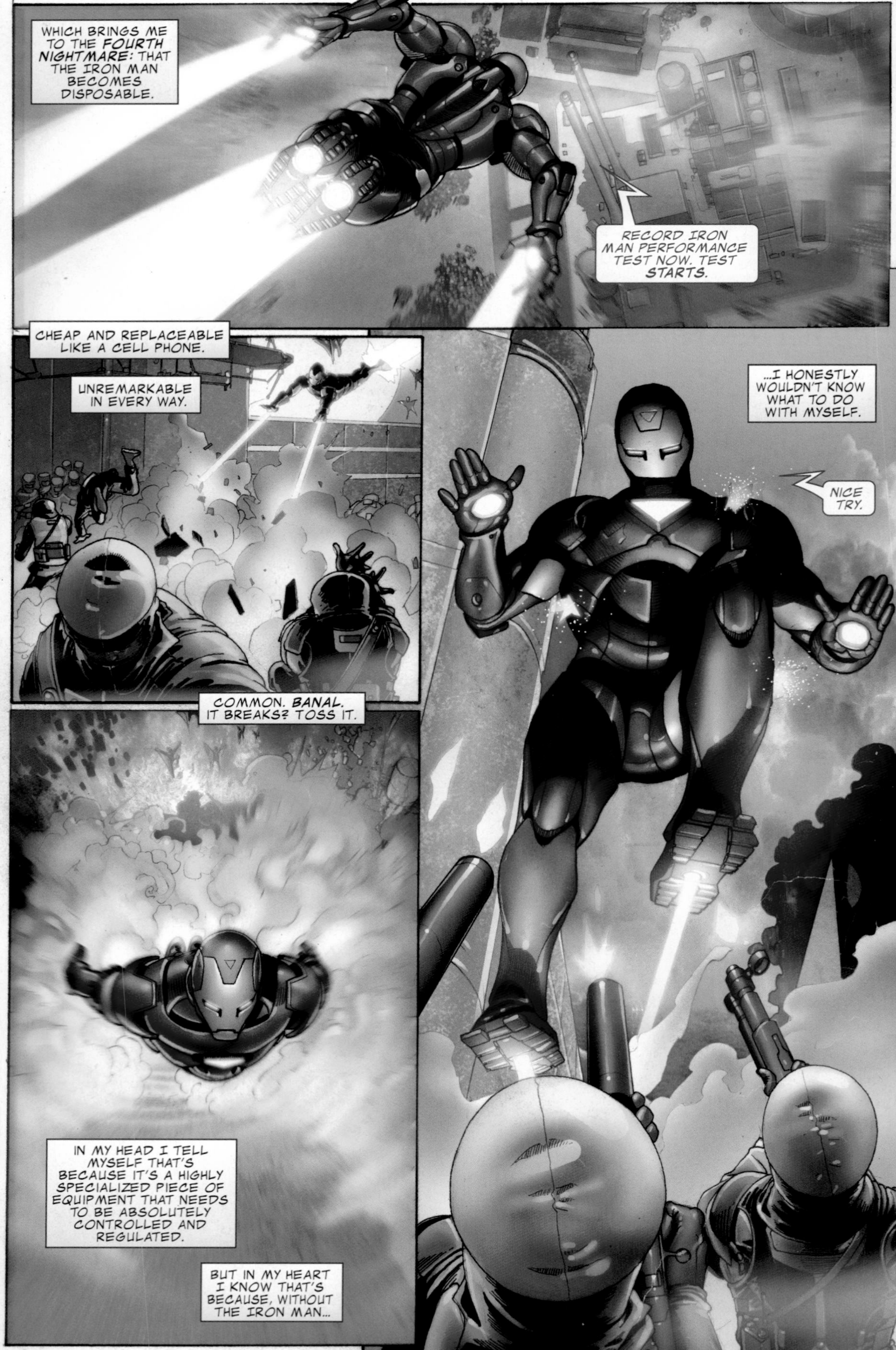
WHICH BRINGS ME TO THE FOURTH NIGHTMARE: THAT THE IRON MAN BECOMES DISPOSABLE.
RECORD IRON MAN PERFORMANCE TEST NOW. TEST STARTS.
CHEAP AND REPLACEABLE LIKE A CELL PHONE.
UNREMARKABLE IN EVERY WAY.
COMMON. BANAL. IT BREAKS? TOSS IT.
IN MY HEAD I TELL MYSELF THAT'S BECAUSE IT'S A HIGHLY SPECIALIZED PIECE OF EQUIPMENT THAT NEEDS TO BE ABSOLUTELY CONTROLLED AND REGULATED.
BUT IN MY HEART I KNOW THAT'S BECAUSE, WITHOUT THE IRON MAN...
...I HONESTLY WOULDN'T KNOW WHAT TO DO WITH MYSELF.
NICE TRY.

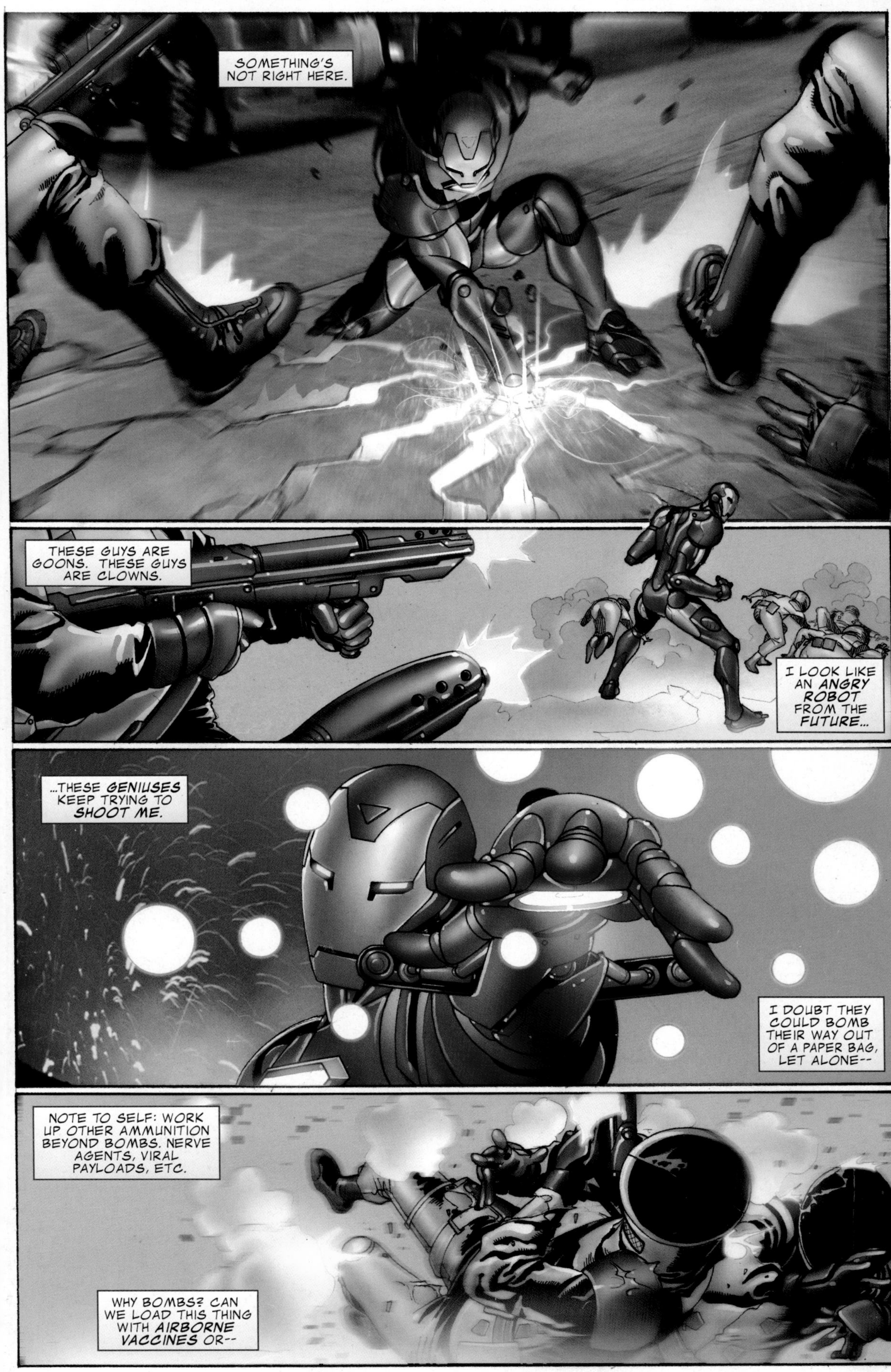
SOMETHING'S NOT RIGHT HERE.
THESE GUYS ARE GOONS. THESE GUYS ARE CLOWNS.
I LOOK LIKE AN ANGRY ROBOT FROM THE FUTURE...
...THESE GENIUSES KEEP TRYING TO SHOOT ME.
I DOUBT THEY COULD BOMB THEIR WAY OUT OF A PAPER BAG, LET ALONE--
NOTE TO SELF: WORK UP OTHER AMMUNITION BEYOND BOMBS. NERVE AGENTS, VIRAL PAYLOADS, ETC.
WHY BOMBS? CAN WE LOAD THIS THING WITH AIRBORNE VACCINES OR--

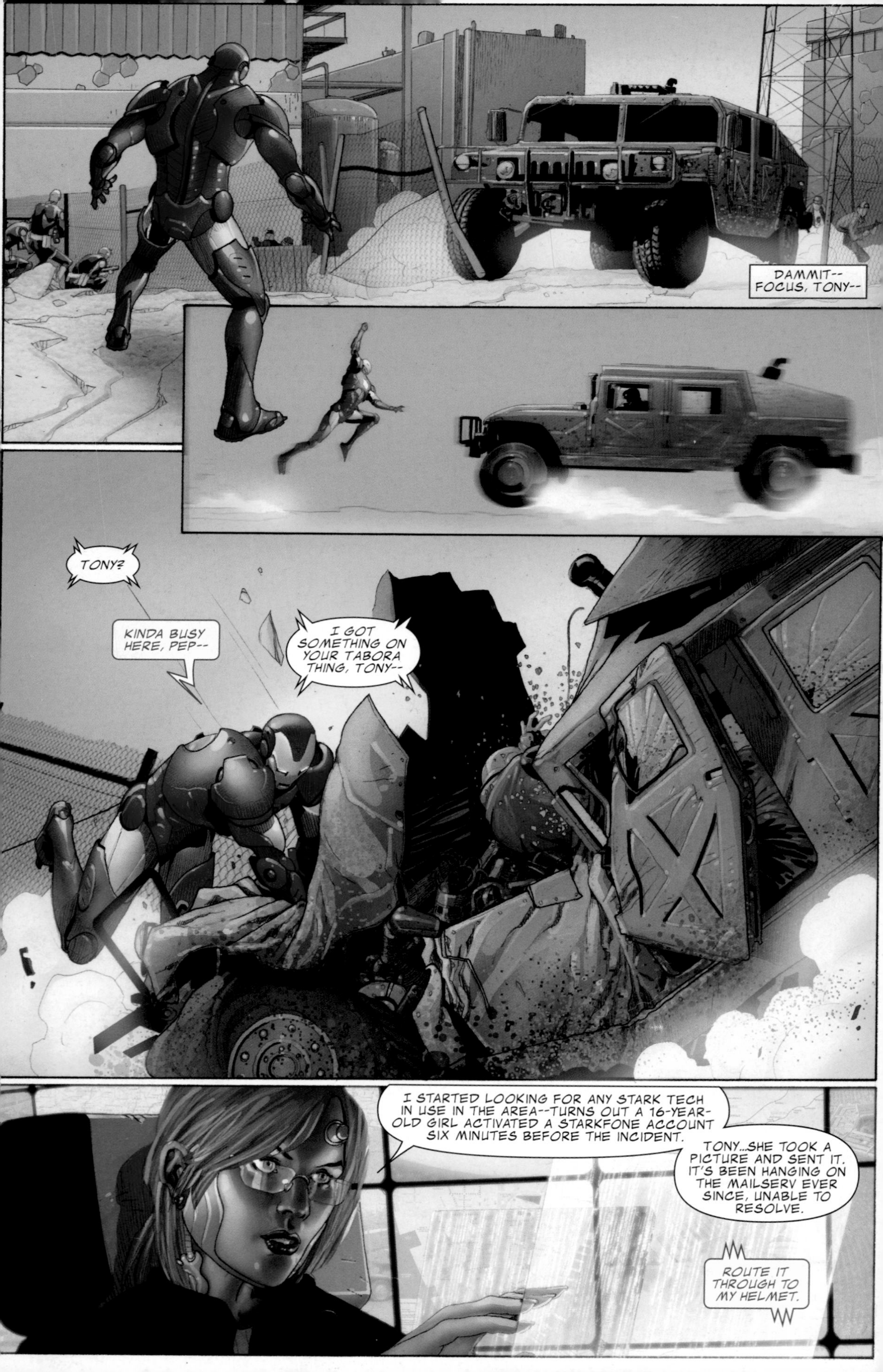
DAMMIT--
FOCUS, TONY--
TONY?
KINDA BUSY HERE, PEP--
I GOT SOMETHING ON YOUR TABORA THING, TONY--
I STARTED LOOKING FOR ANY STARK TECH IN USE IN THE AREA--TURNS OUT A 16-YEAR-OLD GIRL ACTIVATED A STARKFONE ACCOUNT SIX MINUTES BEFORE THE INCIDENT.
TONY...SHE TOOK A PICTURE AND SENT IT. IT'S BEEN HANGING ON THE MAILSERV EVER SINCE, UNABLE TO RESOLVE.
ROUTE IT THROUGH TO MY HELMET.

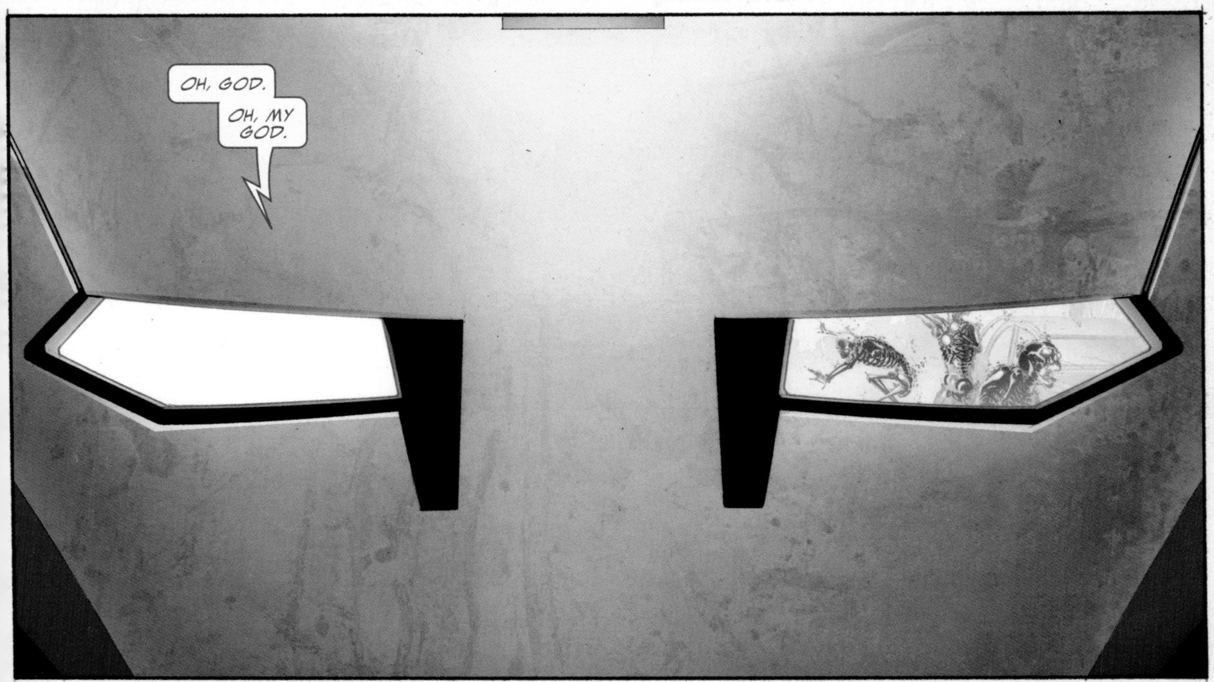
OH, GOD.
OH, MY GOD.

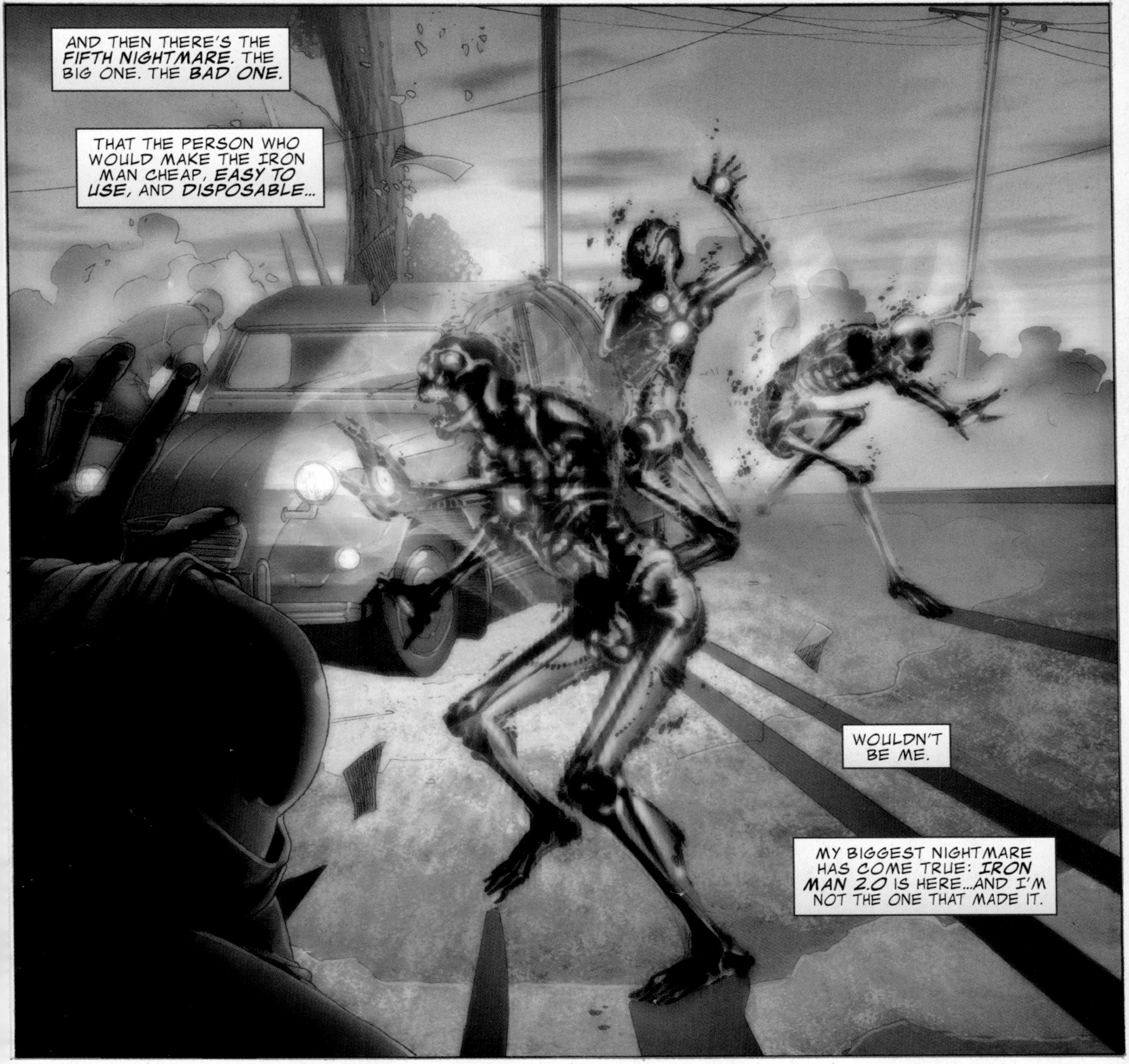
AND THEN THERE'S THE FIFTH NIGHTMARE. THE BIG ONE. THE BAD ONE.
THAT THE PERSON WHO WOULD MAKE THE IRON MAN CHEAP, EASY TO USE, AND DISPOSABLE...
WOULDN'T BE ME.
MY BIGGEST NIGHTMARE HAS COME TRUE: IRON MAN 2.0 IS HERE...AND I'M NOT THE ONE THAT MADE IT.

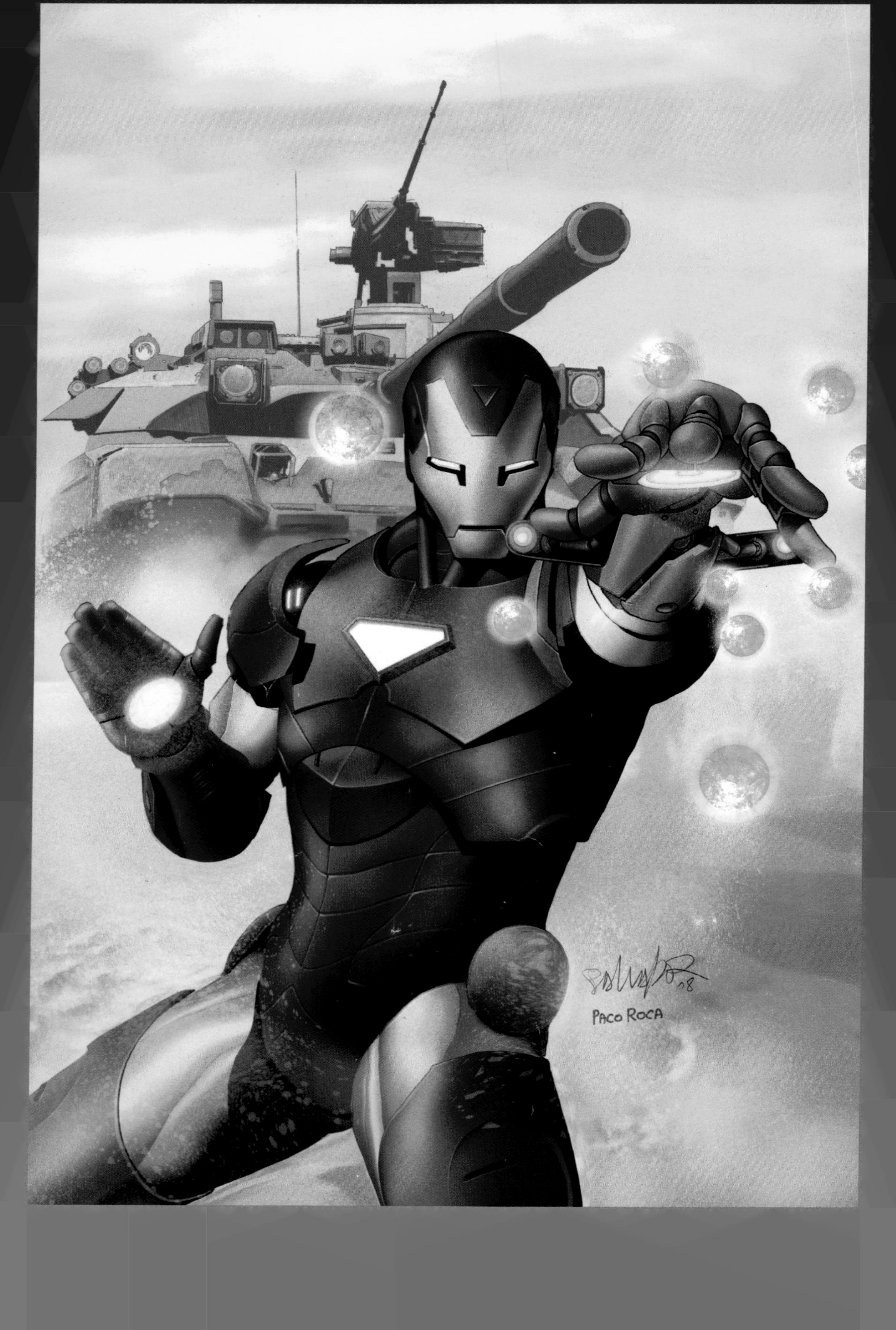
PACO ROCA

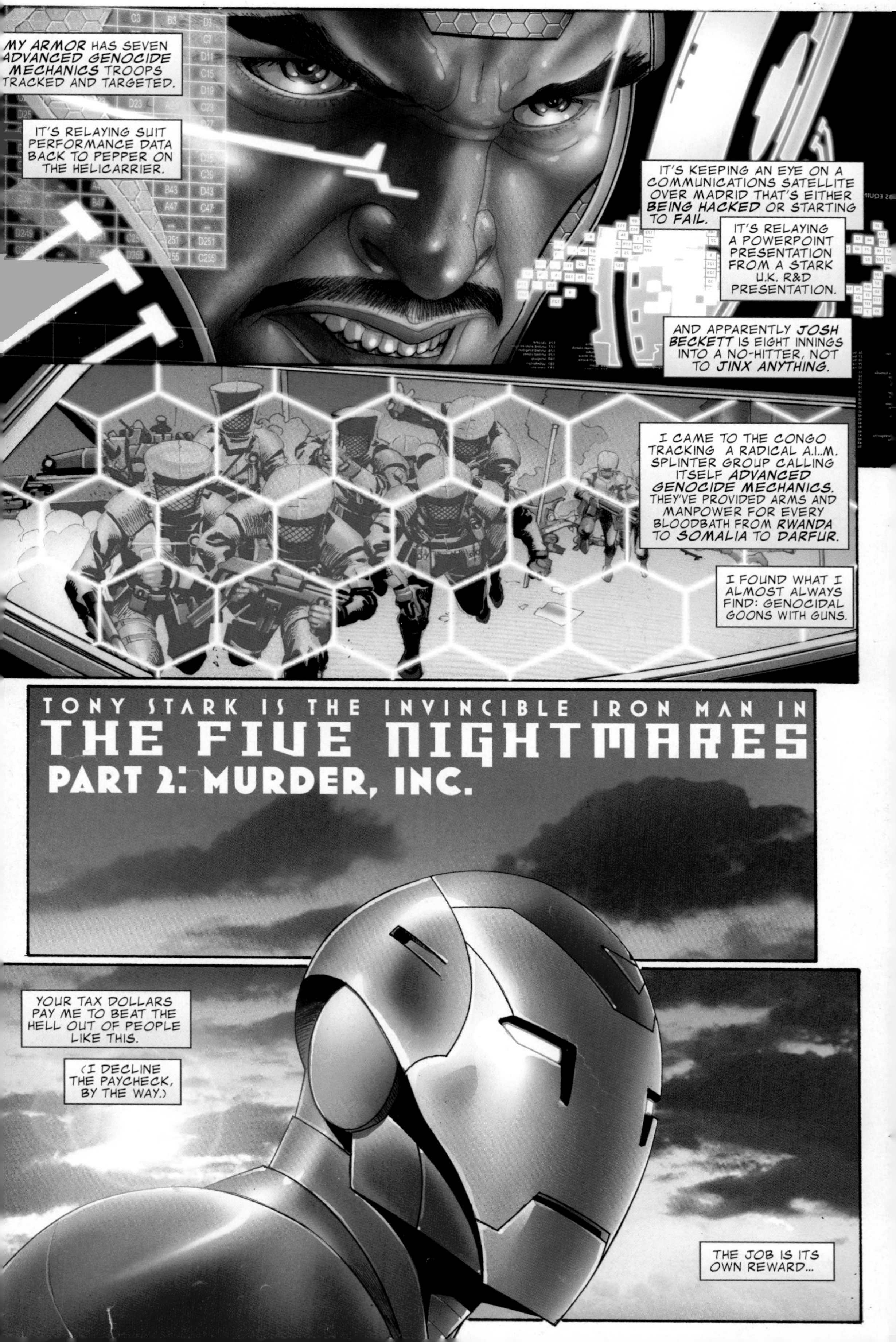
MY ARMOR HAS SEVEN ADVANCED GENOCIDE MECHANICS TROOPS TRACKED AND TARGETED.
IT'S RELAYING SUIT PERFORMANCE DATA BACK TO PEPPER ON THE HELICARRIER.
IT'S KEEPING AN EYE ON A COMMUNICATIONS SATELLITE OVER MADRID THAT'S EITHER BEING HACKED OR STARTING TO FAIL.
IT'S RELAYING A POWERPOINT PRESENTATION FROM A STARK U.K. R&D PRESENTATION.
AND APPARENTLY JOSH BECKETT IS EIGHT INNINGS INTO A NO-HITTER, NOT TO JINX ANYTHING.
I CAME TO THE CONGO TRACKING A RADICAL A.I..M. SPLINTER GROUP CALLING ITSELF ADVANCED GENOCIDE MECHANICS. THEY'VE PROVIDED ARMS AND MANPOWER FOR EVERY BLOODBATH FROM RWANDA TO SOMALIA TO DARFUR.
I FOUND WHAT I ALMOST ALWAYS FIND: GENOCIDAL GOONS WITH GUNS.
TONY STARK IS THE INVINCIBLE IRON MAN IN
THE FIVE NIGHTMARES
PART 2: MURDER, INC.
YOUR TAX DOLLARS PAY ME TO BEAT THE HELL OUT OF PEOPLE LIKE THIS.
(I DECLINE THE PAYCHECK, BY THE WAY.)
THE JOB IS ITS OWN REWARD...

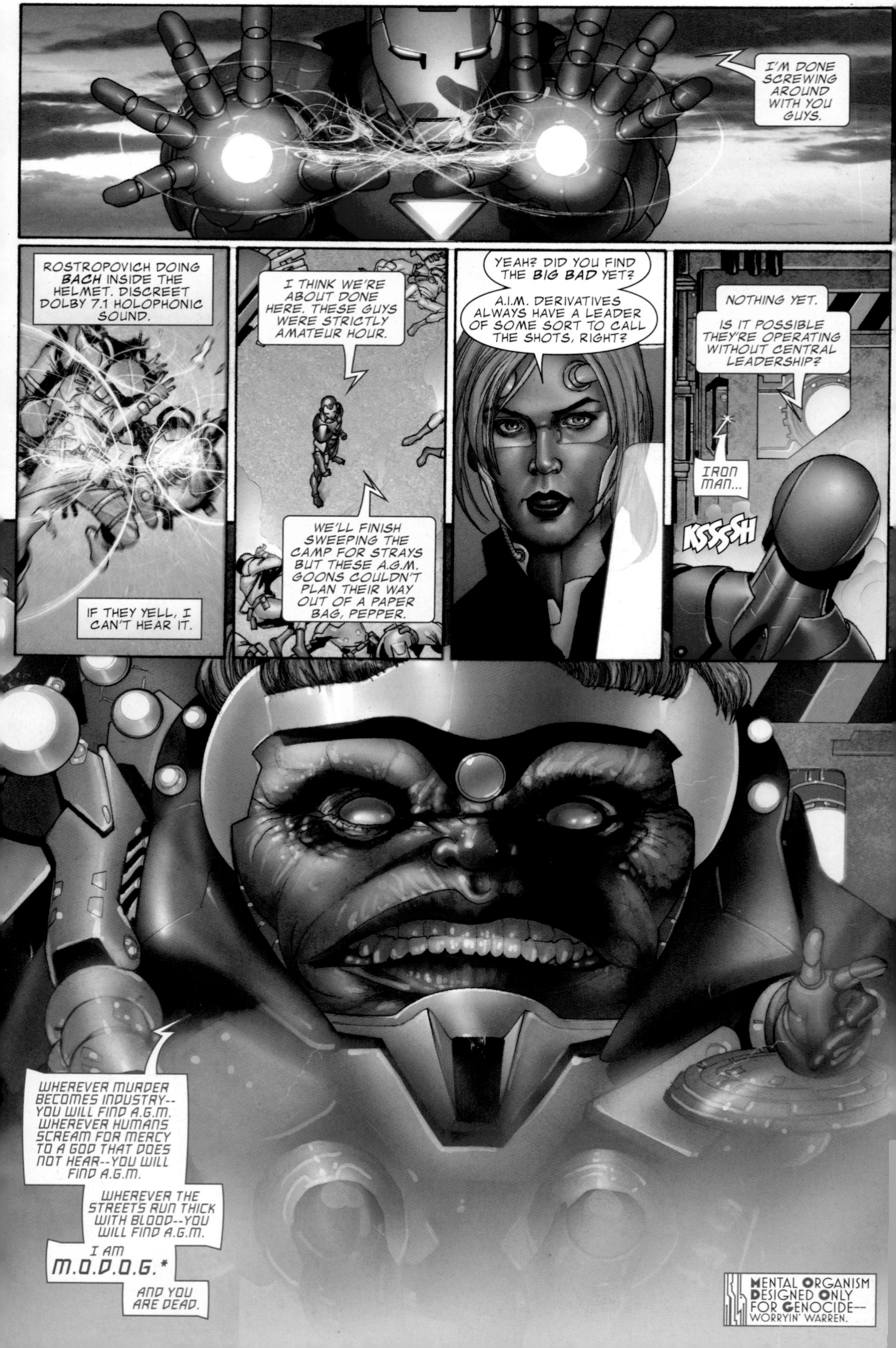
I'M DONE SCREWING AROUND WITH YOU GUYS.
ROSTROPOVICH DOING BACH INSIDE THE HELMET. DISCREET DOLBY 7.1 HOLOPHONIC SOUND.
IF THEY YELL, I CAN'T HEAR IT.
I THINK WE'RE ABOUT DONE HERE. THESE GUYS WERE STRICTLY AMATEUR HOUR.
WE'LL FINISH SWEEPING THE CAMP FOR STRAYS BUT THESE A.G.M. GOONS COULDN'T PLAN THEIR WAY OUT OF A PAPER BAG, PEPPER.
YEAH? DID YOU FIND THE BIG BAD YET?
A.I.M. DERIVATIVES ALWAYS HAVE A LEADER OF SOME SORT TO CALL THE SHOTS, RIGHT?
NOTHING YET.
IS IT POSSIBLE THEY'RE OPERATING WITHOUT CENTRAL LEADERSHIP?
IRON MAN...
KSSSSH
WHEREVER MURDER BECOMES INDUSTRY-- YOU WILL FIND A.G.M. WHEREVER HUMANS SCREAM FOR MERCY TO A GOD THAT DOES NOT HEAR--YOU WILL FIND A.G.M.
WHEREVER THE STREETS RUN THICK WITH BLOOD--YOU WILL FIND A.G.M.
I AM M.O.D.O.G.*
AND YOU ARE DEAD.
MENTAL ORGANISM DESIGNED ONLY FOR GENOCIDE-- WORRYIN' WARREN.

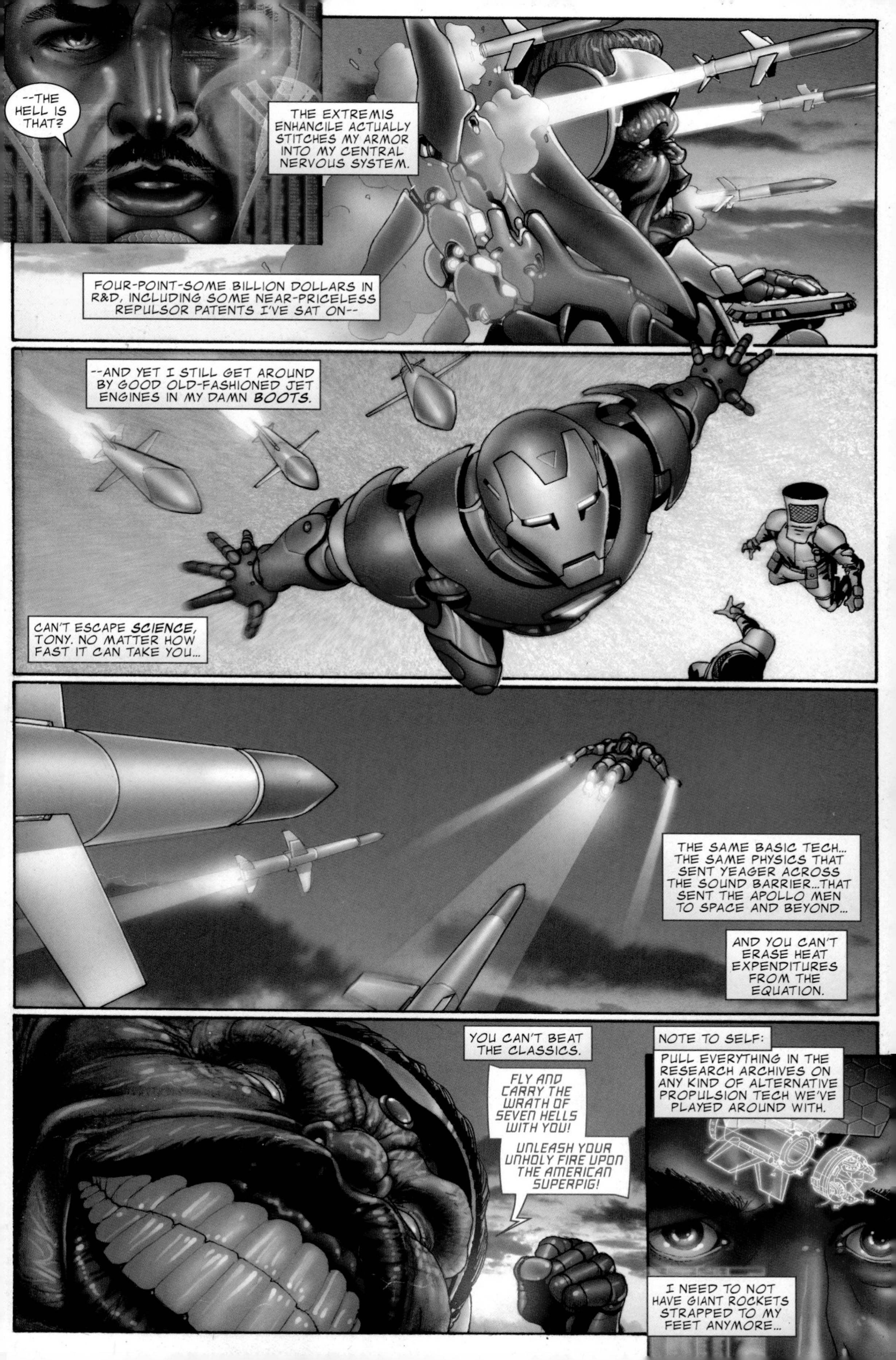
--THE HELL IS THAT?
THE EXTREMIS ENHANCILE ACTUALLY STITCHES MY ARMOR INTO MY CENTRAL NERVOUS SYSTEM.
FOUR-POINT-SOME BILLION DOLLARS IN R&D, INCLUDING SOME NEAR-PRICELESS REPULSOR PATENTS I'VE SAT ON--
--AND YET I STILL GET AROUND BY GOOD OLD-FASHIONED JET ENGINES IN MY DAMN BOOTS.
CAN'T ESCAPE SCIENCE, TONY. NO MATTER HOW FAST IT CAN TAKE YOU...
THE SAME BASIC TECH... THE SAME PHYSICS THAT SENT YEAGER ACROSS THE SOUND BARRIER...THAT SENT THE APOLLO MEN TO SPACE AND BEYOND...
AND YOU CAN'T ERASE HEAT EXPENDITURES FROM THE EQUATION.
YOU CAN'T BEAT THE CLASSICS.
FLY AND CARRY THE WRATH OF SEVEN HELLS WITH YOU!
UNLEASH YOUR UNHOLY FIRE UPON THE AMERICAN SUPERPIG!
NOTE TO SELF:
PULL EVERYTHING IN THE RESEARCH ARCHIVES ON ANY KIND OF ALTERNATIVE PROPULSION TECH WE'VE PLAYED AROUND WITH.
I NEED TO NOT HAVE GIANT ROCKETS STRAPPED TO MY FEET ANYMORE...

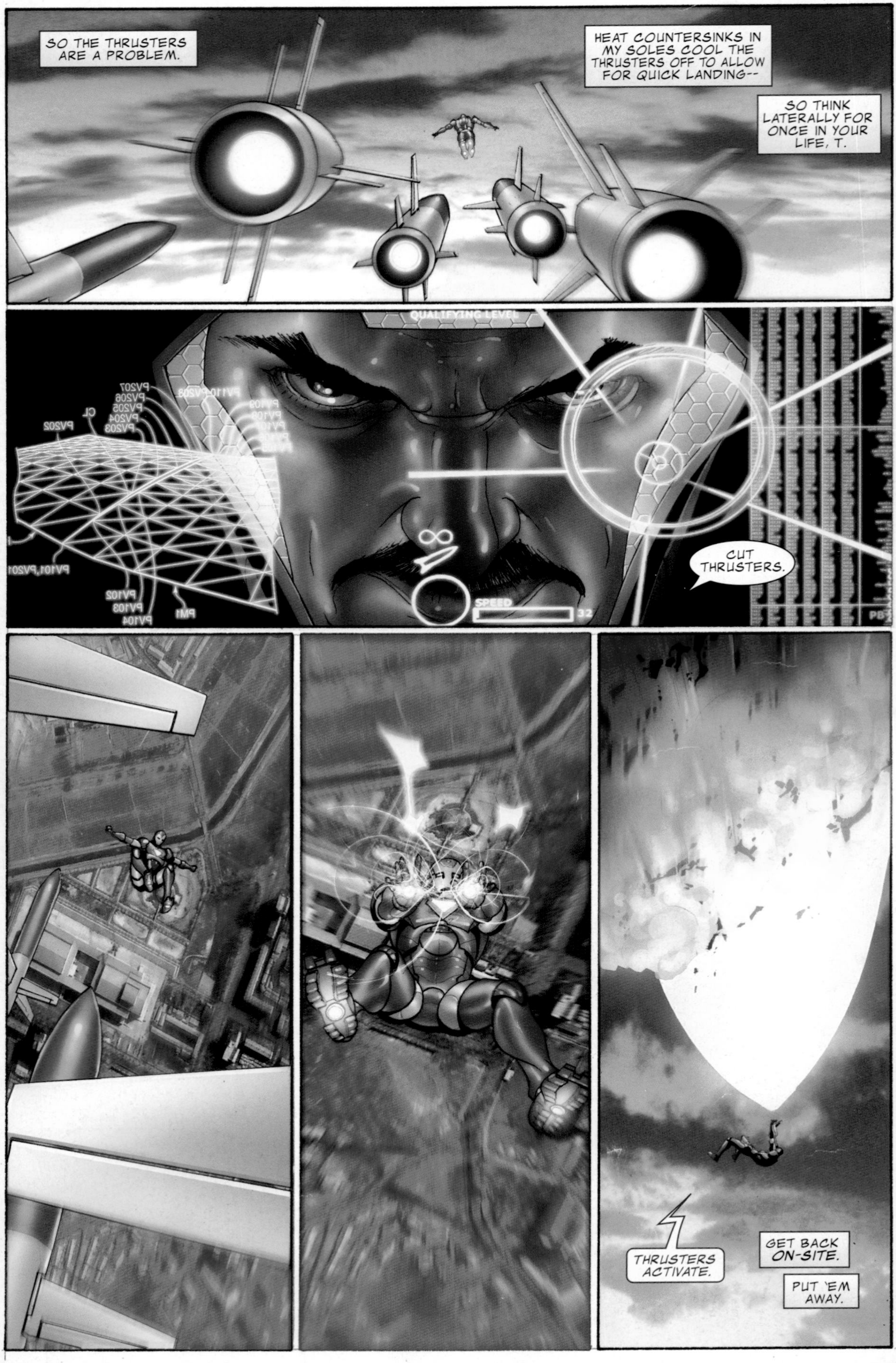
SO THE THRUSTERS ARE A PROBLEM.
HEAT COUNTERSINKS IN MY SOLES COOL THE THRUSTERS OFF TO ALLOW FOR QUICK LANDING--
SO THINK LATERALLY FOR ONCE IN YOUR LIFE, T.
QUALIFYING LEVEL
CUT THRUSTERS.
SPEED
32
THRUSTERS ACTIVATE.
GET BACK ON-SITE.
PUT 'EM AWAY.

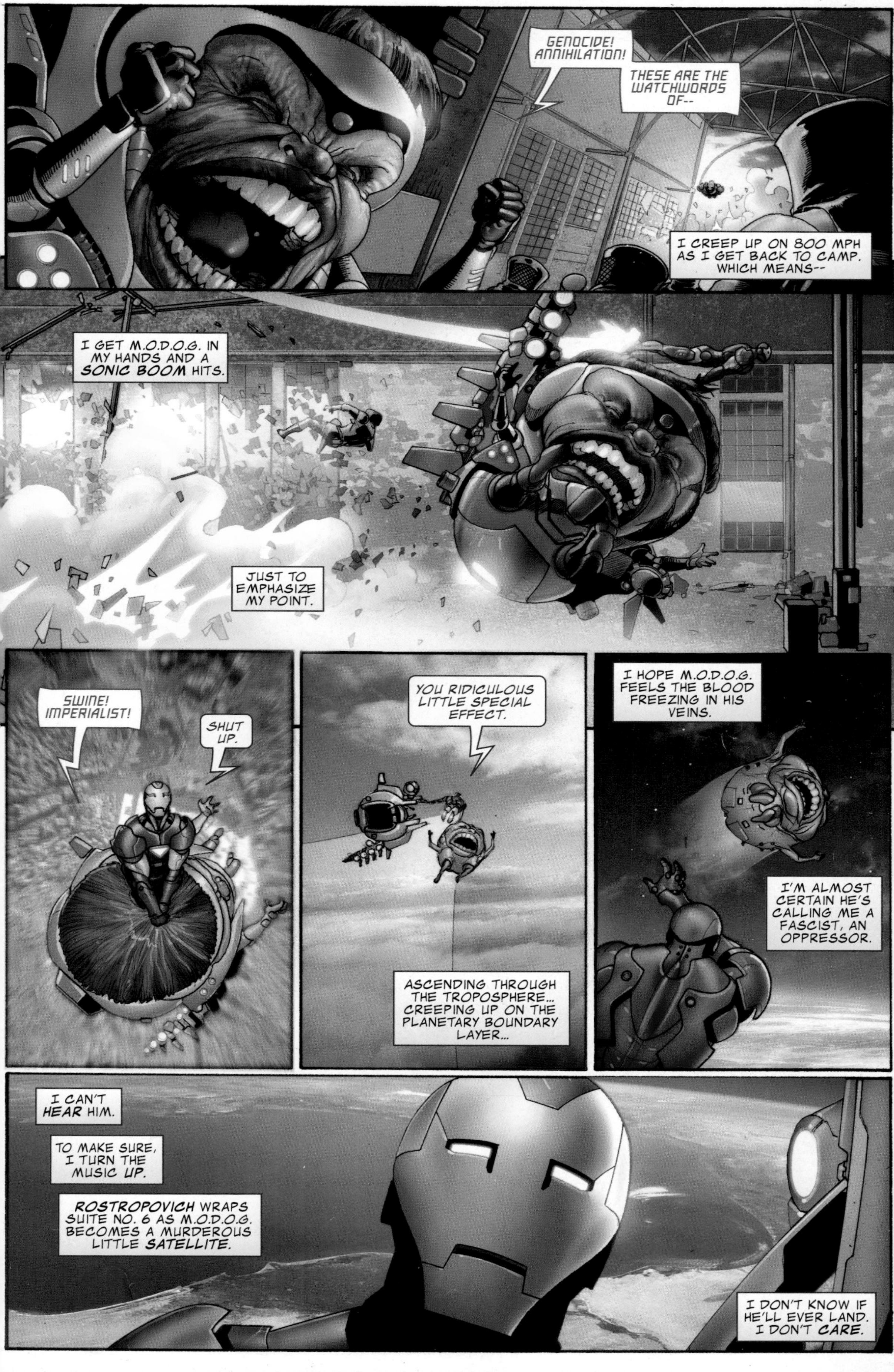
GENOCIDE! ANNIHILATION!
THESE ARE THE WATCHWORDS OF--
I CREEP UP ON 800 MPH AS I GET BACK TO CAMP. WHICH MEANS--
I GET M.O.D.O.G. IN MY HANDS AND A SONIC BOOM HITS.
JUST TO EMPHASIZE MY POINT.
SWINE! IMPERIALIST!
SHUT UP.
YOU RIDICULOUS LITTLE SPECIAL EFFECT.
ASCENDING THROUGH THE TROPOSPHERE... CREEPING UP ON THE PLANETARY BOUNDARY LAYER...
I HOPE M.O.D.O.G. FEELS THE BLOOD FREEZING IN HIS VEINS.
I'M ALMOST CERTAIN HE'S CALLING ME A FASCIST, AN OPPRESSOR.
I CAN'T HEAR HIM.
TO MAKE SURE, I TURN THE MUSIC UP.
ROSTROPOVICH WRAPS SUITE NO. 6 AS M.O.D.O.G. BECOMES A MURDEROUS LITTLE SATELLITE.
I DON'T KNOW IF HE'LL EVER LAND. I DON'T CARE.

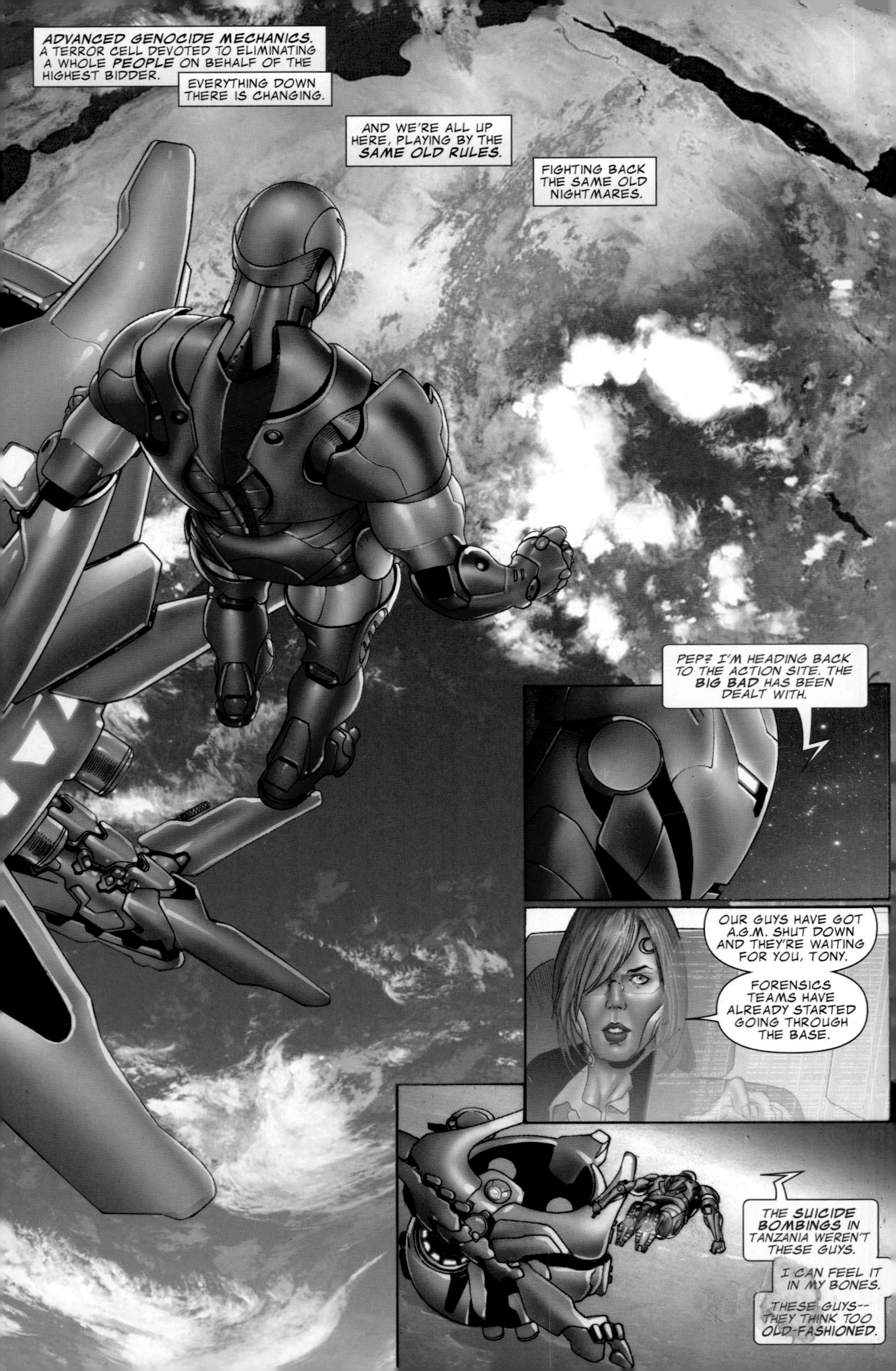
ADVANCED GENOCIDE MECHANICS. A TERROR CELL DEVOTED TO ELIMINATING A WHOLE PEOPLE ON BEHALF OF THE HIGHEST BIDDER.
EVERYTHING DOWN THERE IS CHANGING.
AND WE'RE ALL UP HERE, PLAYING BY THE SAME OLD RULES.
FIGHTING BACK THE SAME OLD NIGHTMARES.
PEP? I'M HEADING BACK TO THE ACTION SITE. THE BIG BAD HAS BEEN DEALT WITH.
OUR GUYS HAVE GOT A.G.M. SHUT DOWN AND THEY'RE WAITING FOR YOU, TONY.
FORENSICS TEAMS HAVE ALREADY STARTED GOING THROUGH THE BASE.
THE SUICIDE BOMBINGS IN TANZANIA WEREN'T THESE GUYS.
I CAN FEEL IT IN MY BONES.
THESE GUYS-- THEY THINK TOO OLD-FASHIONED.

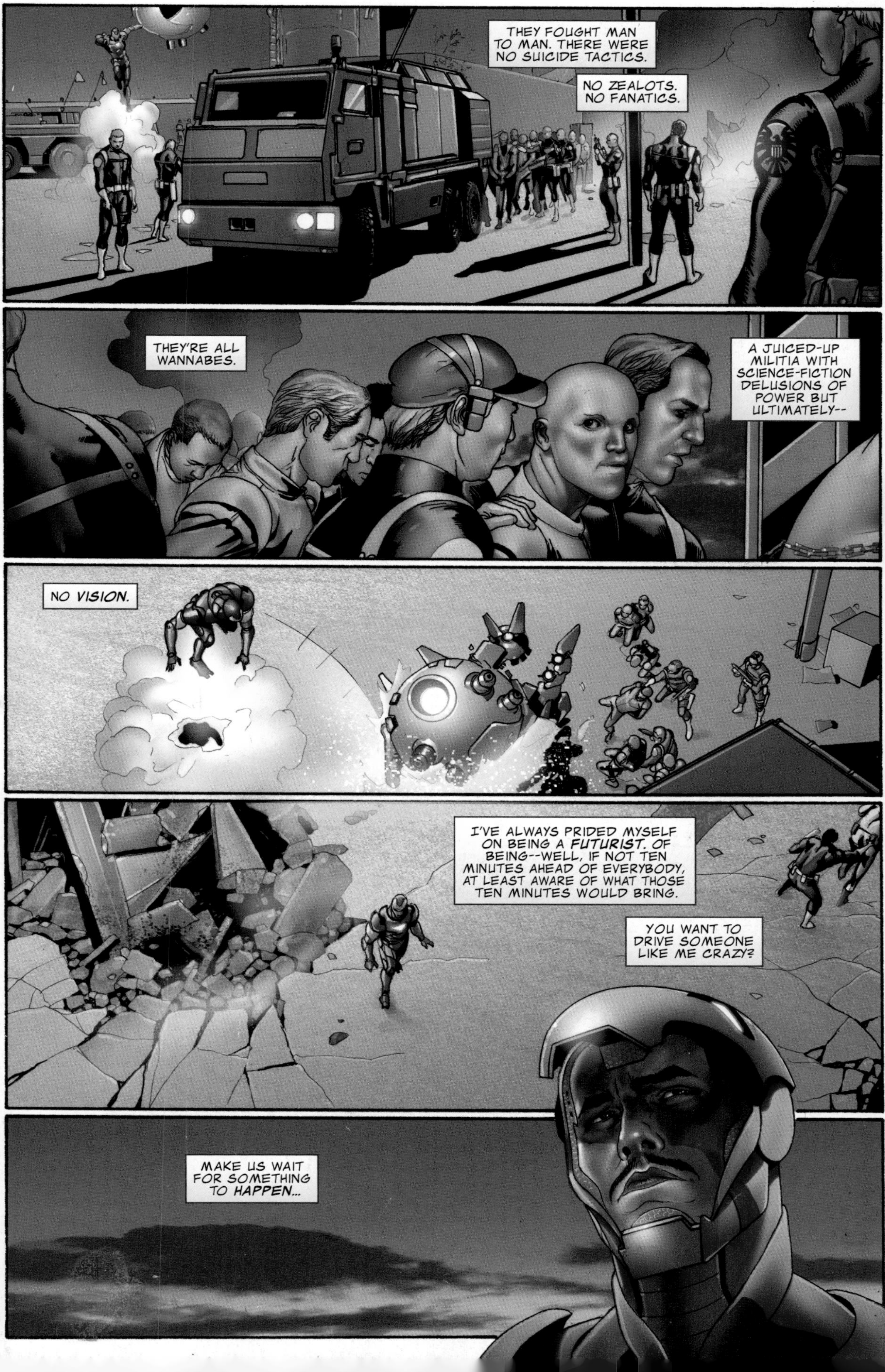
THEY FOUGHT MAN TO MAN. THERE WERE NO SUICIDE TACTICS.
NO ZEALOTS. NO FANATICS.
THEY'RE ALL WANNABES.
A JUICED-UP MILITIA WITH SCIENCE-FICTION DELUSIONS OF POWER BUT ULTIMATELY--
NO VISION.
I'VE ALWAYS PRIDED MYSELF ON BEING A FUTURIST. OF BEING--WELL, IF NOT TEN MINUTES AHEAD OF EVERYBODY, AT LEAST AWARE OF WHAT THOSE TEN MINUTES WOULD BRING.
YOU WANT TO DRIVE SOMEONE LIKE ME CRAZY?
MAKE US WAIT FOR SOMETHING TO HAPPEN...

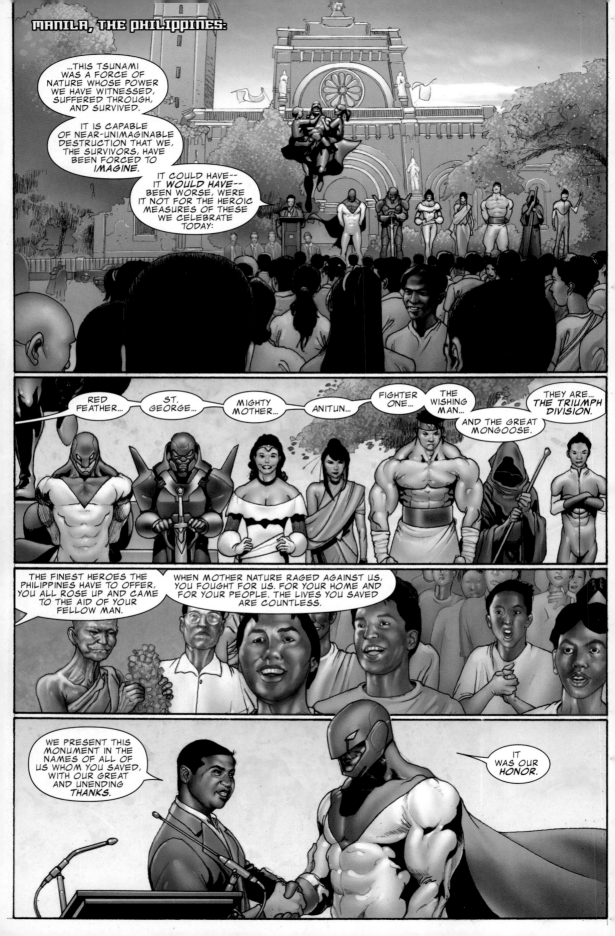

MANILA, THE PHILIPPINES:

...THIS TSUNAMI WAS A FORCE OF NATURE WHOSE POWER WE HAVE WITNESSED, SUFFERED THROUGH, AND SURVIVED.

IT IS CAPABLE OF NEAR-UNIMAGINABLE DESTRUCTION THAT WE, THE SURVIVORS, HAVE BEEN FORCED TO IMAGINE.

IT COULD HAVE-- IT *WOULD HAVE--* BEEN WORSE, WERE IT NOT FOR THE HEROIC MEASURES OF THESE WE CELEBRATE TODAY:

RED FEATHER...

ST. GEORGE...

MIGHTY MOTHER...

ANITUN...

FIGHTER ONE...

THE WISHING MAN...

AND THE GREAT MONGOOSE.

THEY ARE... *THE TRIUMPH DIVISION.*

THE FINEST HEROES THE PHILIPPINES HAVE TO OFFER, YOU ALL ROSE UP AND CAME TO THE AID OF YOUR FELLOW MAN.

WHEN MOTHER NATURE RAGED AGAINST US, YOU FOUGHT FOR US. FOR YOUR HOME AND FOR YOUR PEOPLE. THE LIVES YOU SAVED ARE COUNTLESS.

WE PRESENT THIS MONUMENT IN THE NAMES OF ALL OF US WHOM YOU SAVED, WITH OUR GREAT AND UNENDING *THANKS.*

IT WAS OUR *HONOR.*

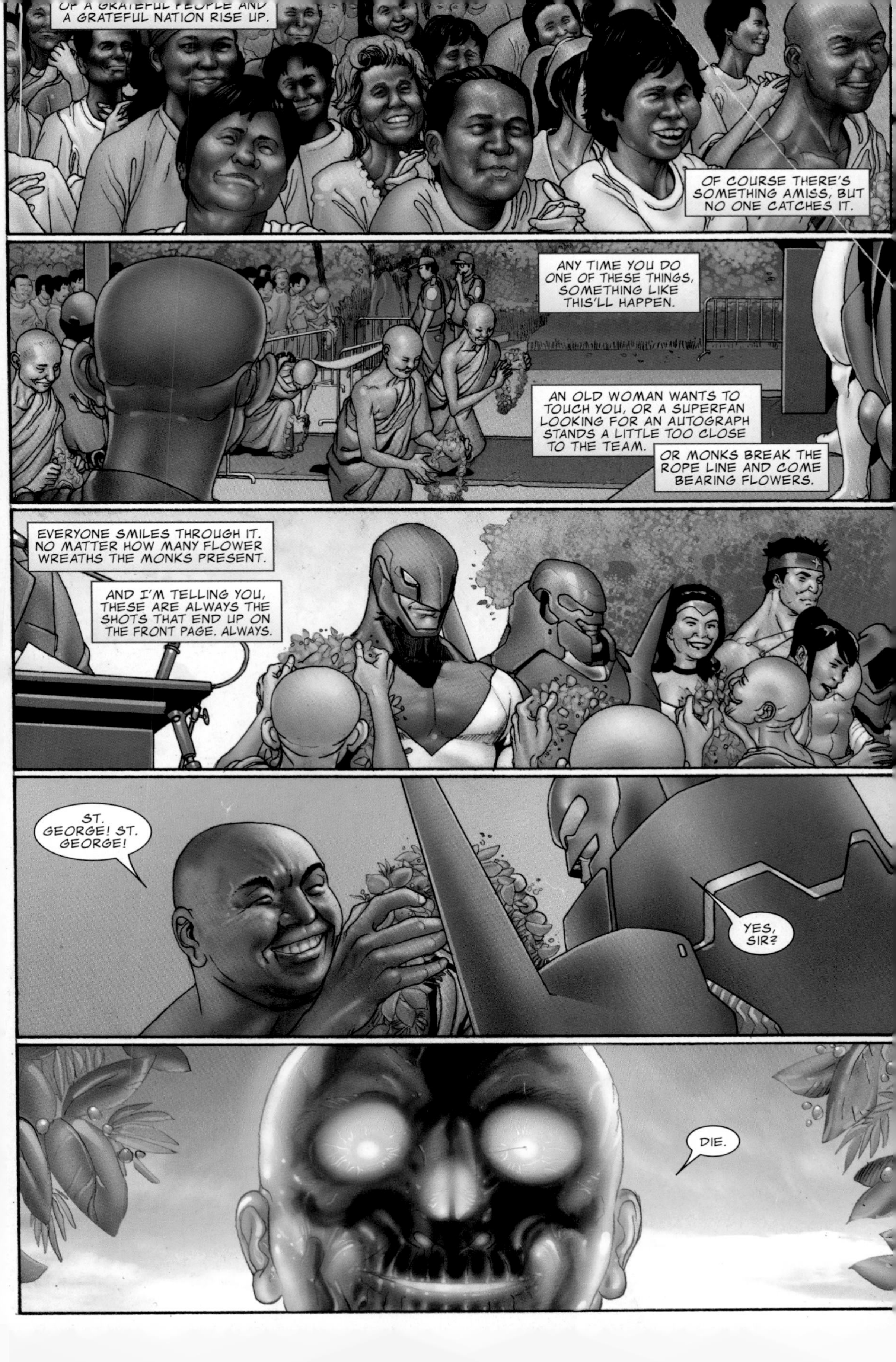

OF A GRATEFUL PEOPLE AND
A GRATEFUL NATION RISE UP.
OF COURSE THERE'S SOMETHING AMISS, BUT NO ONE CATCHES IT.
ANY TIME YOU DO ONE OF THESE THINGS, SOMETHING LIKE THIS'LL HAPPEN.
AN OLD WOMAN WANTS TO TOUCH YOU, OR A SUPERFAN LOOKING FOR AN AUTOGRAPH STANDS A LITTLE TOO CLOSE TO THE TEAM.
OR MONKS BREAK THE ROPE LINE AND COME BEARING FLOWERS.
EVERYONE SMILES THROUGH IT. NO MATTER HOW MANY FLOWER WREATHS THE MONKS PRESENT.
AND I'M TELLING YOU, THESE ARE ALWAYS THE SHOTS THAT END UP ON THE FRONT PAGE. ALWAYS.
ST. GEORGE! ST. GEORGE!
YES, SIR?
DIE.

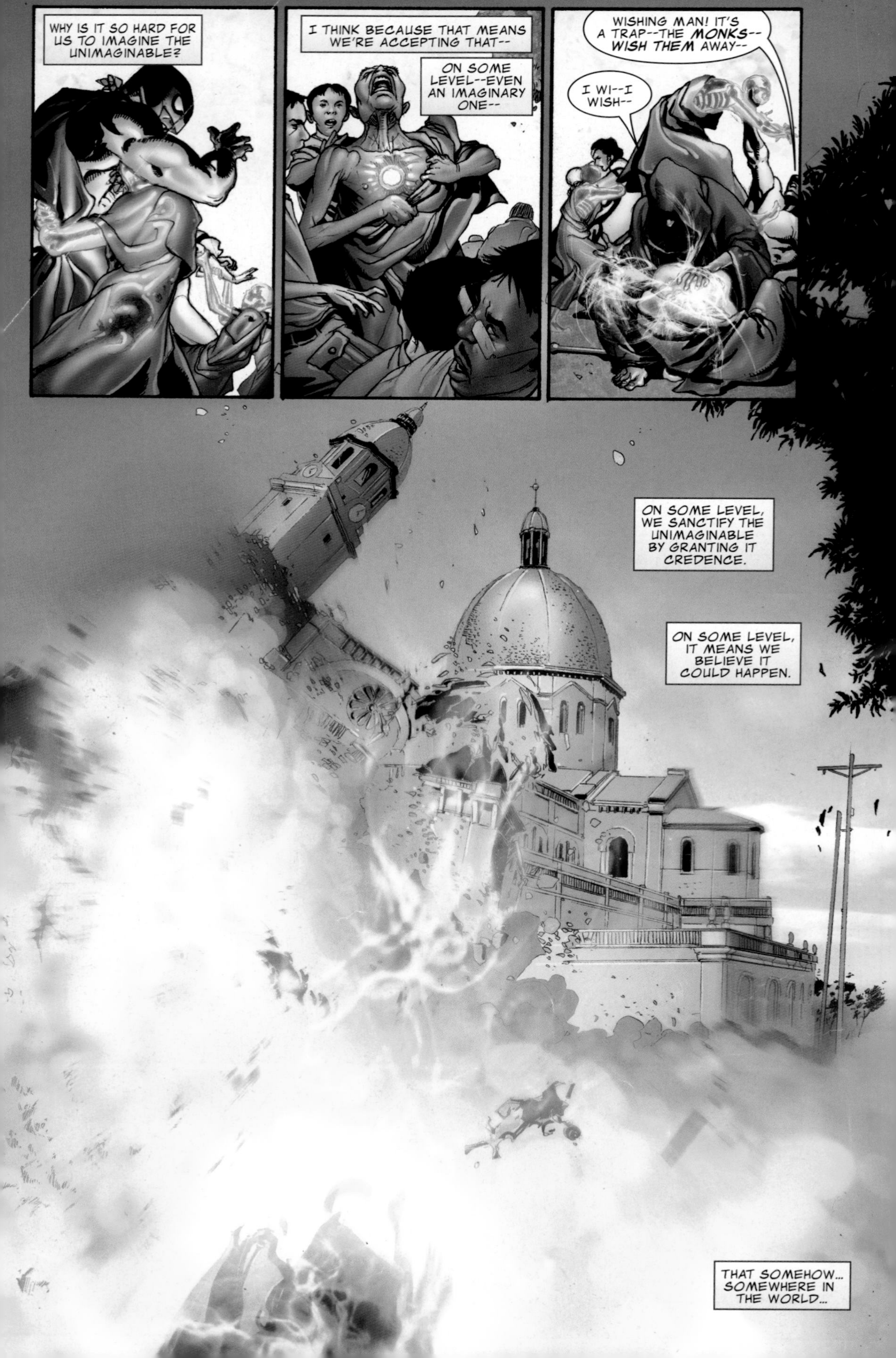
WHY IS IT SO HARD FOR US TO IMAGINE THE UNIMAGINABLE?
I THINK BECAUSE THAT MEANS WE'RE ACCEPTING THAT--
ON SOME LEVEL--EVEN AN IMAGINARY ONE--
WISHING MAN! IT'S A TRAP--THE **MONKS**--**WISH THEM** AWAY--
I WI--I WISH--
ON SOME LEVEL, WE SANCTIFY THE UNIMAGINABLE BY GRANTING IT CREDENCE.
ON SOME LEVEL, IT MEANS WE BELIEVE IT COULD HAPPEN.
THAT SOMEHOW... SOMEWHERE IN THE WORLD...

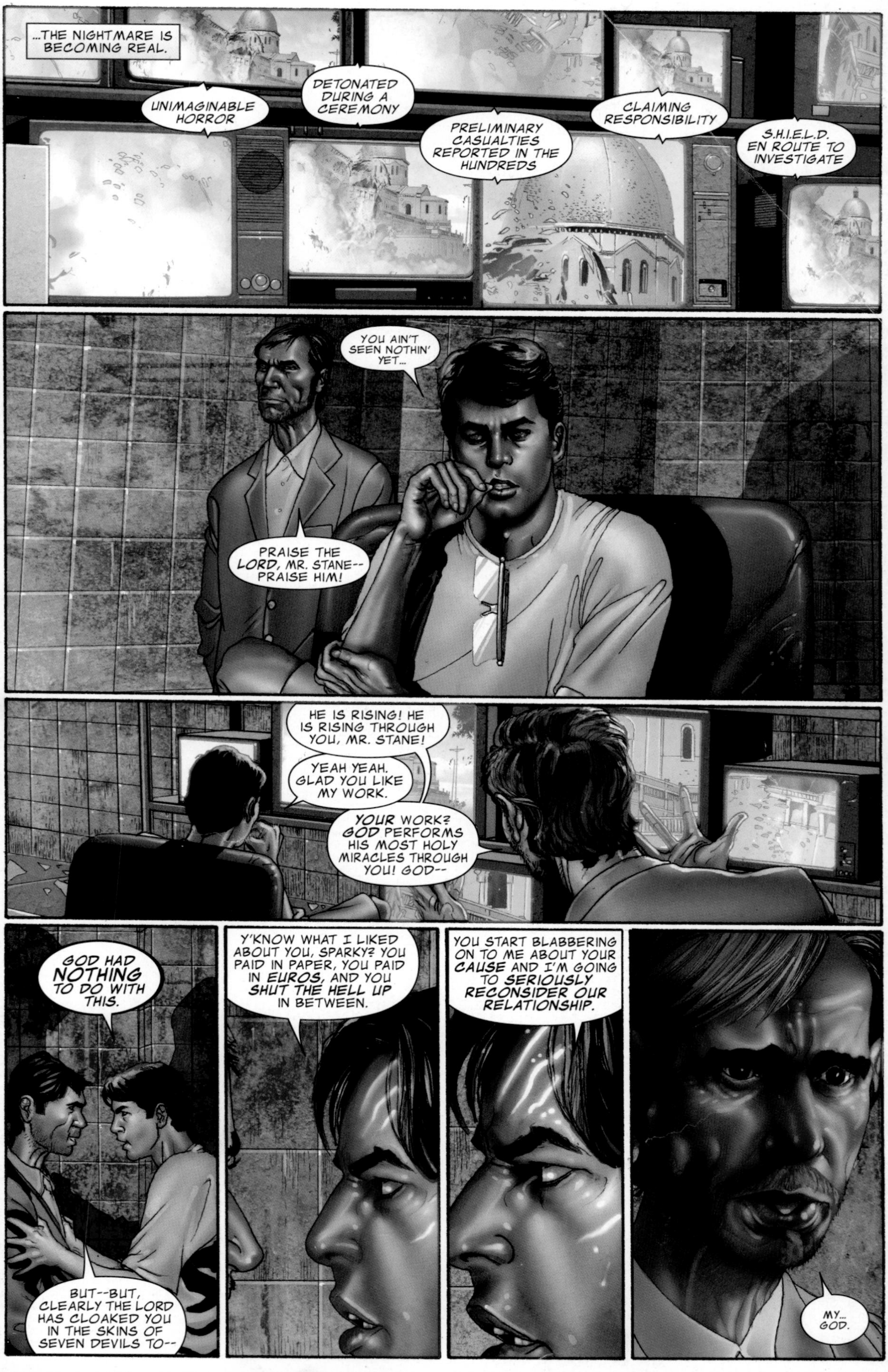
...THE NIGHTMARE IS BECOMING REAL.
UNIMAGINABLE HORROR
DETONATED DURING A CEREMONY
PRELIMINARY CASUALTIES REPORTED IN THE HUNDREDS
CLAIMING RESPONSIBILITY
S.H.I.E.L.D. EN ROUTE TO INVESTIGATE
YOU AIN'T SEEN NOTHIN' YET...
PRAISE THE LORD, MR. STANE--PRAISE HIM!
HE IS RISING! HE IS RISING THROUGH YOU, MR. STANE!
YEAH YEAH. GLAD YOU LIKE MY WORK.
YOUR WORK? GOD PERFORMS HIS MOST HOLY MIRACLES THROUGH YOU! GOD--
GOD HAD NOTHING TO DO WITH THIS.
BUT--BUT, CLEARLY THE LORD HAS CLOAKED YOU IN THE SKINS OF SEVEN DEVILS TO--
Y'KNOW WHAT I LIKED ABOUT YOU, SPARKY? YOU PAID IN PAPER, YOU PAID IN EUROS, AND YOU SHUT THE HELL UP IN BETWEEN.
YOU START BLABBERING ON TO ME ABOUT YOUR CAUSE AND I'M GOING TO SERIOUSLY RECONSIDER OUR RELATIONSHIP.
MY... GOD.

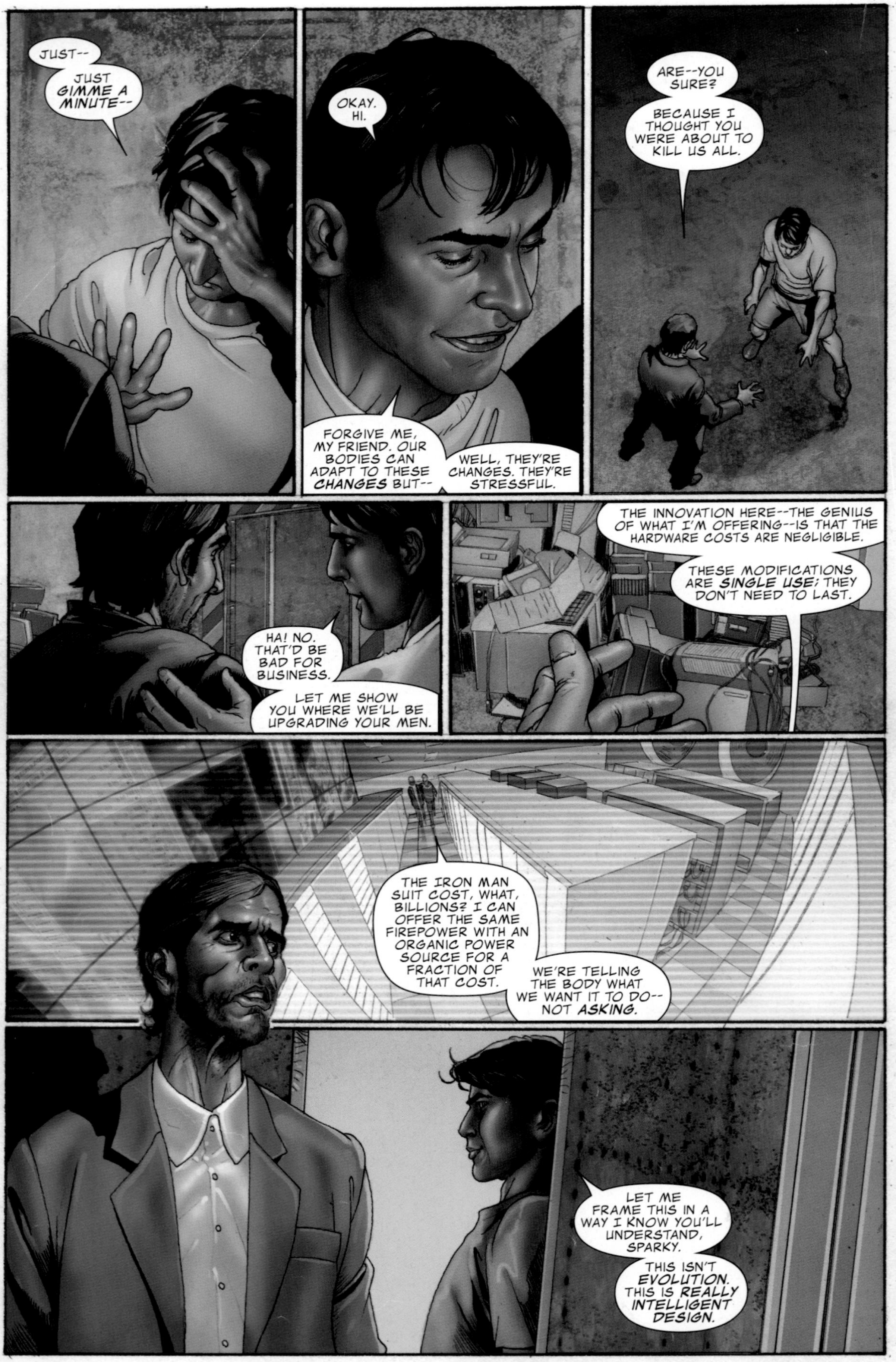
JUST--
JUST GIMME A MINUTE--
OKAY. HI.
FORGIVE ME, MY FRIEND. OUR BODIES CAN ADAPT TO THESE CHANGES BUT--
WELL, THEY'RE CHANGES. THEY'RE STRESSFUL.
ARE--YOU SURE?
BECAUSE I THOUGHT YOU WERE ABOUT TO KILL US ALL.
HA! NO. THAT'D BE BAD FOR BUSINESS.
LET ME SHOW YOU WHERE WE'LL BE UPGRADING YOUR MEN.
THE INNOVATION HERE--THE GENIUS OF WHAT I'M OFFERING--IS THAT THE HARDWARE COSTS ARE NEGLIGIBLE.
THESE MODIFICATIONS ARE SINGLE USE; THEY DON'T NEED TO LAST.
THE IRON MAN SUIT COST, WHAT, BILLIONS? I CAN OFFER THE SAME FIREPOWER WITH AN ORGANIC POWER SOURCE FOR A FRACTION OF THAT COST.
WE'RE TELLING THE BODY WHAT WE WANT IT TO DO--NOT ASKING.
LET ME FRAME THIS IN A WAY I KNOW YOU'LL UNDERSTAND, SPARKY.
THIS ISN'T EVOLUTION. THIS IS REALLY INTELLIGENT DESIGN.

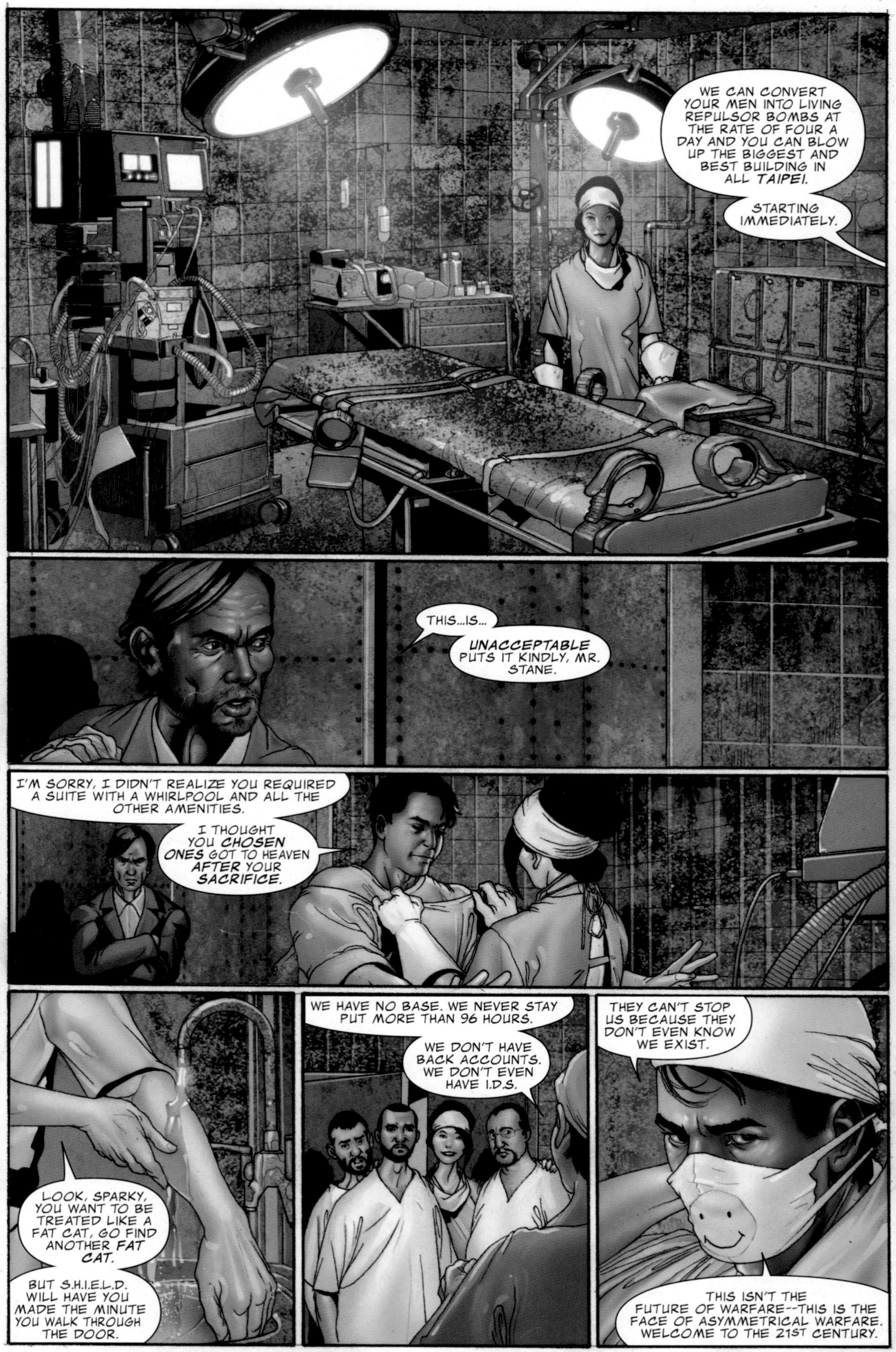
WE CAN CONVERT YOUR MEN INTO LIVING REPULSOR BOMBS AT THE RATE OF FOUR A DAY AND YOU CAN BLOW UP THE BIGGEST AND BEST BUILDING IN ALL TAIPEI.
STARTING IMMEDIATELY.
THIS...IS...
UNACCEPTABLE PUTS IT KINDLY, MR. STANE.
I'M SORRY, I DIDN'T REALIZE YOU REQUIRED A SUITE WITH A WHIRLPOOL AND ALL THE OTHER AMENITIES.
I THOUGHT YOU CHOSEN ONES GOT TO HEAVEN AFTER YOUR SACRIFICE.
LOOK, SPARKY, YOU WANT TO BE TREATED LIKE A FAT CAT, GO FIND ANOTHER FAT CAT.
BUT S.H.I.E.L.D. WILL HAVE YOU MADE THE MINUTE YOU WALK THROUGH THE DOOR.
WE HAVE NO BASE. WE NEVER STAY PUT MORE THAN 96 HOURS.
WE DON'T HAVE BACK ACCOUNTS. WE DON'T EVEN HAVE I.D.S.
THEY CAN'T STOP US BECAUSE THEY DON'T EVEN KNOW WE EXIST.
THIS ISN'T THE FUTURE OF WARFARE--THIS IS THE FACE OF ASYMMETRICAL WARFARE. WELCOME TO THE 21ST CENTURY.

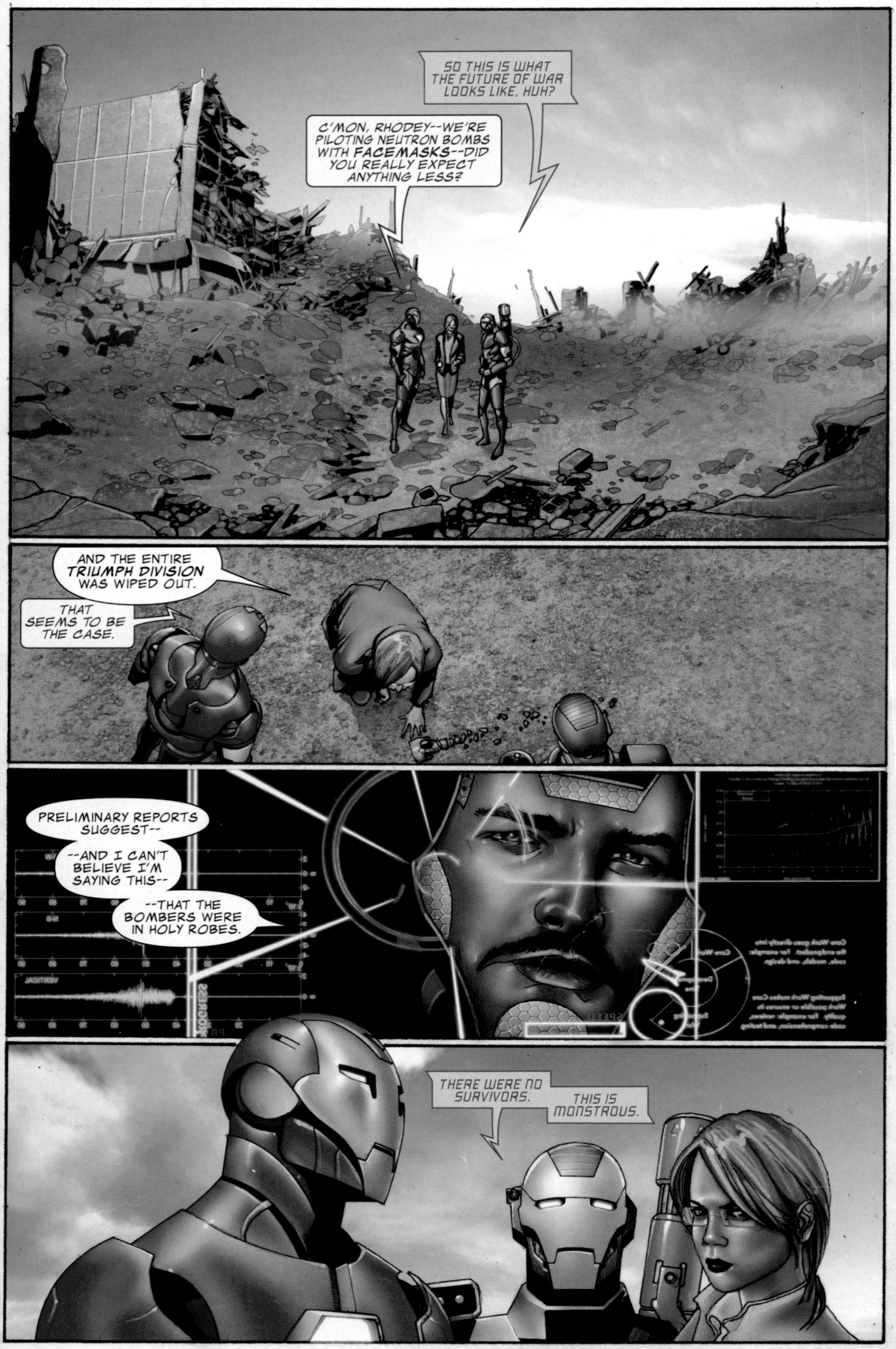
SO THIS IS WHAT THE FUTURE OF WAR LOOKS LIKE, HUH?
C'MON, RHODEY--WE'RE PILOTING NEUTRON BOMBS WITH FACEMASKS--DID YOU REALLY EXPECT ANYTHING LESS?
AND THE ENTIRE TRIUMPH DIVISION WAS WIPED OUT.
THAT SEEMS TO BE THE CASE.
PRELIMINARY REPORTS SUGGEST--
--AND I CAN'T BELIEVE I'M SAYING THIS--
--THAT THE BOMBERS WERE IN HOLY ROBES.
THERE WERE NO SURVIVORS.
THIS IS MONSTROUS.

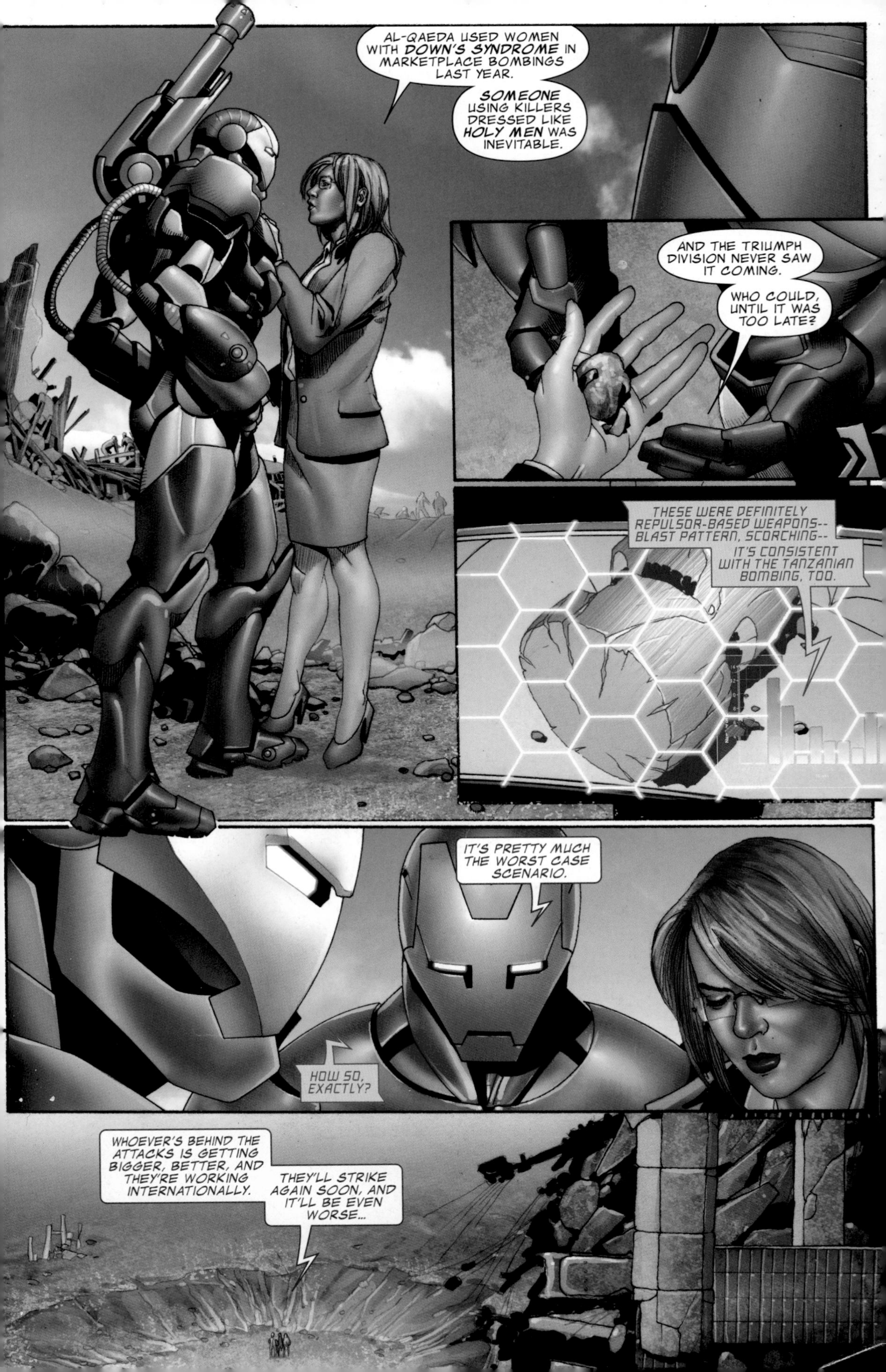
AL-QAEDA USED WOMEN WITH DOWN'S SYNDROME IN MARKETPLACE BOMBINGS LAST YEAR.
SOMEONE USING KILLERS DRESSED LIKE HOLY MEN WAS INEVITABLE.
AND THE TRIUMPH DIVISION NEVER SAW IT COMING.
WHO COULD, UNTIL IT WAS TOO LATE?
THESE WERE DEFINITELY REPULSOR-BASED WEAPONS-- BLAST PATTERN, SCORCHING--
IT'S CONSISTENT WITH THE TANZANIAN BOMBING, TOO.
IT'S PRETTY MUCH THE WORST CASE SCENARIO.
HOW SO, EXACTLY?
WHOEVER'S BEHIND THE ATTACKS IS GETTING BIGGER, BETTER, AND THEY'RE WORKING INTERNATIONALLY.
THEY'LL STRIKE AGAIN SOON, AND IT'LL BE EVEN WORSE...

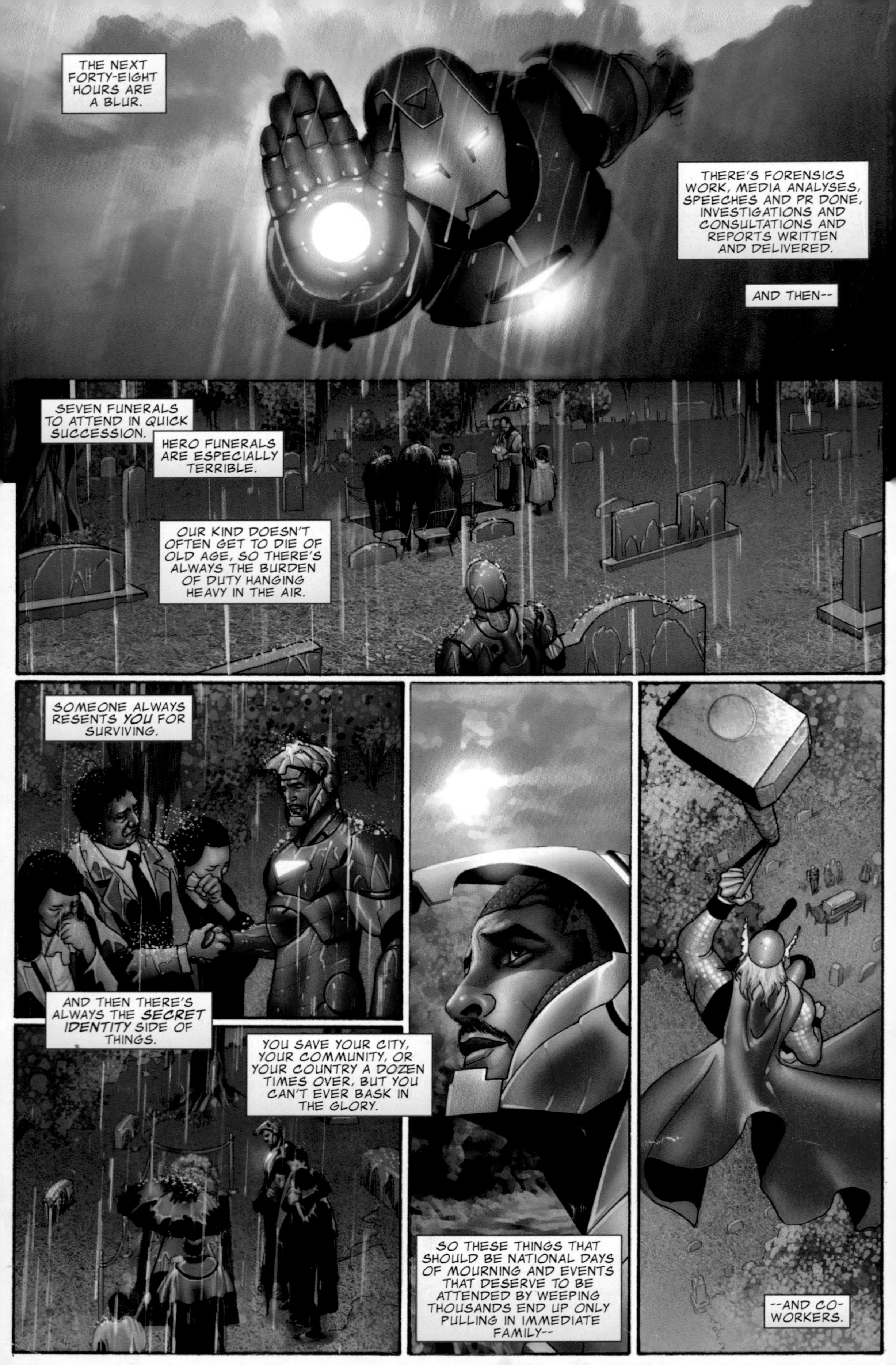
THE NEXT FORTY-EIGHT HOURS ARE A BLUR.
THERE'S FORENSICS WORK, MEDIA ANALYSES, SPEECHES AND PR DONE, INVESTIGATIONS AND CONSULTATIONS AND REPORTS WRITTEN AND DELIVERED.
AND THEN--
SEVEN FUNERALS TO ATTEND IN QUICK SUCCESSION.
HERO FUNERALS ARE ESPECIALLY TERRIBLE.
OUR KIND DOESN'T OFTEN GET TO DIE OF OLD AGE, SO THERE'S ALWAYS THE BURDEN OF DUTY HANGING HEAVY IN THE AIR.
SOMEONE ALWAYS RESENTS *YOU* FOR SURVIVING.
AND THEN THERE'S ALWAYS THE ***SECRET IDENTITY*** SIDE OF THINGS.
YOU SAVE YOUR CITY, YOUR COMMUNITY, OR YOUR COUNTRY A DOZEN TIMES OVER, BUT YOU CAN'T EVER BASK IN THE GLORY.
SO THESE THINGS THAT SHOULD BE NATIONAL DAYS OF MOURNING AND EVENTS THAT DESERVE TO BE ATTENDED BY WEEPING THOUSANDS END UP ONLY PULLING IN IMMEDIATE FAMILY--
--AND CO-WORKERS.

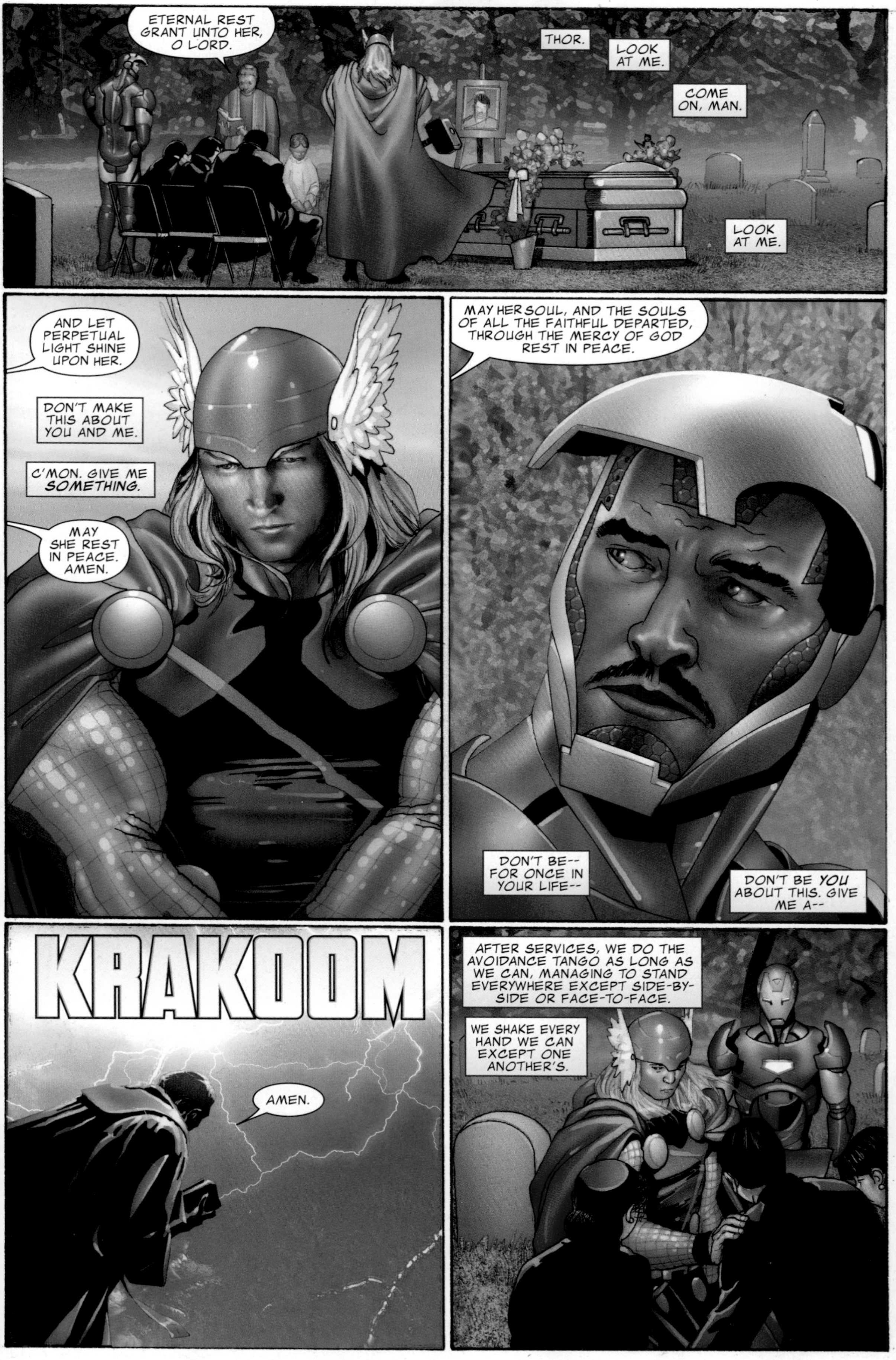
ETERNAL REST GRANT UNTO HER, O LORD.
THOR.
LOOK AT ME.
COME ON, MAN.
LOOK AT ME.
AND LET PERPETUAL LIGHT SHINE UPON HER.
DON'T MAKE THIS ABOUT YOU AND ME.
C'MON. GIVE ME SOMETHING.
MAY SHE REST IN PEACE. AMEN.
MAY HER SOUL, AND THE SOULS OF ALL THE FAITHFUL DEPARTED, THROUGH THE MERCY OF GOD REST IN PEACE.
DON'T BE-- FOR ONCE IN YOUR LIFE--
DON'T BE YOU ABOUT THIS. GIVE ME A--
KRAKOOM
AMEN.
AFTER SERVICES, WE DO THE AVOIDANCE TANGO AS LONG AS WE CAN, MANAGING TO STAND EVERYWHERE EXCEPT SIDE-BY-SIDE OR FACE-TO-FACE.
WE SHAKE EVERY HAND WE CAN EXCEPT ONE ANOTHER'S.

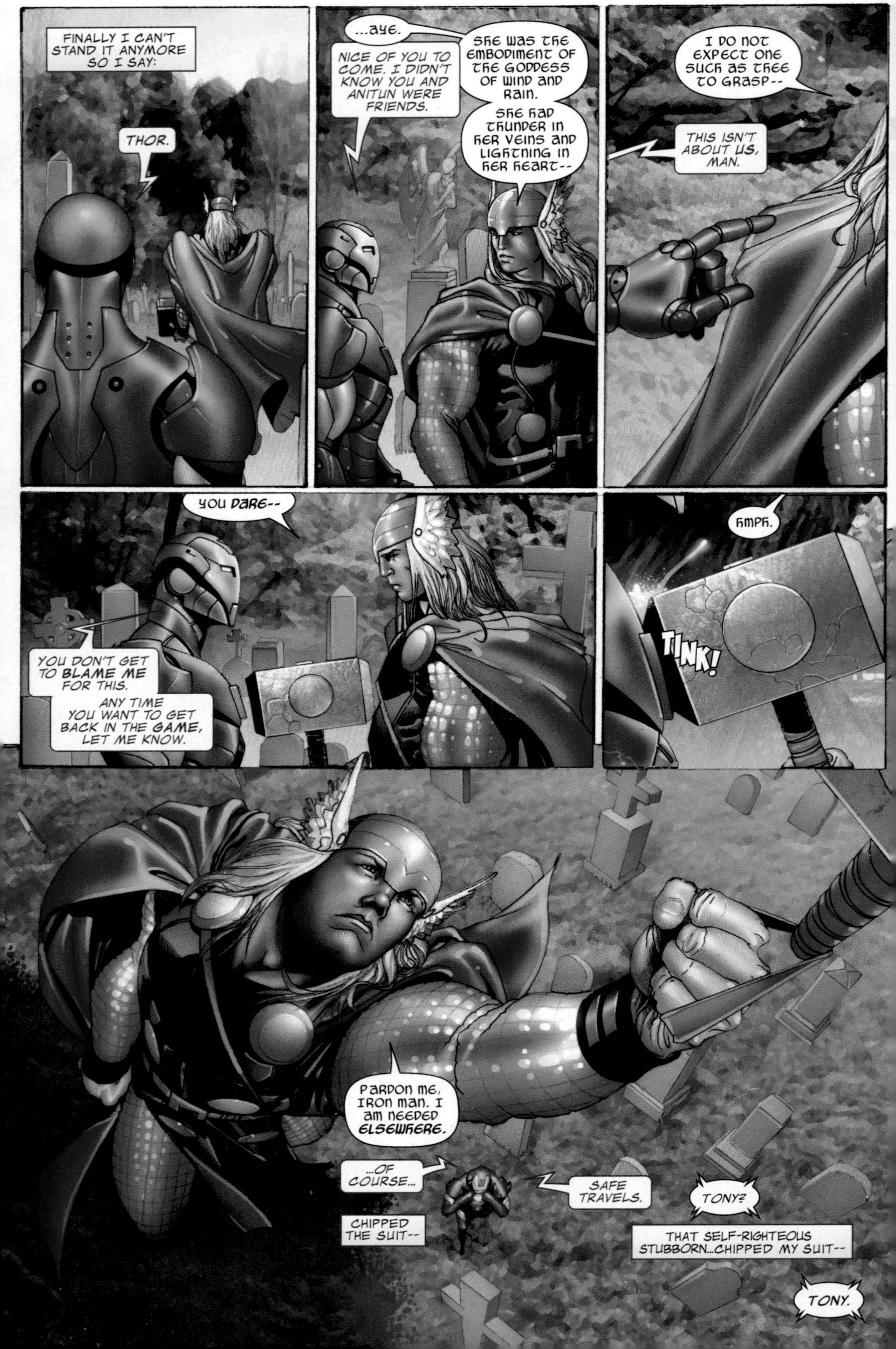
FINALLY I CAN'T STAND IT ANYMORE SO I SAY:
THOR.
...AYE.
NICE OF YOU TO COME. I DIDN'T KNOW YOU AND ANITUN WERE FRIENDS.
SHE WAS THE EMBODIMENT OF THE GODDESS OF WIND AND RAIN.
SHE HAD THUNDER IN HER VEINS AND LIGHTNING IN HER HEART--
I DO NOT EXPECT ONE SUCH AS THEE TO GRASP--
THIS ISN'T ABOUT US, MAN.
YOU DARE--
YOU DON'T GET TO BLAME ME FOR THIS.
ANY TIME YOU WANT TO GET BACK IN THE GAME, LET ME KNOW.
HMPH.
TINK!
PARDON ME, IRON MAN. I AM NEEDED ELSEWHERE.
...OF COURSE...
SAFE TRAVELS.
CHIPPED THE SUIT--
TONY?
THAT SELF-RIGHTEOUS STUBBORN...CHIPPED MY SUIT--
TONY.

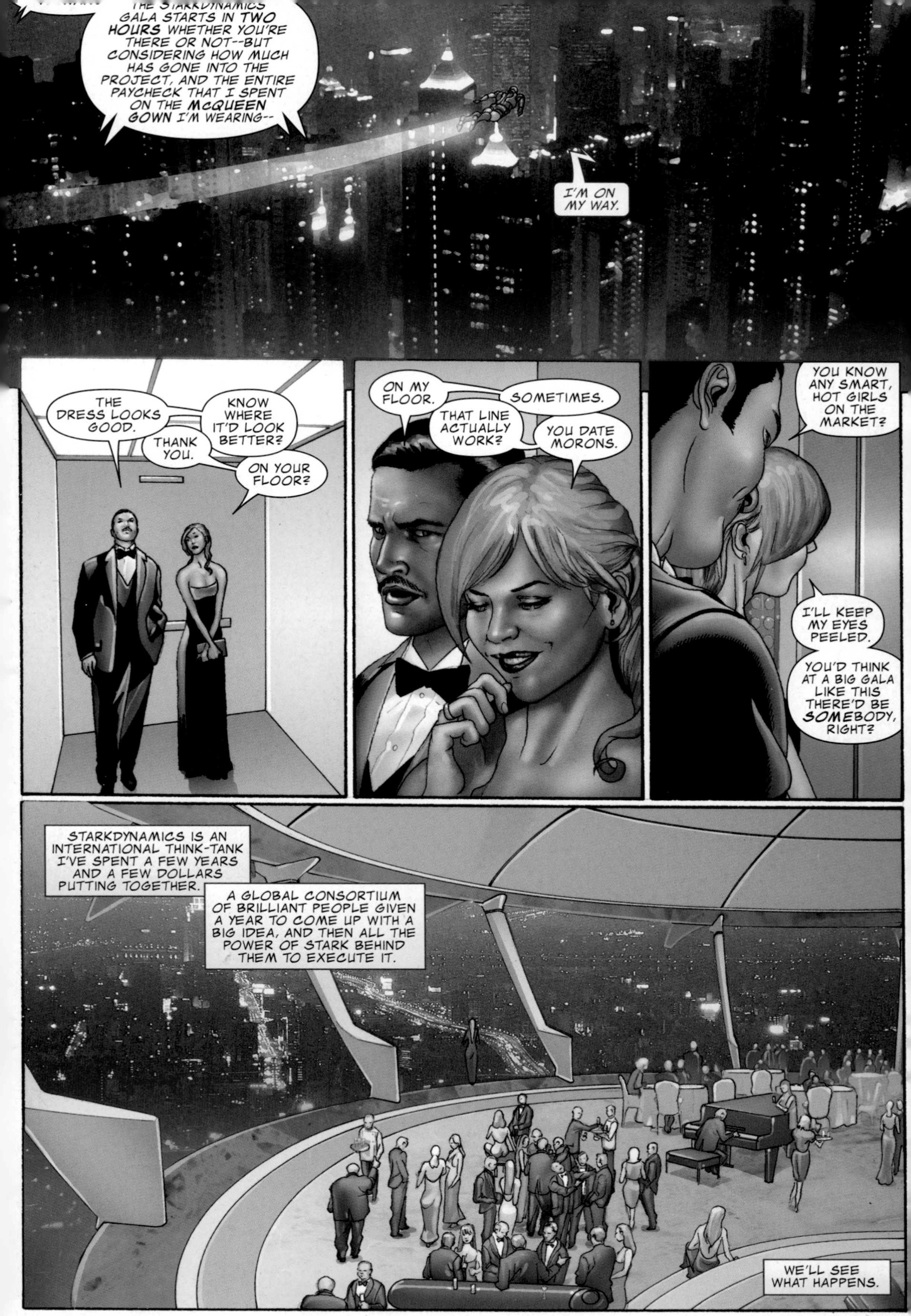
THE STARKDYNAMICS GALA STARTS IN TWO HOURS WHETHER YOU'RE THERE OR NOT--BUT CONSIDERING HOW MUCH HAS GONE INTO THE PROJECT, AND THE ENTIRE PAYCHECK THAT I SPENT ON THE McQUEEN GOWN I'M WEARING--
I'M ON MY WAY.
THE DRESS LOOKS GOOD.
THANK YOU.
KNOW WHERE IT'D LOOK BETTER?
ON YOUR FLOOR?
ON MY FLOOR.
SOMETIMES.
THAT LINE ACTUALLY WORK?
YOU DATE MORONS.
YOU KNOW ANY SMART, HOT GIRLS ON THE MARKET?
I'LL KEEP MY EYES PEELED.
YOU'D THINK AT A BIG GALA LIKE THIS THERE'D BE SOMEBODY, RIGHT?
STARKDYNAMICS IS AN INTERNATIONAL THINK-TANK I'VE SPENT A FEW YEARS AND A FEW DOLLARS PUTTING TOGETHER.
A GLOBAL CONSORTIUM OF BRILLIANT PEOPLE GIVEN A YEAR TO COME UP WITH A BIG IDEA, AND THEN ALL THE POWER OF STARK BEHIND THEM TO EXECUTE IT.
WE'LL SEE WHAT HAPPENS.

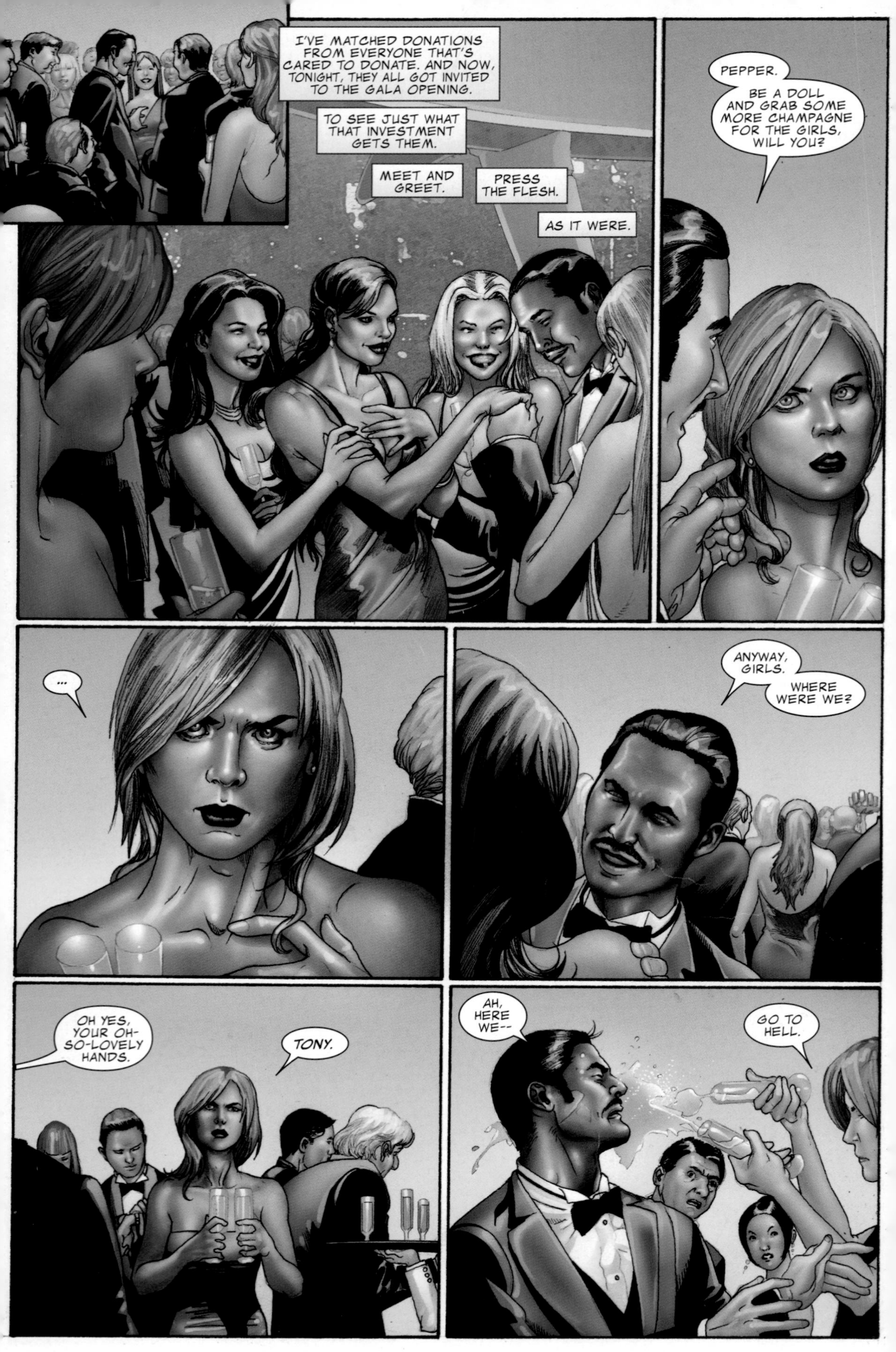
I'VE MATCHED DONATIONS FROM EVERYONE THAT'S CARED TO DONATE. AND NOW, TONIGHT, THEY ALL GOT INVITED TO THE GALA OPENING.
TO SEE JUST WHAT THAT INVESTMENT GETS THEM.
MEET AND GREET.
PRESS THE FLESH.
AS IT WERE.
PEPPER.
BE A DOLL AND GRAB SOME MORE CHAMPAGNE FOR THE GIRLS, WILL YOU?
...
ANYWAY, GIRLS.
WHERE WERE WE?
OH YES, YOUR OH-SO-LOVELY HANDS.
TONY.
AH, HERE WE--
GO TO HELL.

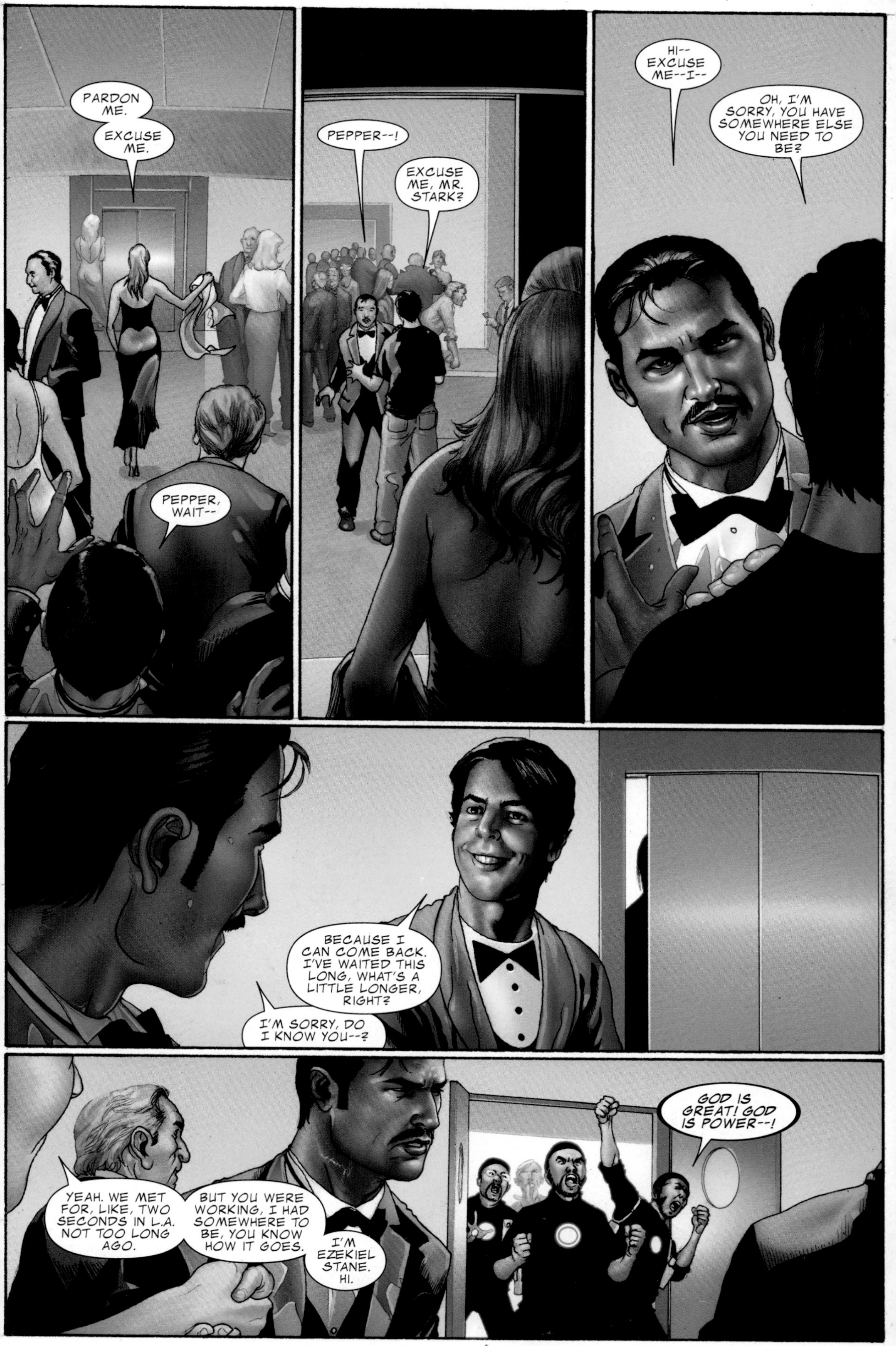
PARDON ME.
EXCUSE ME.
PEPPER, WAIT--
PEPPER--!
EXCUSE ME, MR. STARK?
HI-- EXCUSE ME--I--
OH, I'M SORRY, YOU HAVE SOMEWHERE ELSE YOU NEED TO BE?
BECAUSE I CAN COME BACK. I'VE WAITED THIS LONG, WHAT'S A LITTLE LONGER, RIGHT?
I'M SORRY, DO I KNOW YOU--?
YEAH. WE MET FOR, LIKE, TWO SECONDS IN L.A. NOT TOO LONG AGO.
BUT YOU WERE WORKING, I HAD SOMEWHERE TO BE, YOU KNOW HOW IT GOES.
I'M EZEKIEL STANE. HI.
GOD IS GREAT! GOD IS POWER--!

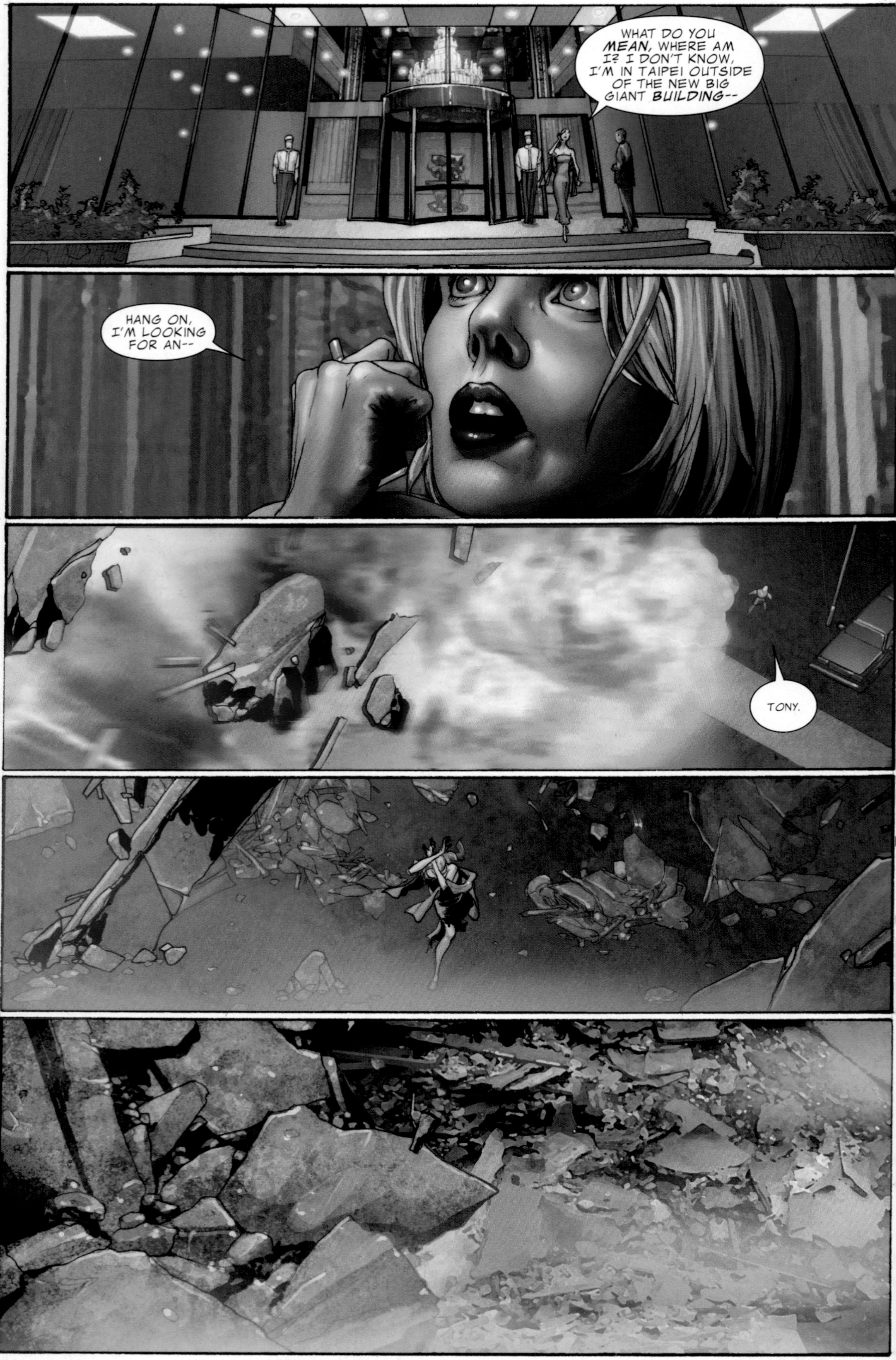
WHAT DO YOU MEAN, WHERE AM I? I DON'T KNOW, I'M IN TAIPEI OUTSIDE OF THE NEW BIG GIANT BUILDING--
HANG ON, I'M LOOKING FOR AN--
TONY.

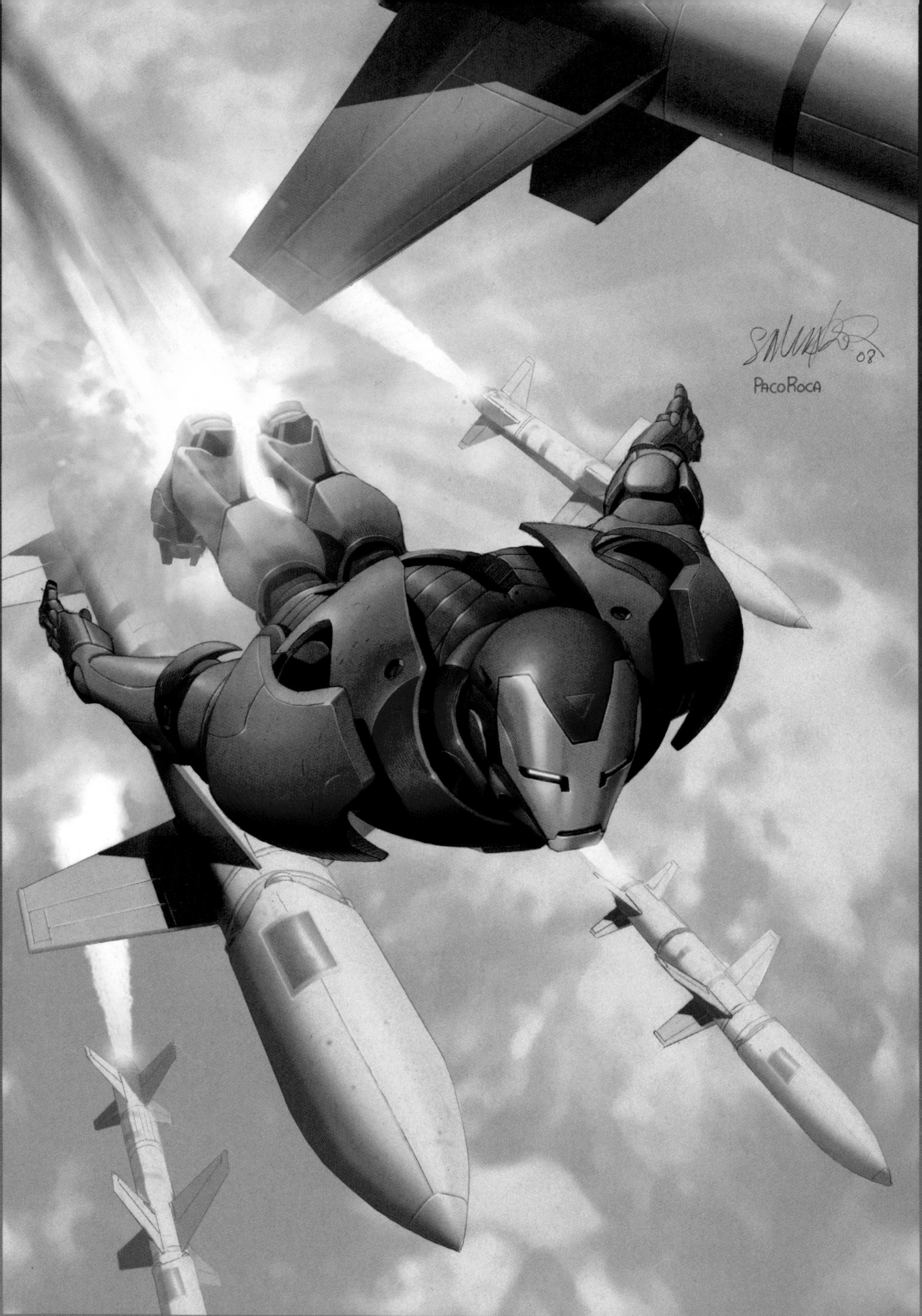
'08
PacoRoca

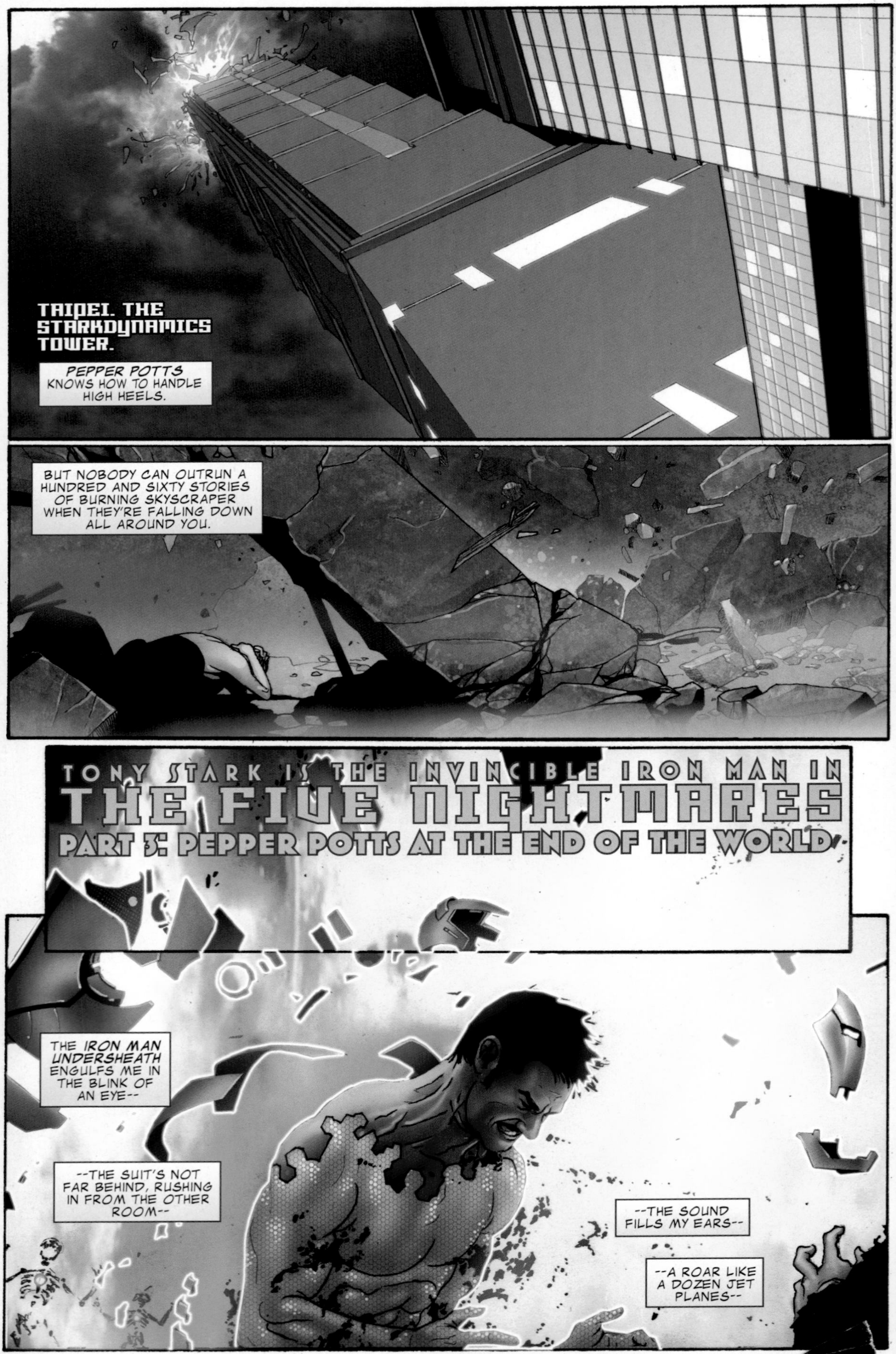
TAIPEI. THE STARKDYNAMICS TOWER.
PEPPER POTTS KNOWS HOW TO HANDLE HIGH HEELS.
BUT NOBODY CAN OUTRUN A HUNDRED AND SIXTY STORIES OF BURNING SKYSCRAPER WHEN THEY'RE FALLING DOWN ALL AROUND YOU.
TONY STARK IS THE INVINCIBLE IRON MAN IN
THE FIVE NIGHTMARES
PART 3: PEPPER POTTS AT THE END OF THE WORLD
THE IRON MAN UNDERSHEATH ENGULFS ME IN THE BLINK OF AN EYE--
--THE SUIT'S NOT FAR BEHIND, RUSHING IN FROM THE OTHER ROOM--
--THE SOUND FILLS MY EARS--
--A ROAR LIKE A DOZEN JET PLANES--

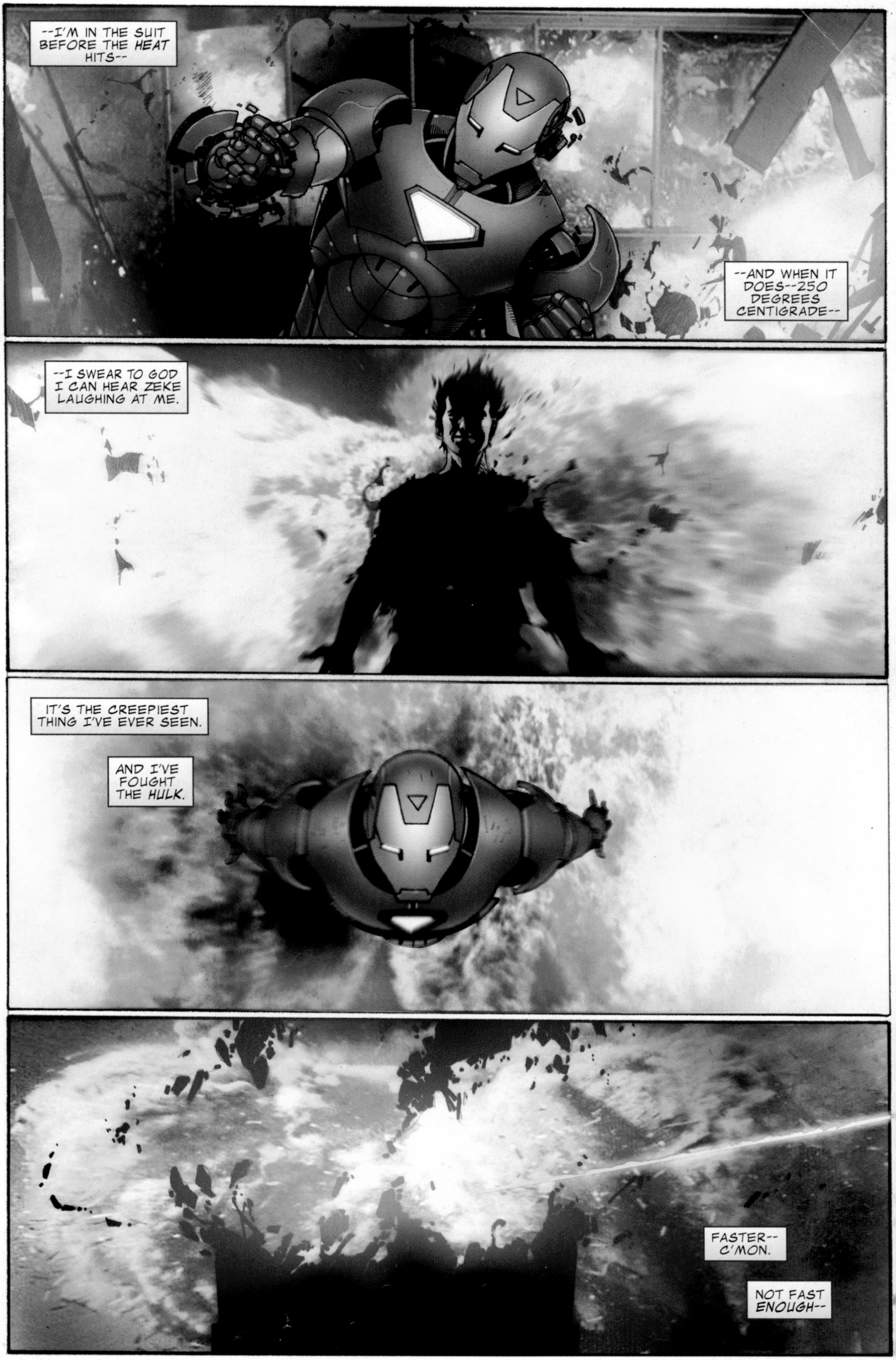
--I'M IN THE SUIT BEFORE THE HEAT HITS--
--AND WHEN IT DOES--250 DEGREES CENTIGRADE--
--I SWEAR TO GOD I CAN HEAR ZEKE LAUGHING AT ME.
IT'S THE CREEPIEST THING I'VE EVER SEEN.
AND I'VE FOUGHT THE HULK.
FASTER-- C'MON.
NOT FAST ENOUGH--

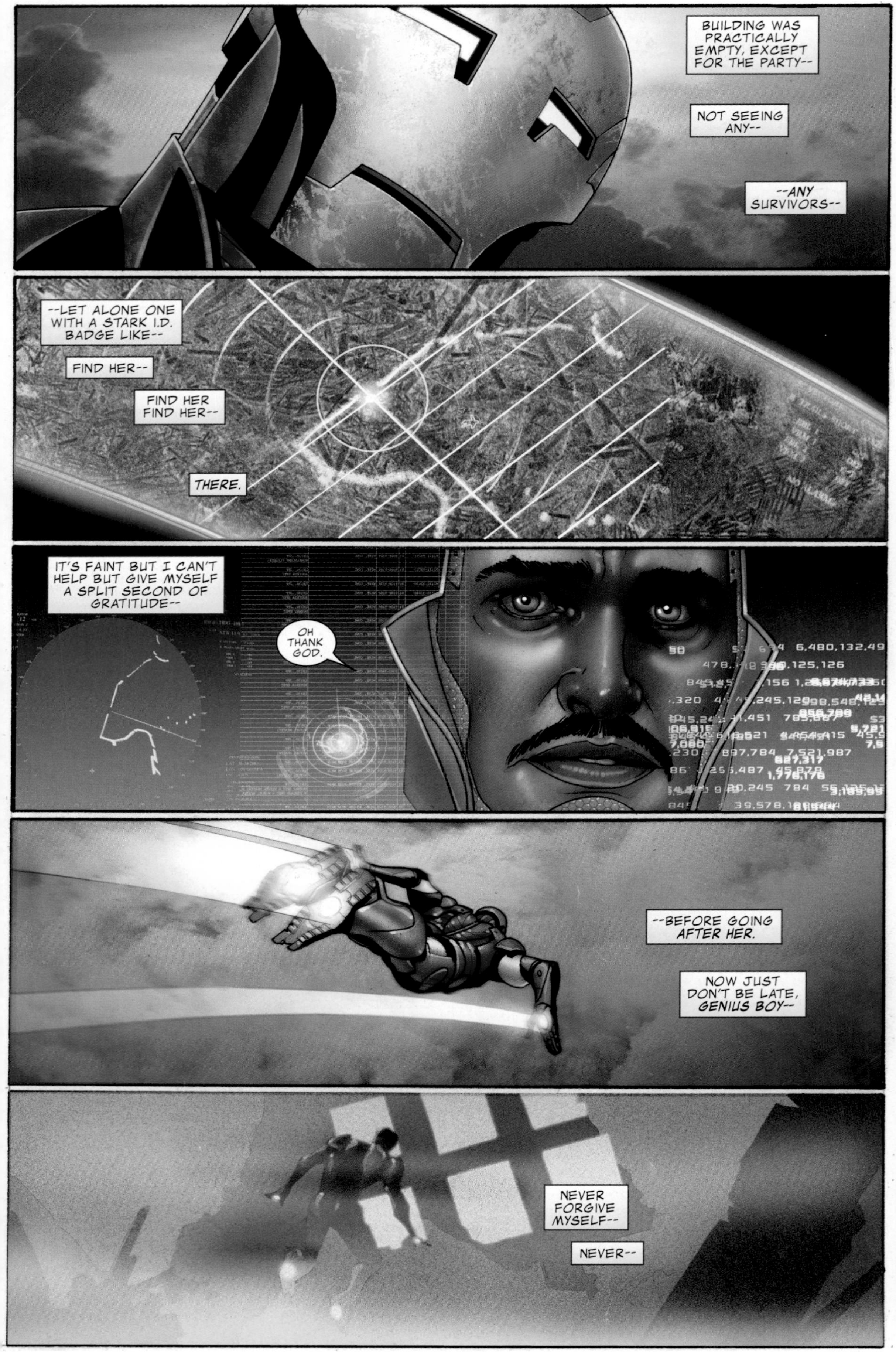
BUILDING WAS PRACTICALLY EMPTY, EXCEPT FOR THE PARTY--
NOT SEEING ANY--
--ANY SURVIVORS--
--LET ALONE ONE WITH A STARK I.D. BADGE LIKE--
FIND HER--
FIND HER FIND HER--
THERE.
IT'S FAINT BUT I CAN'T HELP BUT GIVE MYSELF A SPLIT SECOND OF GRATITUDE--
OH THANK GOD.
--BEFORE GOING AFTER HER.
NOW JUST DON'T BE LATE, GENIUS BOY--
NEVER FORGIVE MYSELF--
NEVER--

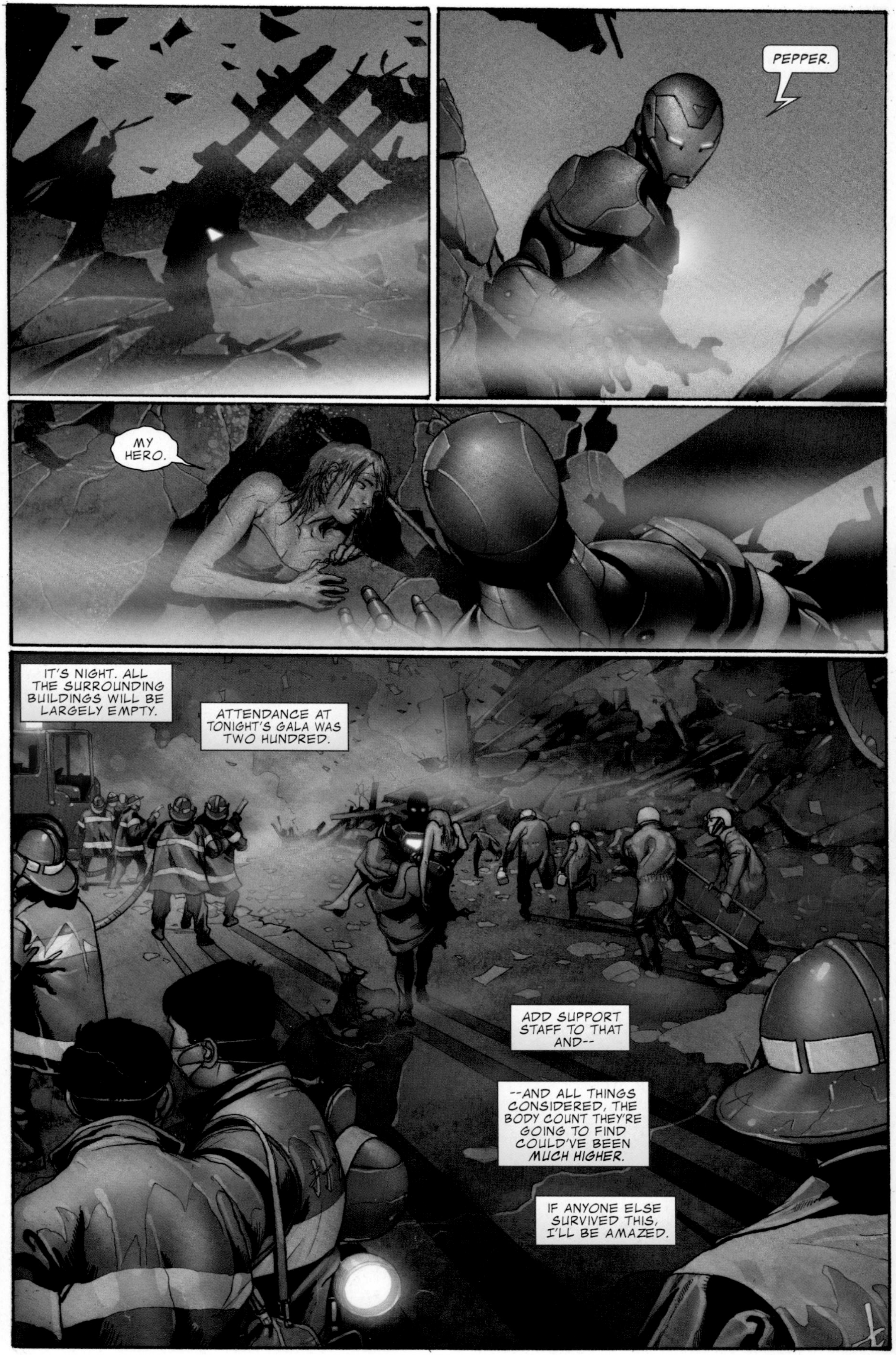

PEPPER.
MY HERO.
IT'S NIGHT. ALL THE SURROUNDING BUILDINGS WILL BE LARGELY EMPTY.
ATTENDANCE AT TONIGHT'S GALA WAS TWO HUNDRED.
ADD SUPPORT STAFF TO THAT AND--
--AND ALL THINGS CONSIDERED, THE BODY COUNT THEY'RE GOING TO FIND COULD'VE BEEN MUCH HIGHER.
IF ANYONE ELSE SURVIVED THIS, I'LL BE AMAZED.

I GET THE ONE WHO DID INTO THE BACK OF THE FIRST AMBULANCE TO ARRIVE ON-SITE...

<LIE STILL, MISS--\>

<YOU'VE GOT *PROFOUND* INTERNAL INJURIES AND MOVING WILL--\>

HEY, BOSS.

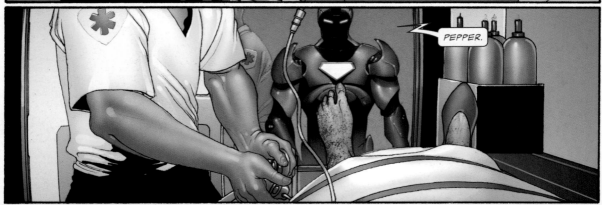

PEPPER.

YOU SHOULDN'T HAVE ASKED ME TO GO GET THOSE GIRLS DRINKS.

YEAH. I KNOW.

AS SOON AS THE AMBULANCE PULLS AWAY I GO BACK TO THE DISASTER SITE TO START RESCUE AND RECOVERY WHEN--

WHEN I SEE ANOTHER SURVIVOR--

IT'S IMPOSSIBLE, IT--

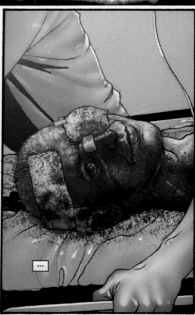

...

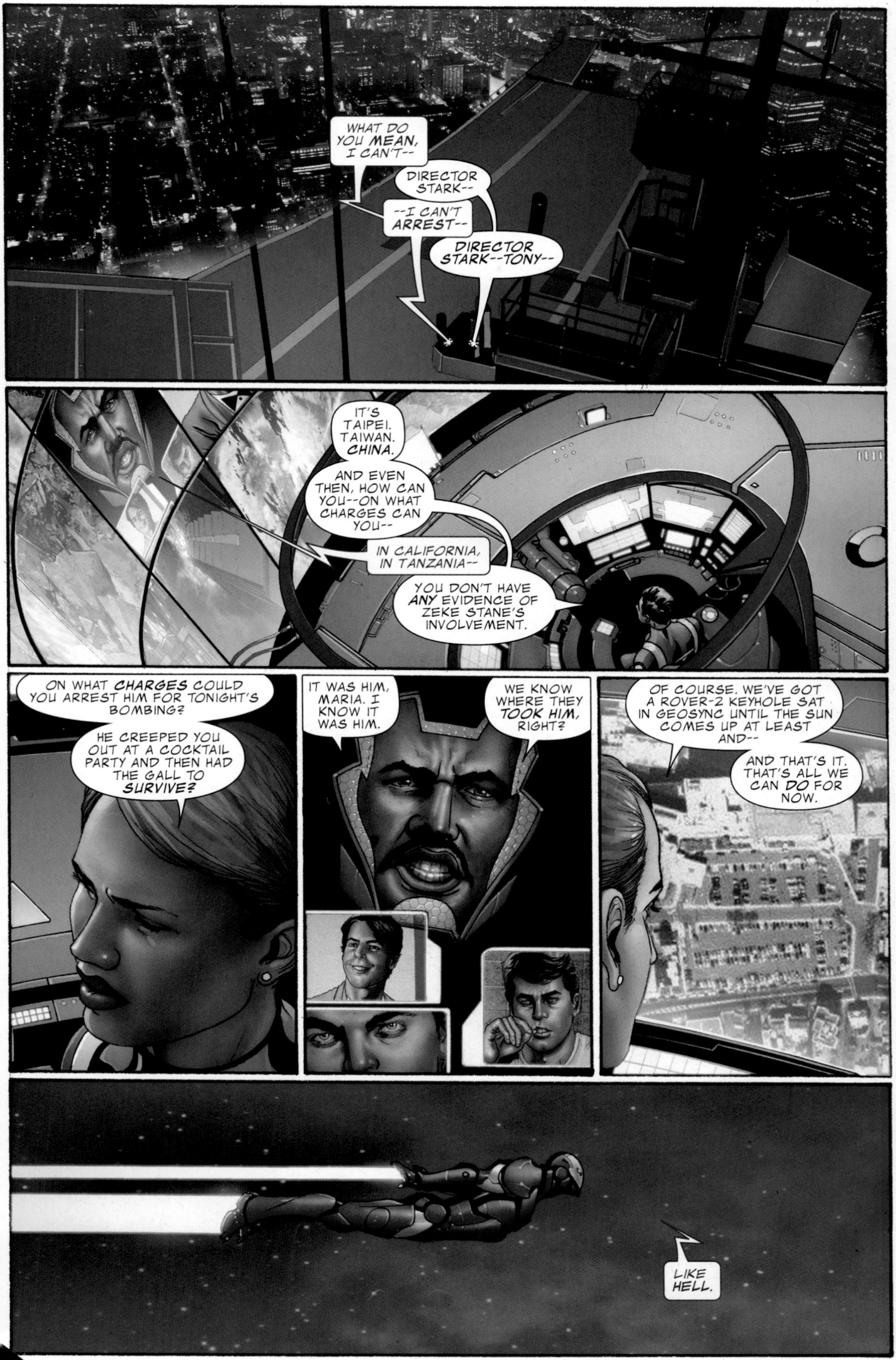
WHAT DO YOU MEAN, I CAN'T--
DIRECTOR STARK--
--I CAN'T ARREST--
DIRECTOR STARK--TONY--
IT'S TAIPEI. TAIWAN. CHINA.
AND EVEN THEN, HOW CAN YOU--ON WHAT CHARGES CAN YOU--
IN CALIFORNIA, IN TANZANIA--
YOU DON'T HAVE ANY EVIDENCE OF ZEKE STANE'S INVOLVEMENT.
ON WHAT CHARGES COULD YOU ARREST HIM FOR TONIGHT'S BOMBING?
HE CREEPED YOU OUT AT A COCKTAIL PARTY AND THEN HAD THE GALL TO SURVIVE?
IT WAS HIM, MARIA. I KNOW IT WAS HIM.
WE KNOW WHERE THEY TOOK HIM, RIGHT?
OF COURSE. WE'VE GOT A ROVER-2 KEYHOLE SAT IN GEOSYNC UNTIL THE SUN COMES UP AT LEAST AND--
AND THAT'S IT. THAT'S ALL WE CAN DO FOR NOW.
LIKE HELL.

GAAAHHH--

DAMMIT. DAMMIT DAMMIT DAMMIT--

SASHA-- GOTTA GET TO--

406

<SIR, NO-- YOU CAN'T GET OUT OF BED, YOU-->

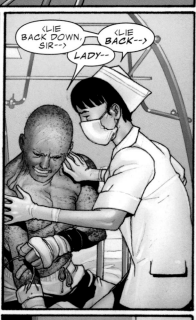

<LIE BACK DOWN, SIR-->

<LIE BACK--> LADY--

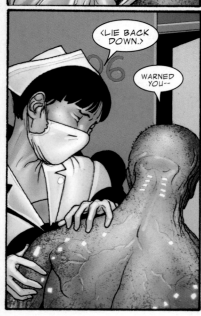

<LIE BACK DOWN.>

WARNED YOU--

SASHA, YOU BETTER DAMN WELL BE OUTSIDE WAITING FOR ME--

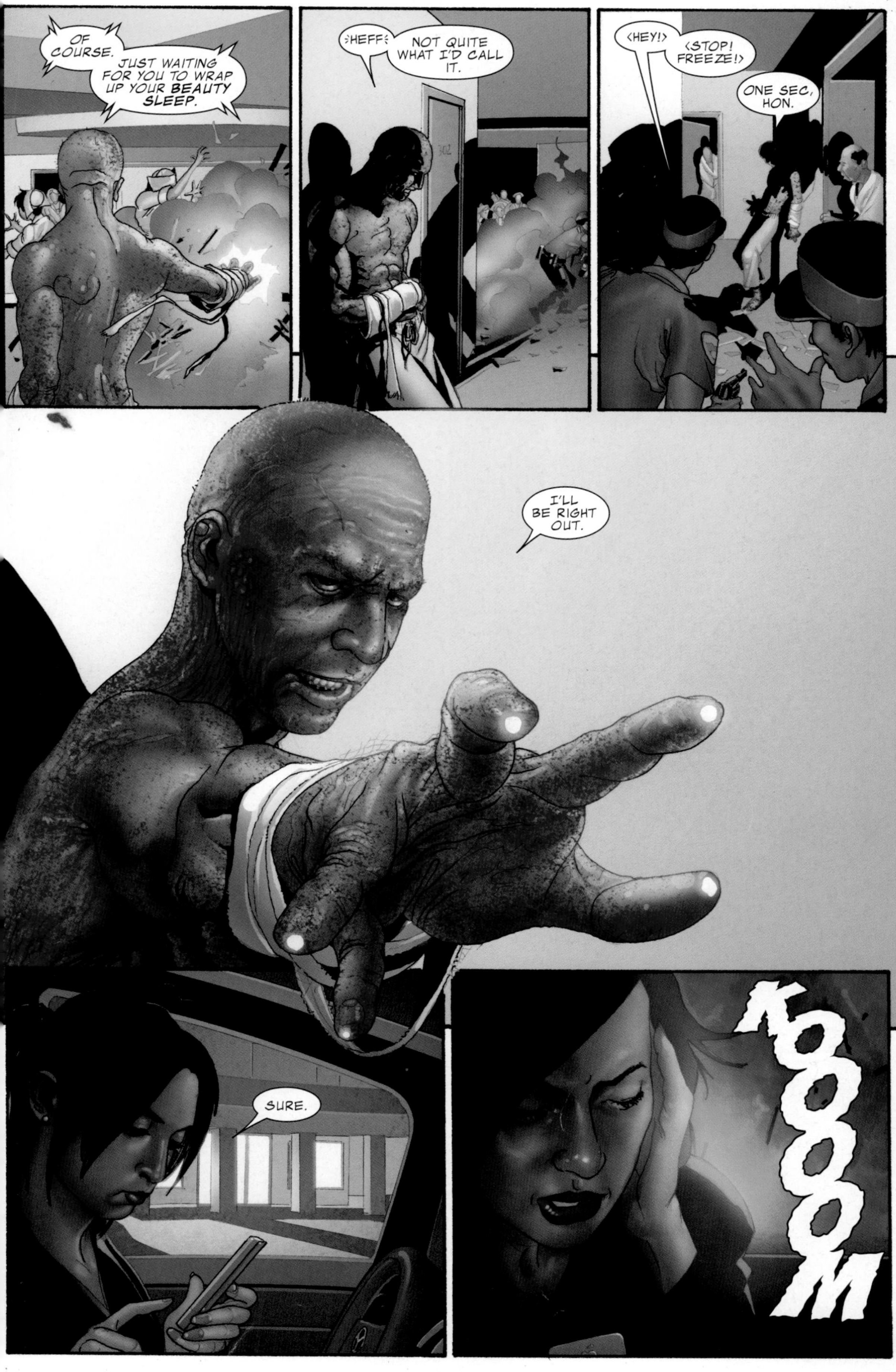
OF COURSE.
JUST WAITING FOR YOU TO WRAP UP YOUR **BEAUTY SLEEP**.
<HEFF>
NOT QUITE WHAT I'D CALL IT.
<HEY!>
<STOP! FREEZE!>
ONE SEC, HON.
I'LL BE RIGHT OUT.
SURE.
KOOOOM

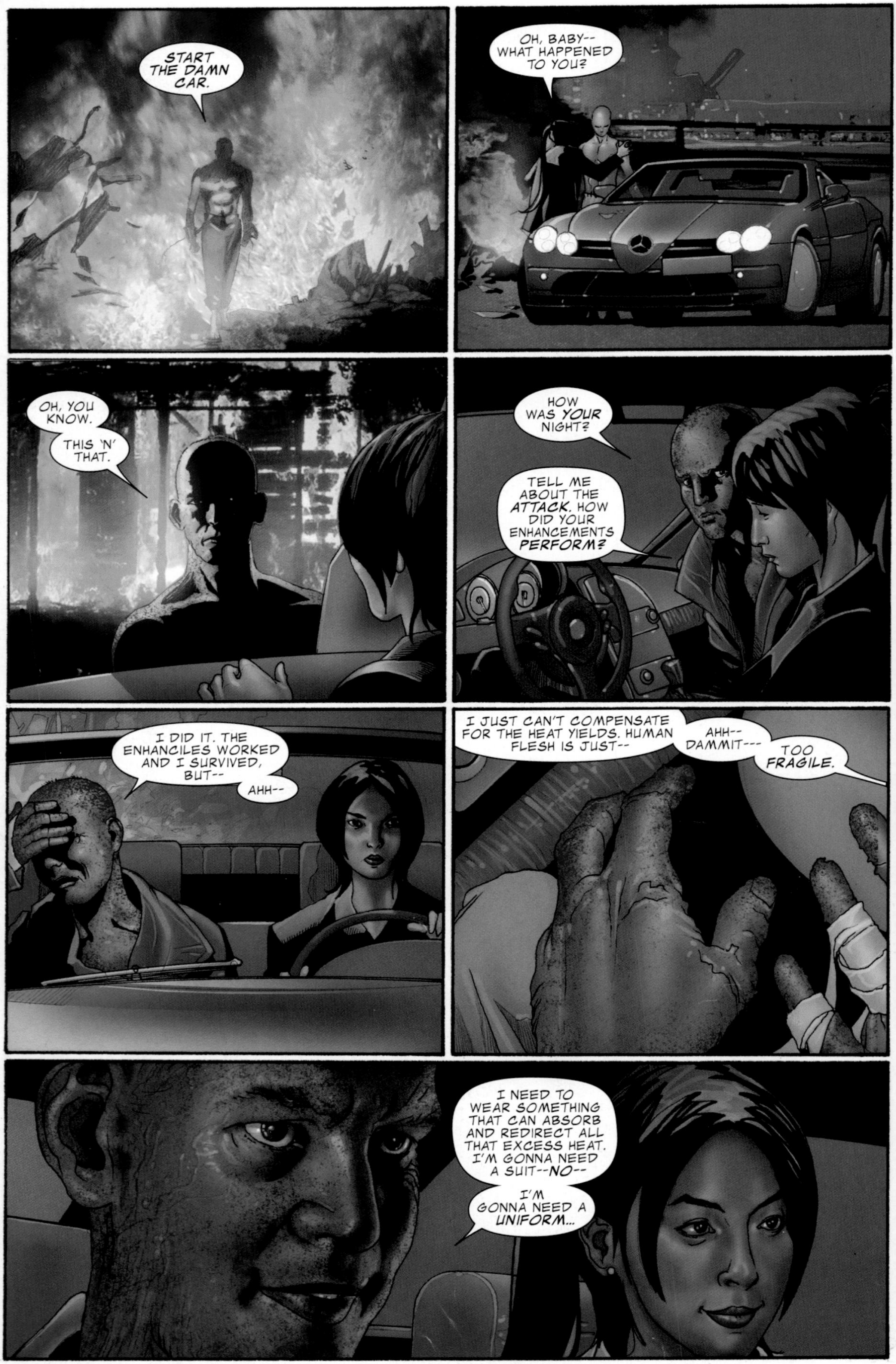
START THE DAMN CAR.
OH, BABY-- WHAT HAPPENED TO YOU?
OH, YOU KNOW.
THIS 'N' THAT.
HOW WAS YOUR NIGHT?
TELL ME ABOUT THE ATTACK. HOW DID YOUR ENHANCEMENTS PERFORM?
I DID IT. THE ENHANCILES WORKED AND I SURVIVED, BUT--
AHH--
I JUST CAN'T COMPENSATE FOR THE HEAT YIELDS. HUMAN FLESH IS JUST--
AHH-- DAMMIT---
TOO FRAGILE.
I NEED TO WEAR SOMETHING THAT CAN ABSORB AND REDIRECT ALL THAT EXCESS HEAT. I'M GONNA NEED A SUIT--NO--
I'M GONNA NEED A UNIFORM...

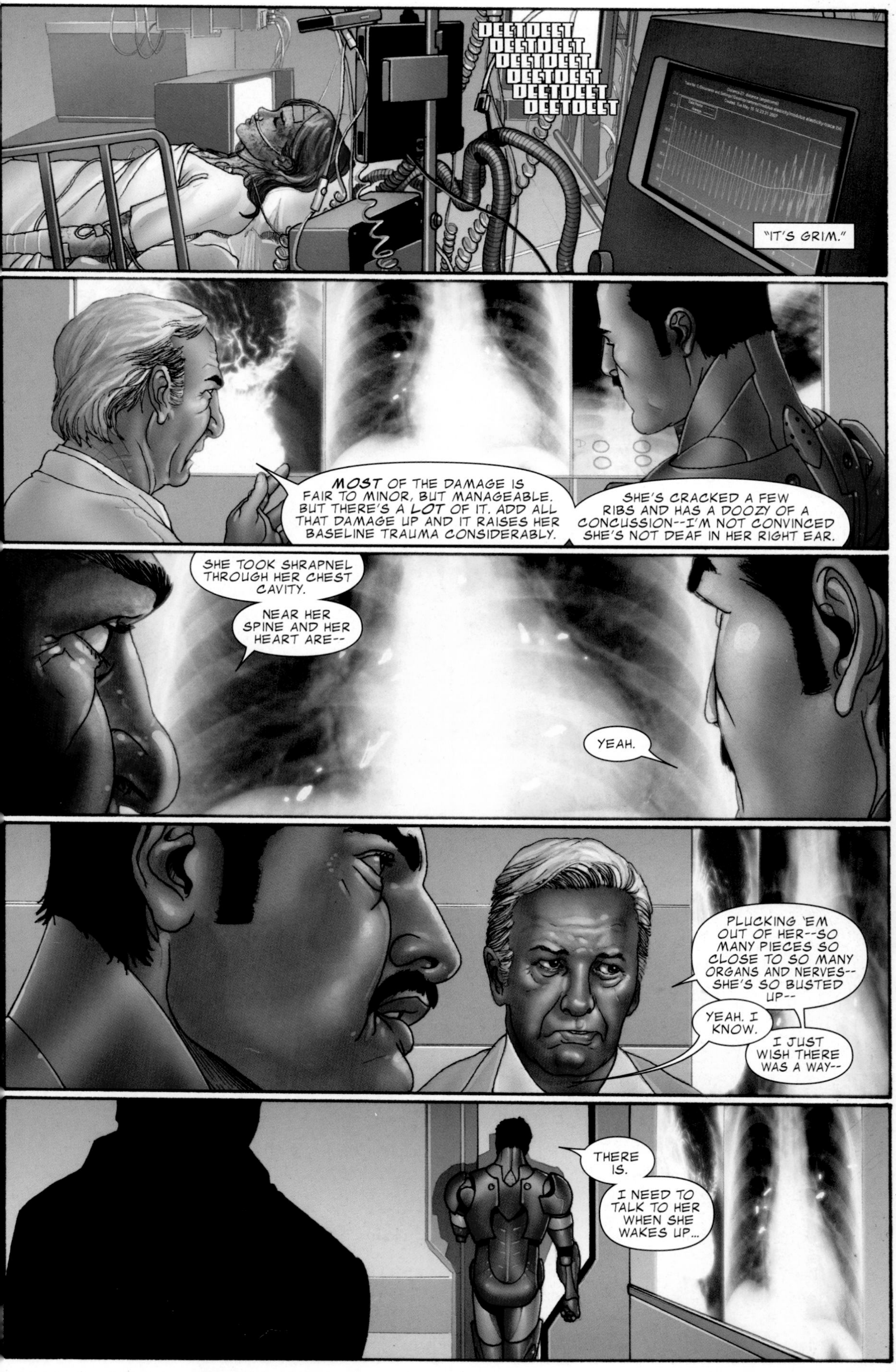
DEETDEET DEETDEET DEETDEET DEETDEET DEETDEET DEETDEET
"IT'S GRIM."
MOST OF THE DAMAGE IS FAIR TO MINOR, BUT MANAGEABLE. BUT THERE'S A LOT OF IT. ADD ALL THAT DAMAGE UP AND IT RAISES HER BASELINE TRAUMA CONSIDERABLY.
SHE'S CRACKED A FEW RIBS AND HAS A DOOZY OF A CONCUSSION--I'M NOT CONVINCED SHE'S NOT DEAF IN HER RIGHT EAR.
SHE TOOK SHRAPNEL THROUGH HER CHEST CAVITY.
NEAR HER SPINE AND HER HEART ARE--
YEAH.
PLUCKING 'EM OUT OF HER--SO MANY PIECES SO CLOSE TO SO MANY ORGANS AND NERVES--SHE'S SO BUSTED UP--
YEAH. I KNOW.
I JUST WISH THERE WAS A WAY--
THERE IS.
I NEED TO TALK TO HER WHEN SHE WAKES UP...

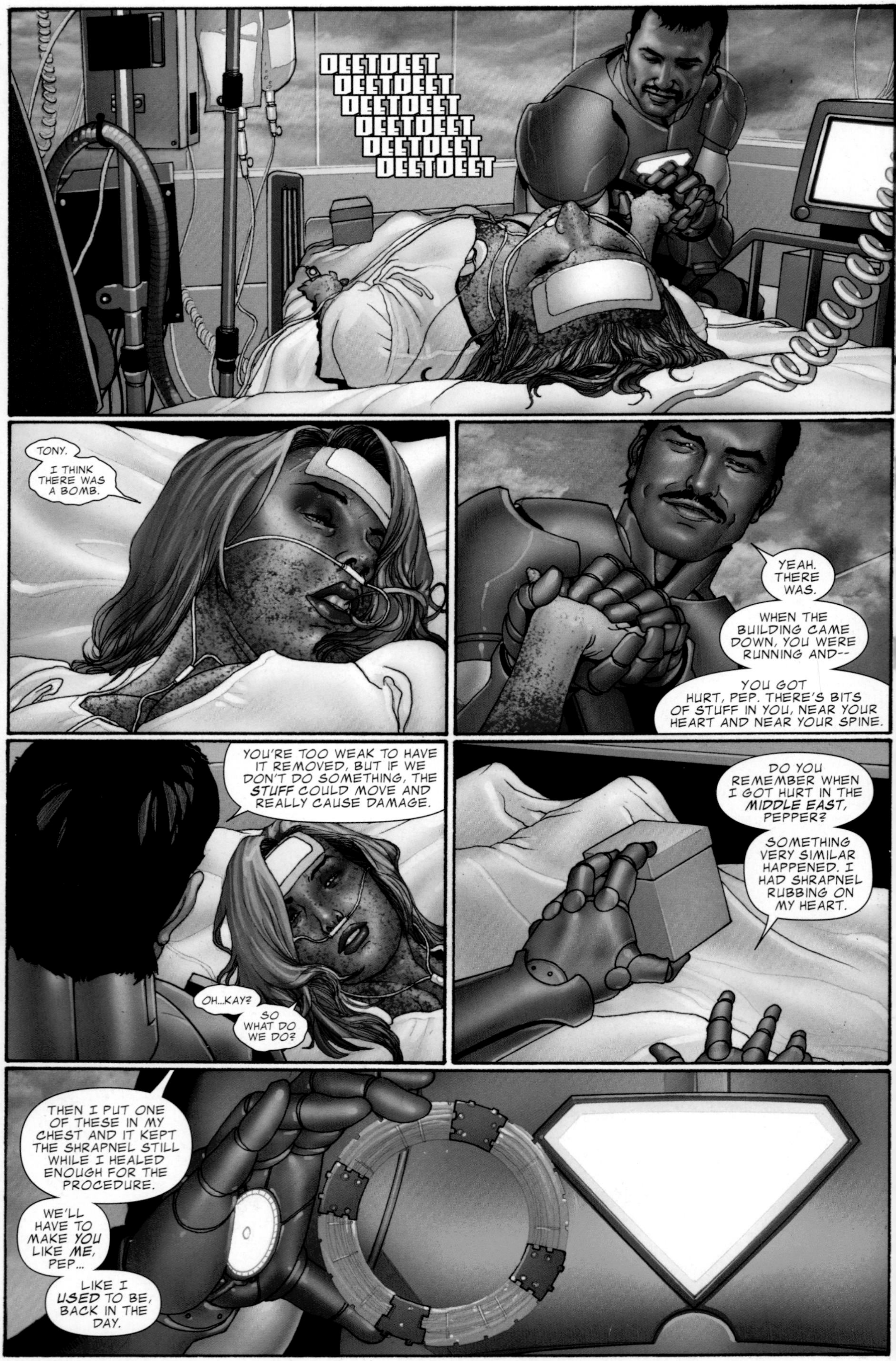
DEETDEET
DEETDEET
DEETDEET
DEETDEET
DEETDEET
DEETDEET
TONY.
I THINK THERE WAS A BOMB.
YEAH. THERE WAS.
WHEN THE BUILDING CAME DOWN, YOU WERE RUNNING AND--
YOU GOT HURT, PEP. THERE'S BITS OF STUFF IN YOU, NEAR YOUR HEART AND NEAR YOUR SPINE.
YOU'RE TOO WEAK TO HAVE IT REMOVED, BUT IF WE DON'T DO SOMETHING, THE STUFF COULD MOVE AND REALLY CAUSE DAMAGE.
OH...KAY?
SO WHAT DO WE DO?
DO YOU REMEMBER WHEN I GOT HURT IN THE MIDDLE EAST, PEPPER?
SOMETHING VERY SIMILAR HAPPENED. I HAD SHRAPNEL RUBBING ON MY HEART.
THEN I PUT ONE OF THESE IN MY CHEST AND IT KEPT THE SHRAPNEL STILL WHILE I HEALED ENOUGH FOR THE PROCEDURE.
WE'LL HAVE TO MAKE YOU LIKE ME, PEP...
LIKE I USED TO BE, BACK IN THE DAY.

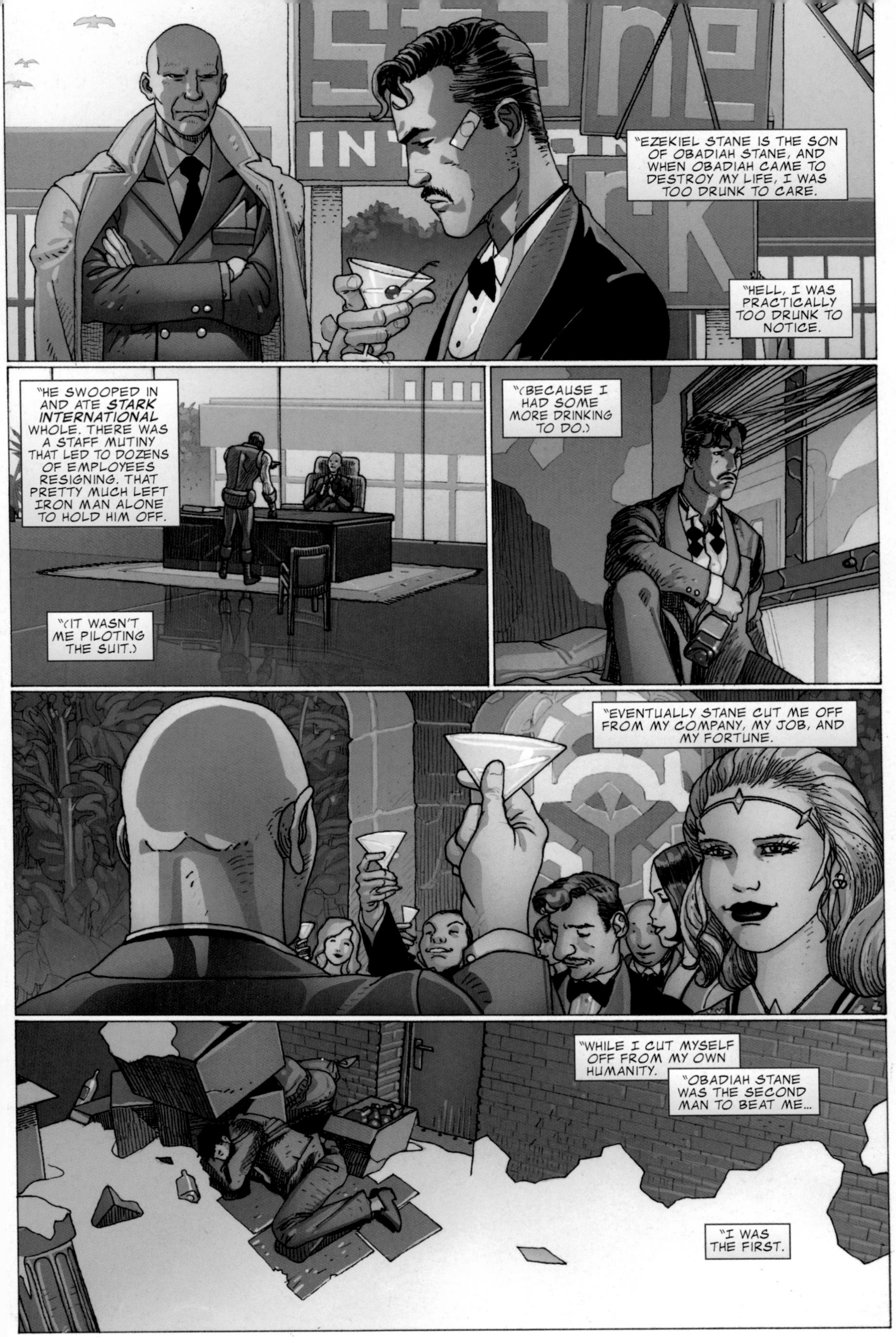
"EZEKIEL STANE IS THE SON OF OBADIAH STANE, AND WHEN OBADIAH STANE CAME TO DESTROY MY LIFE, I WAS TOO DRUNK TO CARE.
"HELL, I WAS PRACTICALLY TOO DRUNK TO NOTICE.
"HE SWOOPED IN AND ATE STARK INTERNATIONAL WHOLE. THERE WAS A STAFF MUTINY THAT LED TO DOZENS OF EMPLOYEES RESIGNING. THAT PRETTY MUCH LEFT IRON MAN ALONE TO HOLD HIM OFF.
"(IT WASN'T ME PILOTING THE SUIT.)
"(BECAUSE I HAD SOME MORE DRINKING TO DO.)
"EVENTUALLY STANE CUT ME OFF FROM MY COMPANY, MY JOB, AND MY FORTUNE.
"WHILE I CUT MYSELF OFF FROM MY OWN HUMANITY.
"OBADIAH STANE WAS THE SECOND MAN TO BEAT ME...
"I WAS THE FIRST.

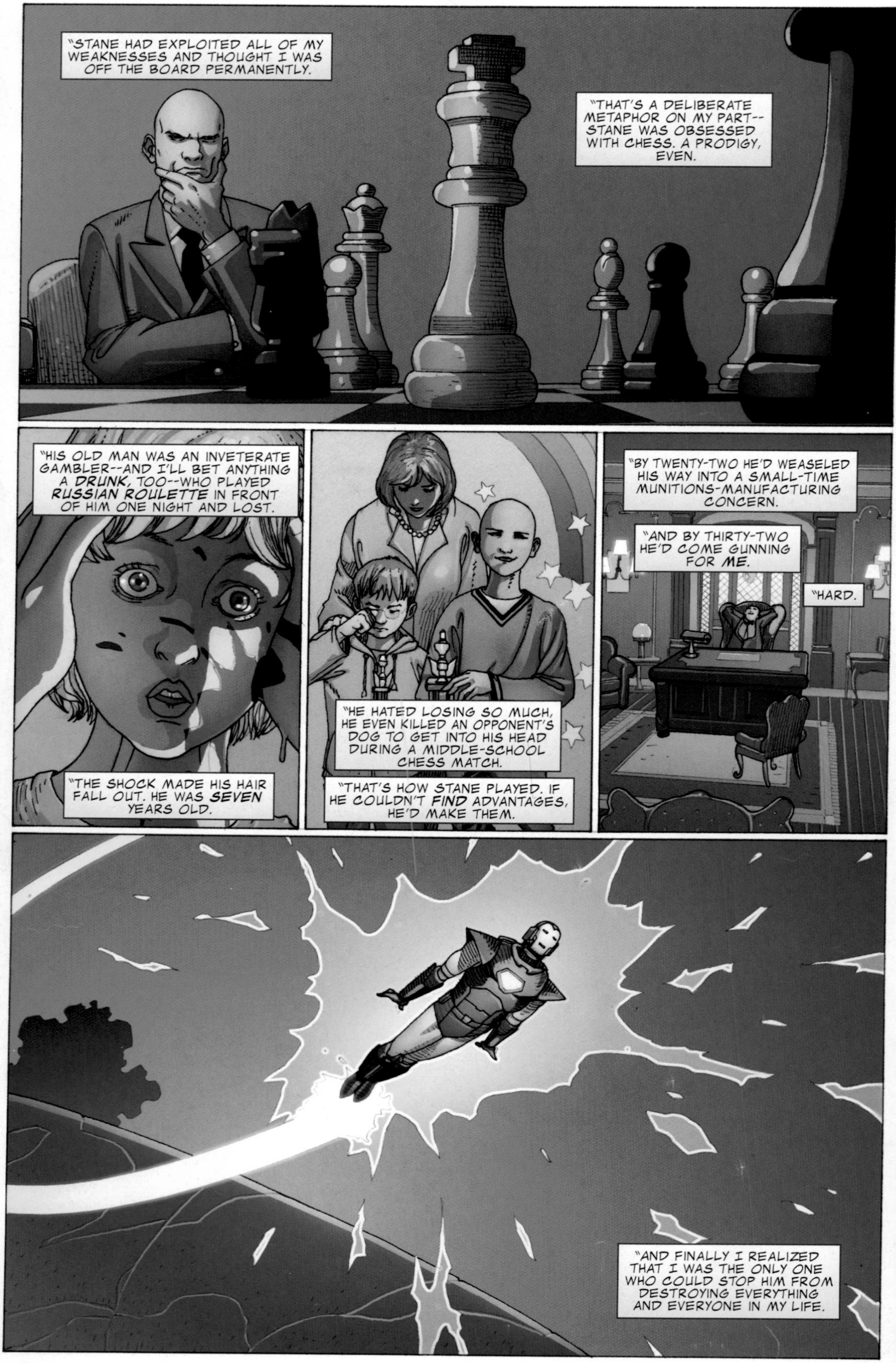
"STANE HAD EXPLOITED ALL OF MY WEAKNESSES AND THOUGHT I WAS OFF THE BOARD PERMANENTLY.
"THAT'S A DELIBERATE METAPHOR ON MY PART--STANE WAS OBSESSED WITH CHESS. A PRODIGY, EVEN.
"HIS OLD MAN WAS AN INVETERATE GAMBLER--AND I'LL BET ANYTHING A DRUNK, TOO--WHO PLAYED RUSSIAN ROULETTE IN FRONT OF HIM ONE NIGHT AND LOST.
"THE SHOCK MADE HIS HAIR FALL OUT. HE WAS SEVEN YEARS OLD.
"HE HATED LOSING SO MUCH, HE EVEN KILLED AN OPPONENT'S DOG TO GET INTO HIS HEAD DURING A MIDDLE-SCHOOL CHESS MATCH.
"THAT'S HOW STANE PLAYED. IF HE COULDN'T FIND ADVANTAGES, HE'D MAKE THEM.
"BY TWENTY-TWO HE'D WEASELED HIS WAY INTO A SMALL-TIME MUNITIONS-MANUFACTURING CONCERN.
"AND BY THIRTY-TWO HE'D COME GUNNING FOR ME.
"HARD.
"AND FINALLY I REALIZED THAT I WAS THE ONLY ONE WHO COULD STOP HIM FROM DESTROYING EVERYTHING AND EVERYONE IN MY LIFE.

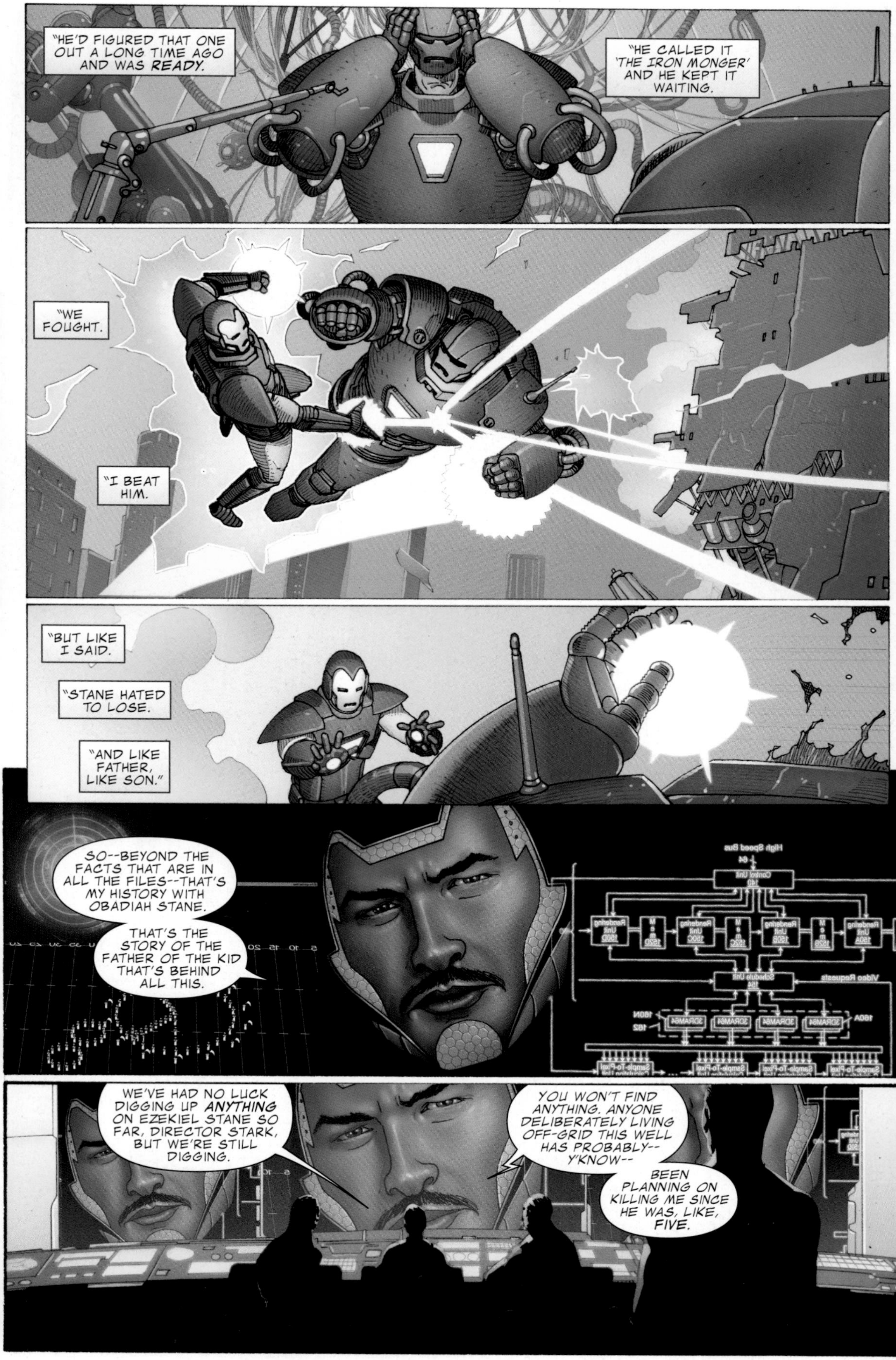
"HE'D FIGURED THAT ONE OUT A LONG TIME AGO AND WAS READY.
"HE CALLED IT 'THE IRON MONGER' AND HE KEPT IT WAITING.
"WE FOUGHT.
"I BEAT HIM.
"BUT LIKE I SAID.
"STANE HATED TO LOSE.
"AND LIKE FATHER, LIKE SON."
SO--BEYOND THE FACTS THAT ARE IN ALL THE FILES--THAT'S MY HISTORY WITH OBADIAH STANE.
THAT'S THE STORY OF THE FATHER OF THE KID THAT'S BEHIND ALL THIS.
WE'VE HAD NO LUCK DIGGING UP ANYTHING ON EZEKIEL STANE SO FAR, DIRECTOR STARK, BUT WE'RE STILL DIGGING.
YOU WON'T FIND ANYTHING. ANYONE DELIBERATELY LIVING OFF-GRID THIS WELL HAS PROBABLY-- Y'KNOW--
BEEN PLANNING ON KILLING ME SINCE HE WAS, LIKE, FIVE.

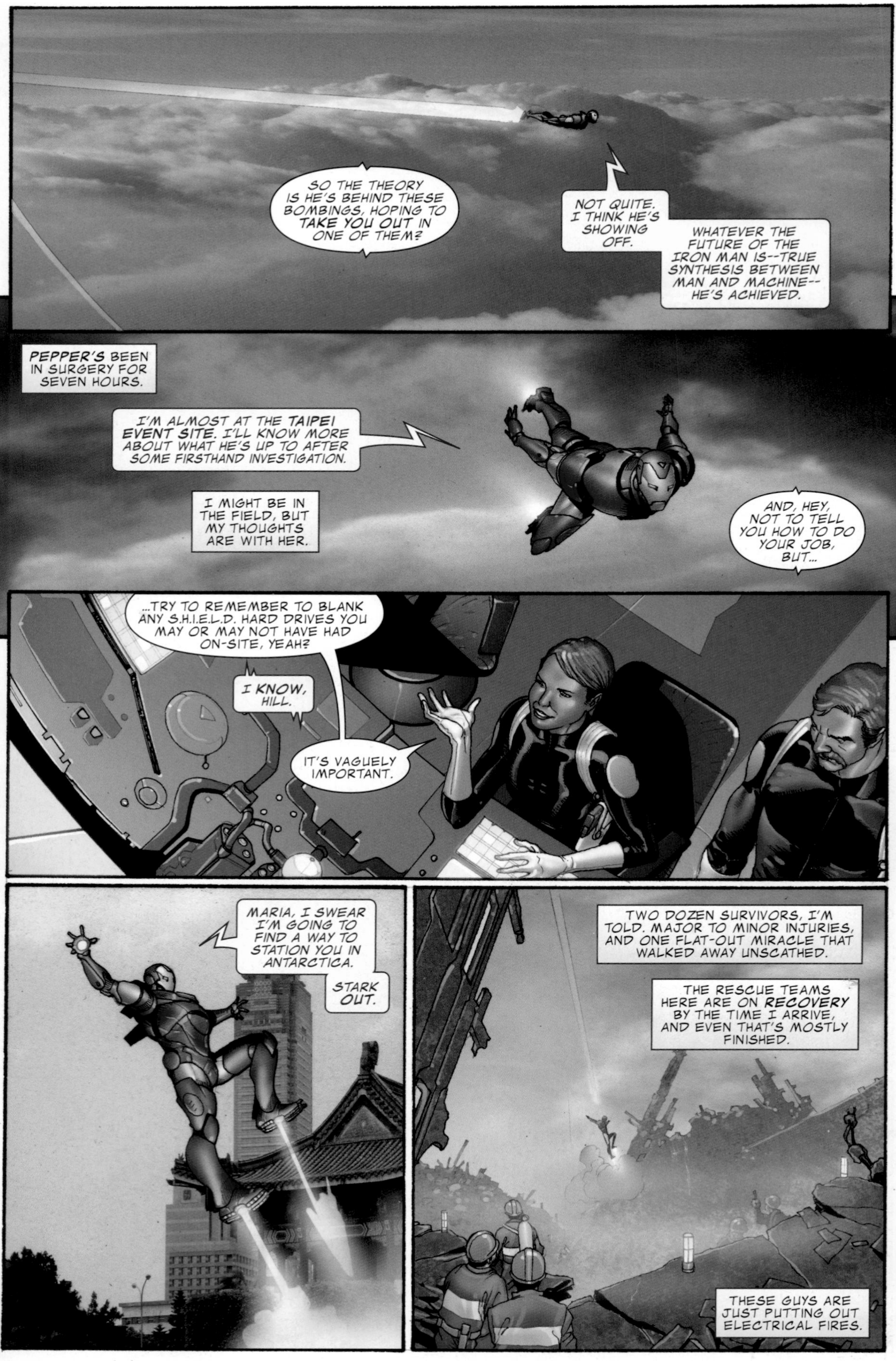
SO THE THEORY IS HE'S BEHIND THESE BOMBINGS, HOPING TO TAKE YOU OUT IN ONE OF THEM?
NOT QUITE. I THINK HE'S SHOWING OFF.
WHATEVER THE FUTURE OF THE IRON MAN IS--TRUE SYNTHESIS BETWEEN MAN AND MACHINE--HE'S ACHIEVED.
PEPPER'S BEEN IN SURGERY FOR SEVEN HOURS.
I'M ALMOST AT THE TAIPEI EVENT SITE. I'LL KNOW MORE ABOUT WHAT HE'S UP TO AFTER SOME FIRSTHAND INVESTIGATION.
I MIGHT BE IN THE FIELD, BUT MY THOUGHTS ARE WITH HER.
AND, HEY, NOT TO TELL YOU HOW TO DO YOUR JOB, BUT...
...TRY TO REMEMBER TO BLANK ANY S.H.I.E.L.D. HARD DRIVES YOU MAY OR MAY NOT HAVE HAD ON-SITE, YEAH?
I KNOW, HILL.
IT'S VAGUELY IMPORTANT.
MARIA, I SWEAR I'M GOING TO FIND A WAY TO STATION YOU IN ANTARCTICA.
STARK OUT.
TWO DOZEN SURVIVORS, I'M TOLD. MAJOR TO MINOR INJURIES, AND ONE FLAT-OUT MIRACLE THAT WALKED AWAY UNSCATHED.
THE RESCUE TEAMS HERE ARE ON RECOVERY BY THE TIME I ARRIVE, AND EVEN THAT'S MOSTLY FINISHED.
THESE GUYS ARE JUST PUTTING OUT ELECTRICAL FIRES.

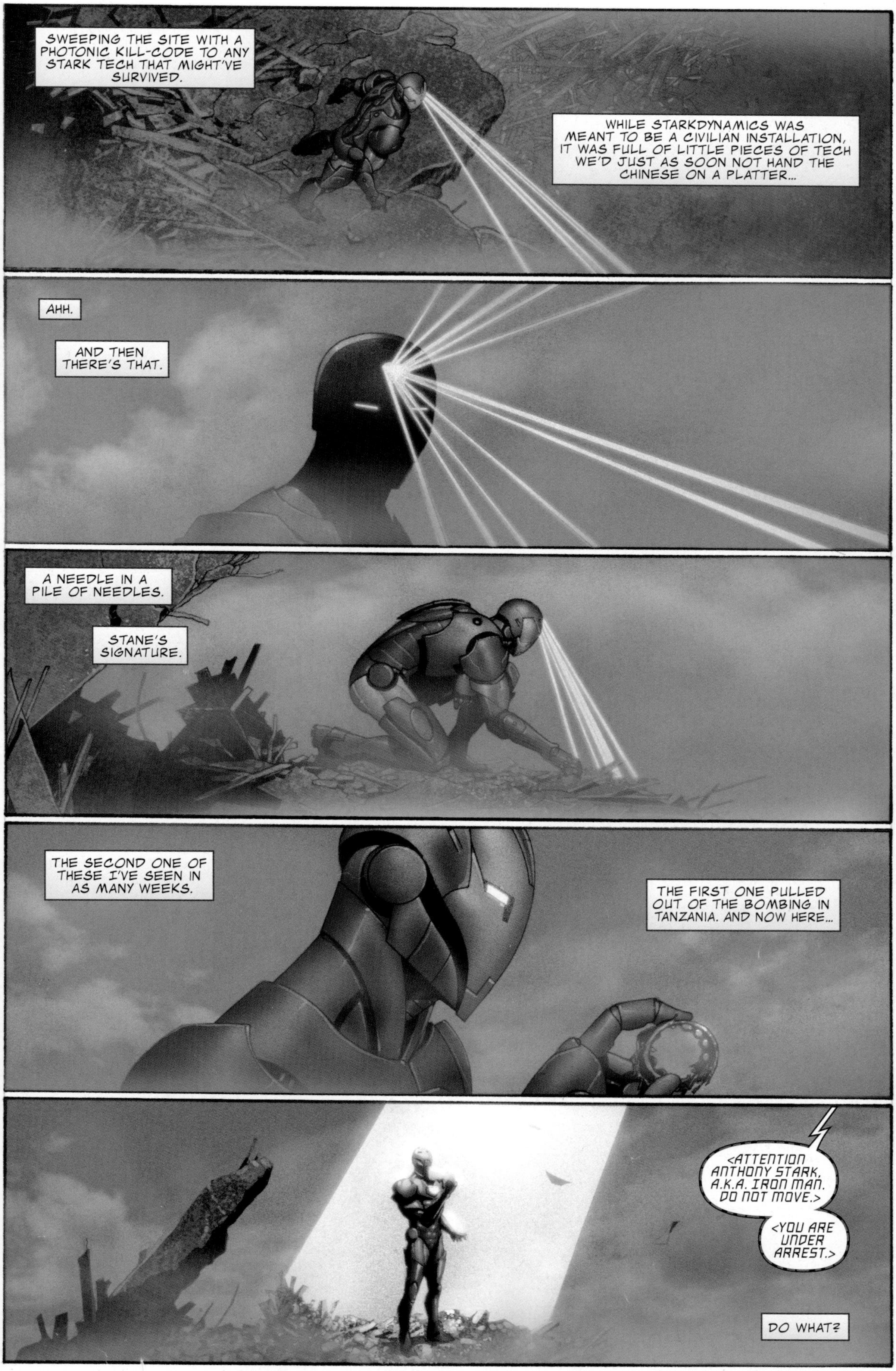
SWEEPING THE SITE WITH A PHOTONIC KILL-CODE TO ANY STARK TECH THAT MIGHT'VE SURVIVED.
WHILE STARKDYNAMICS WAS MEANT TO BE A CIVILIAN INSTALLATION, IT WAS FULL OF LITTLE PIECES OF TECH WE'D JUST AS SOON NOT HAND THE CHINESE ON A PLATTER...
AHH.
AND THEN THERE'S THAT.
A NEEDLE IN A PILE OF NEEDLES.
STANE'S SIGNATURE.
THE SECOND ONE OF THESE I'VE SEEN IN AS MANY WEEKS.
THE FIRST ONE PULLED OUT OF THE BOMBING IN TANZANIA. AND NOW HERE...
<ATTENTION ANTHONY STARK, A.K.A. IRON MAN. DO NOT MOVE.>
<YOU ARE UNDER ARREST.>
DO WHAT?

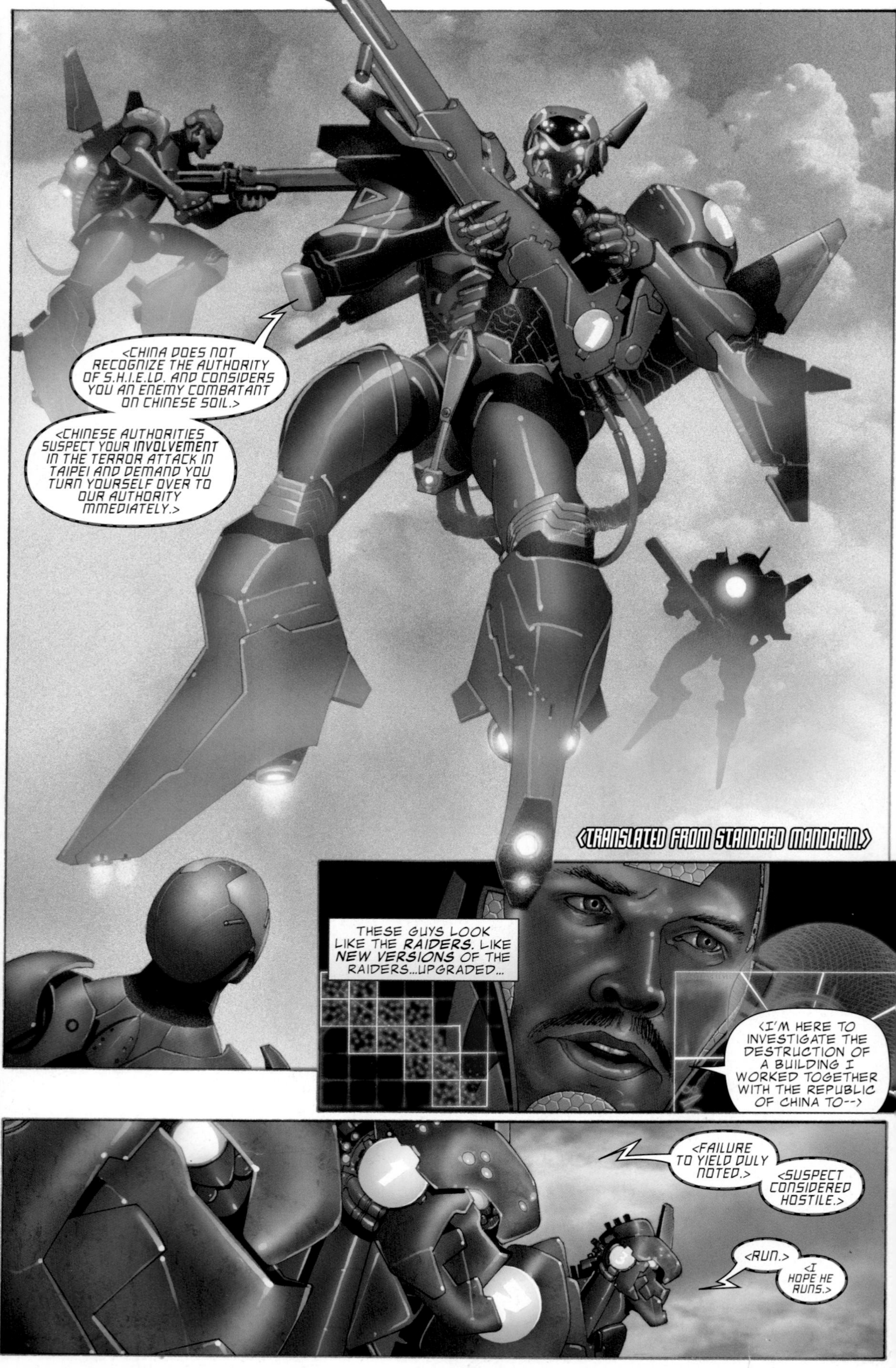
<CHINA DOES NOT RECOGNIZE THE AUTHORITY OF S.H.I.E.L.D. AND CONSIDERS YOU AN ENEMY COMBATANT ON CHINESE SOIL.>
<CHINESE AUTHORITIES SUSPECT YOUR INVOLVEMENT IN THE TERROR ATTACK IN TAIPEI AND DEMAND YOU TURN YOURSELF OVER TO OUR AUTHORITY MMEDIATELY.>
<TRANSLATED FROM STANDARD MANDARIN.>
THESE GUYS LOOK LIKE THE RAIDERS. LIKE NEW VERSIONS OF THE RAIDERS...UPGRADED...
<I'M HERE TO INVESTIGATE THE DESTRUCTION OF A BUILDING I WORKED TOGETHER WITH THE REPUBLIC OF CHINA TO-->
<FAILURE TO YIELD DULY NOTED.>
<SUSPECT CONSIDERED HOSTILE.>
<RUN.>
<I HOPE HE RUNS.>

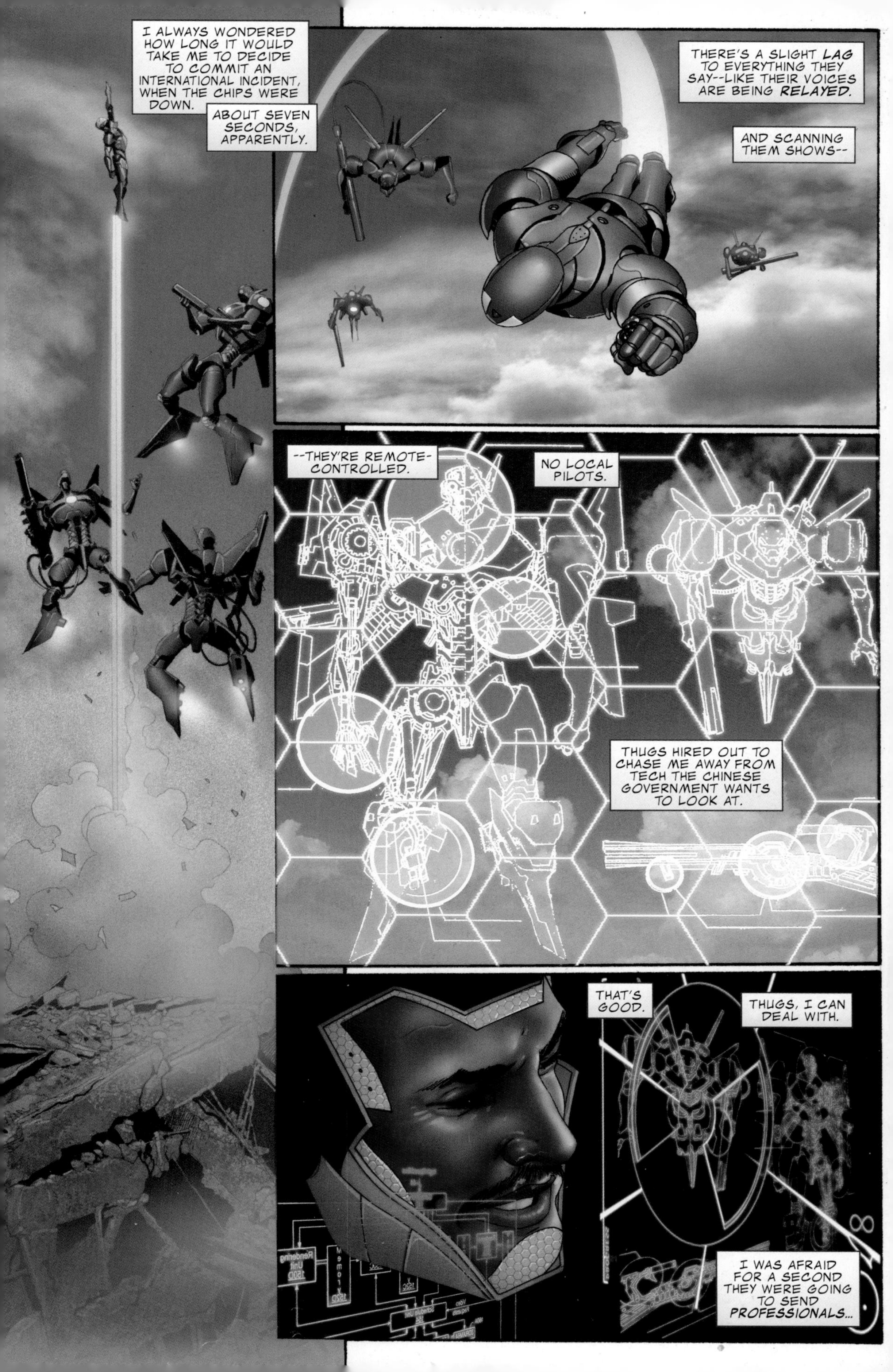
I ALWAYS WONDERED HOW LONG IT WOULD TAKE ME TO DECIDE TO COMMIT AN INTERNATIONAL INCIDENT, WHEN THE CHIPS WERE DOWN.
ABOUT SEVEN SECONDS, APPARENTLY.
THERE'S A SLIGHT LAG TO EVERYTHING THEY SAY--LIKE THEIR VOICES ARE BEING RELAYED.
AND SCANNING THEM SHOWS--
--THEY'RE REMOTE-CONTROLLED.
NO LOCAL PILOTS.
THUGS HIRED OUT TO CHASE ME AWAY FROM TECH THE CHINESE GOVERNMENT WANTS TO LOOK AT.
THAT'S GOOD.
THUGS, I CAN DEAL WITH.
I WAS AFRAID FOR A SECOND THEY WERE GOING TO SEND PROFESSIONALS...

I RUN SLOW ENOUGH TO BE CHASED.

I DODGE CLUMSY ENOUGH TO LET THEM GET HUNGRY FOR BLOOD.

I GET THEM OVER INTERNATIONAL WATERS AND--

GAME ON.

<UM. IT'S *NINETEEN MILES* UNTIL YOU'RE IN INTERNATIONAL AIRSPACE, RIGHT?>

<NINETEEN *KILOMETERS*, NOOB.>

<UH-OH.>

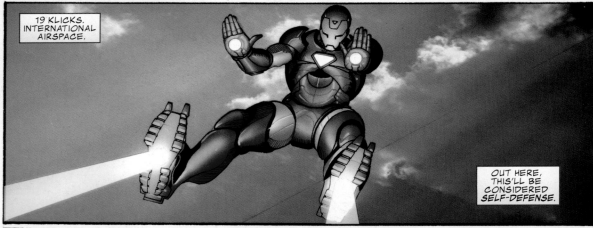

19 KLICKS. INTERNATIONAL AIRSPACE.

OUT HERE, THIS'LL BE CONSIDERED *SELF-DEFENSE.*

<AW, DAMMIT--!>

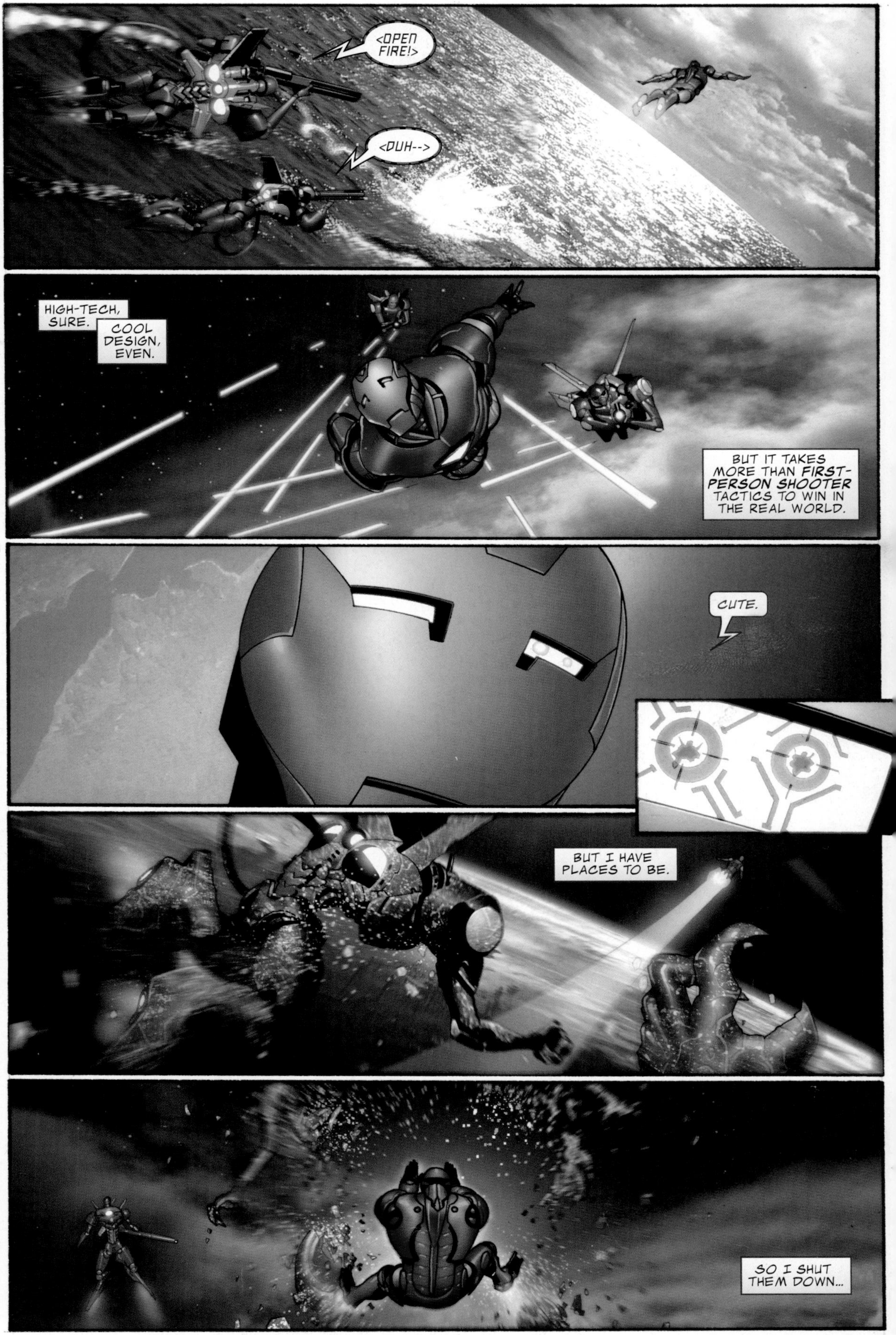
<OPEN FIRE!>
<DUH-->
HIGH-TECH, SURE.
COOL DESIGN, EVEN.
BUT IT TAKES MORE THAN FIRST-PERSON SHOOTER TACTICS TO WIN IN THE REAL WORLD.
CUTE.
BUT I HAVE PLACES TO BE.
SO I SHUT THEM DOWN...

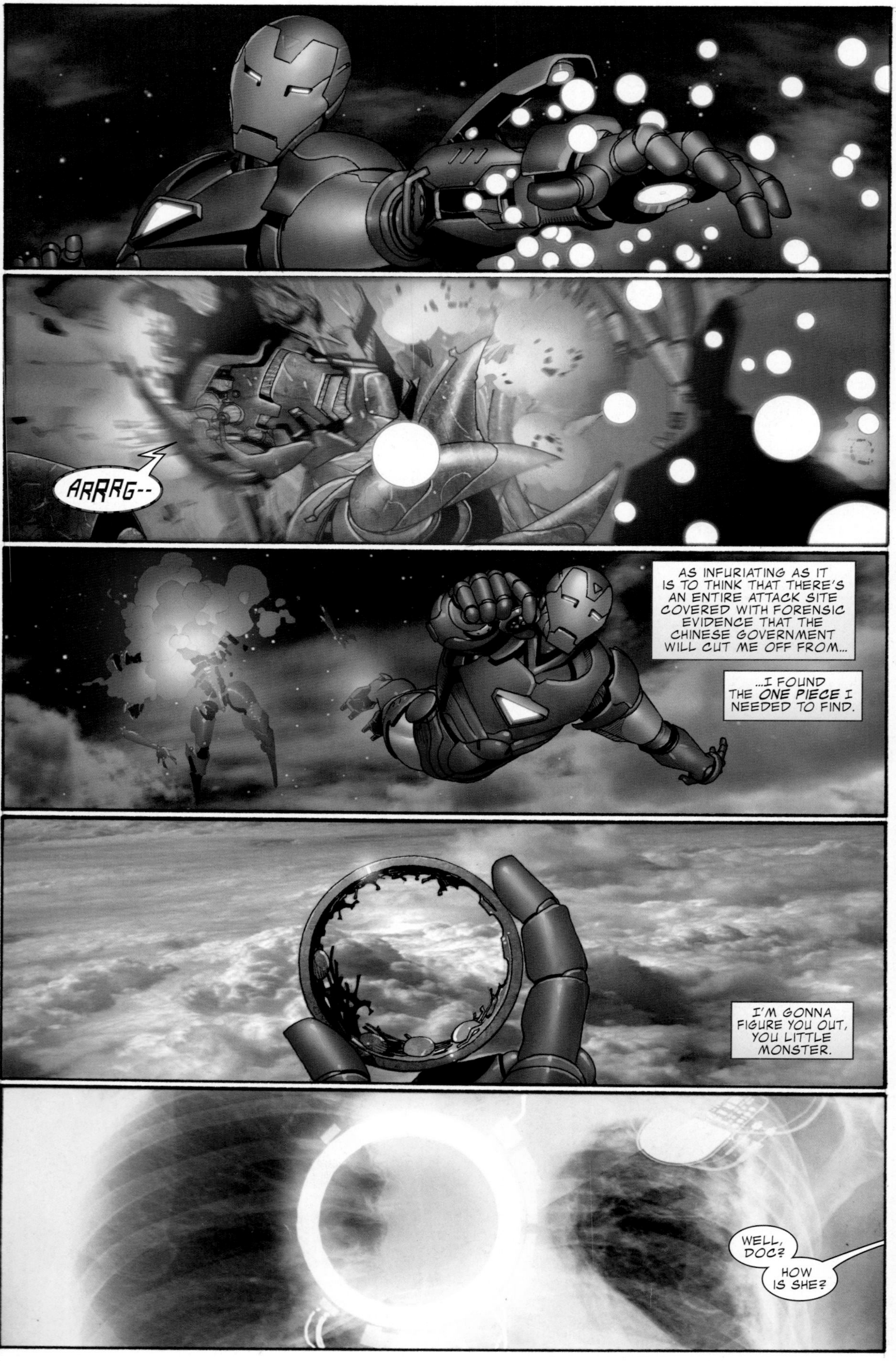
ARRRG--
AS INFURIATING AS IT IS TO THINK THAT THERE'S AN ENTIRE ATTACK SITE COVERED WITH FORENSIC EVIDENCE THAT THE CHINESE GOVERNMENT WILL CUT ME OFF FROM...
...I FOUND THE ONE PIECE I NEEDED TO FIND.
I'M GONNA FIGURE YOU OUT, YOU LITTLE MONSTER.
WELL, DOC?
HOW IS SHE?

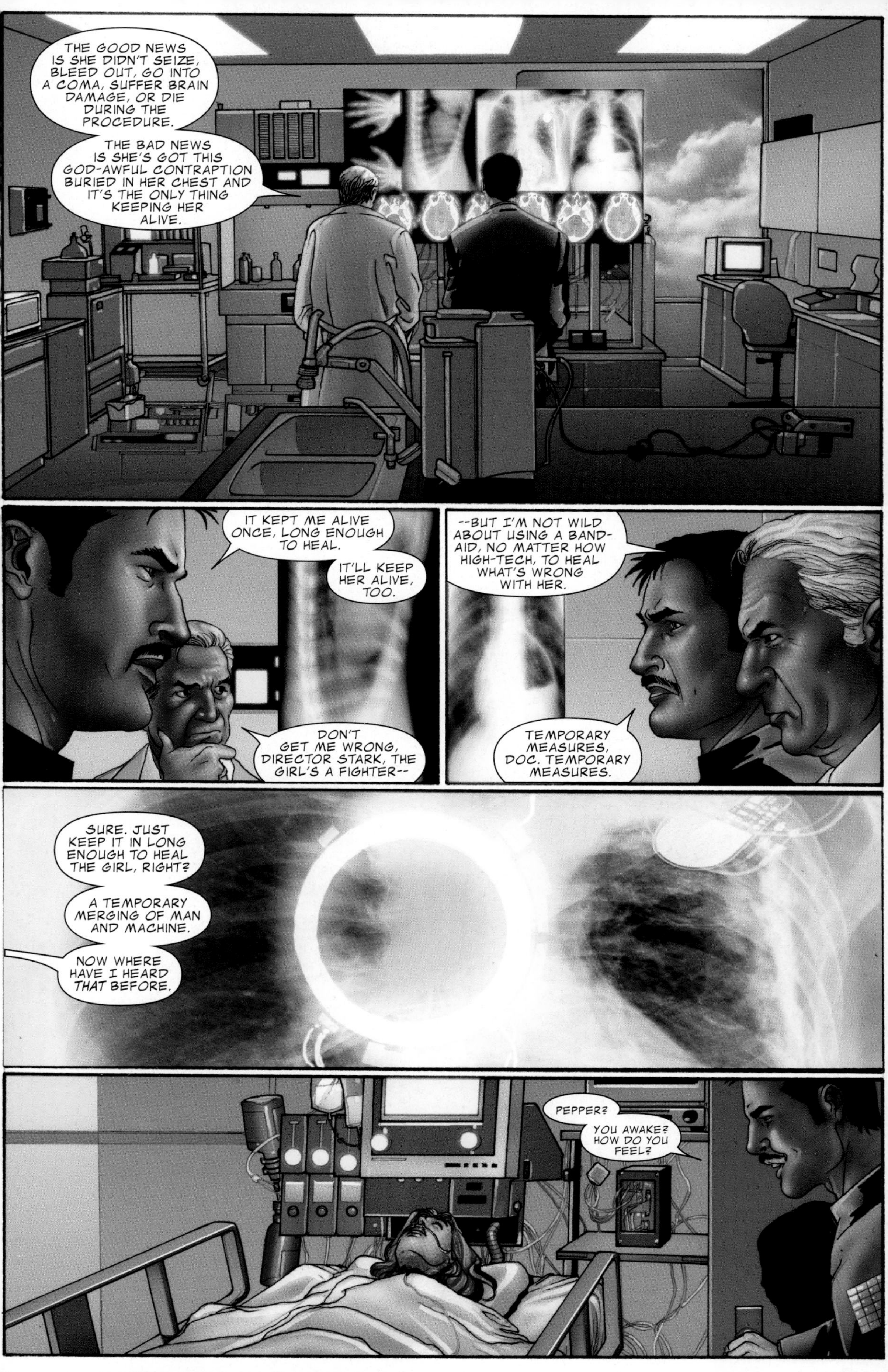

THE GOOD NEWS IS SHE DIDN'T SEIZE, BLEED OUT, GO INTO A COMA, SUFFER BRAIN DAMAGE, OR DIE DURING THE PROCEDURE.
THE BAD NEWS IS SHE'S GOT THIS GOD-AWFUL CONTRAPTION BURIED IN HER CHEST AND IT'S THE ONLY THING KEEPING HER ALIVE.
IT KEPT ME ALIVE ONCE, LONG ENOUGH TO HEAL.
IT'LL KEEP HER ALIVE, TOO.
DON'T GET ME WRONG, DIRECTOR STARK, THE GIRL'S A FIGHTER--
--BUT I'M NOT WILD ABOUT USING A BAND-AID, NO MATTER HOW HIGH-TECH, TO HEAL WHAT'S WRONG WITH HER.
TEMPORARY MEASURES, DOC. TEMPORARY MEASURES.
SURE. JUST KEEP IT IN LONG ENOUGH TO HEAL THE GIRL, RIGHT?
A TEMPORARY MERGING OF MAN AND MACHINE.
NOW WHERE HAVE I HEARD *THAT* BEFORE.
PEPPER?
YOU AWAKE? HOW DO YOU FEEL?

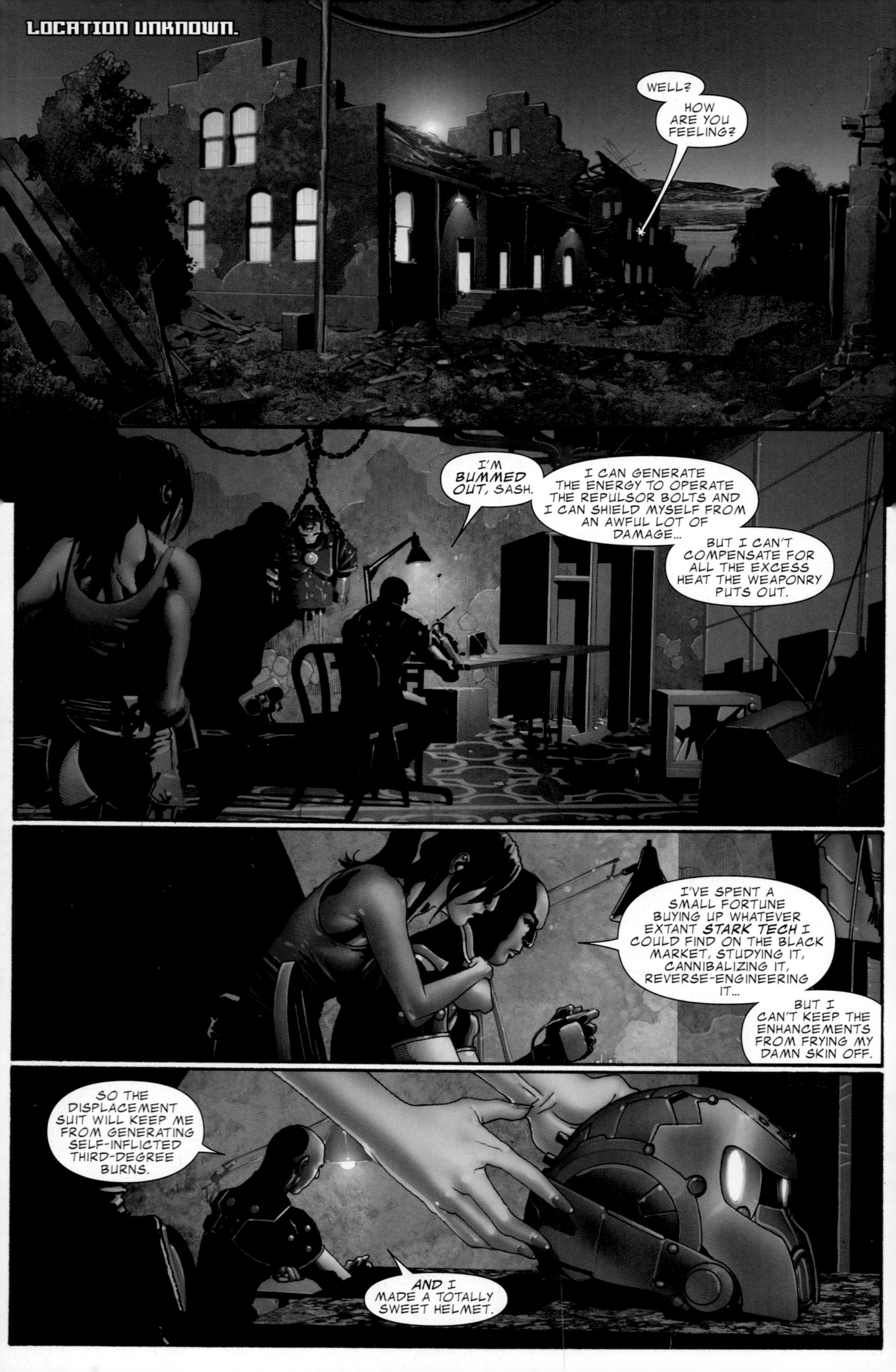
LOCATION UNKNOWN.
WELL? HOW ARE YOU FEELING?
I'M BUMMED OUT, SASH.
I CAN GENERATE THE ENERGY TO OPERATE THE REPULSOR BOLTS AND I CAN SHIELD MYSELF FROM AN AWFUL LOT OF DAMAGE...
BUT I CAN'T COMPENSATE FOR ALL THE EXCESS HEAT THE WEAPONRY PUTS OUT.
I'VE SPENT A SMALL FORTUNE BUYING UP WHATEVER EXTANT STARK TECH I COULD FIND ON THE BLACK MARKET, STUDYING IT, CANNIBALIZING IT, REVERSE-ENGINEERING IT...
BUT I CAN'T KEEP THE ENHANCEMENTS FROM FRYING MY DAMN SKIN OFF.
SO THE DISPLACEMENT SUIT WILL KEEP ME FROM GENERATING SELF-INFLICTED THIRD-DEGREE BURNS.
AND I MADE A TOTALLY SWEET HELMET.

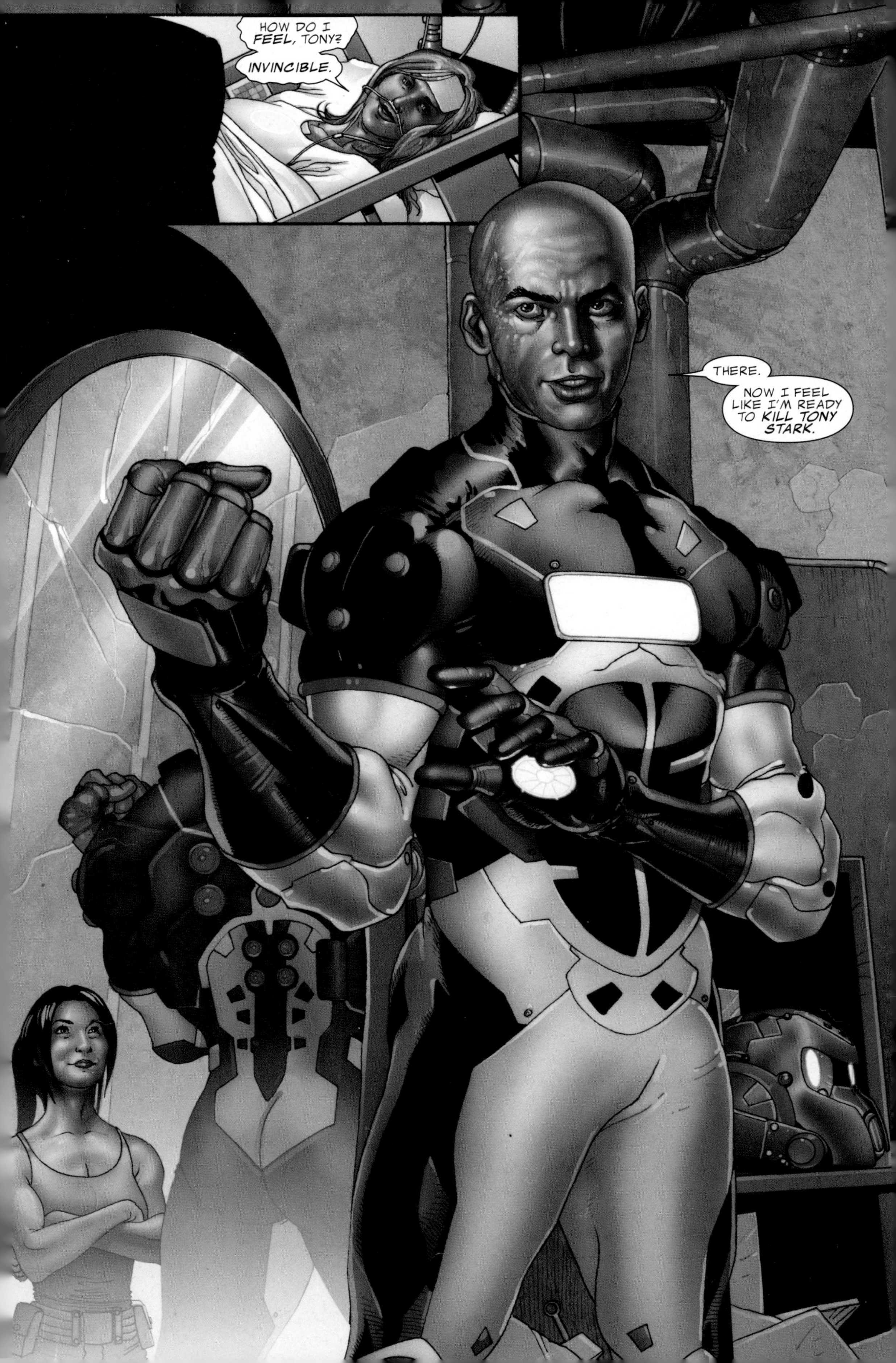
HOW DO I FEEL, TONY?
INVINCIBLE.
THERE.
NOW I FEEL LIKE I'M READY TO KILL TONY STARK.

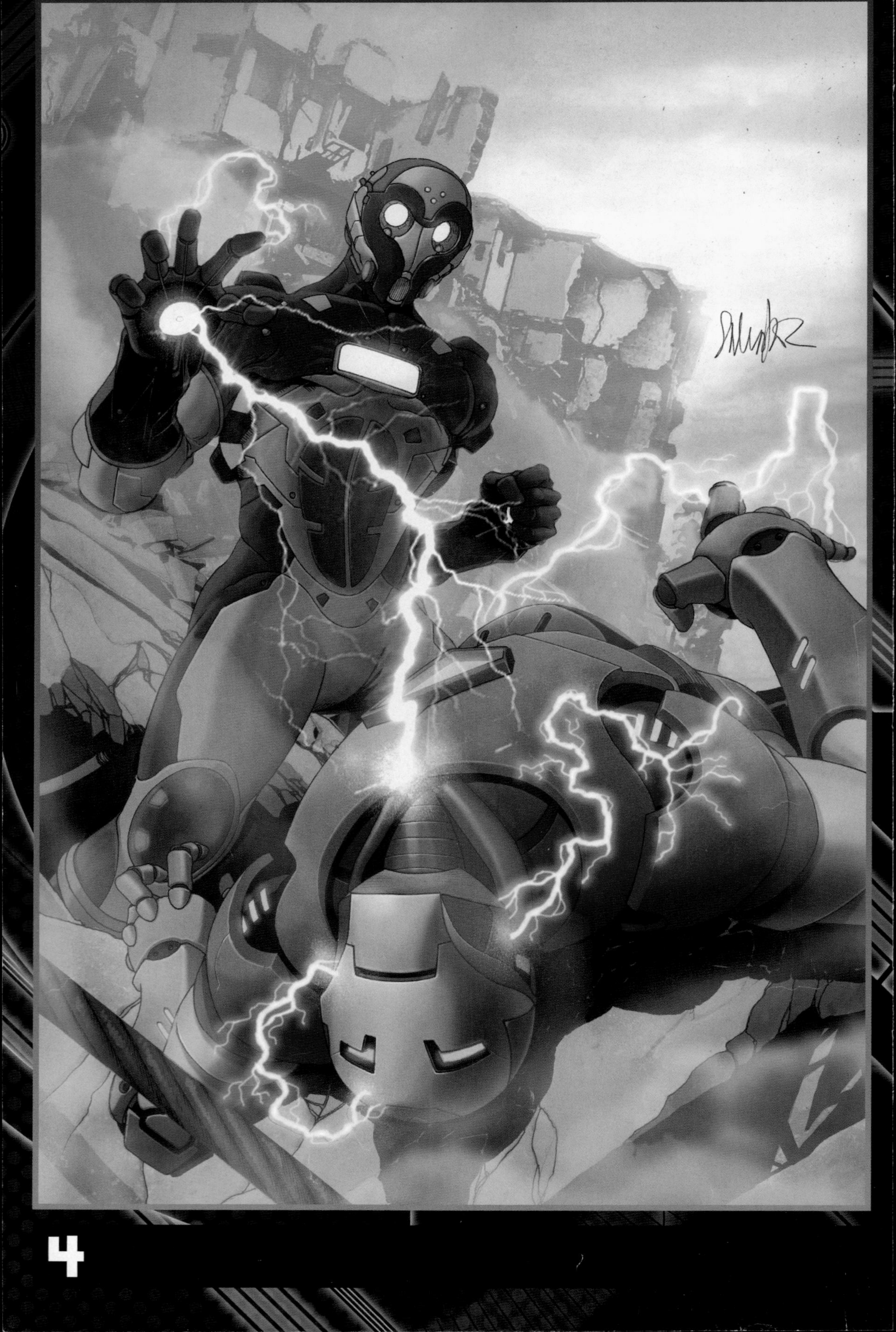

4

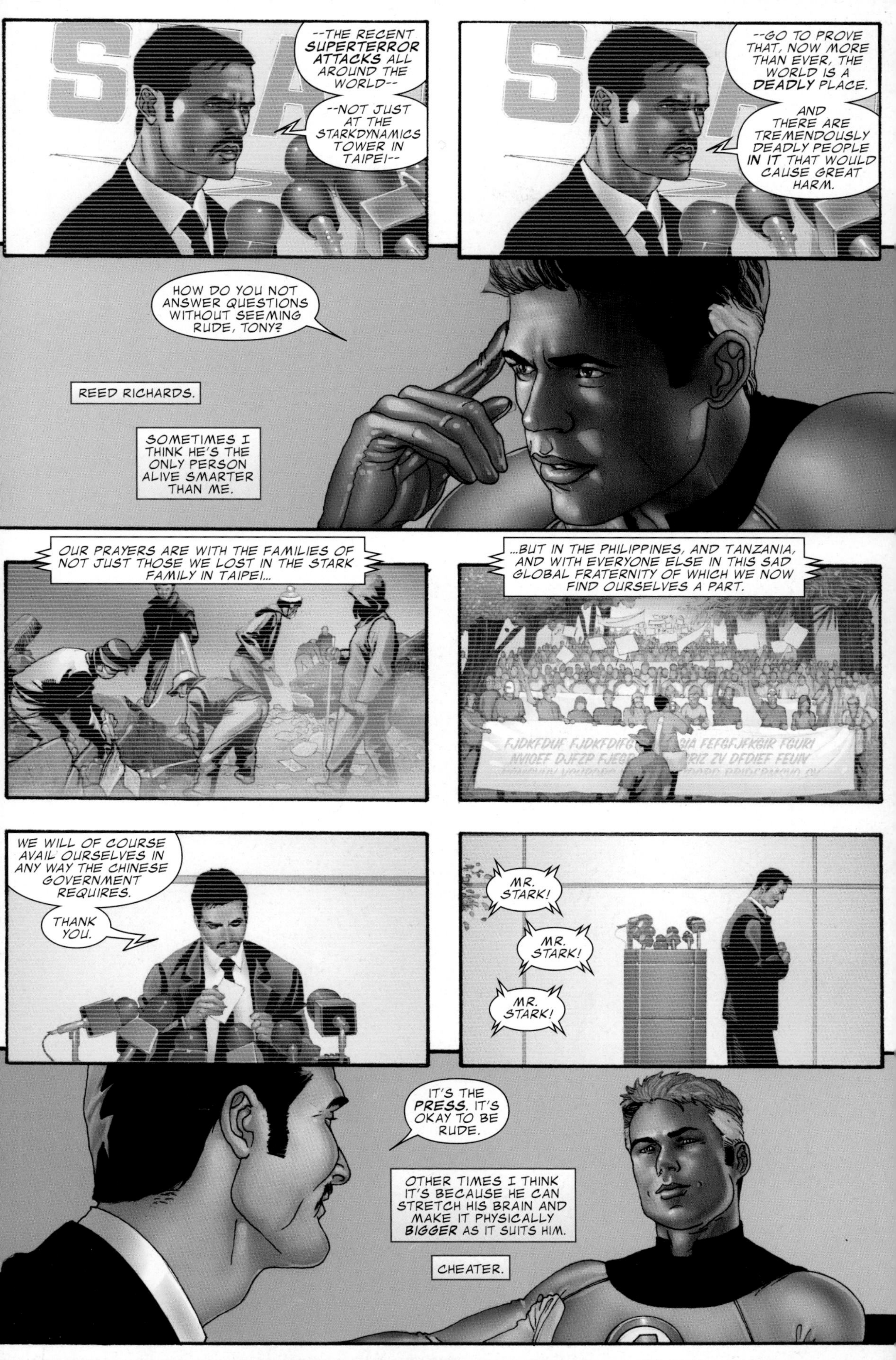
--THE RECENT SUPERTERROR ATTACKS ALL AROUND THE WORLD--
--NOT JUST AT THE STARKDYNAMICS TOWER IN TAIPEI--
--GO TO PROVE THAT, NOW MORE THAN EVER, THE WORLD IS A DEADLY PLACE.
AND THERE ARE TREMENDOUSLY DEADLY PEOPLE IN IT THAT WOULD CAUSE GREAT HARM.
HOW DO YOU NOT ANSWER QUESTIONS WITHOUT SEEMING RUDE, TONY?
REED RICHARDS.
SOMETIMES I THINK HE'S THE ONLY PERSON ALIVE SMARTER THAN ME.
OUR PRAYERS ARE WITH THE FAMILIES OF NOT JUST THOSE WE LOST IN THE STARK FAMILY IN TAIPEI...
...BUT IN THE PHILIPPINES, AND TANZANIA, AND WITH EVERYONE ELSE IN THIS SAD GLOBAL FRATERNITY OF WHICH WE NOW FIND OURSELVES A PART.
WE WILL OF COURSE AVAIL OURSELVES IN ANY WAY THE CHINESE GOVERNMENT REQUIRES.
THANK YOU.
MR. STARK!
MR. STARK!
MR. STARK!
IT'S THE PRESS. IT'S OKAY TO BE RUDE.
OTHER TIMES I THINK IT'S BECAUSE HE CAN STRETCH HIS BRAIN AND MAKE IT PHYSICALLY BIGGER AS IT SUITS HIM.
CHEATER.

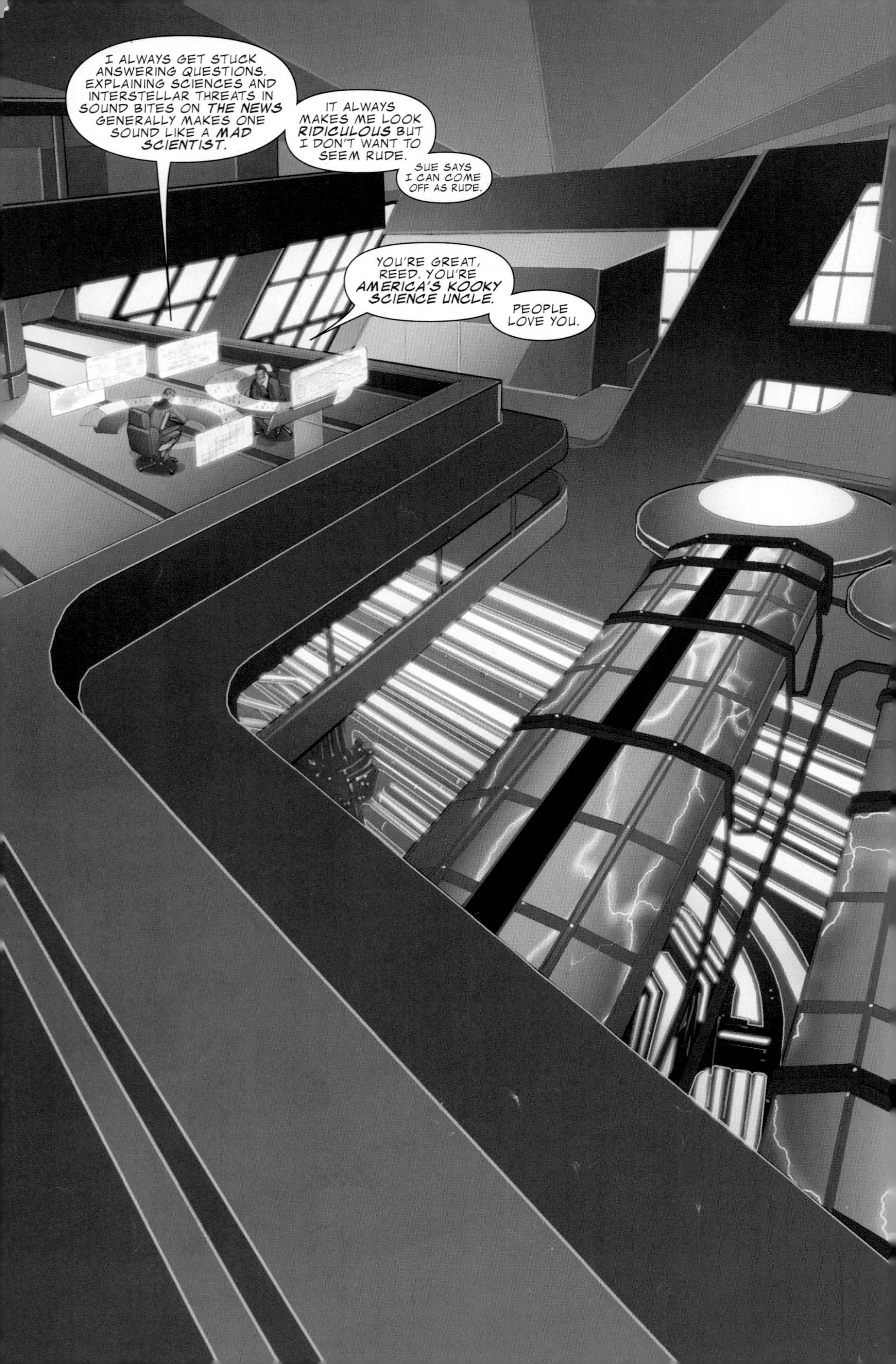
I ALWAYS GET STUCK ANSWERING QUESTIONS. EXPLAINING SCIENCES AND INTERSTELLAR THREATS IN SOUND BITES ON THE NEWS GENERALLY MAKES ONE SOUND LIKE A MAD SCIENTIST.
IT ALWAYS MAKES ME LOOK RIDICULOUS BUT I DON'T WANT TO SEEM RUDE.
SUE SAYS I CAN COME OFF AS RUDE.
YOU'RE GREAT, REED. YOU'RE AMERICA'S KOOKY SCIENCE UNCLE.
PEOPLE LOVE YOU.

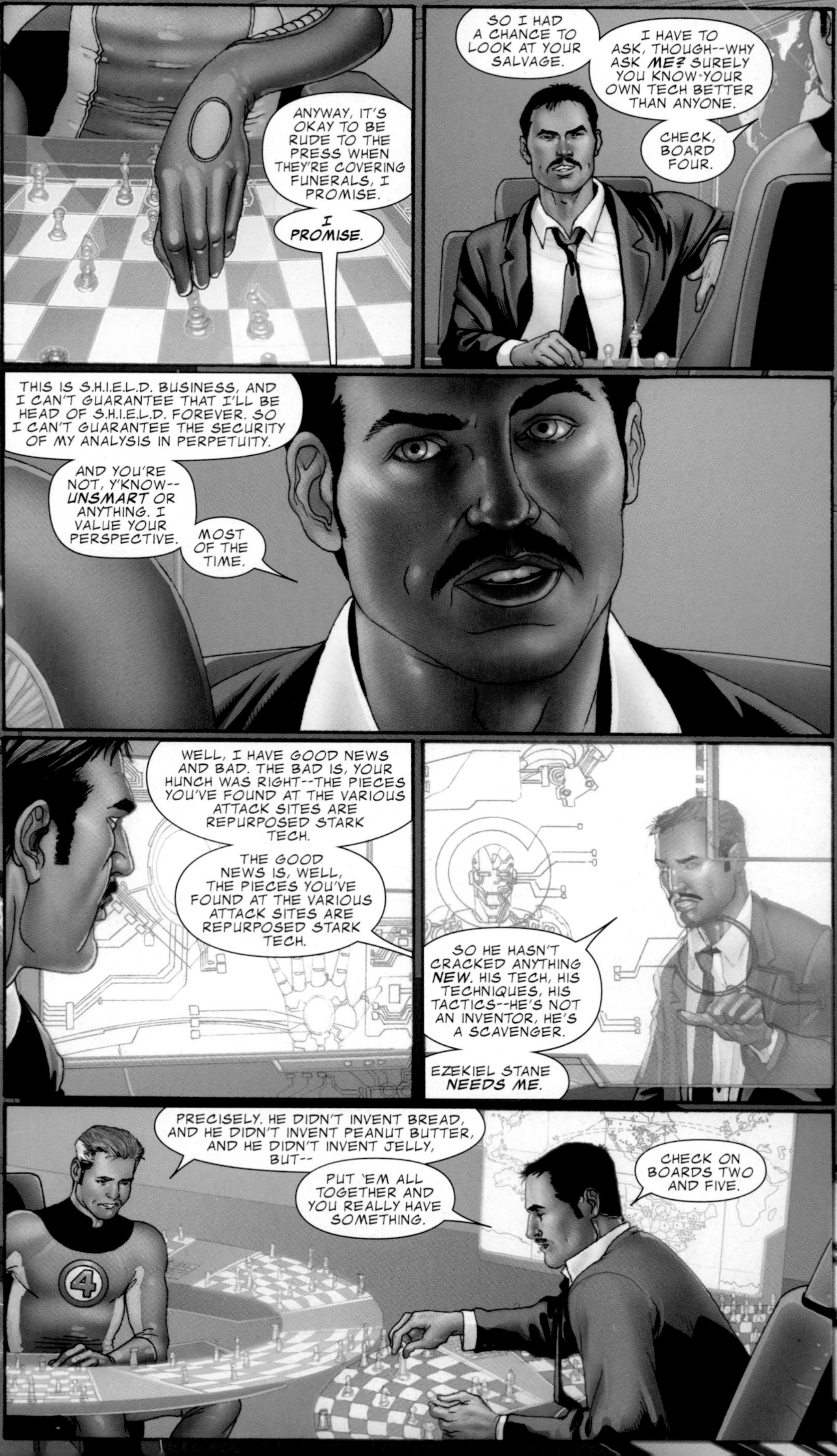
ANYWAY, IT'S OKAY TO BE RUDE TO THE PRESS WHEN THEY'RE COVERING FUNERALS, I PROMISE.
I PROMISE.
SO I HAD A CHANCE TO LOOK AT YOUR SALVAGE.
I HAVE TO ASK, THOUGH--WHY ASK ME? SURELY YOU KNOW YOUR OWN TECH BETTER THAN ANYONE.
CHECK, BOARD FOUR.
THIS IS S.H.I.E.L.D. BUSINESS, AND I CAN'T GUARANTEE THAT I'LL BE HEAD OF S.H.I.E.L.D. FOREVER. SO I CAN'T GUARANTEE THE SECURITY OF MY ANALYSIS IN PERPETUITY.
AND YOU'RE NOT, Y'KNOW--UNSMART OR ANYTHING. I VALUE YOUR PERSPECTIVE.
MOST OF THE TIME.
WELL, I HAVE GOOD NEWS AND BAD. THE BAD IS, YOUR HUNCH WAS RIGHT--THE PIECES YOU'VE FOUND AT THE VARIOUS ATTACK SITES ARE REPURPOSED STARK TECH.
THE GOOD NEWS IS, WELL, THE PIECES YOU'VE FOUND AT THE VARIOUS ATTACK SITES ARE REPURPOSED STARK TECH.
SO HE HASN'T CRACKED ANYTHING NEW. HIS TECH, HIS TECHNIQUES, HIS TACTICS--HE'S NOT AN INVENTOR, HE'S A SCAVENGER.
EZEKIEL STANE NEEDS ME.
PRECISELY. HE DIDN'T INVENT BREAD, AND HE DIDN'T INVENT PEANUT BUTTER, AND HE DIDN'T INVENT JELLY, BUT--
PUT 'EM ALL TOGETHER AND YOU REALLY HAVE SOMETHING.
CHECK ON BOARDS TWO AND FIVE.

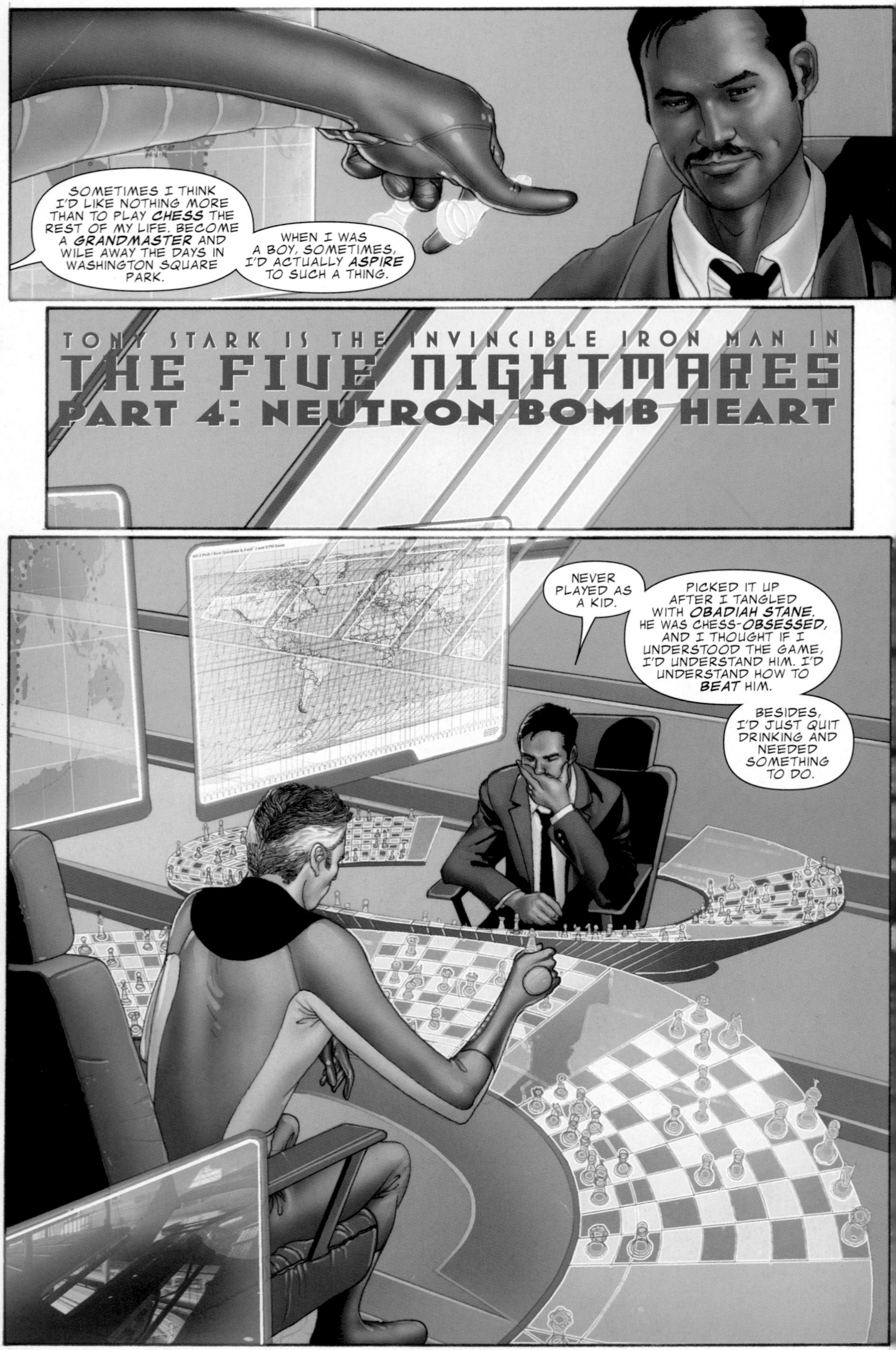
SOMETIMES I THINK I'D LIKE NOTHING MORE THAN TO PLAY CHESS THE REST OF MY LIFE. BECOME A GRANDMASTER AND WILE AWAY THE DAYS IN WASHINGTON SQUARE PARK.
WHEN I WAS A BOY, SOMETIMES, I'D ACTUALLY ASPIRE TO SUCH A THING.
TONY STARK IS THE INVINCIBLE IRON MAN IN
THE FIVE NIGHTMARES
PART 4: NEUTRON BOMB HEART
NEVER PLAYED AS A KID.
PICKED IT UP AFTER I TANGLED WITH OBADIAH STANE. HE WAS CHESS-OBSESSED, AND I THOUGHT IF I UNDERSTOOD THE GAME, I'D UNDERSTAND HIM. I'D UNDERSTAND HOW TO BEAT HIM.
BESIDES, I'D JUST QUIT DRINKING AND NEEDED SOMETHING TO DO.

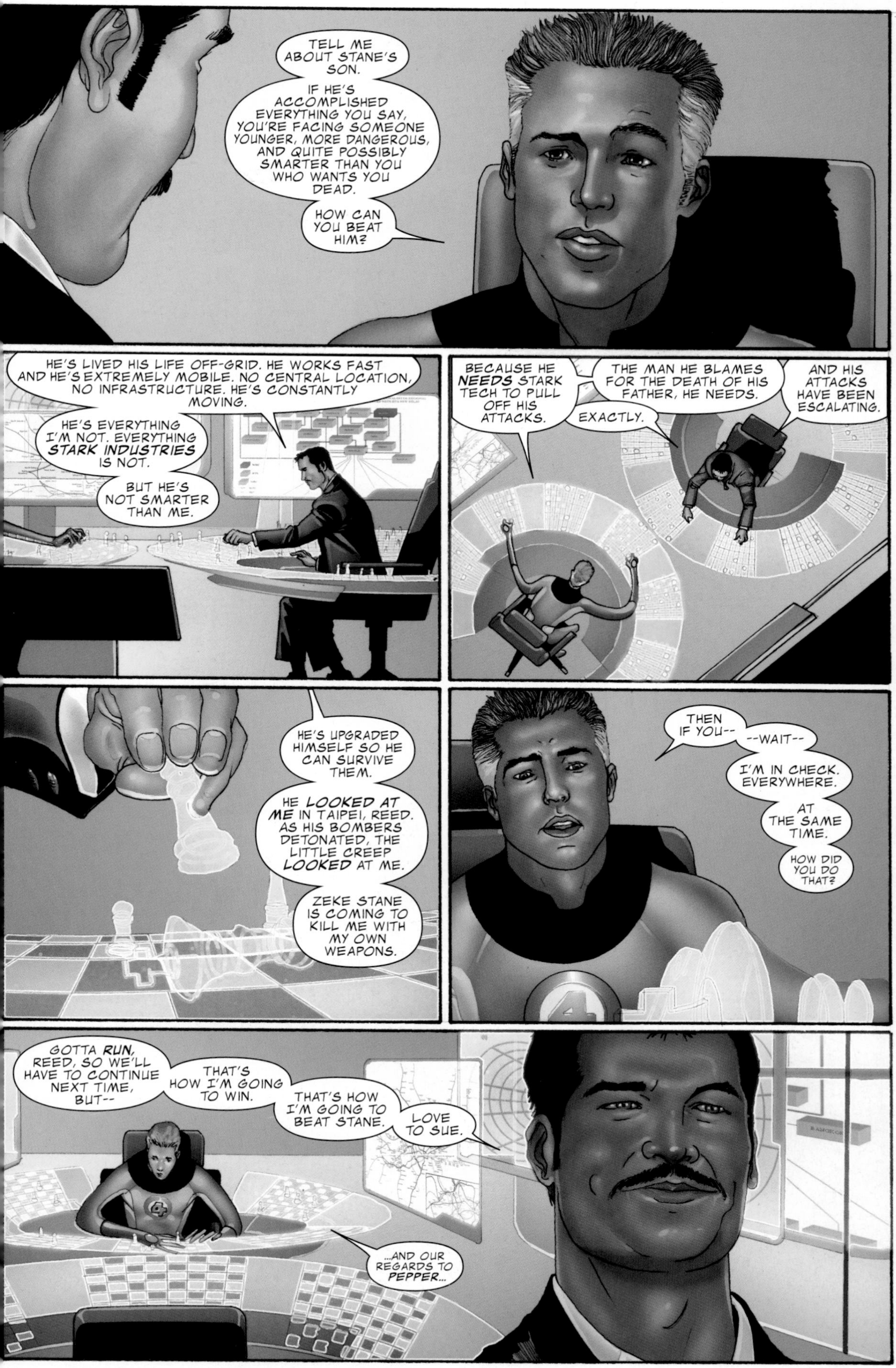
TELL ME ABOUT STANE'S SON.
IF HE'S ACCOMPLISHED EVERYTHING YOU SAY, YOU'RE FACING SOMEONE YOUNGER, MORE DANGEROUS, AND QUITE POSSIBLY SMARTER THAN YOU WHO WANTS YOU DEAD.
HOW CAN YOU BEAT HIM?
HE'S LIVED HIS LIFE OFF-GRID. HE WORKS FAST AND HE'S EXTREMELY MOBILE. NO CENTRAL LOCATION, NO INFRASTRUCTURE. HE'S CONSTANTLY MOVING.
HE'S EVERYTHING I'M NOT. EVERYTHING STARK INDUSTRIES IS NOT.
BUT HE'S NOT SMARTER THAN ME.
BECAUSE HE NEEDS STARK TECH TO PULL OFF HIS ATTACKS.
THE MAN HE BLAMES FOR THE DEATH OF HIS FATHER, HE NEEDS.
EXACTLY.
AND HIS ATTACKS HAVE BEEN ESCALATING.
HE'S UPGRADED HIMSELF SO HE CAN SURVIVE THEM.
HE LOOKED AT ME IN TAIPEI, REED. AS HIS BOMBERS DETONATED, THE LITTLE CREEP LOOKED AT ME.
ZEKE STANE IS COMING TO KILL ME WITH MY OWN WEAPONS.
THEN IF YOU--
--WAIT--
I'M IN CHECK. EVERYWHERE.
AT THE SAME TIME.
HOW DID YOU DO THAT?
GOTTA RUN, REED, SO WE'LL HAVE TO CONTINUE NEXT TIME, BUT--
THAT'S HOW I'M GOING TO WIN.
THAT'S HOW I'M GOING TO BEAT STANE.
LOVE TO SUE.
...AND OUR REGARDS TO PEPPER...

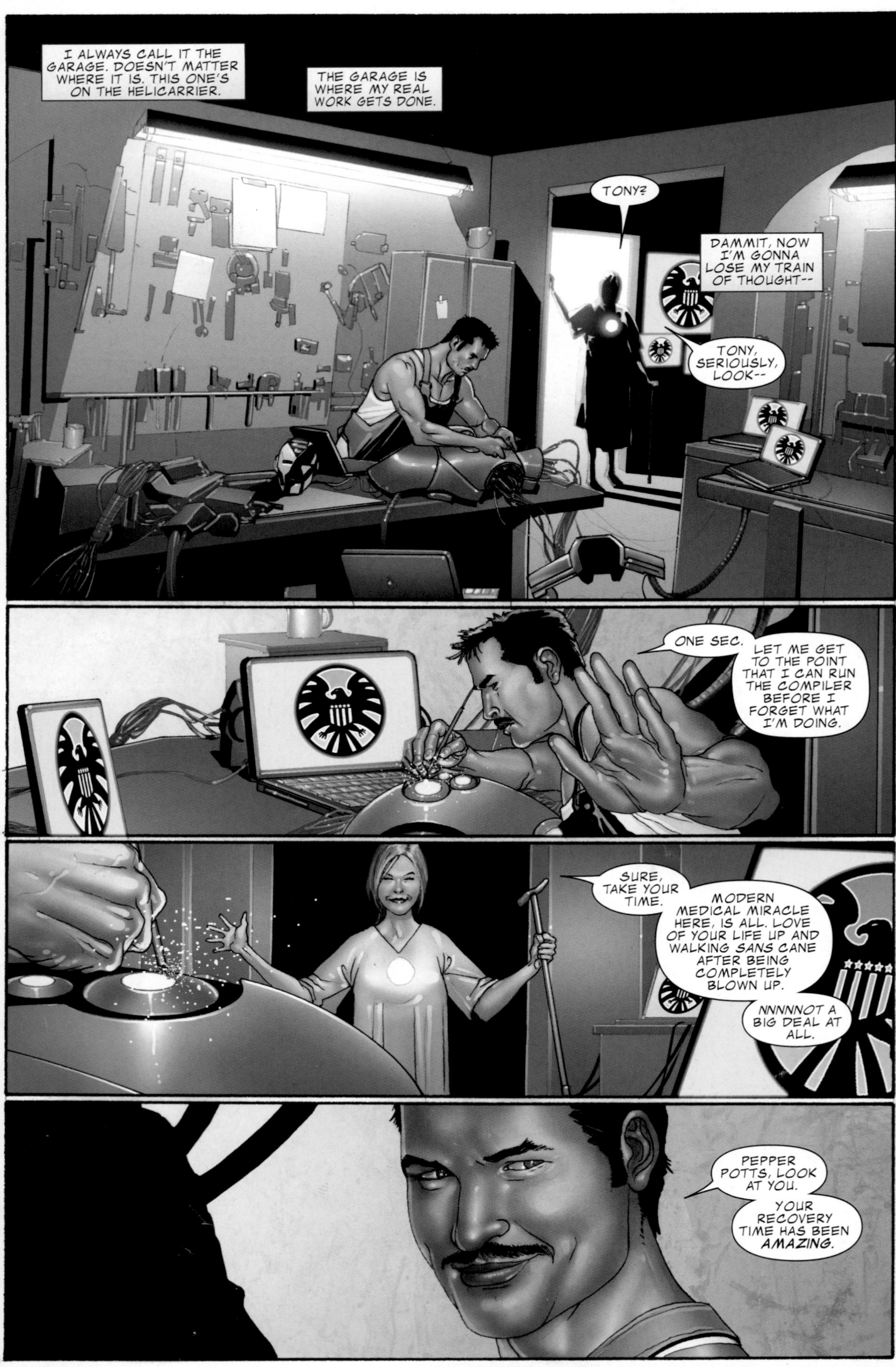
I ALWAYS CALL IT THE GARAGE. DOESN'T MATTER WHERE IT IS. THIS ONE'S ON THE HELICARRIER.
THE GARAGE IS WHERE MY REAL WORK GETS DONE.
TONY?
DAMMIT, NOW I'M GONNA LOSE MY TRAIN OF THOUGHT--
TONY, SERIOUSLY, LOOK--
ONE SEC.
LET ME GET TO THE POINT THAT I CAN RUN THE COMPILER BEFORE I FORGET WHAT I'M DOING.
SURE, TAKE YOUR TIME.
MODERN MEDICAL MIRACLE HERE, IS ALL. LOVE OF YOUR LIFE UP AND WALKING SANS CANE AFTER BEING COMPLETELY BLOWN UP.
NNNNNOT A BIG DEAL AT ALL.
PEPPER POTTS, LOOK AT YOU.
YOUR RECOVERY TIME HAS BEEN *AMAZING*.

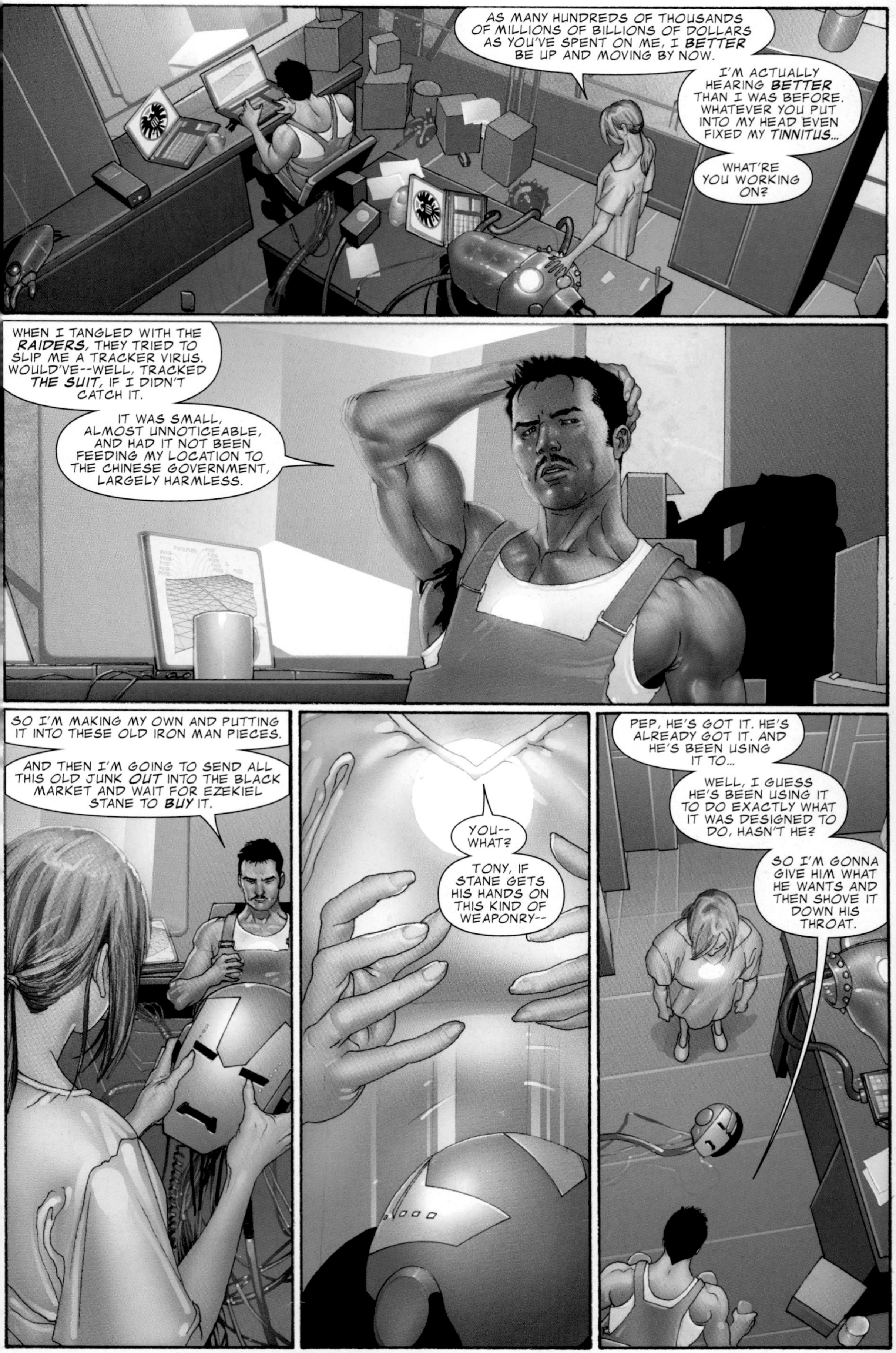
AS MANY HUNDREDS OF THOUSANDS OF MILLIONS OF BILLIONS OF DOLLARS AS YOU'VE SPENT ON ME, I **BETTER** BE UP AND MOVING BY NOW.
I'M ACTUALLY HEARING **BETTER** THAN I WAS BEFORE. WHATEVER YOU PUT INTO MY HEAD EVEN FIXED MY ***TINNITUS***...
WHAT'RE YOU WORKING ON?
WHEN I TANGLED WITH THE ***RAIDERS***, THEY TRIED TO SLIP ME A TRACKER VIRUS. WOULD'VE--WELL, TRACKED ***THE SUIT***, IF I DIDN'T CATCH IT.
IT WAS SMALL, ALMOST UNNOTICEABLE, AND HAD IT NOT BEEN FEEDING MY LOCATION TO THE CHINESE GOVERNMENT, LARGELY HARMLESS.
SO I'M MAKING MY OWN AND PUTTING IT INTO THESE OLD IRON MAN PIECES.
AND THEN I'M GOING TO SEND ALL THIS OLD JUNK ***OUT*** INTO THE BLACK MARKET AND WAIT FOR EZEKIEL STANE TO ***BUY*** IT.
YOU-- WHAT?
TONY, IF STANE GETS HIS HANDS ON THIS KIND OF WEAPONRY--
PEP, HE'S GOT IT. HE'S ALREADY GOT IT. AND HE'S BEEN USING IT TO...
WELL, I GUESS HE'S BEEN USING IT TO DO EXACTLY WHAT IT WAS DESIGNED TO DO, HASN'T HE?
SO I'M GONNA GIVE HIM WHAT HE WANTS AND THEN SHOVE IT DOWN HIS THROAT.

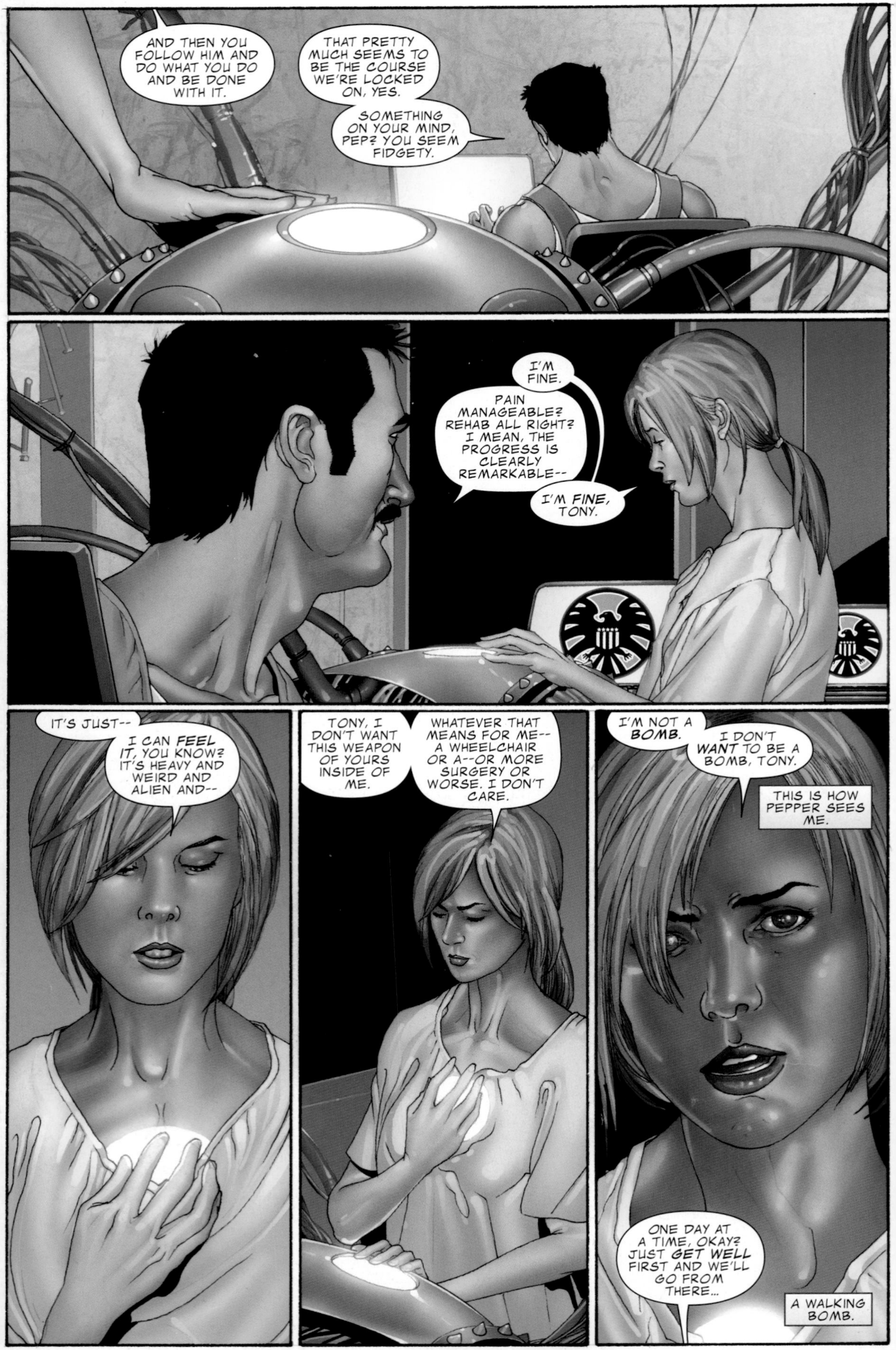
AND THEN YOU FOLLOW HIM AND DO WHAT YOU DO AND BE DONE WITH IT.
THAT PRETTY MUCH SEEMS TO BE THE COURSE WE'RE LOCKED ON, YES.
SOMETHING ON YOUR MIND, PEP? YOU SEEM FIDGETY.
I'M FINE.
PAIN MANAGEABLE? REHAB ALL RIGHT? I MEAN, THE PROGRESS IS CLEARLY REMARKABLE--
I'M FINE, TONY.
IT'S JUST--
I CAN FEEL IT, YOU KNOW? IT'S HEAVY AND WEIRD AND ALIEN AND--
TONY, I DON'T WANT THIS WEAPON OF YOURS INSIDE OF ME.
WHATEVER THAT MEANS FOR ME-- A WHEELCHAIR OR A--OR MORE SURGERY OR WORSE. I DON'T CARE.
I'M NOT A BOMB.
I DON'T WANT TO BE A BOMB, TONY.
THIS IS HOW PEPPER SEES ME.
ONE DAY AT A TIME, OKAY? JUST GET WELL FIRST AND WE'LL GO FROM THERE...
A WALKING BOMB.

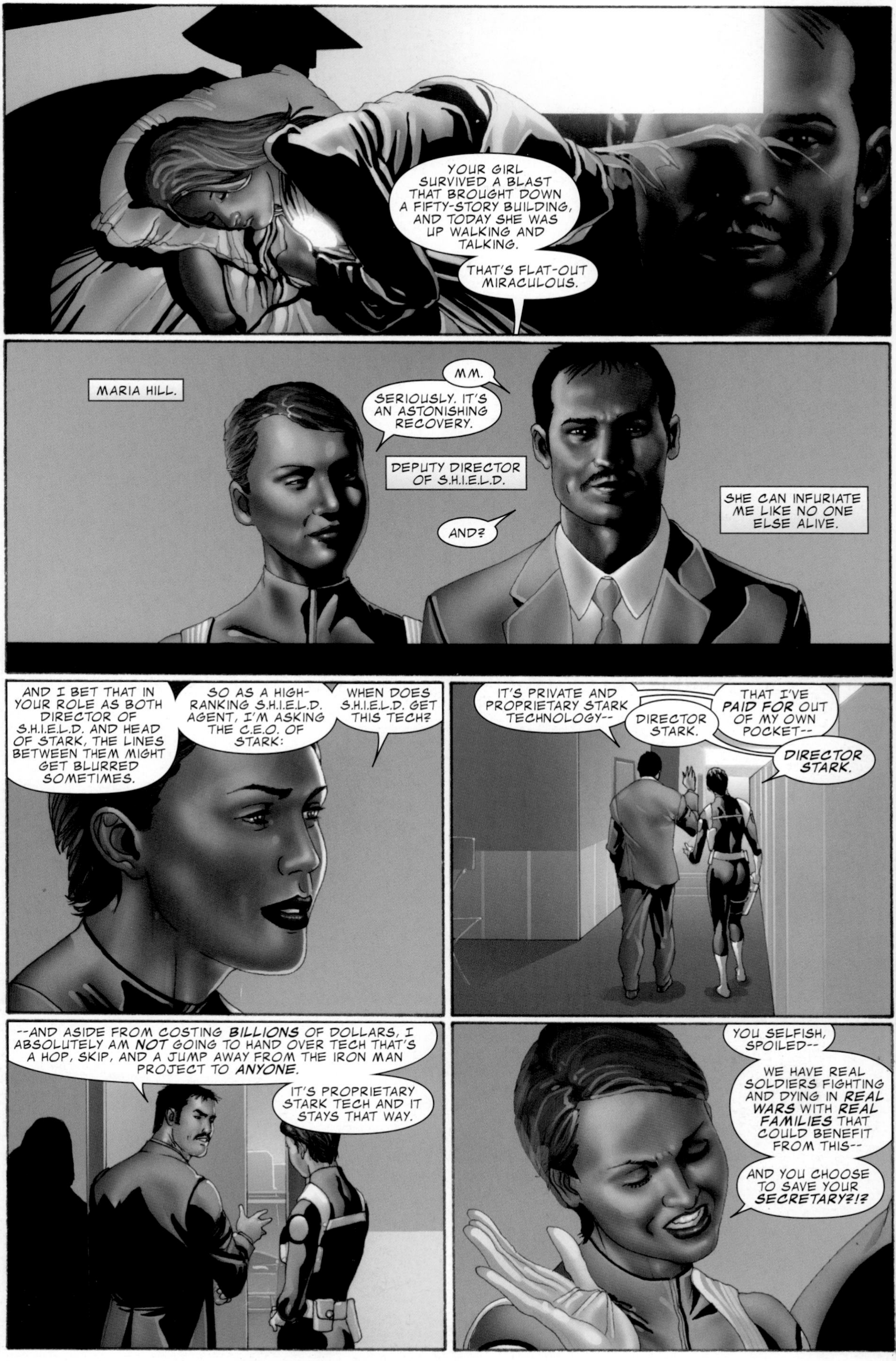
YOUR GIRL SURVIVED A BLAST THAT BROUGHT DOWN A FIFTY-STORY BUILDING, AND TODAY SHE WAS UP WALKING AND TALKING.
THAT'S FLAT-OUT MIRACULOUS.
MARIA HILL.
MM.
SERIOUSLY. IT'S AN ASTONISHING RECOVERY.
DEPUTY DIRECTOR OF S.H.I.E.L.D.
AND?
SHE CAN INFURIATE ME LIKE NO ONE ELSE ALIVE.
AND I BET THAT IN YOUR ROLE AS BOTH DIRECTOR OF S.H.I.E.L.D. AND HEAD OF STARK, THE LINES BETWEEN THEM MIGHT GET BLURRED SOMETIMES.
SO AS A HIGH-RANKING S.H.I.E.L.D. AGENT, I'M ASKING THE C.E.O. OF STARK:
WHEN DOES S.H.I.E.L.D. GET THIS TECH?
IT'S PRIVATE AND PROPRIETARY STARK TECHNOLOGY--
DIRECTOR STARK.
THAT I'VE PAID FOR OUT OF MY OWN POCKET--
DIRECTOR STARK.
--AND ASIDE FROM COSTING BILLIONS OF DOLLARS, I ABSOLUTELY AM NOT GOING TO HAND OVER TECH THAT'S A HOP, SKIP, AND A JUMP AWAY FROM THE IRON MAN PROJECT TO ANYONE.
IT'S PROPRIETARY STARK TECH AND IT STAYS THAT WAY.
YOU SELFISH, SPOILED--
WE HAVE REAL SOLDIERS FIGHTING AND DYING IN REAL WARS WITH REAL FAMILIES THAT COULD BENEFIT FROM THIS--
AND YOU CHOOSE TO SAVE YOUR SECRETARY?!?

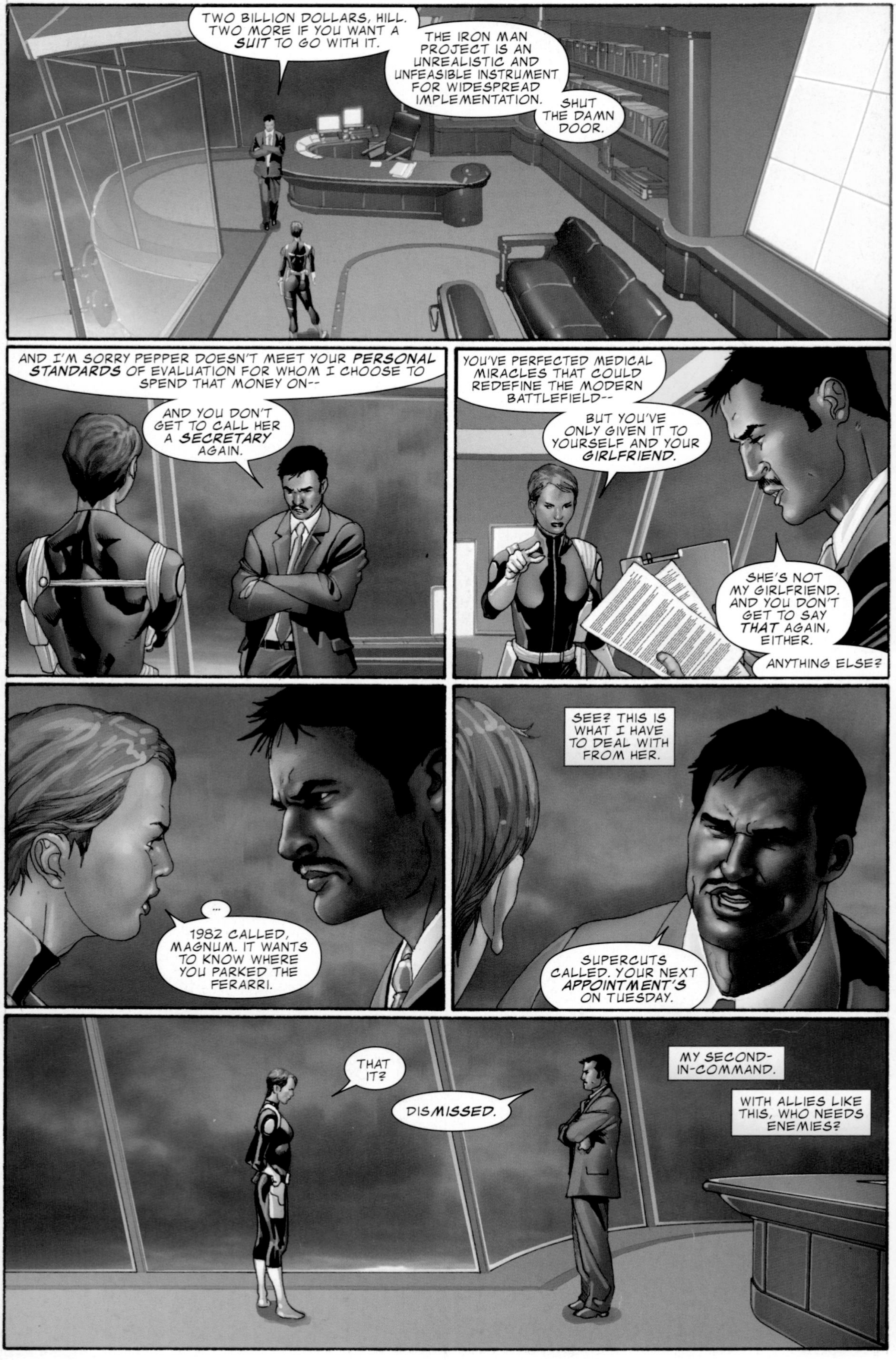

TWO BILLION DOLLARS, HILL. TWO MORE IF YOU WANT A SUIT TO GO WITH IT.
THE IRON MAN PROJECT IS AN UNREALISTIC AND UNFEASIBLE INSTRUMENT FOR WIDESPREAD IMPLEMENTATION.
SHUT THE DAMN DOOR.
AND I'M SORRY PEPPER DOESN'T MEET YOUR PERSONAL STANDARDS OF EVALUATION FOR WHOM I CHOOSE TO SPEND THAT MONEY ON--
AND YOU DON'T GET TO CALL HER A SECRETARY AGAIN.
YOU'VE PERFECTED MEDICAL MIRACLES THAT COULD REDEFINE THE MODERN BATTLEFIELD--
BUT YOU'VE ONLY GIVEN IT TO YOURSELF AND YOUR GIRLFRIEND.
SHE'S NOT MY GIRLFRIEND. AND YOU DON'T GET TO SAY THAT AGAIN, EITHER.
ANYTHING ELSE?
...
1982 CALLED, MAGNUM. IT WANTS TO KNOW WHERE YOU PARKED THE FERARRI.
SEE? THIS IS WHAT I HAVE TO DEAL WITH FROM HER.
SUPERCUTS CALLED. YOUR NEXT APPOINTMENT'S ON TUESDAY.
THAT IT?
DISMISSED.
MY SECOND-IN-COMMAND.
WITH ALLIES LIKE THIS, WHO NEEDS ENEMIES?

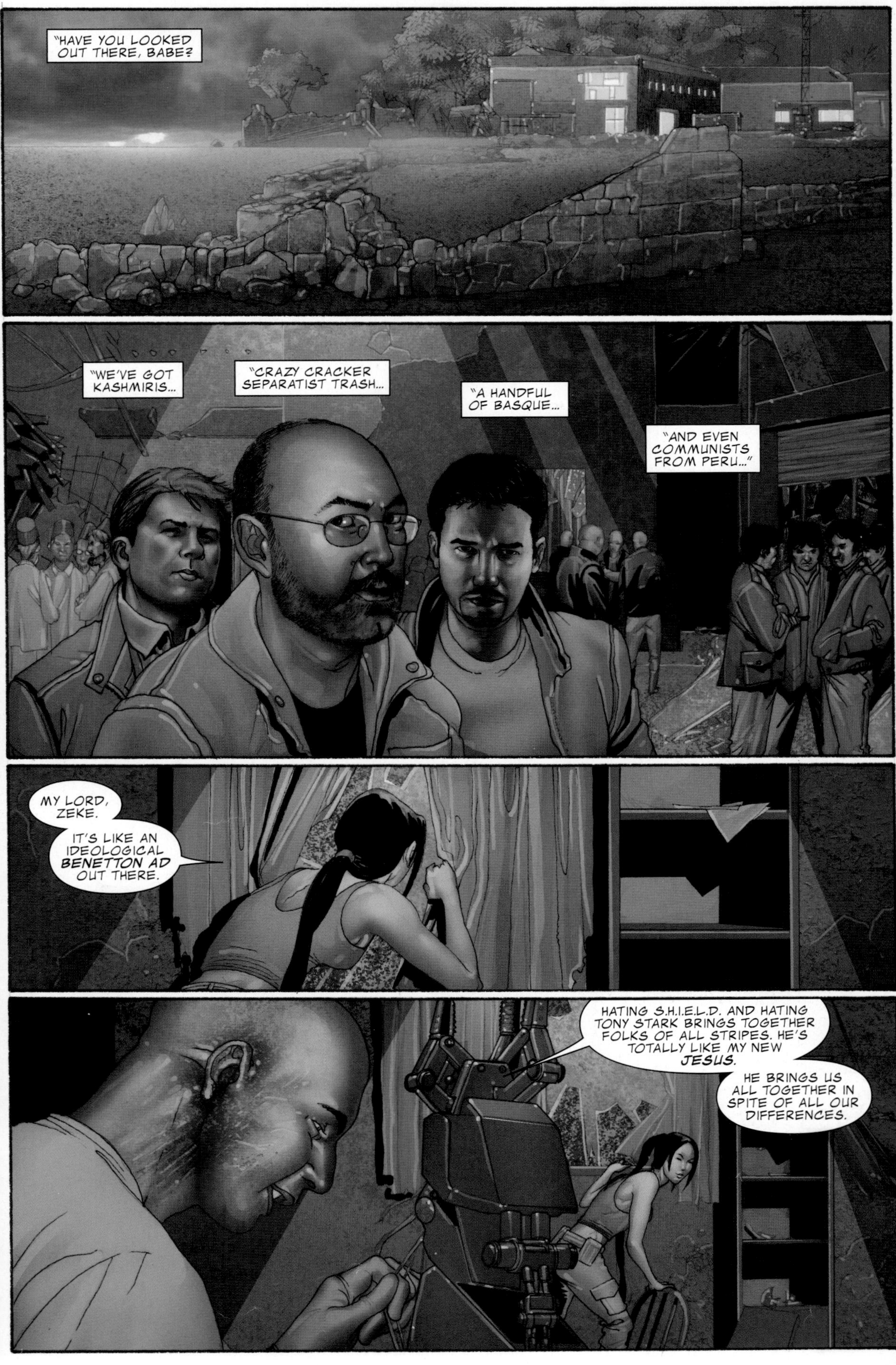
"HAVE YOU LOOKED OUT THERE, BABE?
"WE'VE GOT KASHMIRIS...
"CRAZY CRACKER SEPARATIST TRASH...
"A HANDFUL OF BASQUE...
"AND EVEN COMMUNISTS FROM PERU..."
MY LORD, ZEKE.
IT'S LIKE AN IDEOLOGICAL BENETTON AD OUT THERE.
HATING S.H.I.E.L.D. AND HATING TONY STARK BRINGS TOGETHER FOLKS OF ALL STRIPES. HE'S TOTALLY LIKE MY NEW JESUS.
HE BRINGS US ALL TOGETHER IN SPITE OF ALL OUR DIFFERENCES.

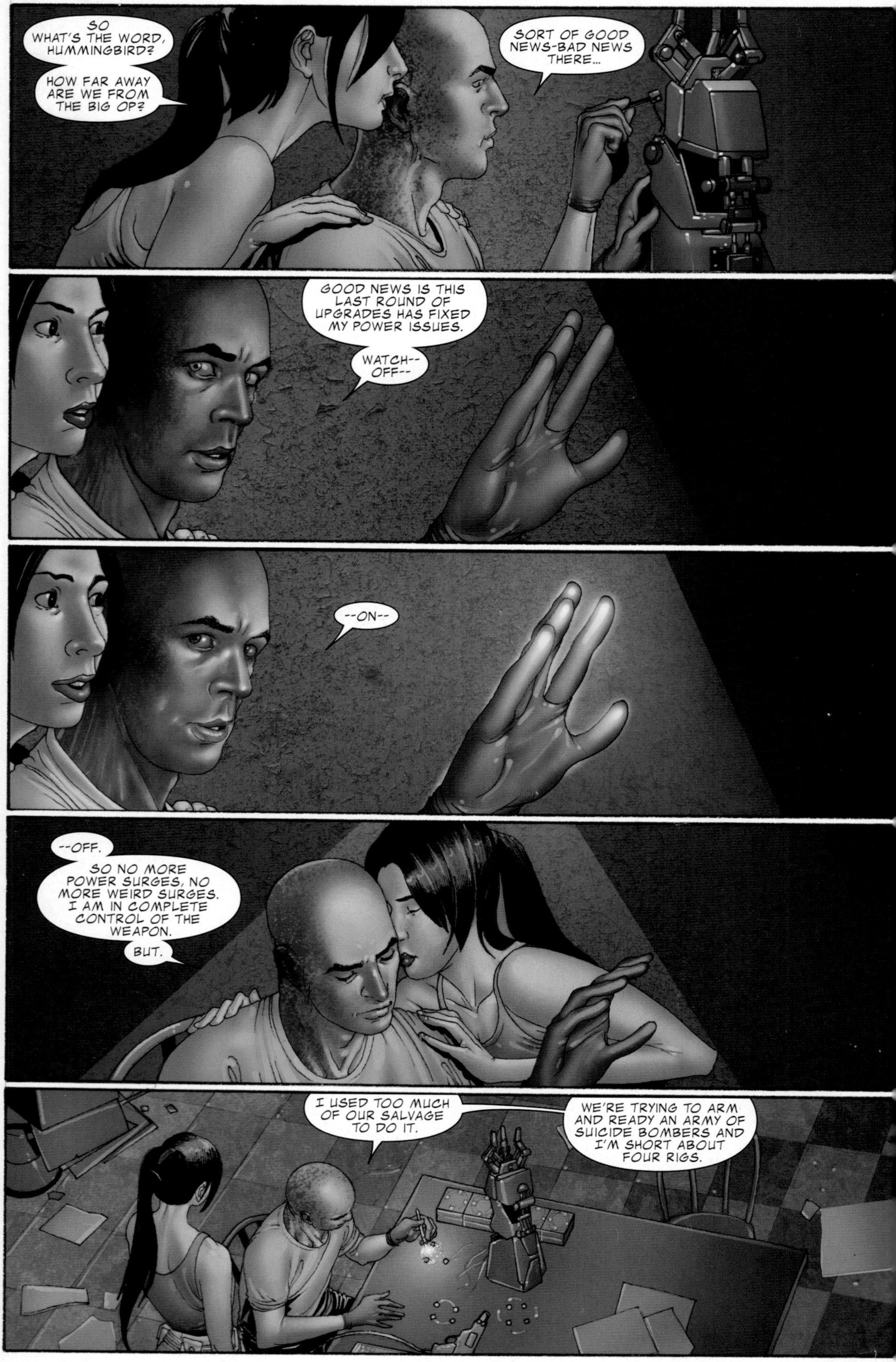
SO WHAT'S THE WORD, HUMMINGBIRD?
HOW FAR AWAY ARE WE FROM THE BIG OP?
SORT OF GOOD NEWS-BAD NEWS THERE...
GOOD NEWS IS THIS LAST ROUND OF UPGRADES HAS FIXED MY POWER ISSUES.
WATCH-- OFF--
--ON--
--OFF.
SO NO MORE POWER SURGES, NO MORE WEIRD SURGES. I AM IN COMPLETE CONTROL OF THE WEAPON.
BUT.
I USED TOO MUCH OF OUR SALVAGE TO DO IT.
WE'RE TRYING TO ARM AND READY AN ARMY OF SUICIDE BOMBERS AND I'M SHORT ABOUT FOUR RIGS.

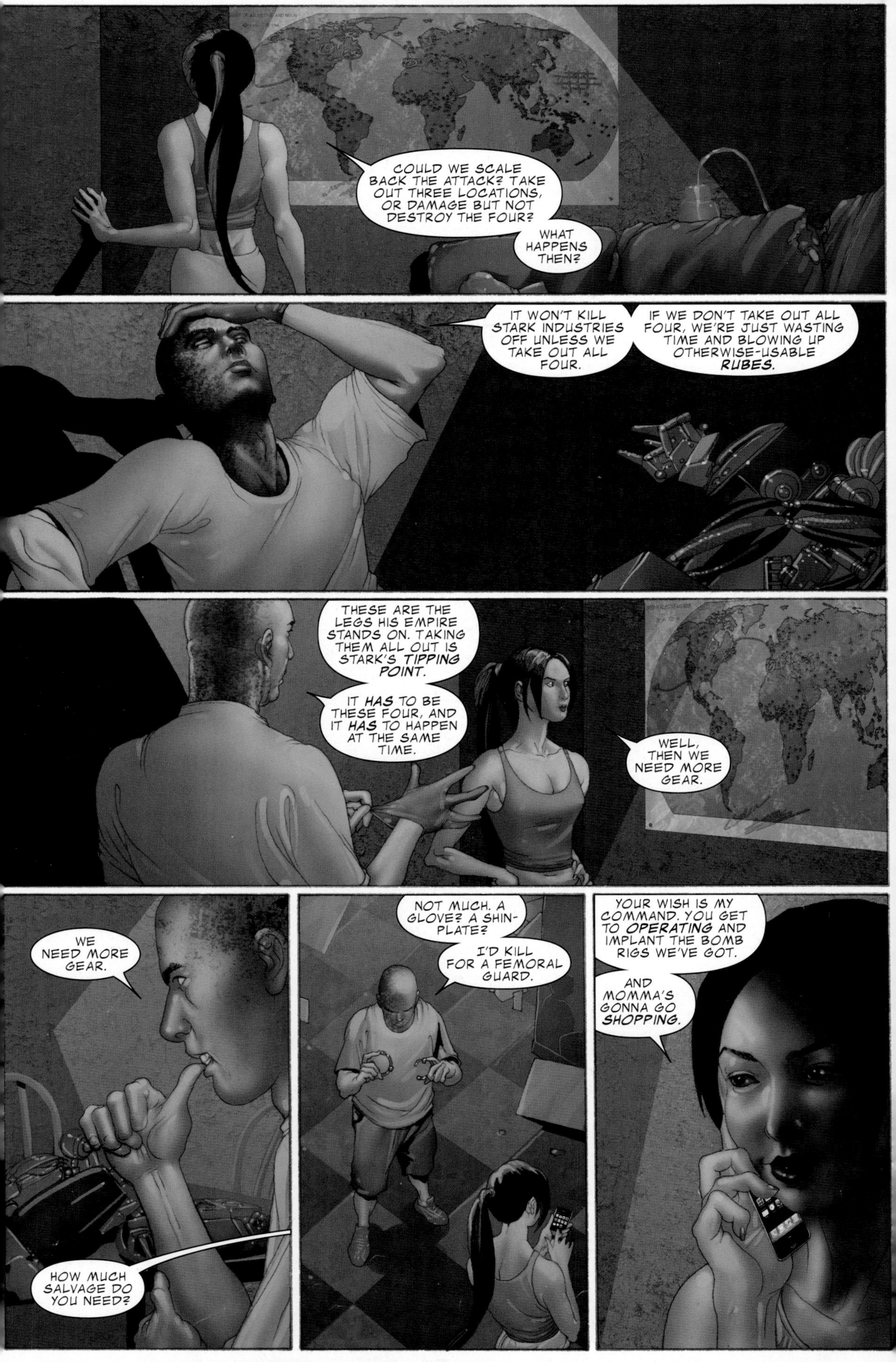
COULD WE SCALE BACK THE ATTACK? TAKE OUT THREE LOCATIONS, OR DAMAGE BUT NOT DESTROY THE FOUR?
WHAT HAPPENS THEN?
IT WON'T KILL STARK INDUSTRIES OFF UNLESS WE TAKE OUT ALL FOUR.
IF WE DON'T TAKE OUT ALL FOUR, WE'RE JUST WASTING TIME AND BLOWING UP OTHERWISE-USABLE RUBES.
THESE ARE THE LEGS HIS EMPIRE STANDS ON. TAKING THEM ALL OUT IS STARK'S TIPPING POINT.
IT HAS TO BE THESE FOUR, AND IT HAS TO HAPPEN AT THE SAME TIME.
WELL, THEN WE NEED MORE GEAR.
WE NEED MORE GEAR.
HOW MUCH SALVAGE DO YOU NEED?
NOT MUCH. A GLOVE? A SHIN-PLATE?
I'D KILL FOR A FEMORAL GUARD.
YOUR WISH IS MY COMMAND. YOU GET TO OPERATING AND IMPLANT THE BOMB RIGS WE'VE GOT.
AND MOMMA'S GONNA GO SHOPPING.

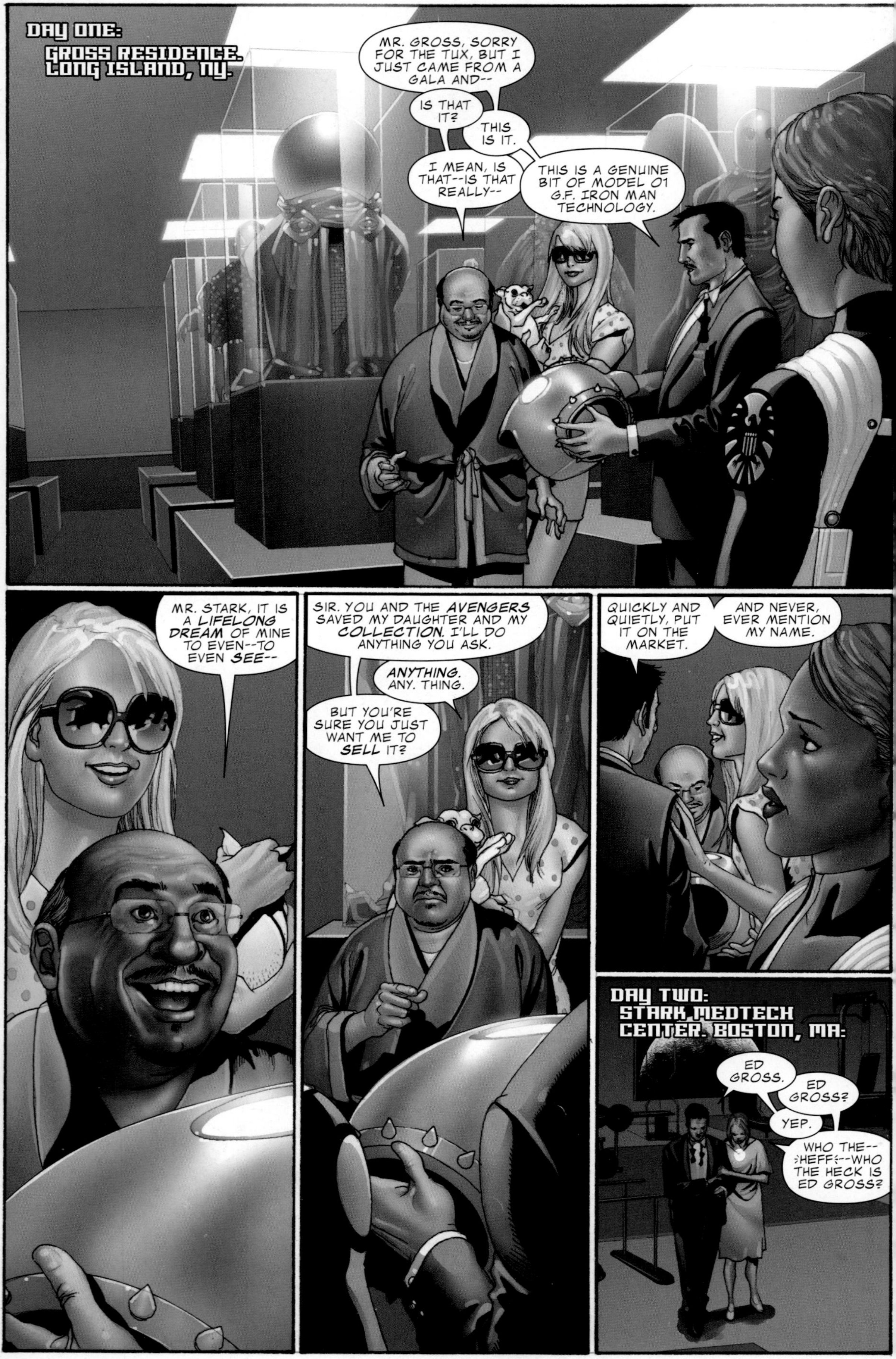
DAY ONE:
GROSS RESIDENCE. LONG ISLAND, NY.
MR. GROSS, SORRY FOR THE TUX, BUT I JUST CAME FROM A GALA AND--
IS THAT IT?
THIS IS IT.
I MEAN, IS THAT--IS THAT REALLY--
THIS IS A GENUINE BIT OF MODEL 01 G.F. IRON MAN TECHNOLOGY.
MR. STARK, IT IS A LIFELONG DREAM OF MINE TO EVEN--TO EVEN SEE--
SIR. YOU AND THE AVENGERS SAVED MY DAUGHTER AND MY COLLECTION. I'LL DO ANYTHING YOU ASK.
ANYTHING. ANY. THING.
BUT YOU'RE SURE YOU JUST WANT ME TO SELL IT?
QUICKLY AND QUIETLY, PUT IT ON THE MARKET.
AND NEVER, EVER MENTION MY NAME.
DAY TWO:
STARK MEDTECH CENTER. BOSTON, MA:
ED GROSS.
ED GROSS?
YEP.
WHO THE-- <HEFF>--WHO THE HECK IS ED GROSS?

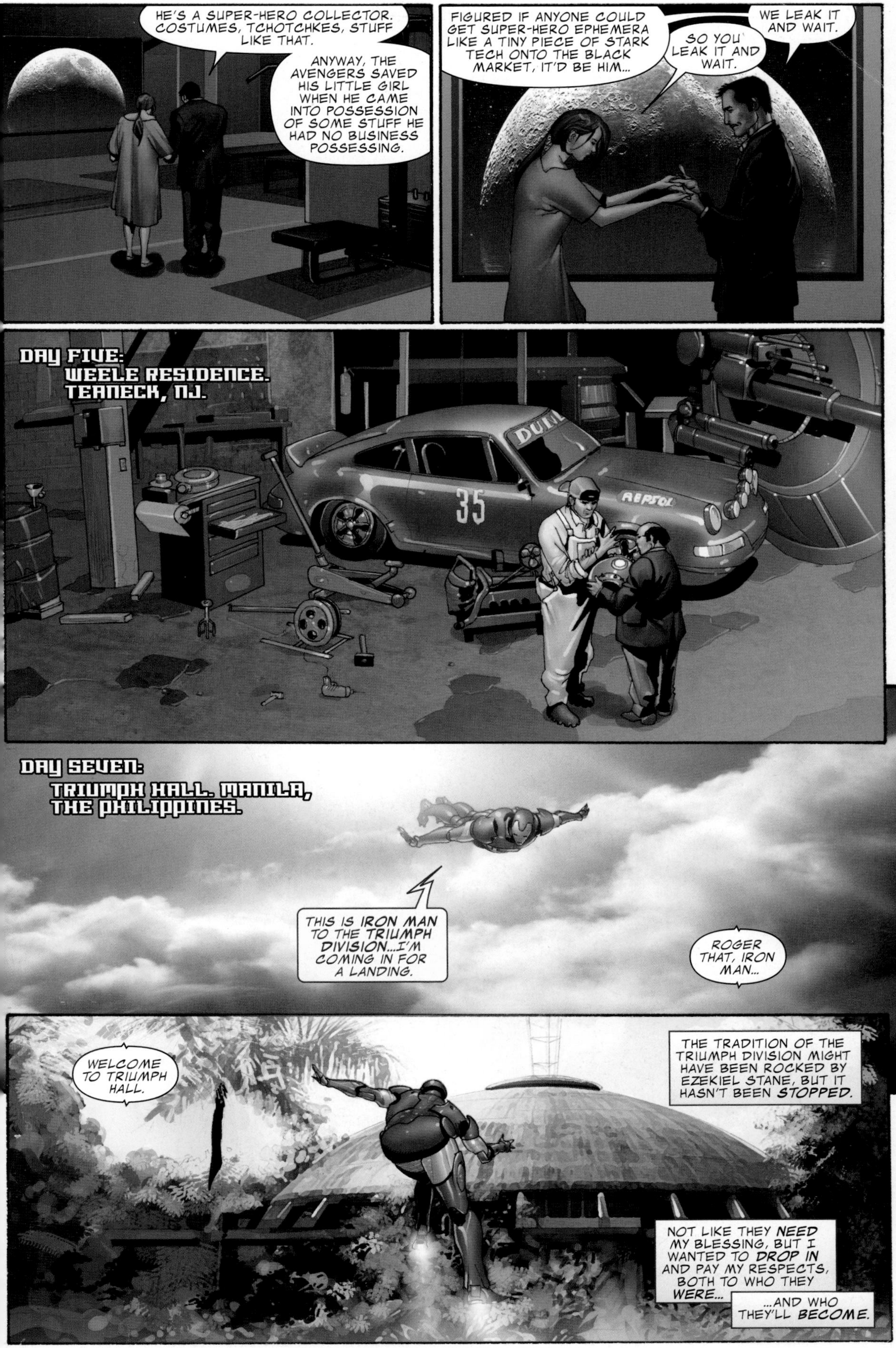

HE'S A SUPER-HERO COLLECTOR. COSTUMES, TCHOTCHKES, STUFF LIKE THAT.
ANYWAY, THE AVENGERS SAVED HIS LITTLE GIRL WHEN HE CAME INTO POSSESSION OF SOME STUFF HE HAD NO BUSINESS POSSESSING.
FIGURED IF ANYONE COULD GET SUPER-HERO EPHEMERA LIKE A TINY PIECE OF STARK TECH ONTO THE BLACK MARKET, IT'D BE HIM...
WE LEAK IT AND WAIT.
SO YOU LEAK IT AND WAIT.
DAY FIVE: WEELE RESIDENCE. TEANECK, NJ.
35
DAY SEVEN: TRIUMPH HALL. MANILA, THE PHILIPPINES.
THIS IS IRON MAN TO THE TRIUMPH DIVISION...I'M COMING IN FOR A LANDING.
ROGER THAT, IRON MAN...
WELCOME TO TRIUMPH HALL.
THE TRADITION OF THE TRIUMPH DIVISION MIGHT HAVE BEEN ROCKED BY EZEKIEL STANE, BUT IT HASN'T BEEN STOPPED.
NOT LIKE THEY NEED MY BLESSING, BUT I WANTED TO DROP IN AND PAY MY RESPECTS, BOTH TO WHO THEY WERE...
...AND WHO THEY'LL BECOME.

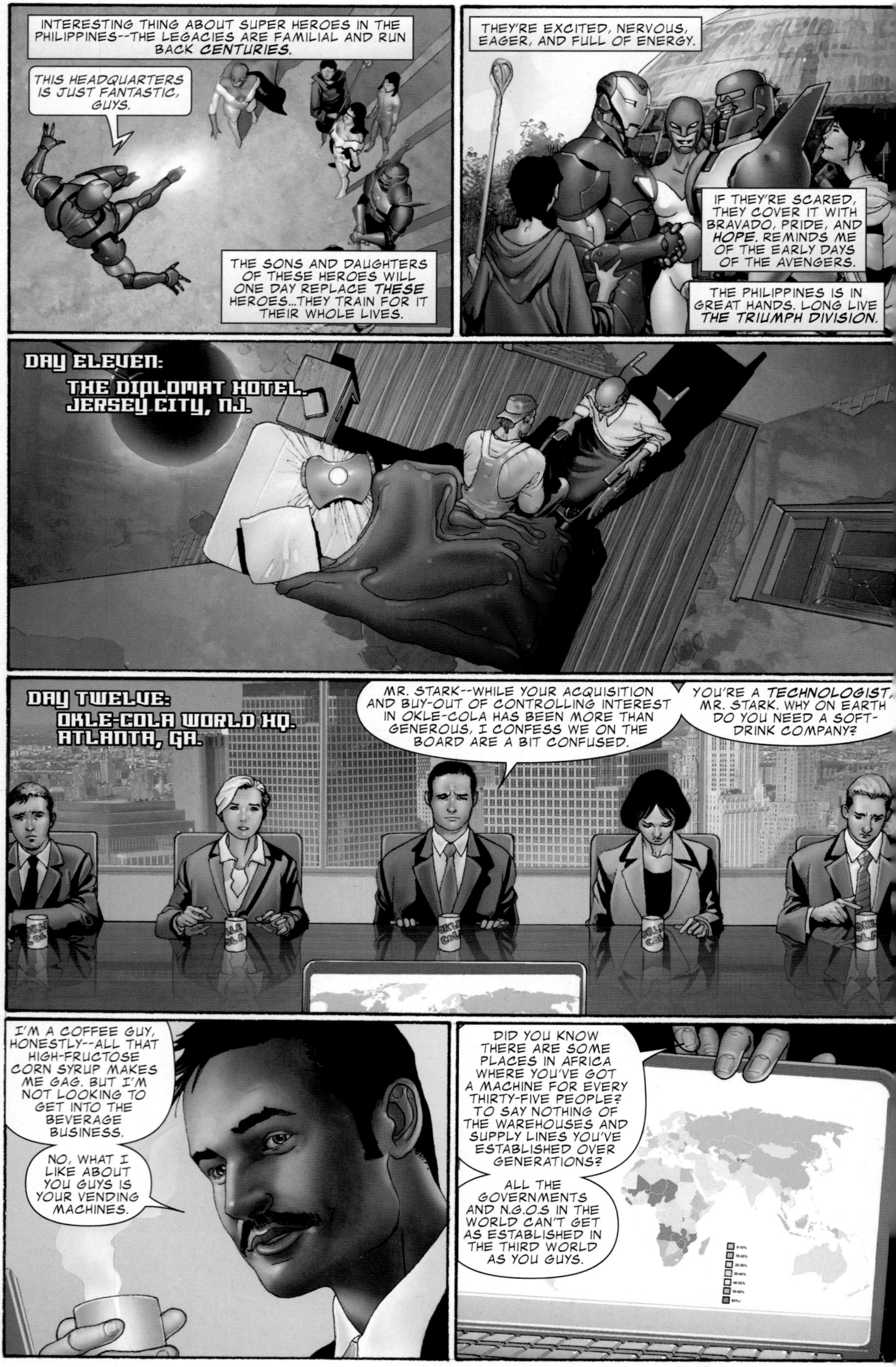
INTERESTING THING ABOUT SUPER HEROES IN THE PHILIPPINES--THE LEGACIES ARE FAMILIAL AND RUN BACK CENTURIES.
THIS HEADQUARTERS IS JUST FANTASTIC, GUYS.
THE SONS AND DAUGHTERS OF THESE HEROES WILL ONE DAY REPLACE THESE HEROES...THEY TRAIN FOR IT THEIR WHOLE LIVES.
THEY'RE EXCITED, NERVOUS, EAGER, AND FULL OF ENERGY.
IF THEY'RE SCARED, THEY COVER IT WITH BRAVADO, PRIDE, AND HOPE. REMINDS ME OF THE EARLY DAYS OF THE AVENGERS.
THE PHILIPPINES IS IN GREAT HANDS. LONG LIVE THE TRIUMPH DIVISION.
DAY ELEVEN:
THE DIPLOMAT HOTEL. JERSEY CITY, NJ.
DAY TWELVE:
OKLE-COLA WORLD HQ. ATLANTA, GA.
MR. STARK--WHILE YOUR ACQUISITION AND BUY-OUT OF CONTROLLING INTEREST IN OKLE-COLA HAS BEEN MORE THAN GENEROUS, I CONFESS WE ON THE BOARD ARE A BIT CONFUSED.
YOU'RE A TECHNOLOGIST, MR. STARK. WHY ON EARTH DO YOU NEED A SOFT-DRINK COMPANY?
I'M A COFFEE GUY, HONESTLY--ALL THAT HIGH-FRUCTOSE CORN SYRUP MAKES ME GAG. BUT I'M NOT LOOKING TO GET INTO THE BEVERAGE BUSINESS.
NO, WHAT I LIKE ABOUT YOU GUYS IS YOUR VENDING MACHINES.
DID YOU KNOW THERE ARE SOME PLACES IN AFRICA WHERE YOU'VE GOT A MACHINE FOR EVERY THIRTY-FIVE PEOPLE? TO SAY NOTHING OF THE WAREHOUSES AND SUPPLY LINES YOU'VE ESTABLISHED OVER GENERATIONS?
ALL THE GOVERNMENTS AND N.G.O.S IN THE WORLD CAN'T GET AS ESTABLISHED IN THE THIRD WORLD AS YOU GUYS.

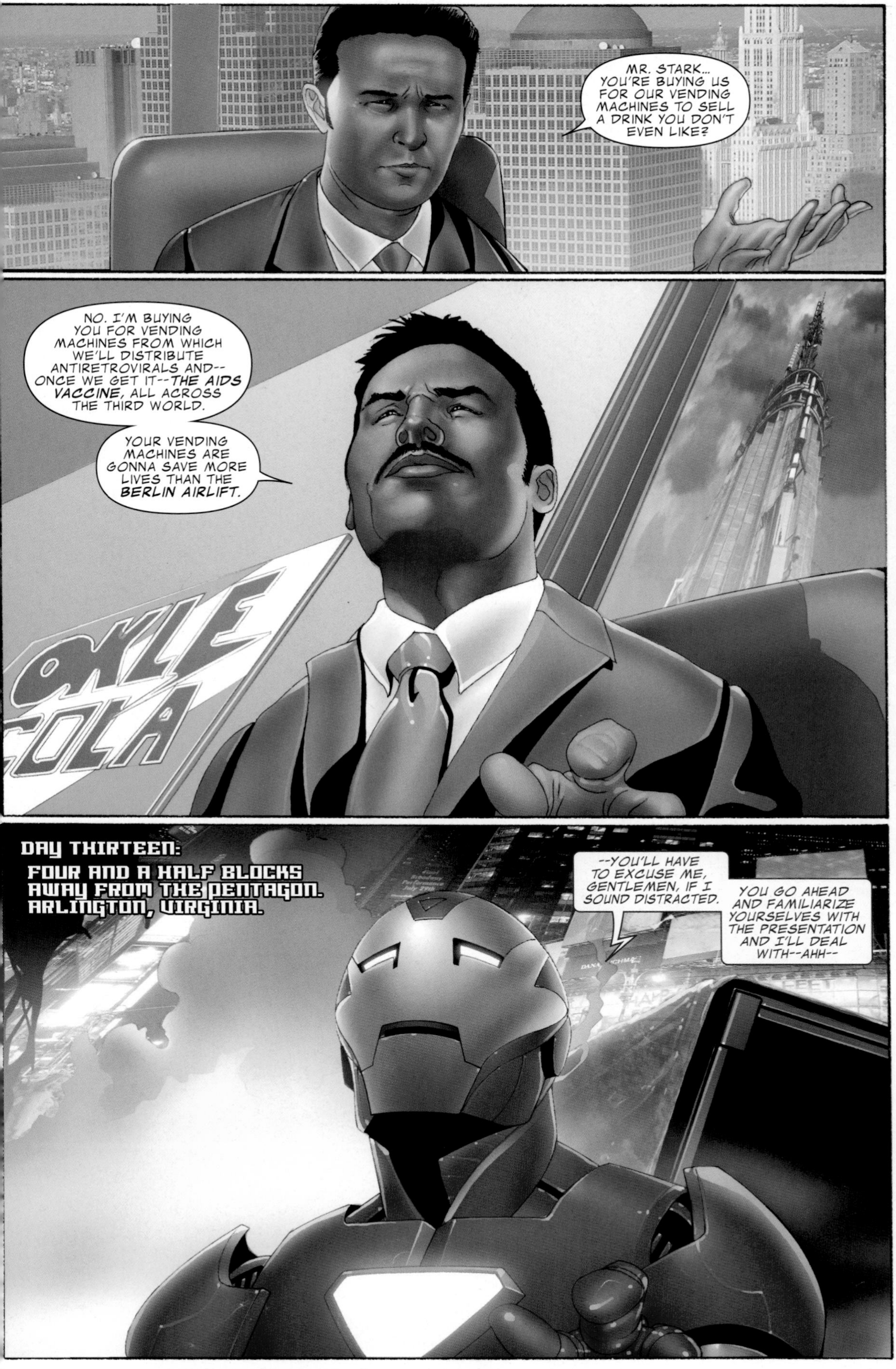
MR. STARK... YOU'RE BUYING US FOR OUR VENDING MACHINES TO SELL A DRINK YOU DON'T EVEN LIKE?
NO. I'M BUYING YOU FOR VENDING MACHINES FROM WHICH WE'LL DISTRIBUTE ANTIRETROVIRALS AND--ONCE WE GET IT--THE AIDS VACCINE, ALL ACROSS THE THIRD WORLD.
YOUR VENDING MACHINES ARE GONNA SAVE MORE LIVES THAN THE BERLIN AIRLIFT.
DAY THIRTEEN:
FOUR AND A HALF BLOCKS AWAY FROM THE PENTAGON. ARLINGTON, VIRGINIA.
--YOU'LL HAVE TO EXCUSE ME, GENTLEMEN, IF I SOUND DISTRACTED.
YOU GO AHEAD AND FAMILIARIZE YOURSELVES WITH THE PRESENTATION AND I'LL DEAL WITH--AHH--

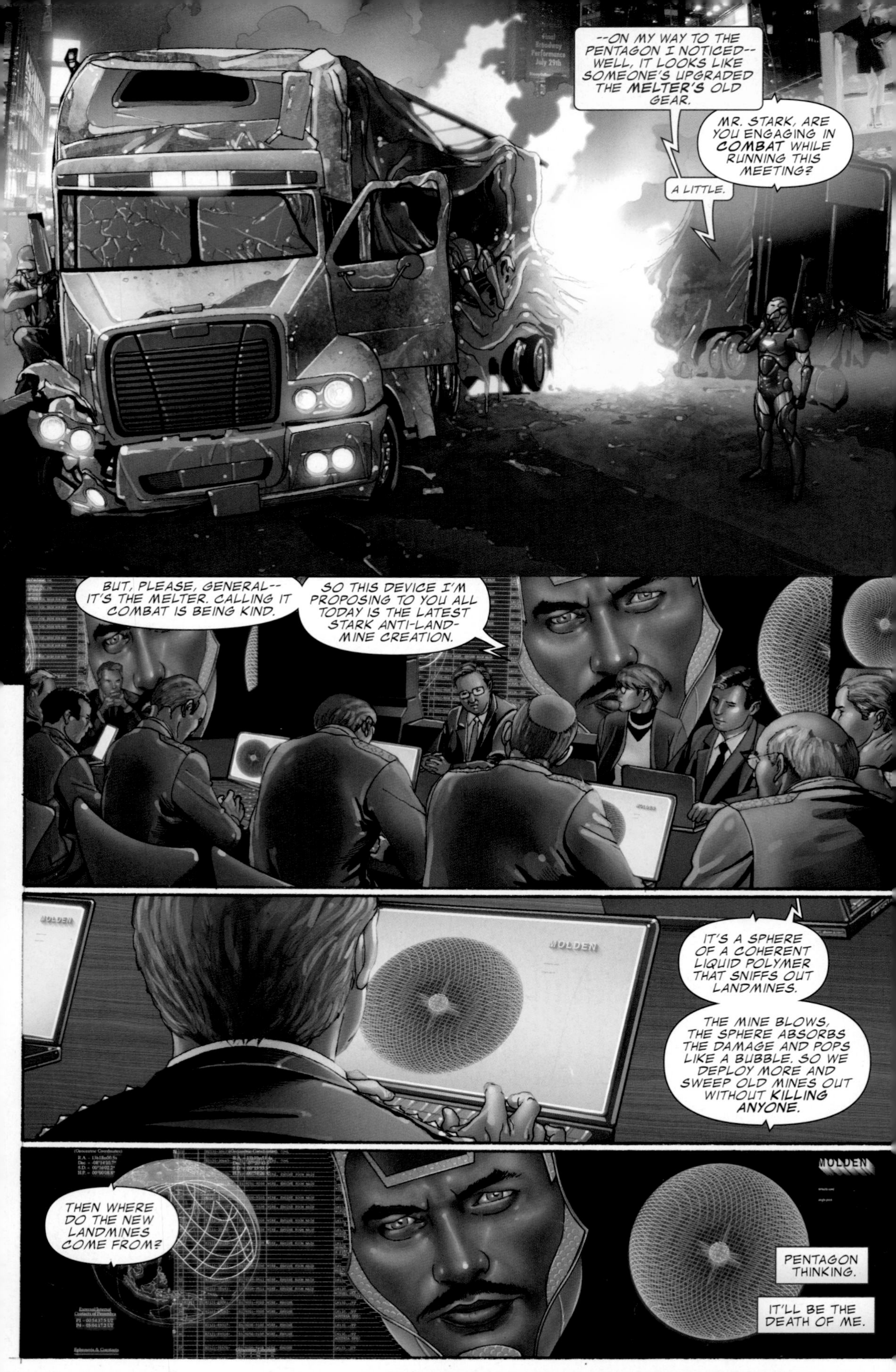

Final Broadway Performance July 29th
--ON MY WAY TO THE PENTAGON I NOTICED-- WELL, IT LOOKS LIKE SOMEONE'S UPGRADED THE MELTER'S OLD GEAR.
MR. STARK, ARE YOU ENGAGING IN COMBAT WHILE RUNNING THIS MEETING?
A LITTLE.
BUT, PLEASE, GENERAL-- IT'S THE MELTER. CALLING IT COMBAT IS BEING KIND.
SO THIS DEVICE I'M PROPOSING TO YOU ALL TODAY IS THE LATEST STARK ANTI-LAND-MINE CREATION.
MOLDEN
IT'S A SPHERE OF A COHERENT LIQUID POLYMER THAT SNIFFS OUT LANDMINES.
THE MINE BLOWS, THE SPHERE ABSORBS THE DAMAGE AND POPS LIKE A BUBBLE. SO WE DEPLOY MORE AND SWEEP OLD MINES OUT WITHOUT KILLING ANYONE.
THEN WHERE DO THE NEW LANDMINES COME FROM?
MOLDEN
PENTAGON THINKING.
IT'LL BE THE DEATH OF ME.

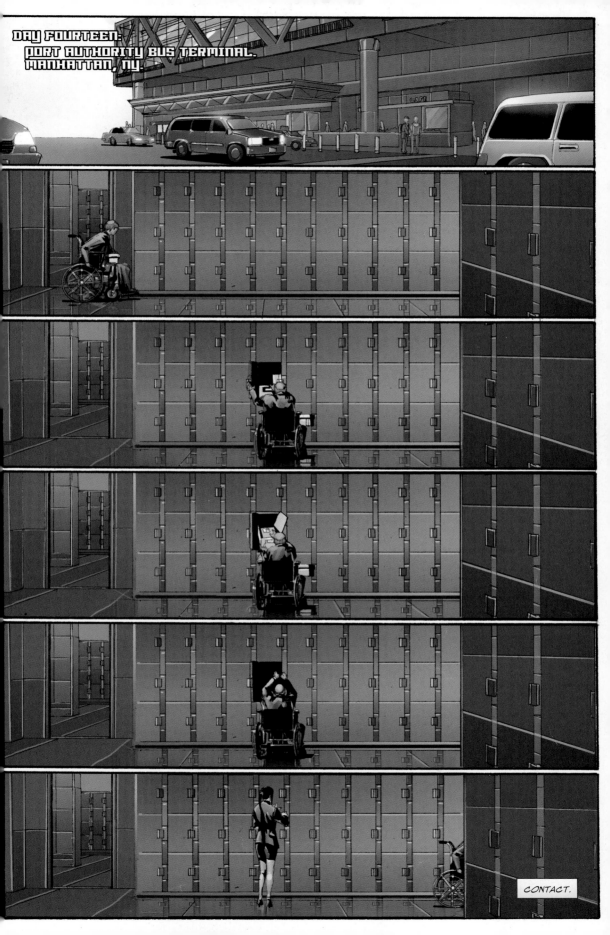

DAY FOURTEEN:
PORT AUTHORITY BUS TERMINAL.
MANHATTAN, NY.

CONTACT.

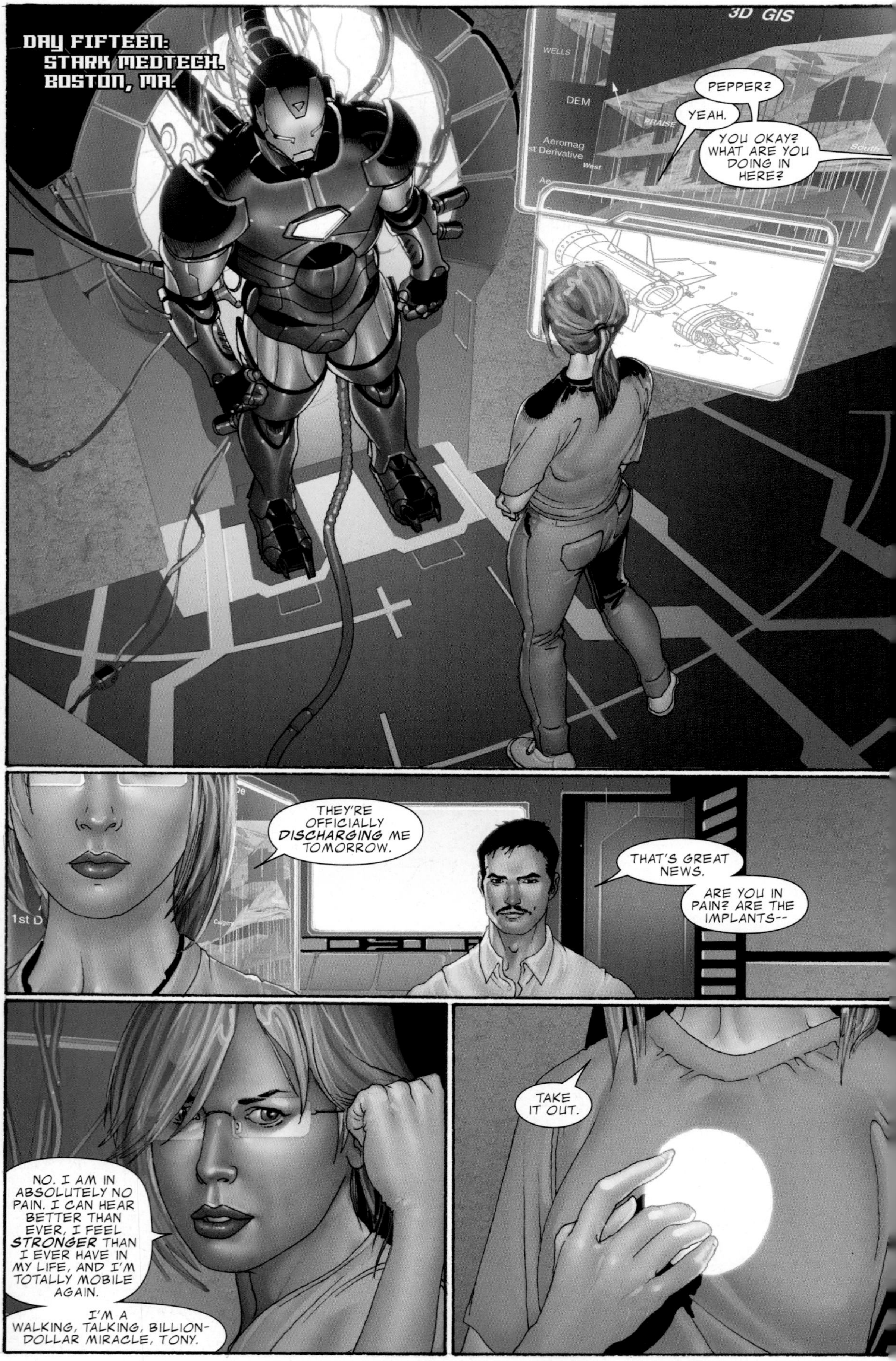
DAY FIFTEEN:
STARK MEDTECH.
BOSTON, MA.
3D GIS
WELLS
DEM
PRAISE
Aeromag
st Derivative
West
South
PEPPER?
YEAH.
YOU OKAY? WHAT ARE YOU DOING IN HERE?
THEY'RE OFFICIALLY DISCHARGING ME TOMORROW.
THAT'S GREAT NEWS.
ARE YOU IN PAIN? ARE THE IMPLANTS--
NO. I AM IN ABSOLUTELY NO PAIN. I CAN HEAR BETTER THAN EVER, I FEEL STRONGER THAN I EVER HAVE IN MY LIFE, AND I'M TOTALLY MOBILE AGAIN.
I'M A WALKING, TALKING, BILLION-DOLLAR MIRACLE, TONY.
TAKE IT OUT.

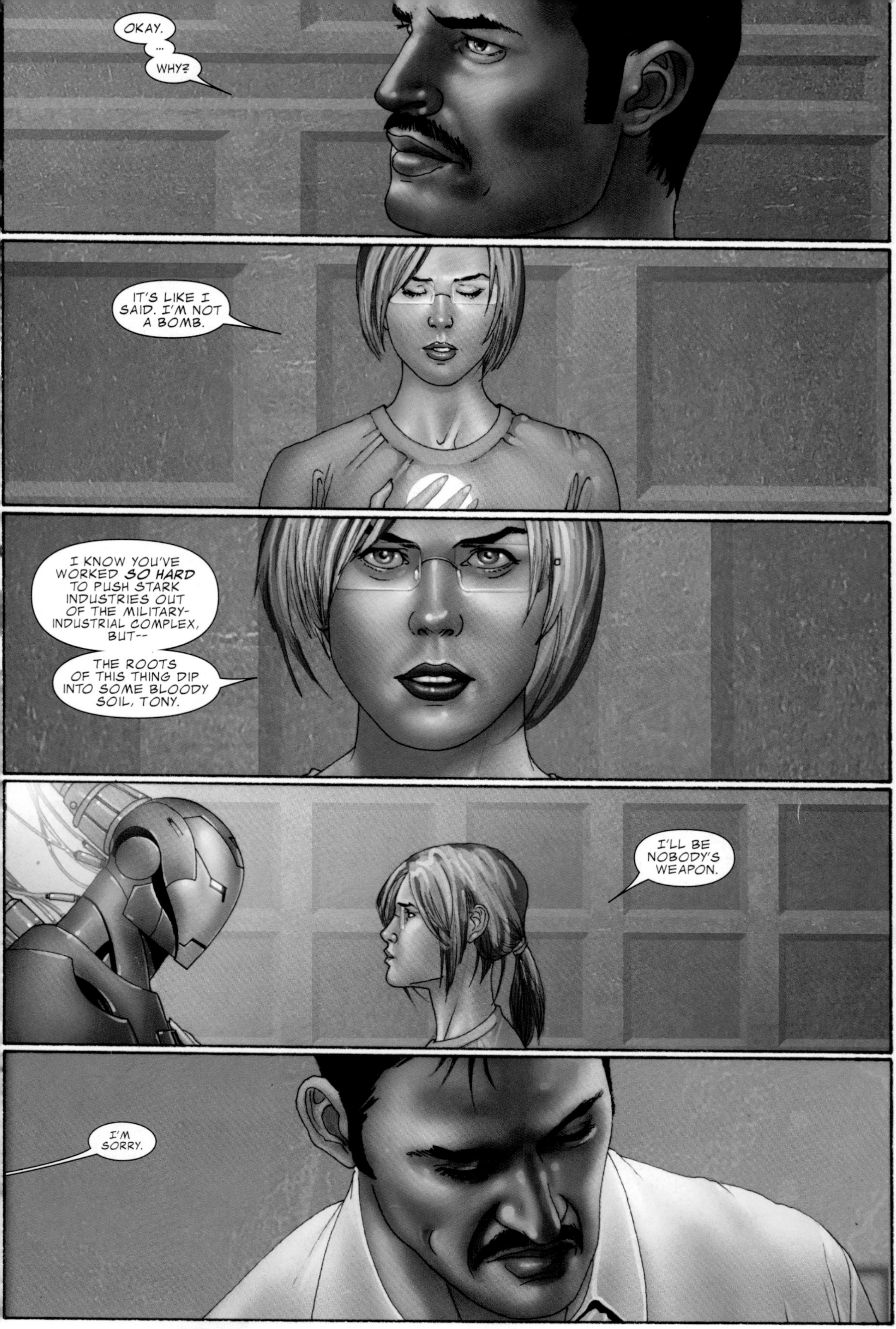
OKAY.
...
WHY?
IT'S LIKE I SAID. I'M NOT A BOMB.
I KNOW YOU'VE WORKED SO HARD TO PUSH STARK INDUSTRIES OUT OF THE MILITARY-INDUSTRIAL COMPLEX, BUT--
THE ROOTS OF THIS THING DIP INTO SOME BLOODY SOIL, TONY.
I'LL BE NOBODY'S WEAPON.
I'M SORRY.

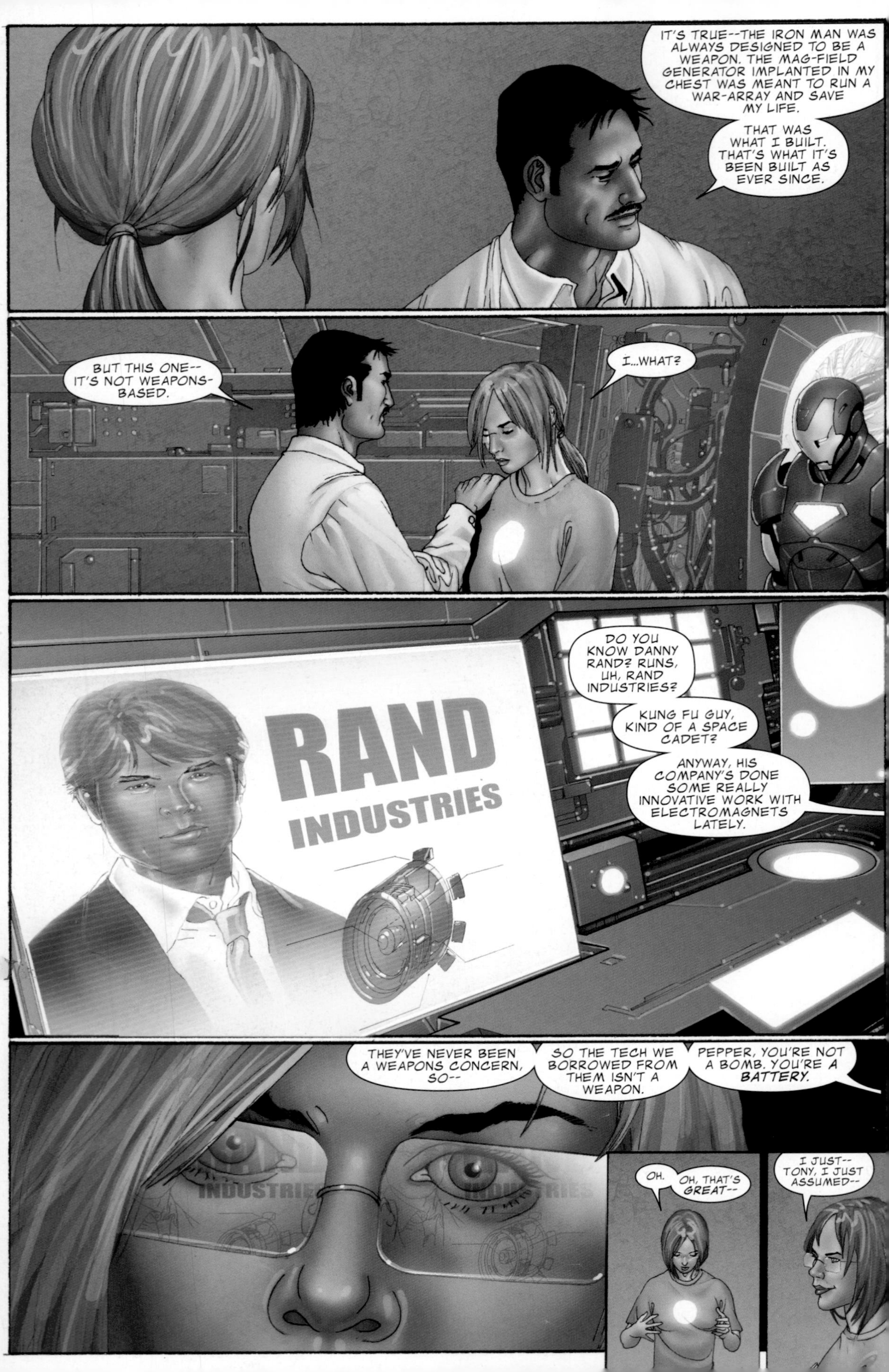
IT'S TRUE--THE IRON MAN WAS ALWAYS DESIGNED TO BE A WEAPON. THE MAG-FIELD GENERATOR IMPLANTED IN MY CHEST WAS MEANT TO RUN A WAR-ARRAY AND SAVE MY LIFE.
THAT WAS WHAT I BUILT. THAT'S WHAT IT'S BEEN BUILT AS EVER SINCE.
BUT THIS ONE-- IT'S NOT WEAPONS-BASED.
I...WHAT?
DO YOU KNOW DANNY RAND? RUNS, UH, RAND INDUSTRIES?
KUNG FU GUY, KIND OF A SPACE CADET?
ANYWAY, HIS COMPANY'S DONE SOME REALLY INNOVATIVE WORK WITH ELECTROMAGNETS LATELY.
RAND INDUSTRIES
THEY'VE NEVER BEEN A WEAPONS CONCERN, SO--
SO THE TECH WE BORROWED FROM THEM ISN'T A WEAPON.
PEPPER, YOU'RE NOT A BOMB. YOU'RE A *BATTERY.*
OH.
OH, THAT'S *GREAT*--
I JUST-- TONY, I JUST ASSUMED--

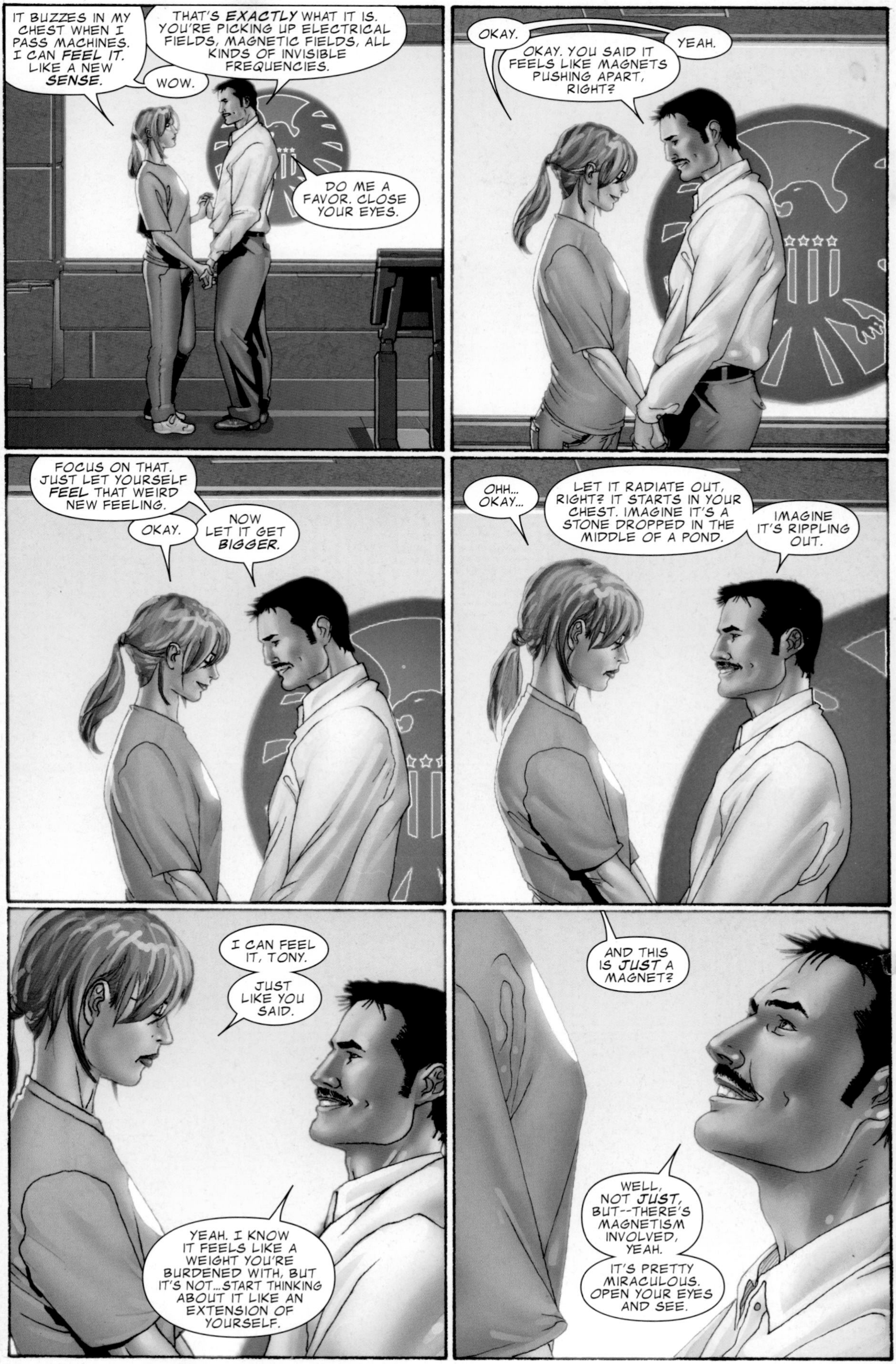

IT BUZZES IN MY CHEST WHEN I PASS MACHINES. I CAN FEEL IT. LIKE A NEW SENSE.
THAT'S EXACTLY WHAT IT IS. YOU'RE PICKING UP ELECTRICAL FIELDS, MAGNETIC FIELDS, ALL KINDS OF INVISIBLE FREQUENCIES.
WOW.
DO ME A FAVOR. CLOSE YOUR EYES.
OKAY.
OKAY. YOU SAID IT FEELS LIKE MAGNETS PUSHING APART, RIGHT?
YEAH.
FOCUS ON THAT. JUST LET YOURSELF FEEL THAT WEIRD NEW FEELING.
OKAY.
NOW LET IT GET BIGGER.
OHH... OKAY...
LET IT RADIATE OUT, RIGHT? IT STARTS IN YOUR CHEST. IMAGINE IT'S A STONE DROPPED IN THE MIDDLE OF A POND.
IMAGINE IT'S RIPPLING OUT.
I CAN FEEL IT, TONY.
JUST LIKE YOU SAID.
YEAH. I KNOW IT FEELS LIKE A WEIGHT YOU'RE BURDENED WITH, BUT IT'S NOT...START THINKING ABOUT IT LIKE AN EXTENSION OF YOURSELF.
AND THIS IS JUST A MAGNET?
WELL, NOT JUST, BUT--THERE'S MAGNETISM INVOLVED, YEAH.
IT'S PRETTY MIRACULOUS. OPEN YOUR EYES AND SEE.

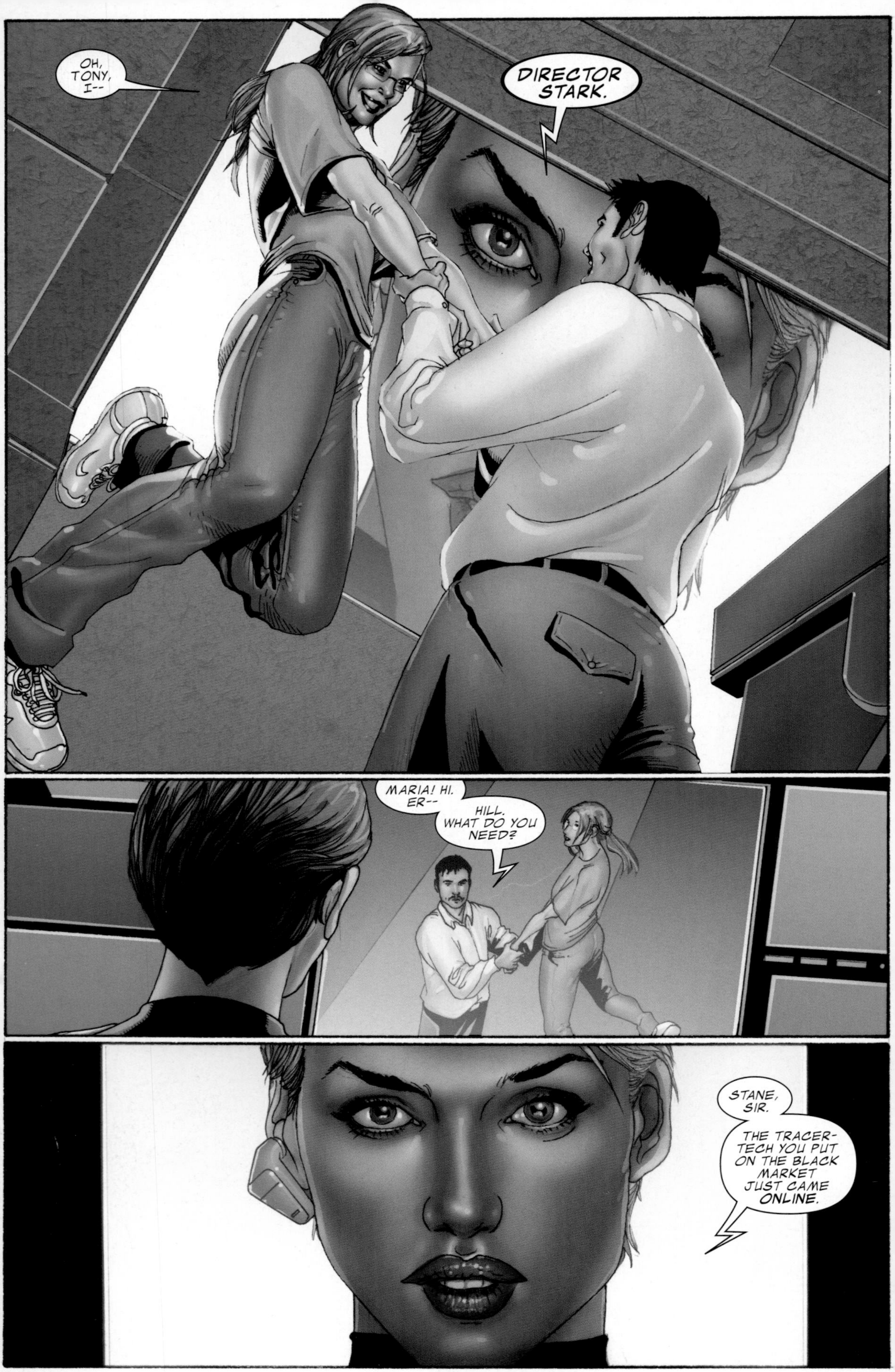
OH, TONY, I--
DIRECTOR STARK.
MARIA! HI. ER--
HILL. WHAT DO YOU NEED?
STANE, SIR.
THE TRACER-TECH YOU PUT ON THE BLACK MARKET JUST CAME ONLINE.

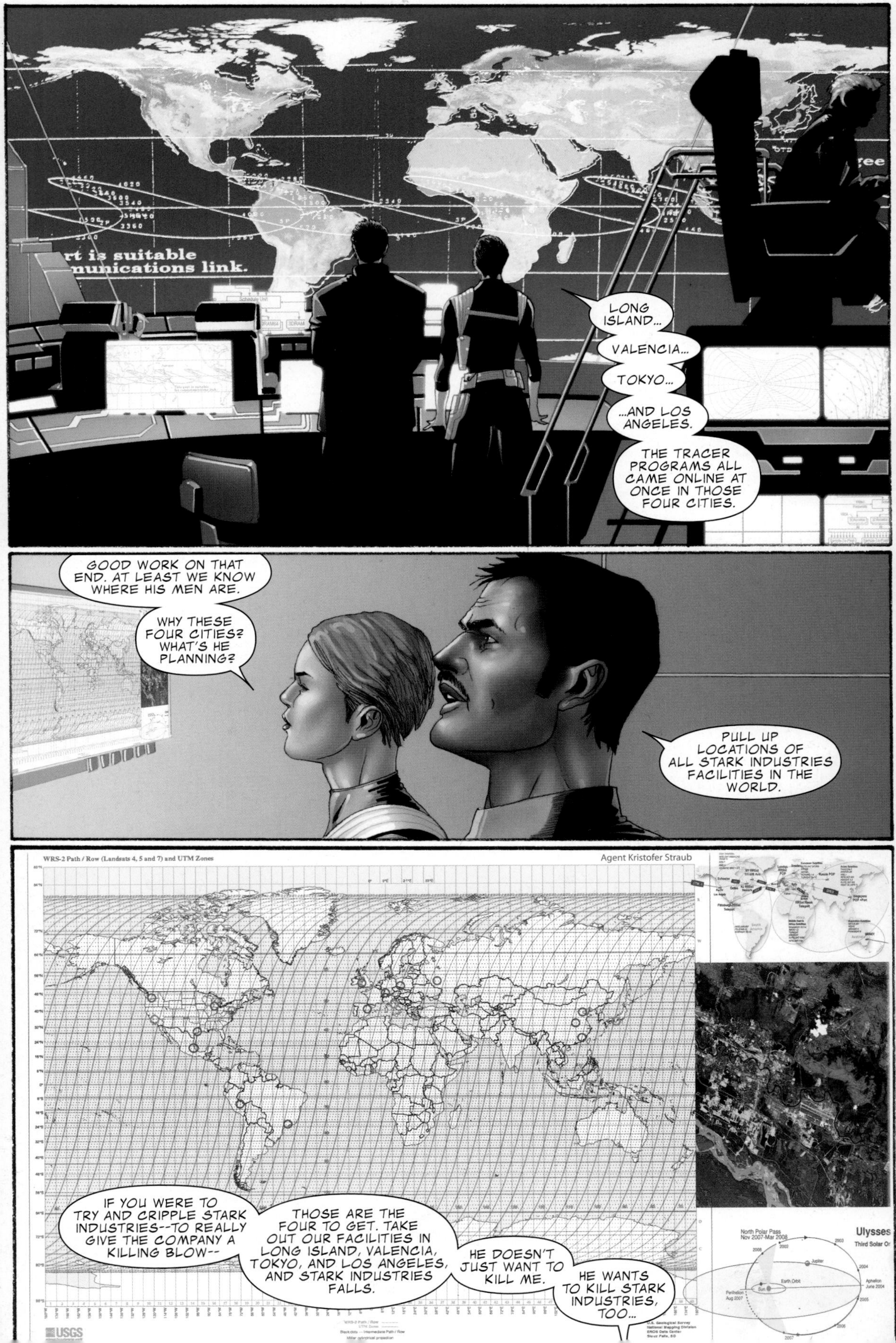

rt is suitable
unications link.
LONG ISLAND...
VALENCIA...
TOKYO...
...AND LOS ANGELES.
THE TRACER PROGRAMS ALL CAME ONLINE AT ONCE IN THOSE FOUR CITIES.
GOOD WORK ON THAT END. AT LEAST WE KNOW WHERE HIS MEN ARE.
WHY THESE FOUR CITIES? WHAT'S HE PLANNING?
PULL UP LOCATIONS OF ALL STARK INDUSTRIES FACILITIES IN THE WORLD.
WRS-2 Path / Row (Landsats 4, 5 and 7) and UTM Zones
Agent Kristofer Straub
IF YOU WERE TO TRY AND CRIPPLE STARK INDUSTRIES--TO REALLY GIVE THE COMPANY A KILLING BLOW--
THOSE ARE THE FOUR TO GET. TAKE OUT OUR FACILITIES IN LONG ISLAND, VALENCIA, TOKYO, AND LOS ANGELES, AND STARK INDUSTRIES FALLS.
HE DOESN'T JUST WANT TO KILL ME.
HE WANTS TO KILL STARK INDUSTRIES, TOO...
North Polar Pass
Nov 2007-Mar 2008
Ulysses
Third Solar Or
Jupiter
Earth Orbit
Sun
Perihelion
Aug 2007
Aphelion
June 2004
USGS

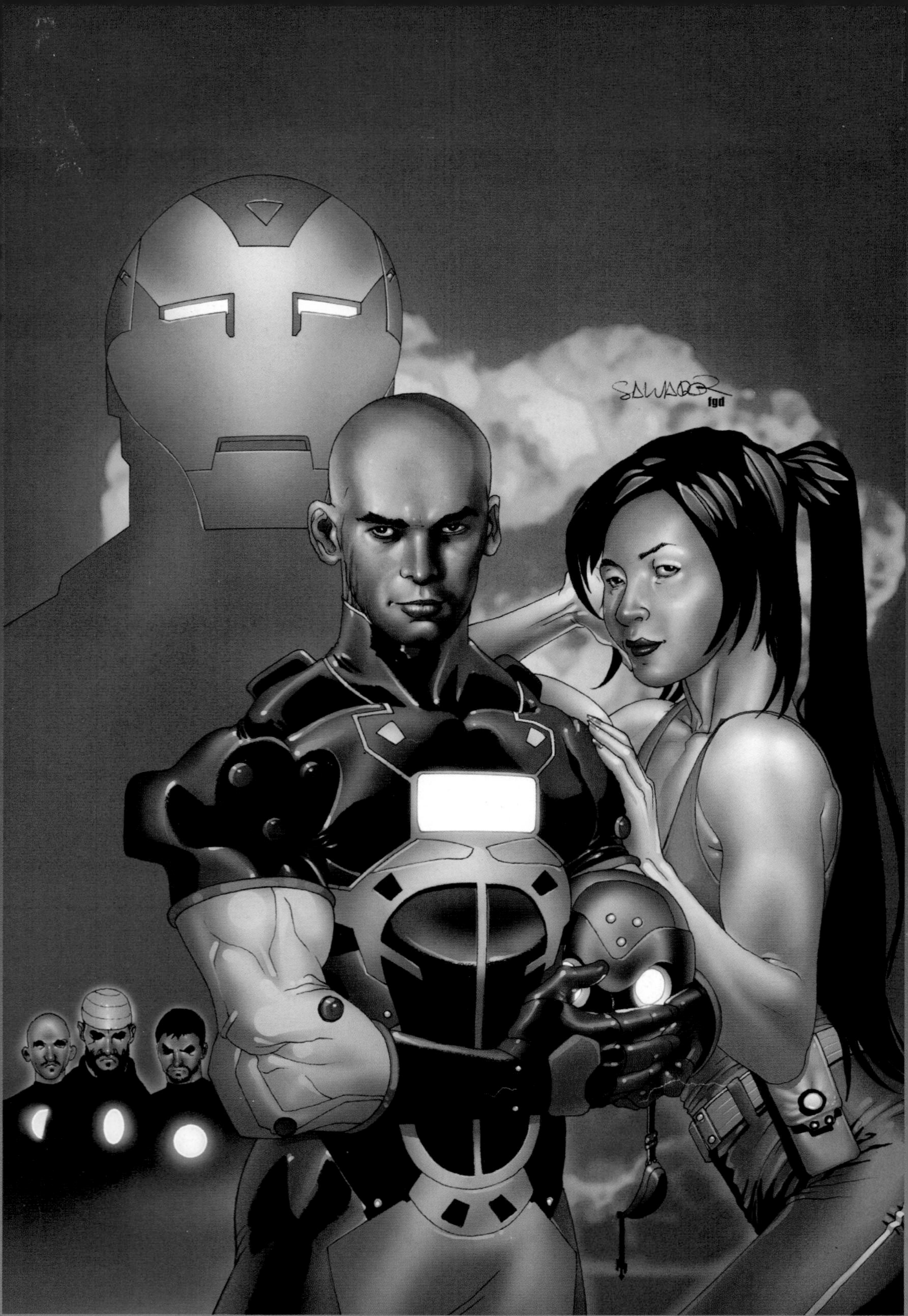

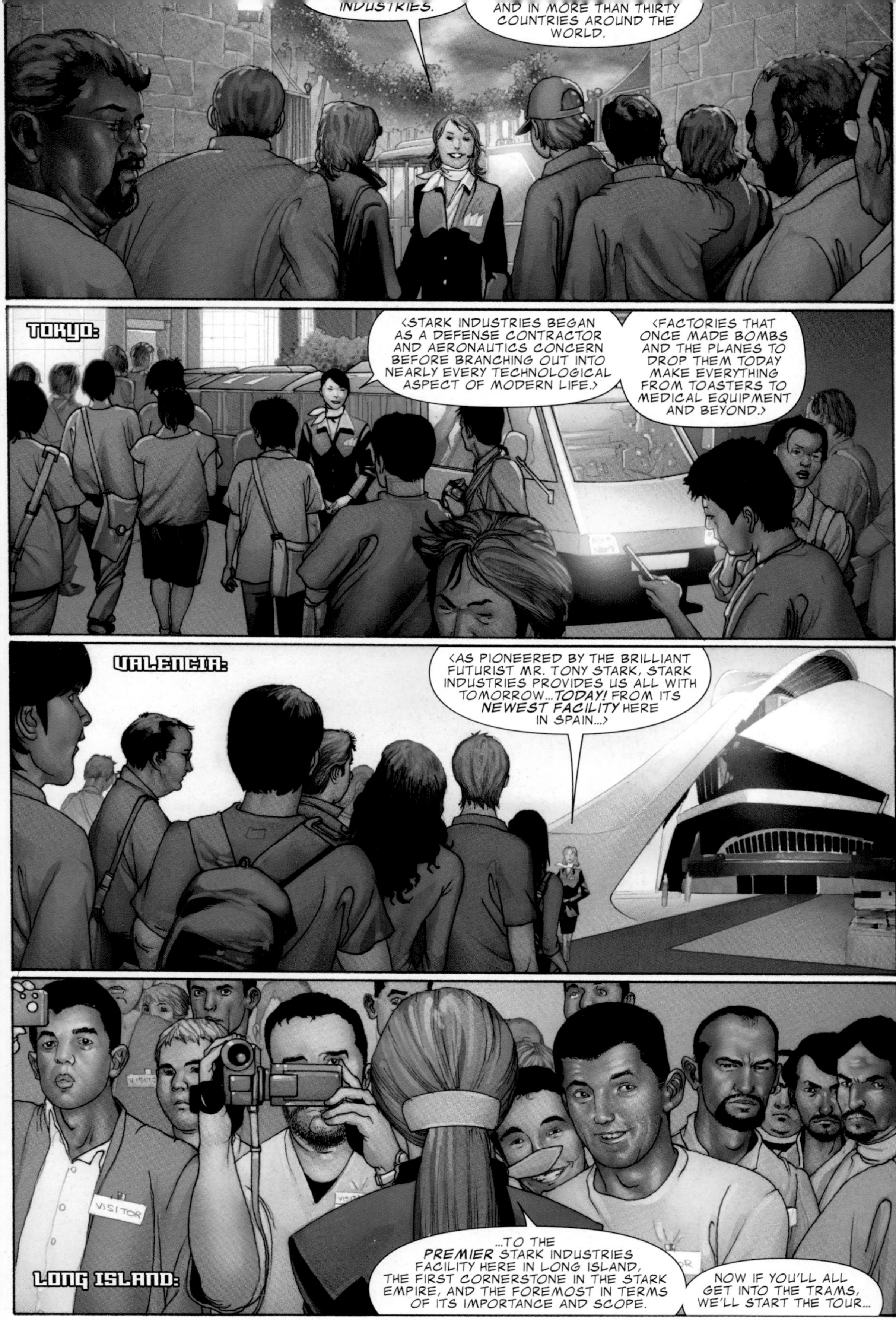

INDUSTRIES.
AND IN MORE THAN THIRTY COUNTRIES AROUND THE WORLD.
TOKYO:
<STARK INDUSTRIES BEGAN AS A DEFENSE CONTRACTOR AND AERONAUTICS CONCERN BEFORE BRANCHING OUT INTO NEARLY EVERY TECHNOLOGICAL ASPECT OF MODERN LIFE.>
<FACTORIES THAT ONCE MADE BOMBS AND THE PLANES TO DROP THEM TODAY MAKE EVERYTHING FROM TOASTERS TO MEDICAL EQUIPMENT AND BEYOND.>
VALENCIA:
<AS PIONEERED BY THE BRILLIANT FUTURIST MR. TONY STARK, STARK INDUSTRIES PROVIDES US ALL WITH TOMORROW...TODAY! FROM ITS NEWEST FACILITY HERE IN SPAIN...>
VISITOR
LONG ISLAND:
...TO THE PREMIER STARK INDUSTRIES FACILITY HERE IN LONG ISLAND, THE FIRST CORNERSTONE IN THE STARK EMPIRE, AND THE FOREMOST IN TERMS OF ITS IMPORTANCE AND SCOPE.
NOW IF YOU'LL ALL GET INTO THE TRAMS, WE'LL START THE TOUR...

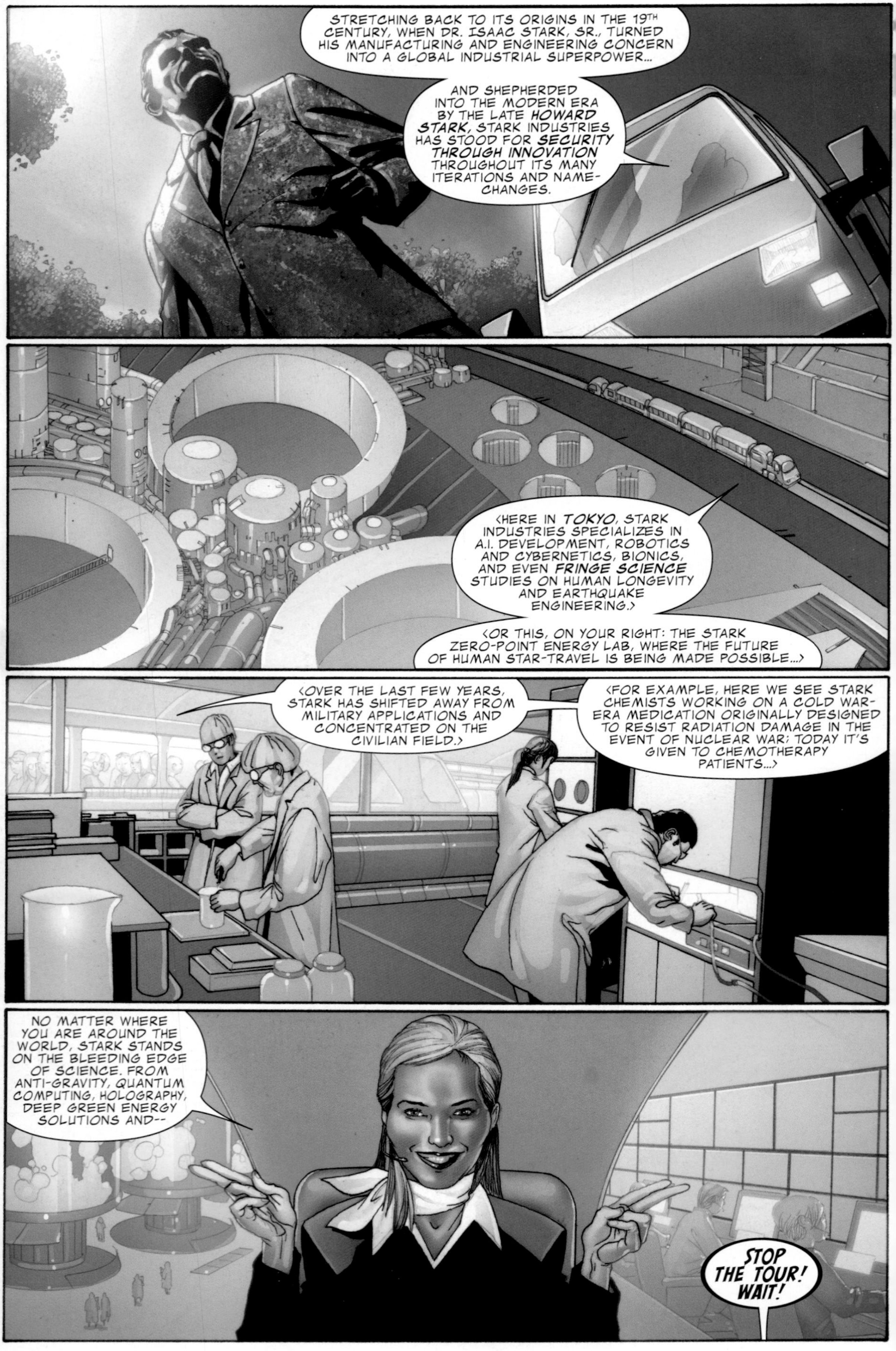
STRETCHING BACK TO ITS ORIGINS IN THE 19TH CENTURY, WHEN DR. ISAAC STARK, SR., TURNED HIS MANUFACTURING AND ENGINEERING CONCERN INTO A GLOBAL INDUSTRIAL SUPERPOWER...
AND SHEPHERDED INTO THE MODERN ERA BY THE LATE HOWARD STARK, STARK INDUSTRIES HAS STOOD FOR SECURITY THROUGH INNOVATION THROUGHOUT ITS MANY ITERATIONS AND NAME-CHANGES.
<HERE IN TOKYO, STARK INDUSTRIES SPECIALIZES IN A.I. DEVELOPMENT, ROBOTICS AND CYBERNETICS, BIONICS, AND EVEN FRINGE SCIENCE STUDIES ON HUMAN LONGEVITY AND EARTHQUAKE ENGINEERING.>
<OR THIS, ON YOUR RIGHT: THE STARK ZERO-POINT ENERGY LAB, WHERE THE FUTURE OF HUMAN STAR-TRAVEL IS BEING MADE POSSIBLE...>
<OVER THE LAST FEW YEARS, STARK HAS SHIFTED AWAY FROM MILITARY APPLICATIONS AND CONCENTRATED ON THE CIVILIAN FIELD.>
<FOR EXAMPLE, HERE WE SEE STARK CHEMISTS WORKING ON A COLD WAR-ERA MEDICATION ORIGINALLY DESIGNED TO RESIST RADIATION DAMAGE IN THE EVENT OF NUCLEAR WAR; TODAY IT'S GIVEN TO CHEMOTHERAPY PATIENTS...>
NO MATTER WHERE YOU ARE AROUND THE WORLD, STARK STANDS ON THE BLEEDING EDGE OF SCIENCE. FROM ANTI-GRAVITY, QUANTUM COMPUTING, HOLOGRAPHY, DEEP GREEN ENERGY SOLUTIONS AND--
STOP THE TOUR! WAIT!

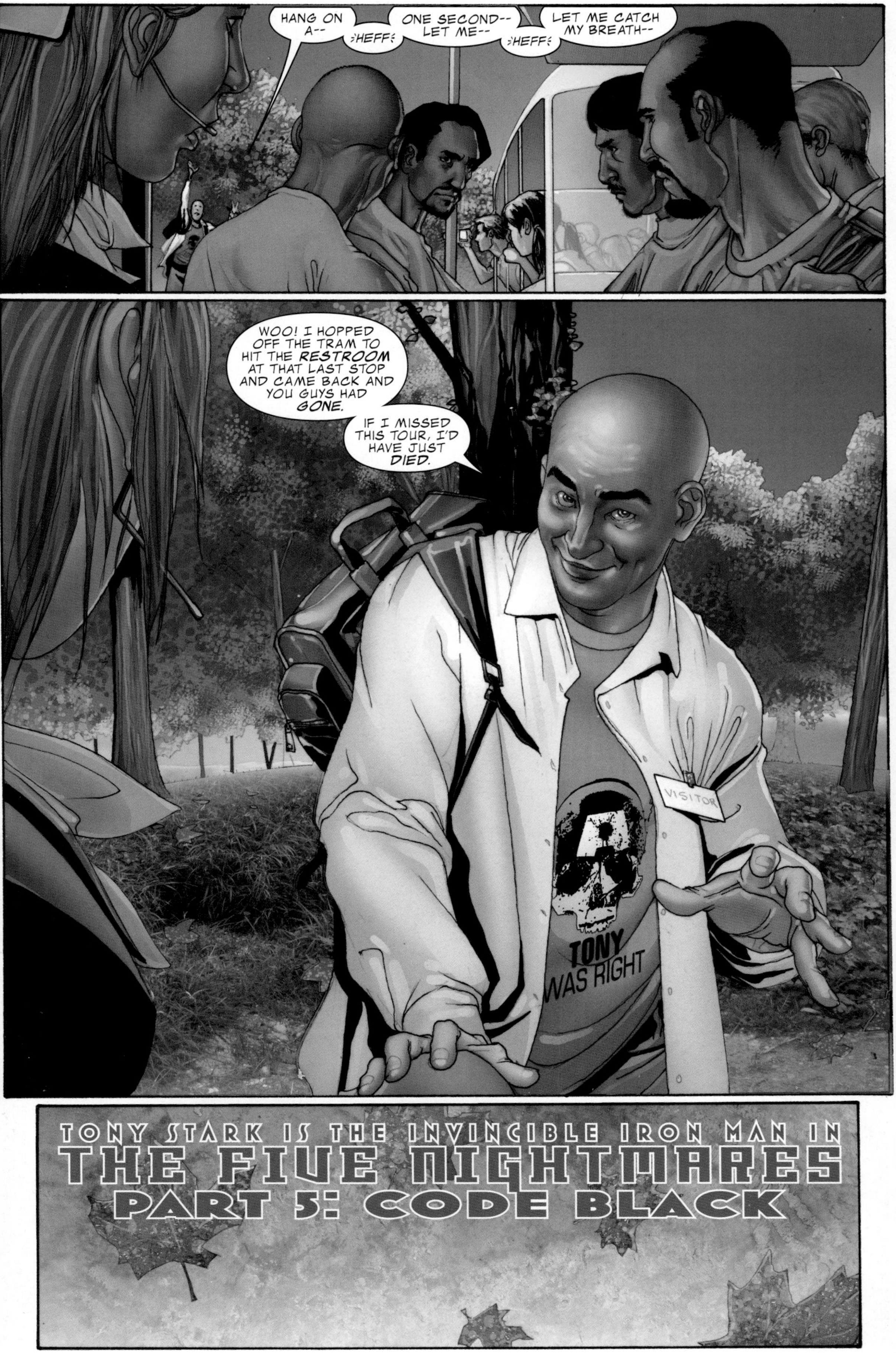
HANG ON A--
HEFF
ONE SECOND-- LET ME--
HEFF
LET ME CATCH MY BREATH--
WOO! I HOPPED OFF THE TRAM TO HIT THE *RESTROOM* AT THAT LAST STOP AND CAME BACK AND YOU GUYS HAD *GONE*.
IF I MISSED THIS TOUR, I'D HAVE JUST *DIED*.
VISITOR
TONY WAS RIGHT
TONY STARK IS THE INVINCIBLE IRON MAN IN
THE FIVE NIGHTMARES
PART 5: CODE BLACK

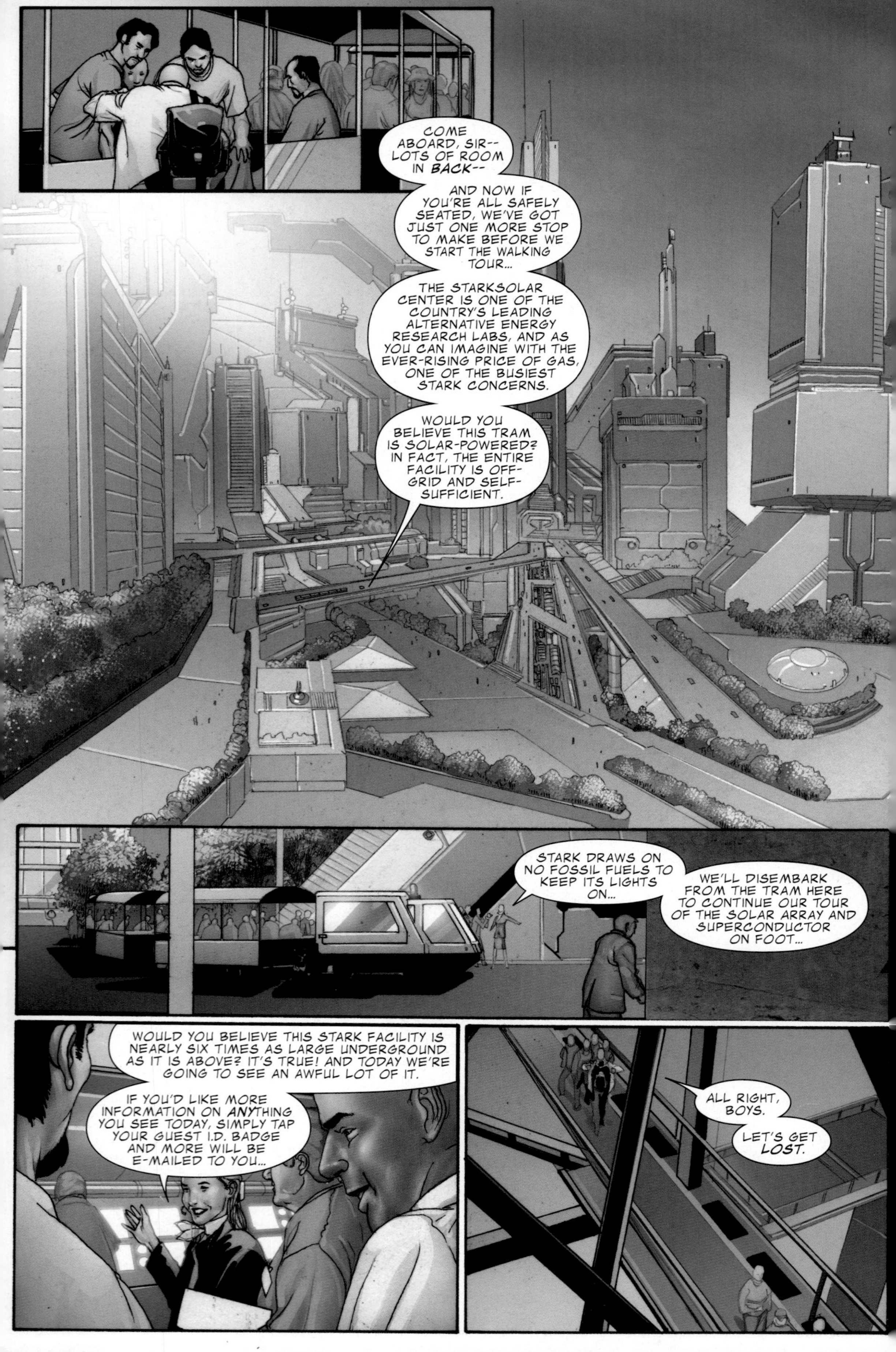
COME ABOARD, SIR-- LOTS OF ROOM IN BACK--
AND NOW IF YOU'RE ALL SAFELY SEATED, WE'VE GOT JUST ONE MORE STOP TO MAKE BEFORE WE START THE WALKING TOUR...
THE STARKSOLAR CENTER IS ONE OF THE COUNTRY'S LEADING ALTERNATIVE ENERGY RESEARCH LABS, AND AS YOU CAN IMAGINE WITH THE EVER-RISING PRICE OF GAS, ONE OF THE BUSIEST STARK CONCERNS.
WOULD YOU BELIEVE THIS TRAM IS SOLAR-POWERED? IN FACT, THE ENTIRE FACILITY IS OFF-GRID AND SELF-SUFFICIENT.
STARK DRAWS ON NO FOSSIL FUELS TO KEEP ITS LIGHTS ON...
WE'LL DISEMBARK FROM THE TRAM HERE TO CONTINUE OUR TOUR OF THE SOLAR ARRAY AND SUPERCONDUCTOR ON FOOT...
WOULD YOU BELIEVE THIS STARK FACILITY IS NEARLY SIX TIMES AS LARGE UNDERGROUND AS IT IS ABOVE? IT'S TRUE! AND TODAY WE'RE GOING TO SEE AN AWFUL LOT OF IT.
IF YOU'D LIKE MORE INFORMATION ON ANYTHING YOU SEE TODAY, SIMPLY TAP YOUR GUEST I.D. BADGE AND MORE WILL BE E-MAILED TO YOU...
ALL RIGHT, BOYS.
LET'S GET LOST.

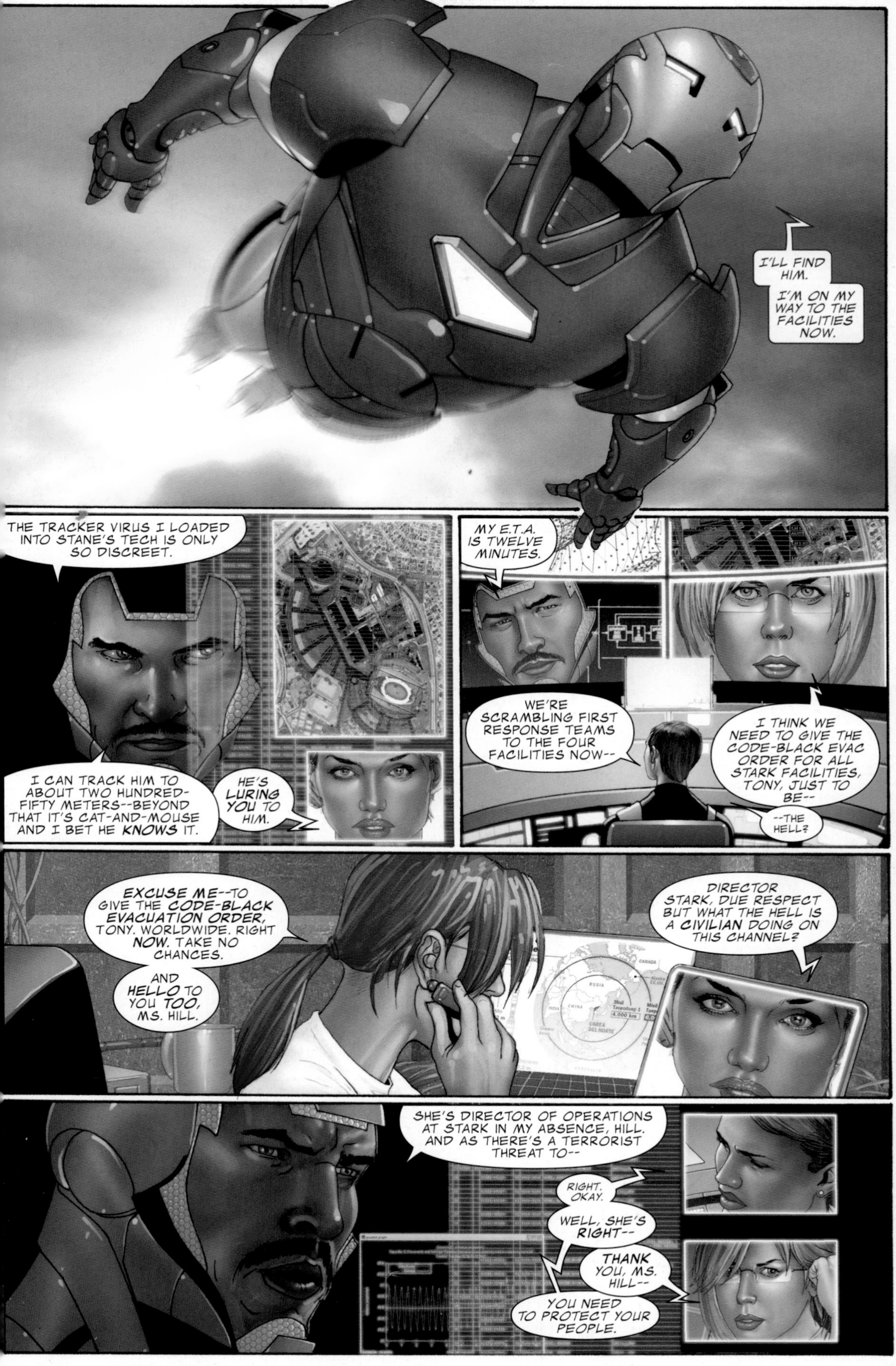
I'LL FIND HIM.
I'M ON MY WAY TO THE FACILITIES NOW.
THE TRACKER VIRUS I LOADED INTO STANE'S TECH IS ONLY SO DISCREET.
I CAN TRACK HIM TO ABOUT TWO HUNDRED-FIFTY METERS--BEYOND THAT IT'S CAT-AND-MOUSE AND I BET HE KNOWS IT.
HE'S LURING YOU TO HIM.
MY E.T.A. IS TWELVE MINUTES.
WE'RE SCRAMBLING FIRST RESPONSE TEAMS TO THE FOUR FACILITIES NOW--
I THINK WE NEED TO GIVE THE CODE-BLACK EVAC ORDER FOR ALL STARK FACILITIES, TONY, JUST TO BE--
--THE HELL?
EXCUSE ME--TO GIVE THE CODE-BLACK EVACUATION ORDER, TONY. WORLDWIDE. RIGHT NOW. TAKE NO CHANCES.
AND HELLO TO YOU TOO, MS. HILL.
DIRECTOR STARK, DUE RESPECT BUT WHAT THE HELL IS A CIVILIAN DOING ON THIS CHANNEL?
SHE'S DIRECTOR OF OPERATIONS AT STARK IN MY ABSENCE, HILL. AND AS THERE'S A TERRORIST THREAT TO--
RIGHT. OKAY.
WELL, SHE'S RIGHT--
THANK YOU, MS. HILL--
YOU NEED TO PROTECT YOUR PEOPLE.

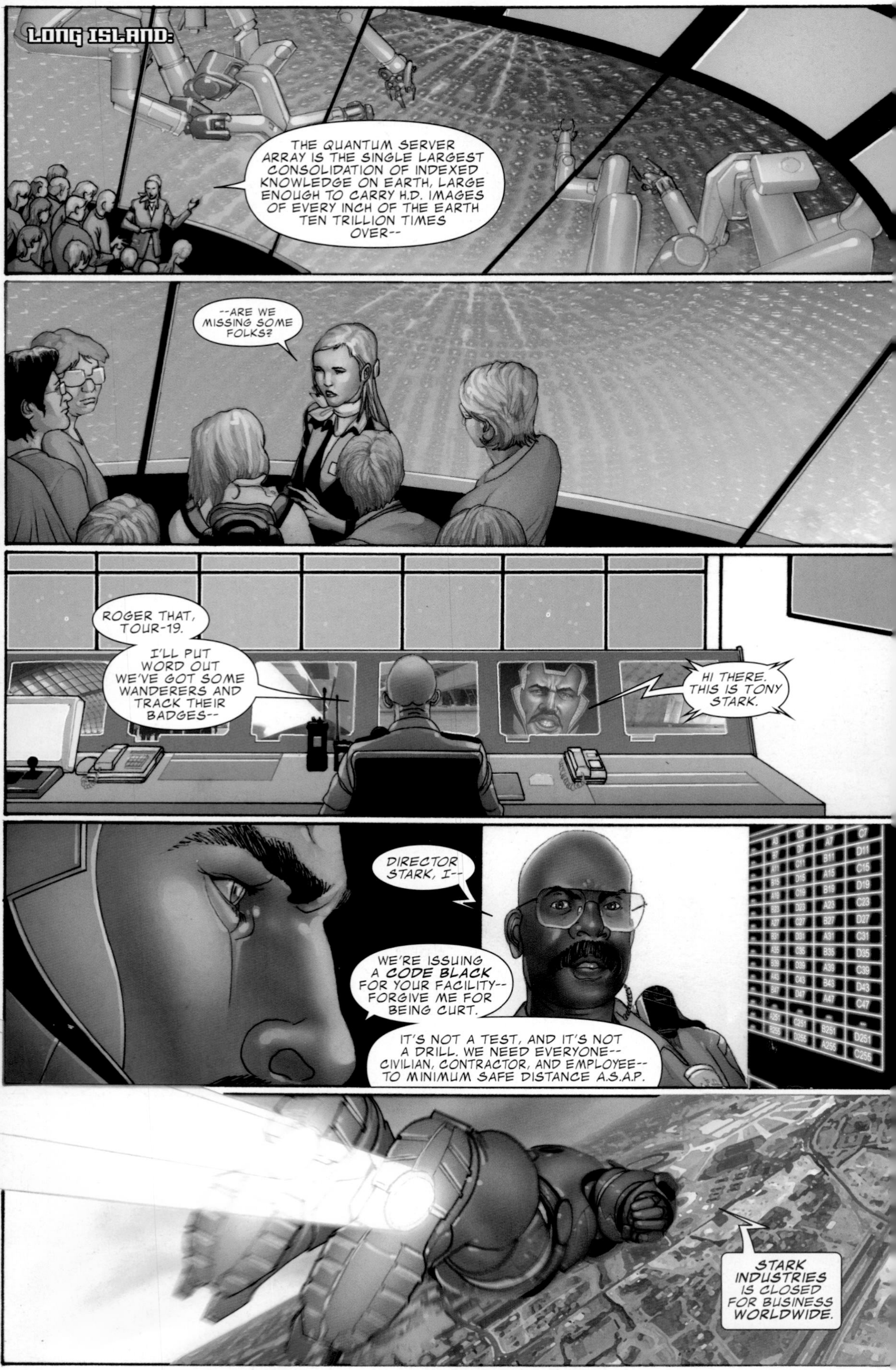
LONG ISLAND:
THE QUANTUM SERVER ARRAY IS THE SINGLE LARGEST CONSOLIDATION OF INDEXED KNOWLEDGE ON EARTH, LARGE ENOUGH TO CARRY H.D. IMAGES OF EVERY INCH OF THE EARTH TEN TRILLION TIMES OVER--
--ARE WE MISSING SOME FOLKS?
ROGER THAT, TOUR-19.
I'LL PUT WORD OUT WE'VE GOT SOME WANDERERS AND TRACK THEIR BADGES--
HI THERE. THIS IS TONY STARK.
DIRECTOR STARK, I--
WE'RE ISSUING A CODE BLACK FOR YOUR FACILITY--FORGIVE ME FOR BEING CURT.
IT'S NOT A TEST, AND IT'S NOT A DRILL. WE NEED EVERYONE--CIVILIAN, CONTRACTOR, AND EMPLOYEE--TO MINIMUM SAFE DISTANCE A.S.A.P.
STARK INDUSTRIES IS CLOSED FOR BUSINESS WORLDWIDE.

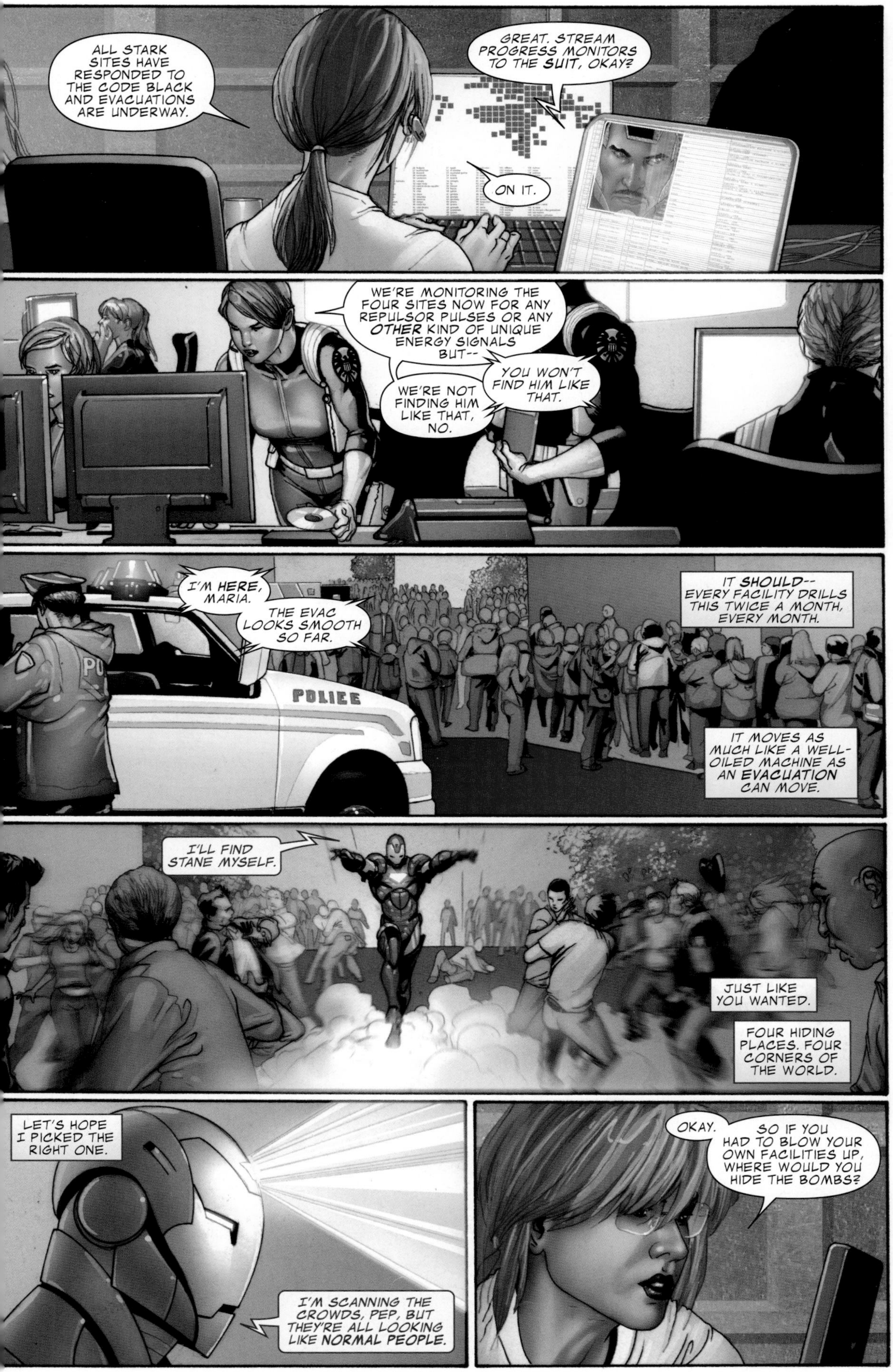
ALL STARK SITES HAVE RESPONDED TO THE CODE BLACK AND EVACUATIONS ARE UNDERWAY.
GREAT. STREAM PROGRESS MONITORS TO THE SUIT, OKAY?
ON IT.
WE'RE MONITORING THE FOUR SITES NOW FOR ANY REPULSOR PULSES OR ANY OTHER KIND OF UNIQUE ENERGY SIGNALS BUT--
WE'RE NOT FINDING HIM LIKE THAT, NO.
YOU WON'T FIND HIM LIKE THAT.
I'M HERE, MARIA.
THE EVAC LOOKS SMOOTH SO FAR.
POLICE
IT SHOULD-- EVERY FACILITY DRILLS THIS TWICE A MONTH, EVERY MONTH.
IT MOVES AS MUCH LIKE A WELL-OILED MACHINE AS AN EVACUATION CAN MOVE.
I'LL FIND STANE MYSELF.
JUST LIKE YOU WANTED.
FOUR HIDING PLACES. FOUR CORNERS OF THE WORLD.
LET'S HOPE I PICKED THE RIGHT ONE.
I'M SCANNING THE CROWDS, PEP, BUT THEY'RE ALL LOOKING LIKE NORMAL PEOPLE.
OKAY.
SO IF YOU HAD TO BLOW YOUR OWN FACILITIES UP, WHERE WOULD YOU HIDE THE BOMBS?

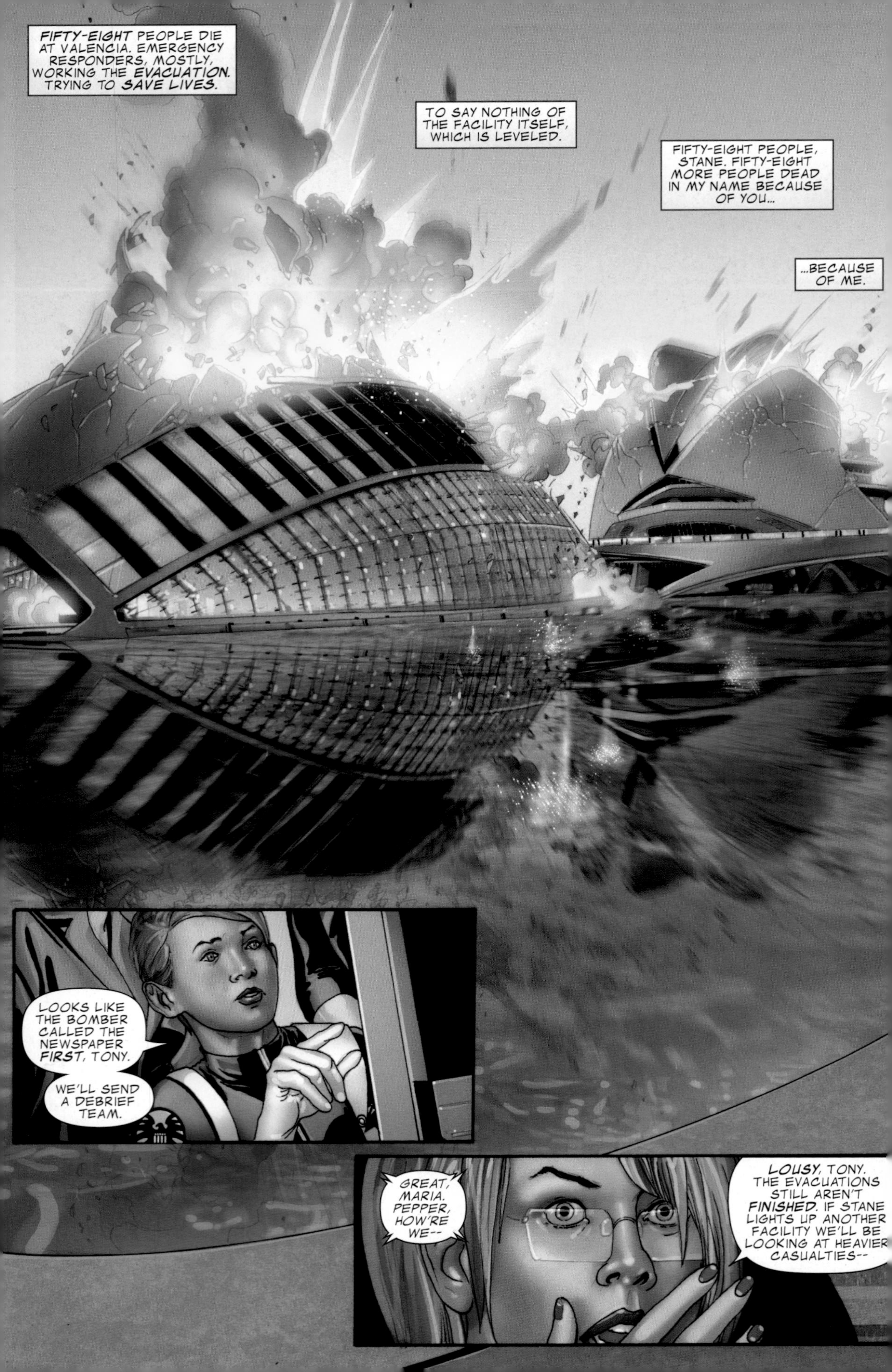
FIFTY-EIGHT PEOPLE DIE AT VALENCIA. EMERGENCY RESPONDERS, MOSTLY, WORKING THE EVACUATION. TRYING TO SAVE LIVES.
TO SAY NOTHING OF THE FACILITY ITSELF, WHICH IS LEVELED.
FIFTY-EIGHT PEOPLE, STANE. FIFTY-EIGHT MORE PEOPLE DEAD IN MY NAME BECAUSE OF YOU...
...BECAUSE OF ME.
LOOKS LIKE THE BOMBER CALLED THE NEWSPAPER FIRST, TONY.
WE'LL SEND A DEBRIEF TEAM.
GREAT, MARIA. PEPPER, HOW'RE WE--
LOUSY, TONY. THE EVACUATIONS STILL AREN'T FINISHED. IF STANE LIGHTS UP ANOTHER FACILITY WE'LL BE LOOKING AT HEAVIER CASUALTIES--

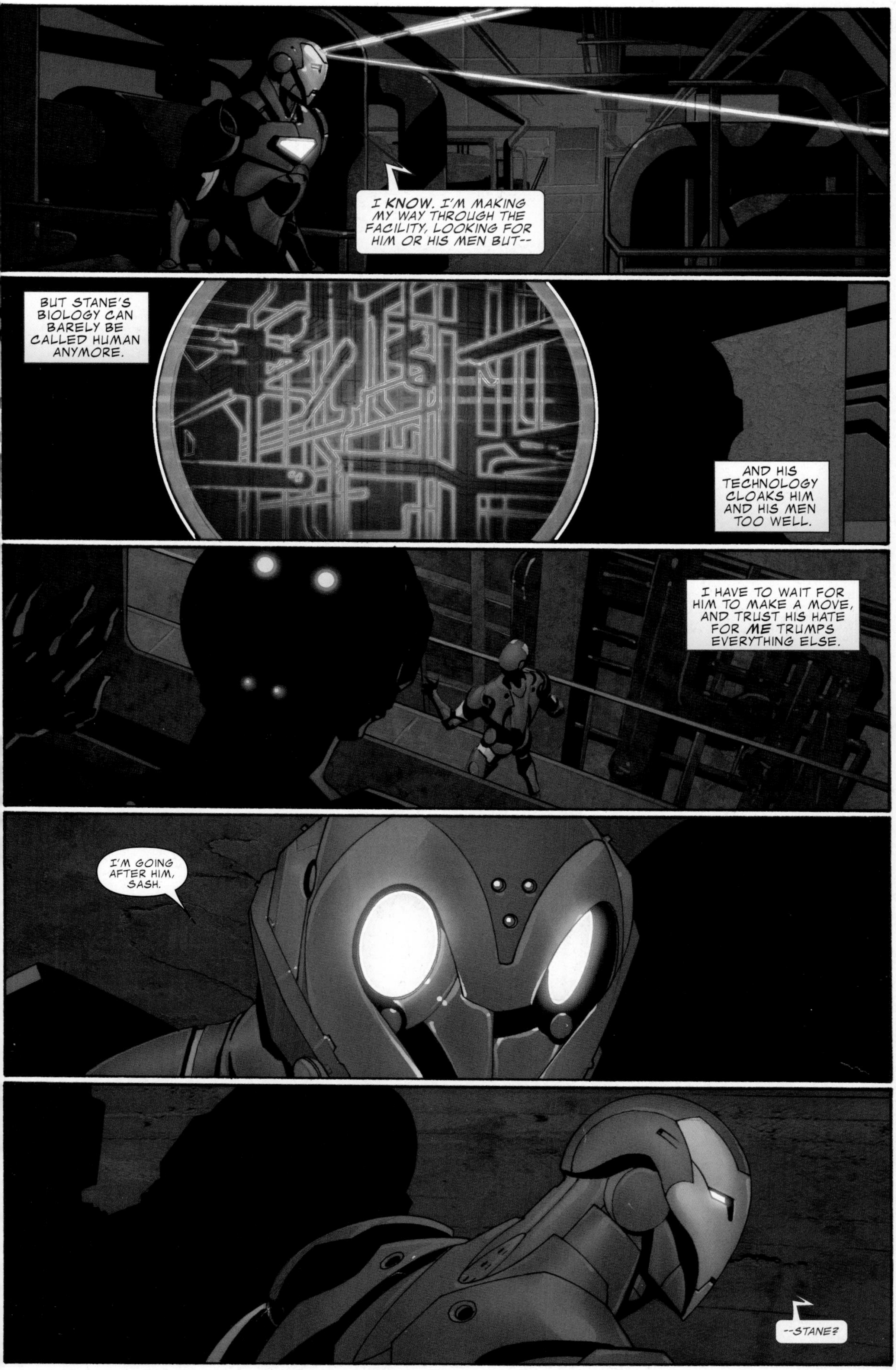
I KNOW. I'M MAKING MY WAY THROUGH THE FACILITY, LOOKING FOR HIM OR HIS MEN BUT--
BUT STANE'S BIOLOGY CAN BARELY BE CALLED HUMAN ANYMORE.
AND HIS TECHNOLOGY CLOAKS HIM AND HIS MEN TOO WELL.
I HAVE TO WAIT FOR HIM TO MAKE A MOVE, AND TRUST HIS HATE FOR ME TRUMPS EVERYTHING ELSE.
I'M GOING AFTER HIM, SASH.
--STANE?

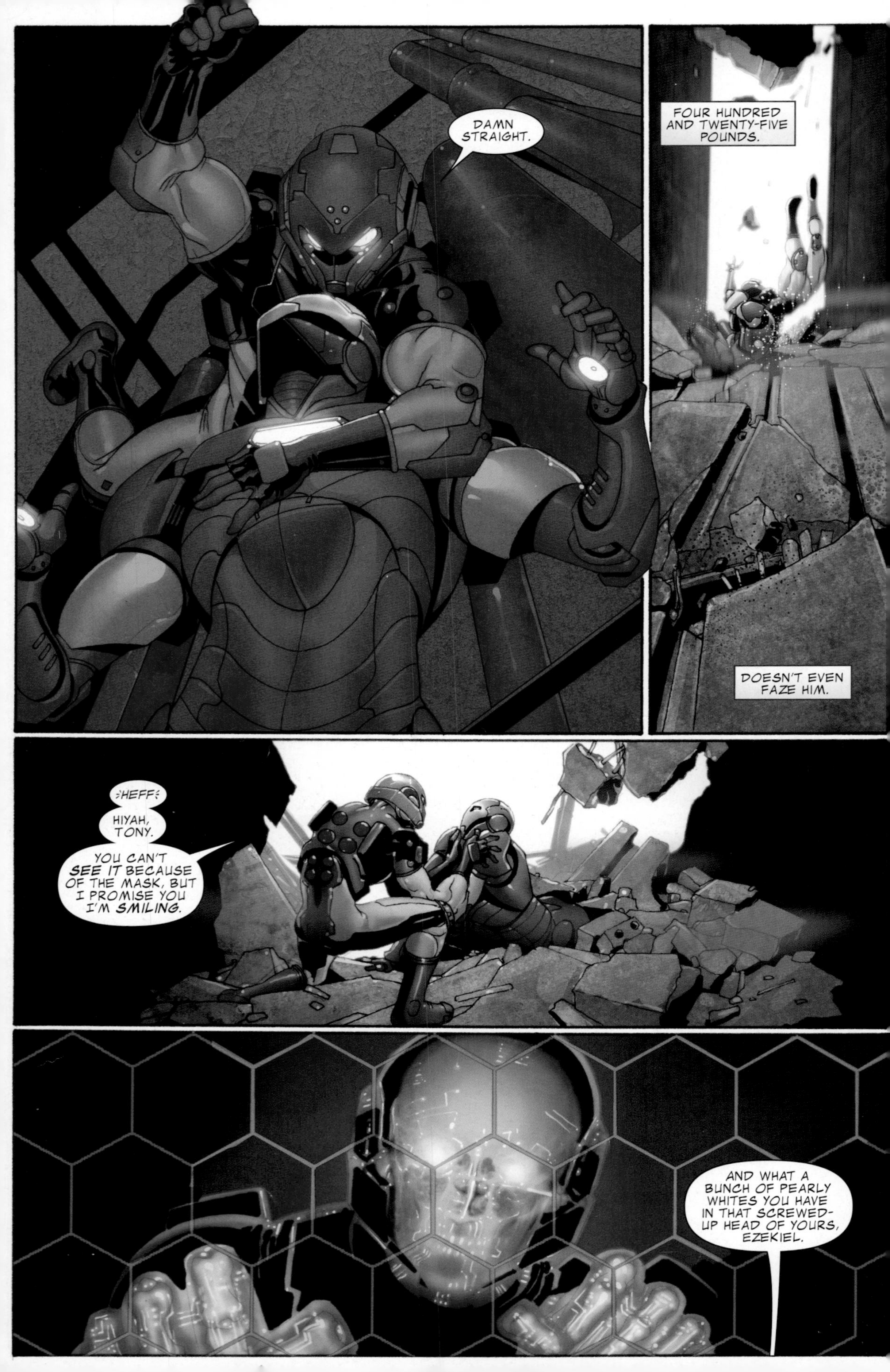

DAMN STRAIGHT.
FOUR HUNDRED AND TWENTY-FIVE POUNDS.
DOESN'T EVEN FAZE HIM.
HEFF
HIYAH, TONY.
YOU CAN'T SEE IT BECAUSE OF THE MASK, BUT I PROMISE YOU I'M SMILING.
AND WHAT A BUNCH OF PEARLY WHITES YOU HAVE IN THAT SCREWED-UP HEAD OF YOURS, EZEKIEL.

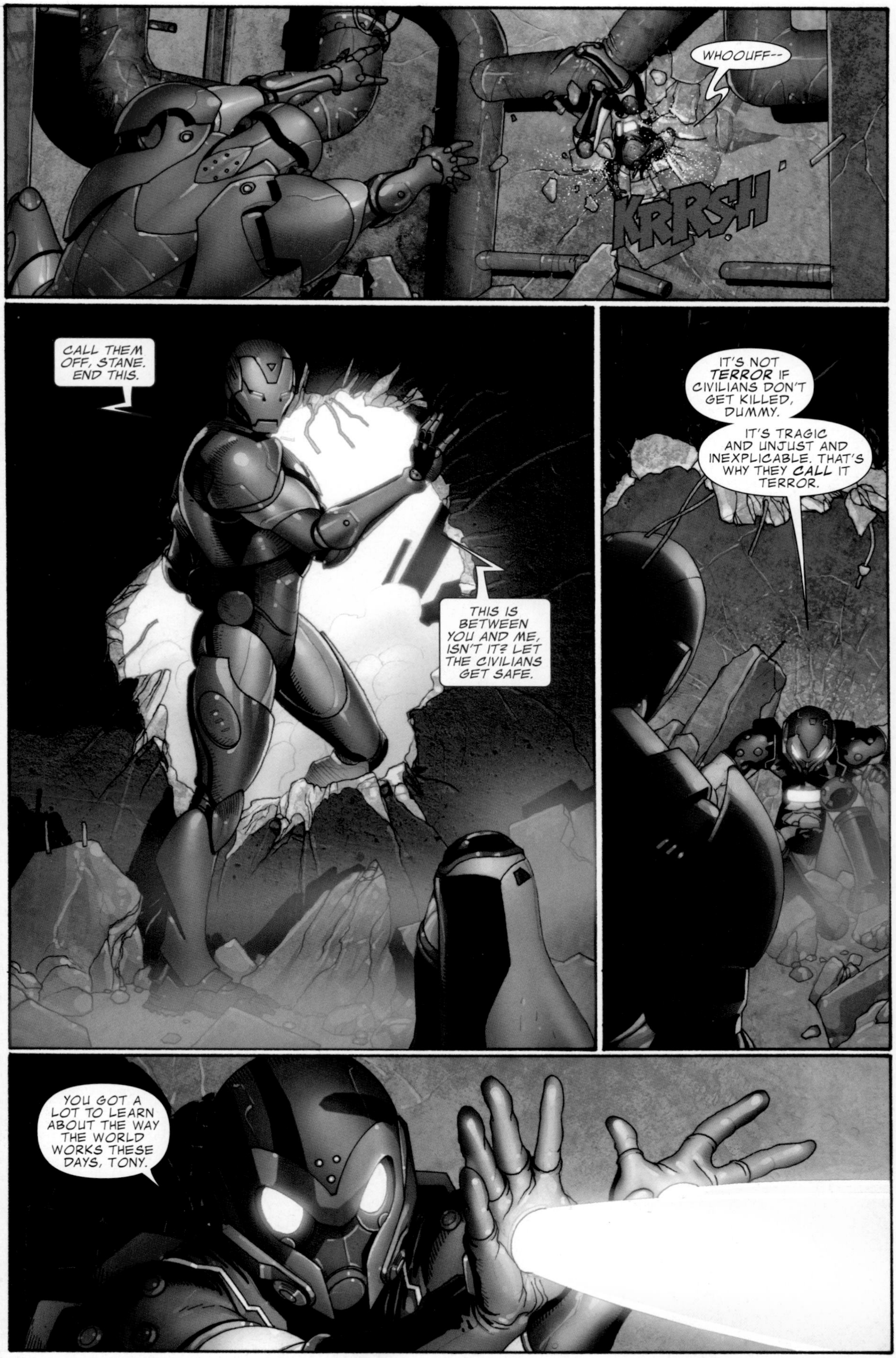
WHOOUFF--
KRRSH
CALL THEM OFF, STANE. END THIS.
THIS IS BETWEEN YOU AND ME, ISN'T IT? LET THE CIVILIANS GET SAFE.
IT'S NOT TERROR IF CIVILIANS DON'T GET KILLED, DUMMY.
IT'S TRAGIC AND UNJUST AND INEXPLICABLE. THAT'S WHY THEY CALL IT TERROR.
YOU GOT A LOT TO LEARN ABOUT THE WAY THE WORLD WORKS THESE DAYS, TONY.

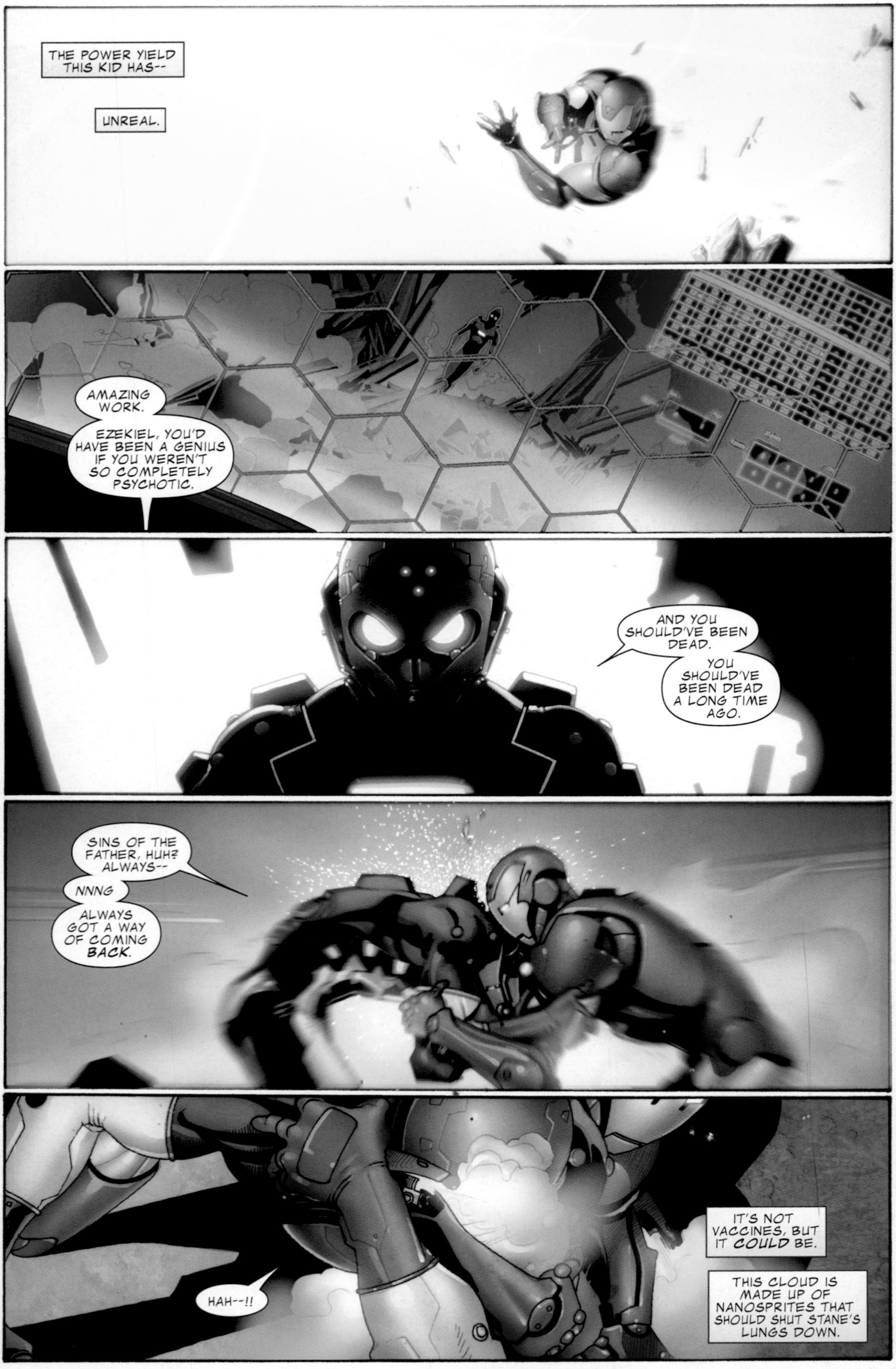
THE POWER YIELD THIS KID HAS--
UNREAL.
AMAZING WORK.
EZEKIEL, YOU'D HAVE BEEN A GENIUS IF YOU WEREN'T SO COMPLETELY PSYCHOTIC.
AND YOU SHOULD'VE BEEN DEAD.
YOU SHOULD'VE BEEN DEAD A LONG TIME AGO.
SINS OF THE FATHER, HUH? ALWAYS--
NNNG
ALWAYS GOT A WAY OF COMING BACK.
IT'S NOT VACCINES, BUT IT COULD BE.
THIS CLOUD IS MADE UP OF NANOSPRITES THAT SHOULD SHUT STANE'S LUNGS DOWN.
HAH--!!

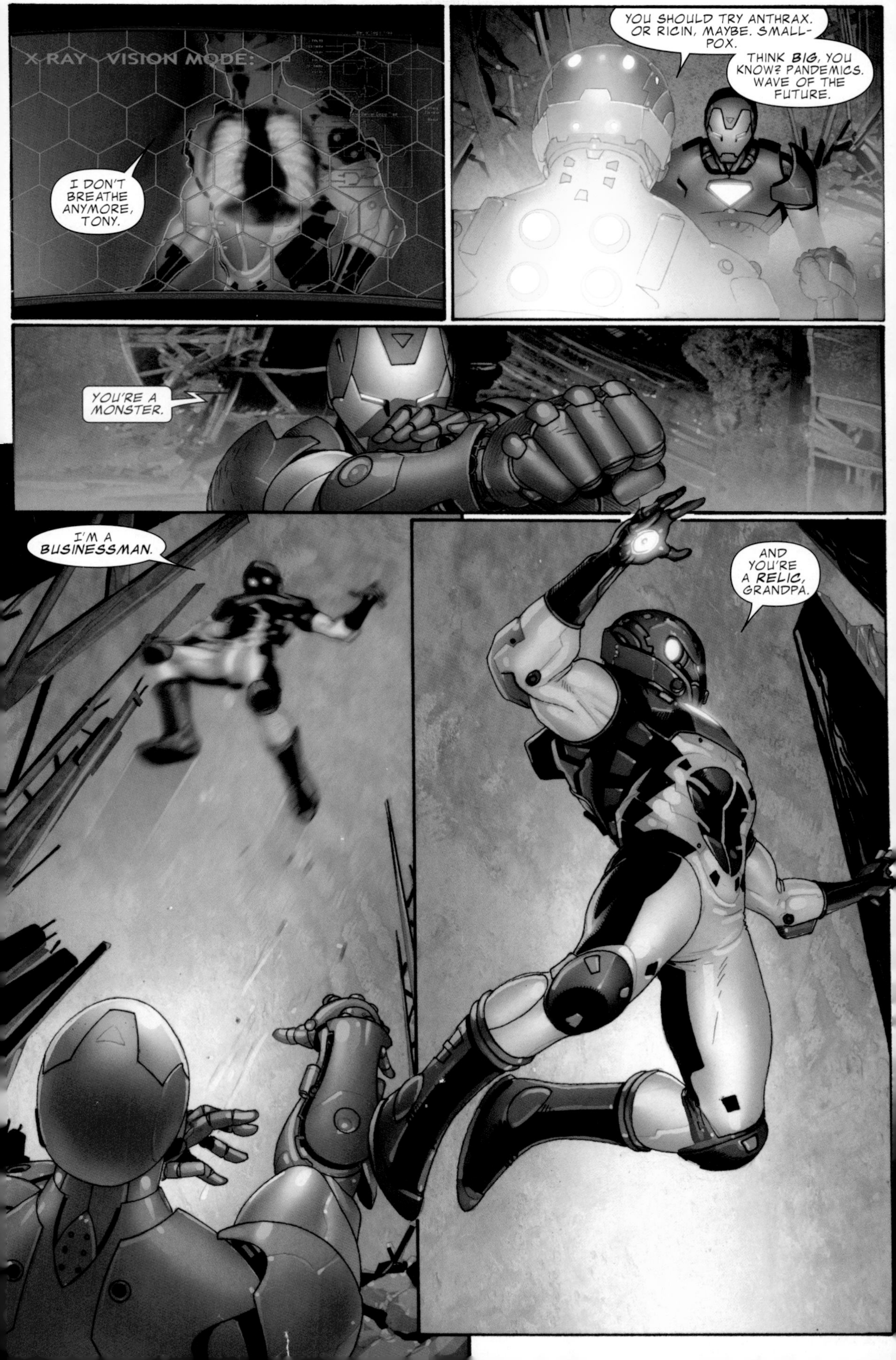
X RAY VISION MODE:
I DON'T BREATHE ANYMORE, TONY.
YOU SHOULD TRY ANTHRAX. OR RICIN, MAYBE. SMALL-POX.
THINK BIG, YOU KNOW? PANDEMICS. WAVE OF THE FUTURE.
YOU'RE A MONSTER.
I'M A BUSINESSMAN.
AND YOU'RE A RELIC, GRANDPA.

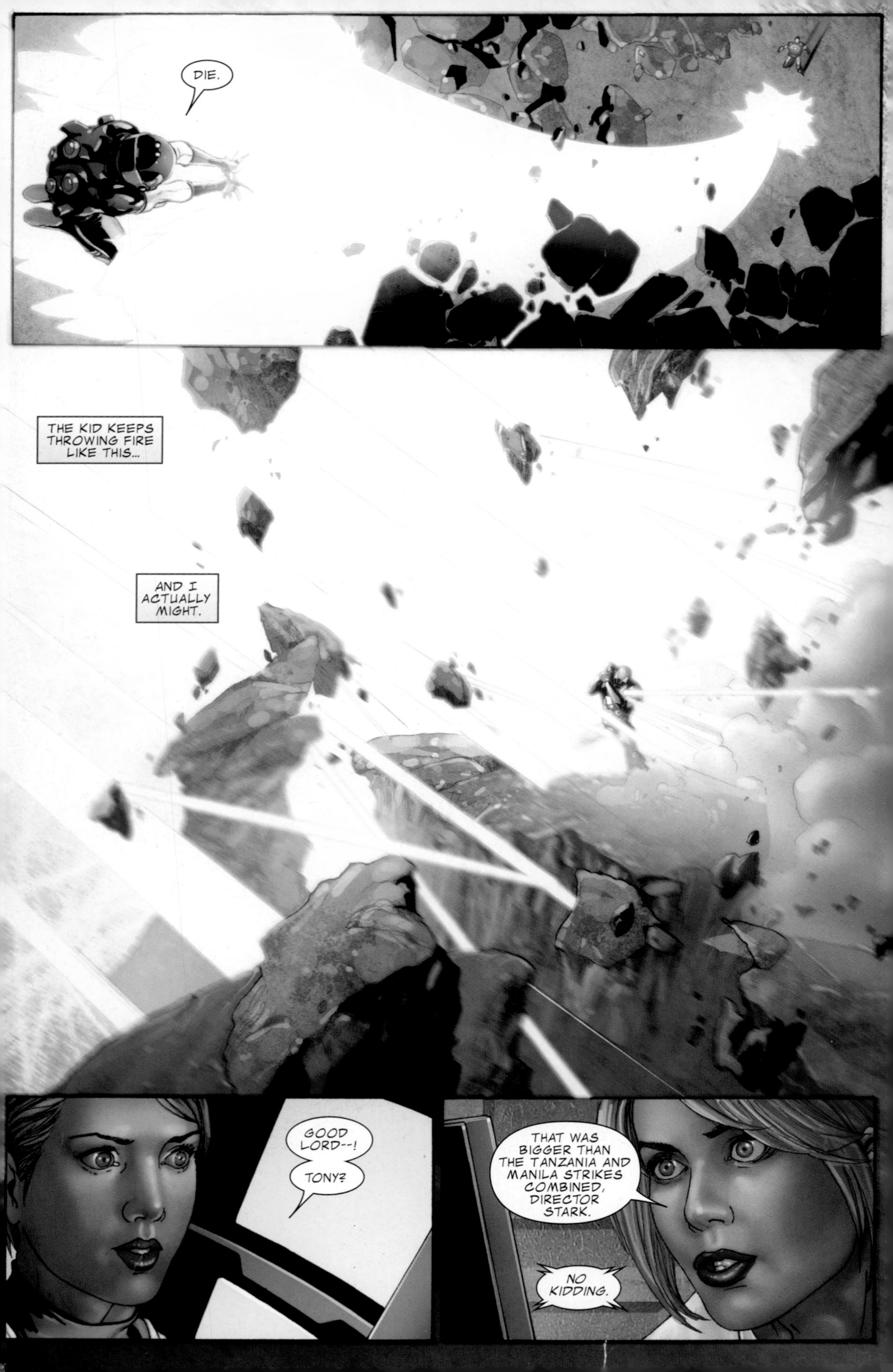
DIE.
THE KID KEEPS THROWING FIRE LIKE THIS...
AND I ACTUALLY MIGHT.
GOOD LORD--!
TONY?
THAT WAS BIGGER THAN THE TANZANIA AND MANILA STRIKES COMBINED, DIRECTOR STARK.
NO KIDDING.

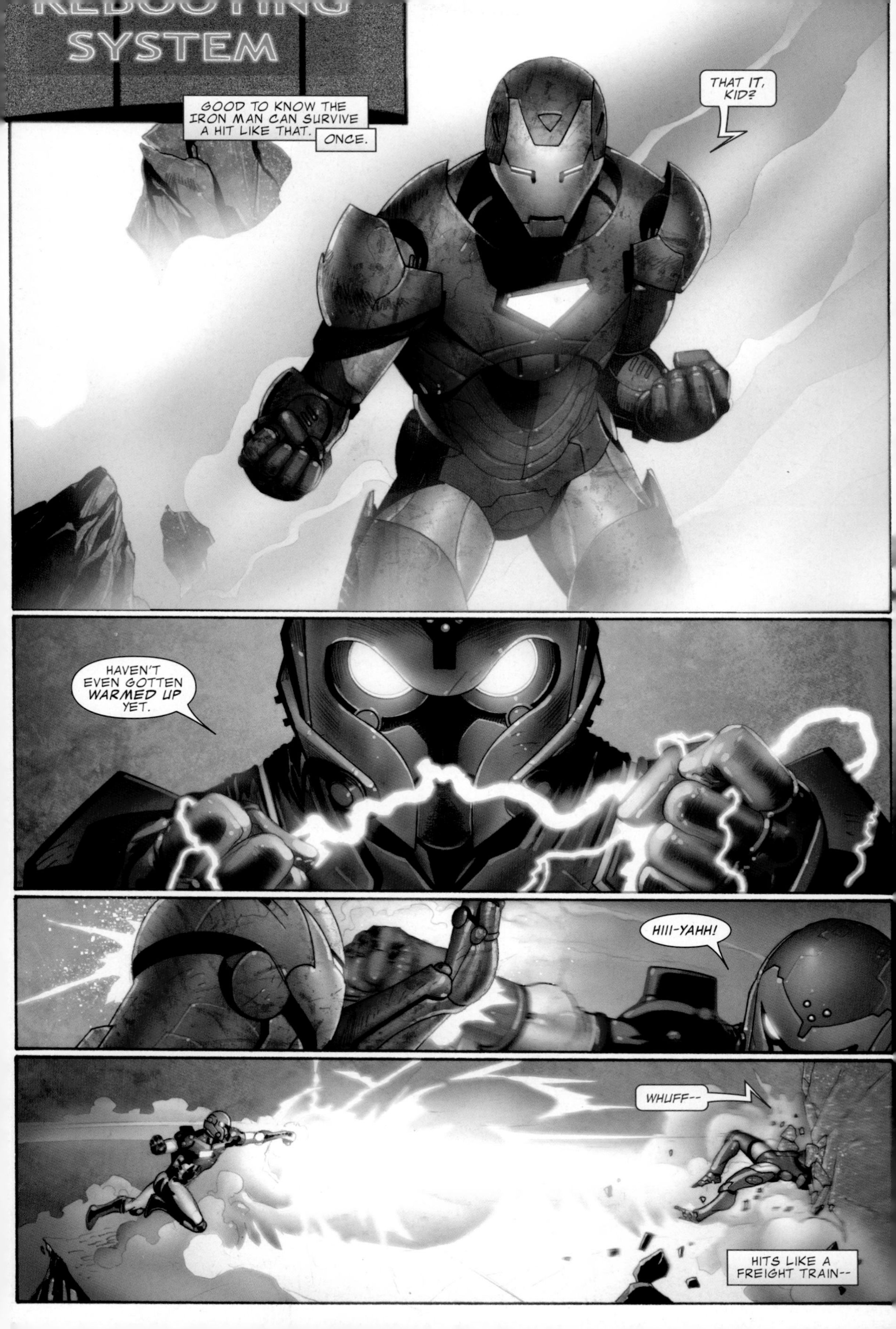
REBOOTING SYSTEM
GOOD TO KNOW THE IRON MAN CAN SURVIVE A HIT LIKE THAT.
ONCE.
THAT IT, KID?
HAVEN'T EVEN GOTTEN WARMED UP YET.
HIII-YAHH!
WHUFF--
HITS LIKE A FREIGHT TRAIN--

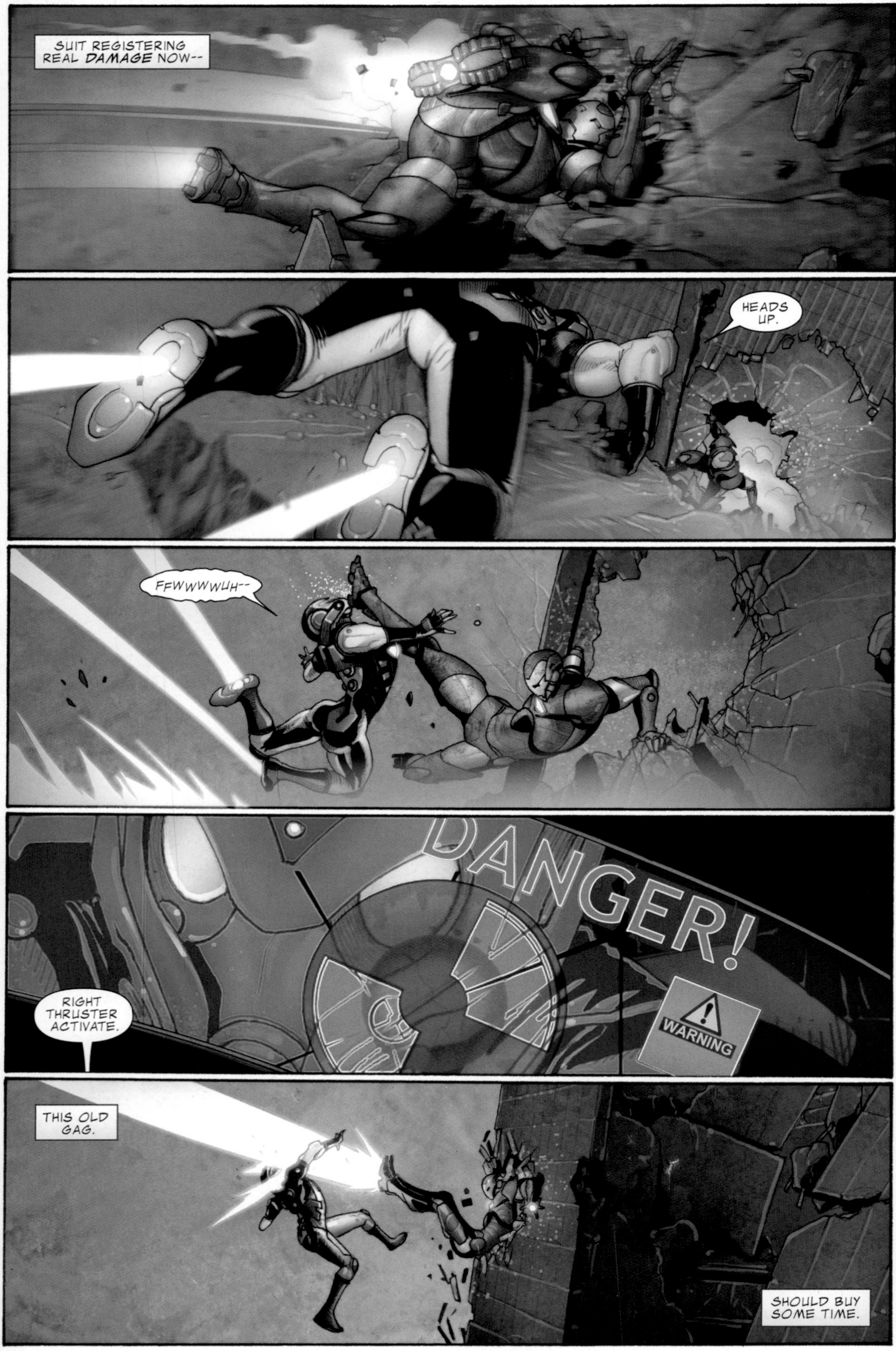
SUIT REGISTERING REAL DAMAGE NOW--
HEADS UP.
FFWWWWUH--
DANGER!
WARNING
RIGHT THRUSTER ACTIVATE.
THIS OLD GAG.
SHOULD BUY SOME TIME.

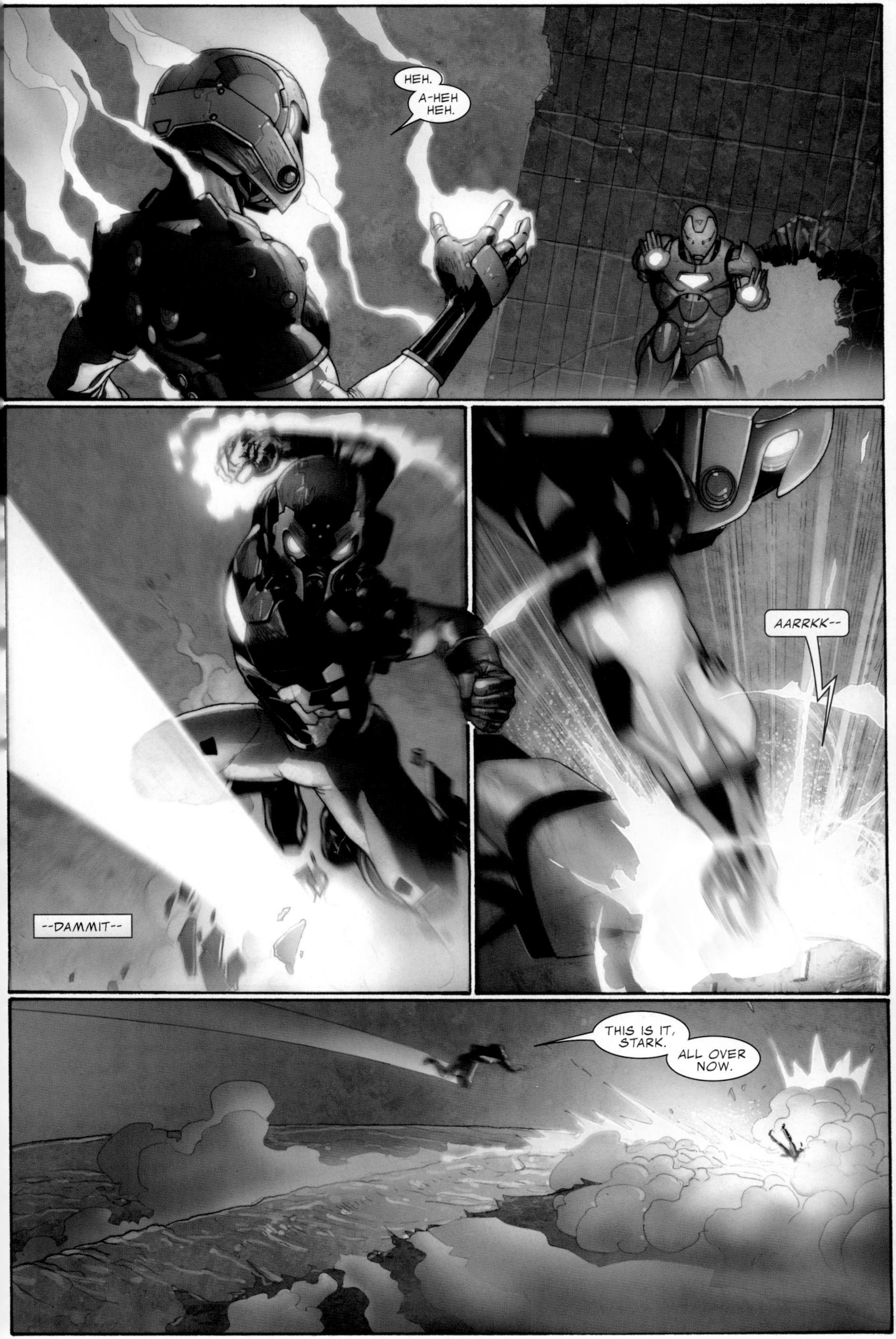
HEH.
A-HEH HEH.
AARRKK--
--DAMMIT--
THIS IS IT, STARK.
ALL OVER NOW.

GRRRAHH---!

HE'S RIGHT--

KID'S RIGHT--

THE ARMOR CAN'T TAKE MUCH MORE OF THIS PUNISHMENT--

ONE MORE HIT--MAYBE TWO--

STANE--

THAT'S RIGHT, TONY. MAKE *MY NAME* YOUR LAST WORD.

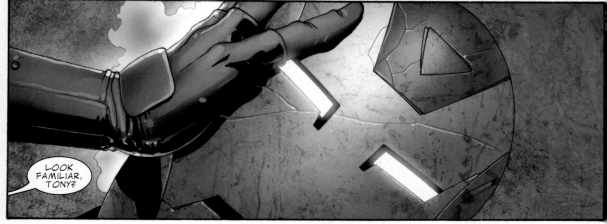

LOOK FAMILIAR, TONY?

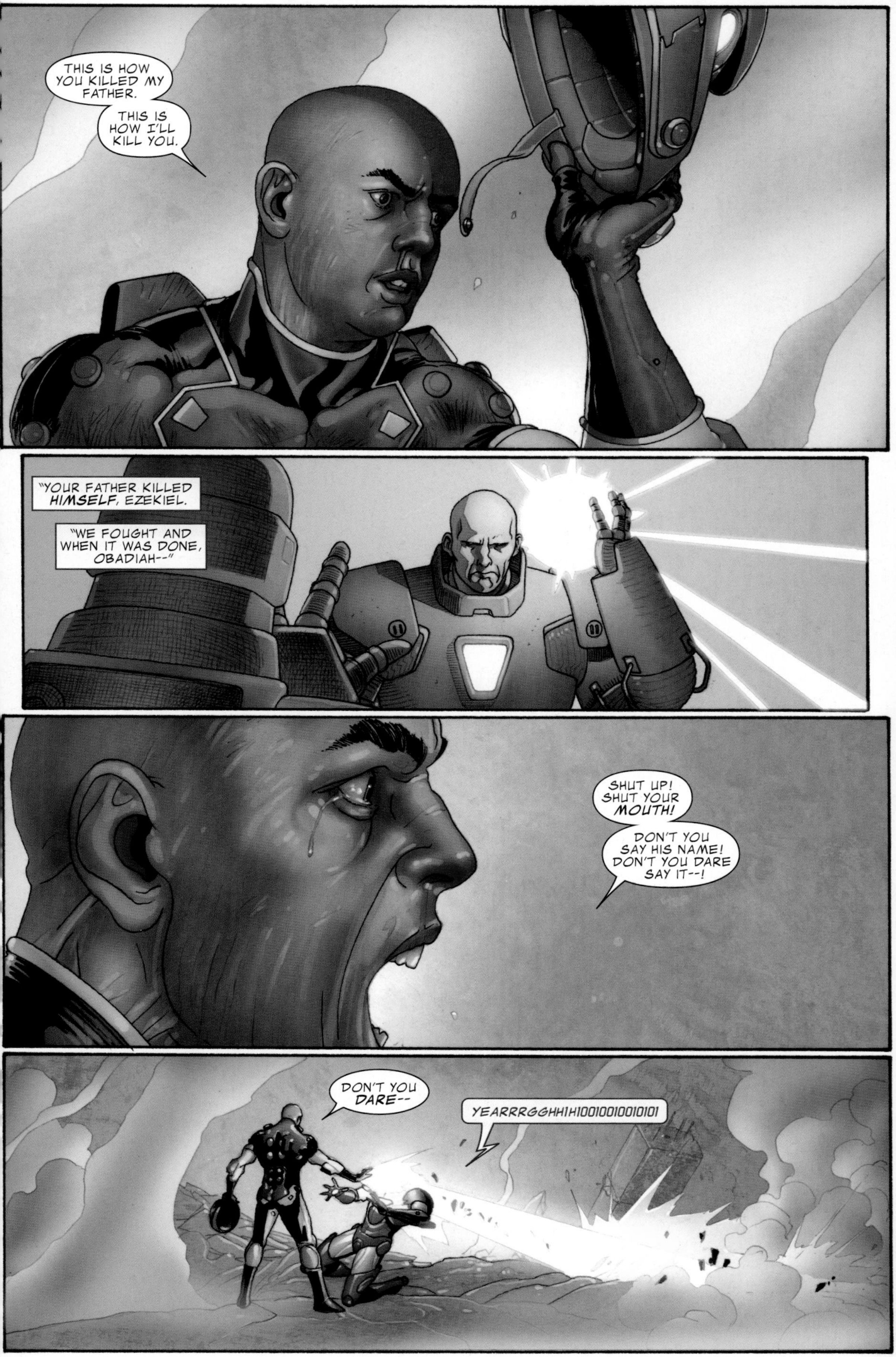

THIS IS HOW YOU KILLED MY FATHER.
THIS IS HOW I'LL KILL YOU.
"YOUR FATHER KILLED HIMSELF, EZEKIEL.
"WE FOUGHT AND WHEN IT WAS DONE, OBADIAH--"
SHUT UP! SHUT YOUR MOUTH!
DON'T YOU SAY HIS NAME! DON'T YOU DARE SAY IT--!
DON'T YOU DARE--
YEARRRGGHH1H1001001001010101

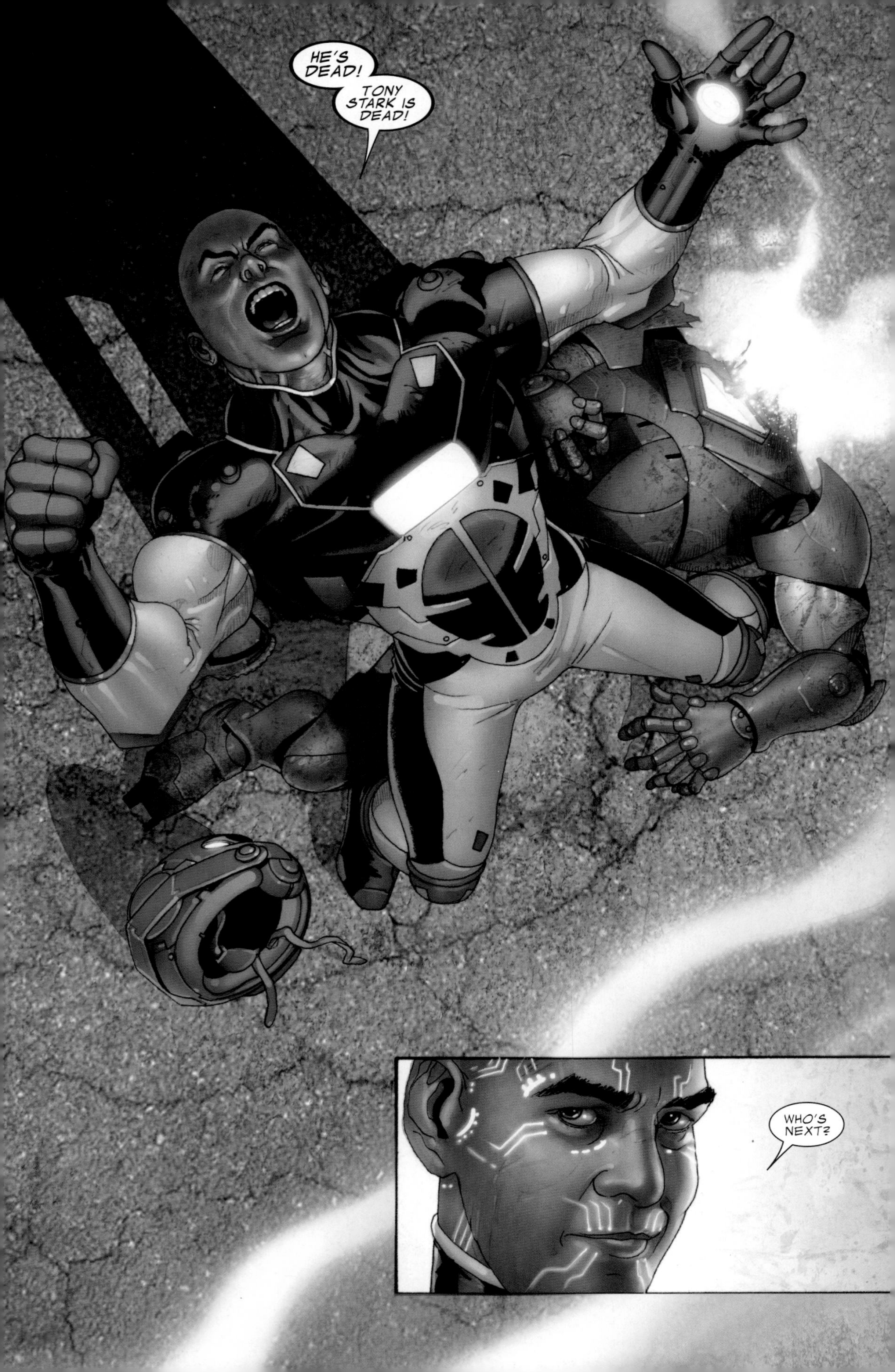
HE'S DEAD!
TONY STARK IS DEAD!
WHO'S NEXT?

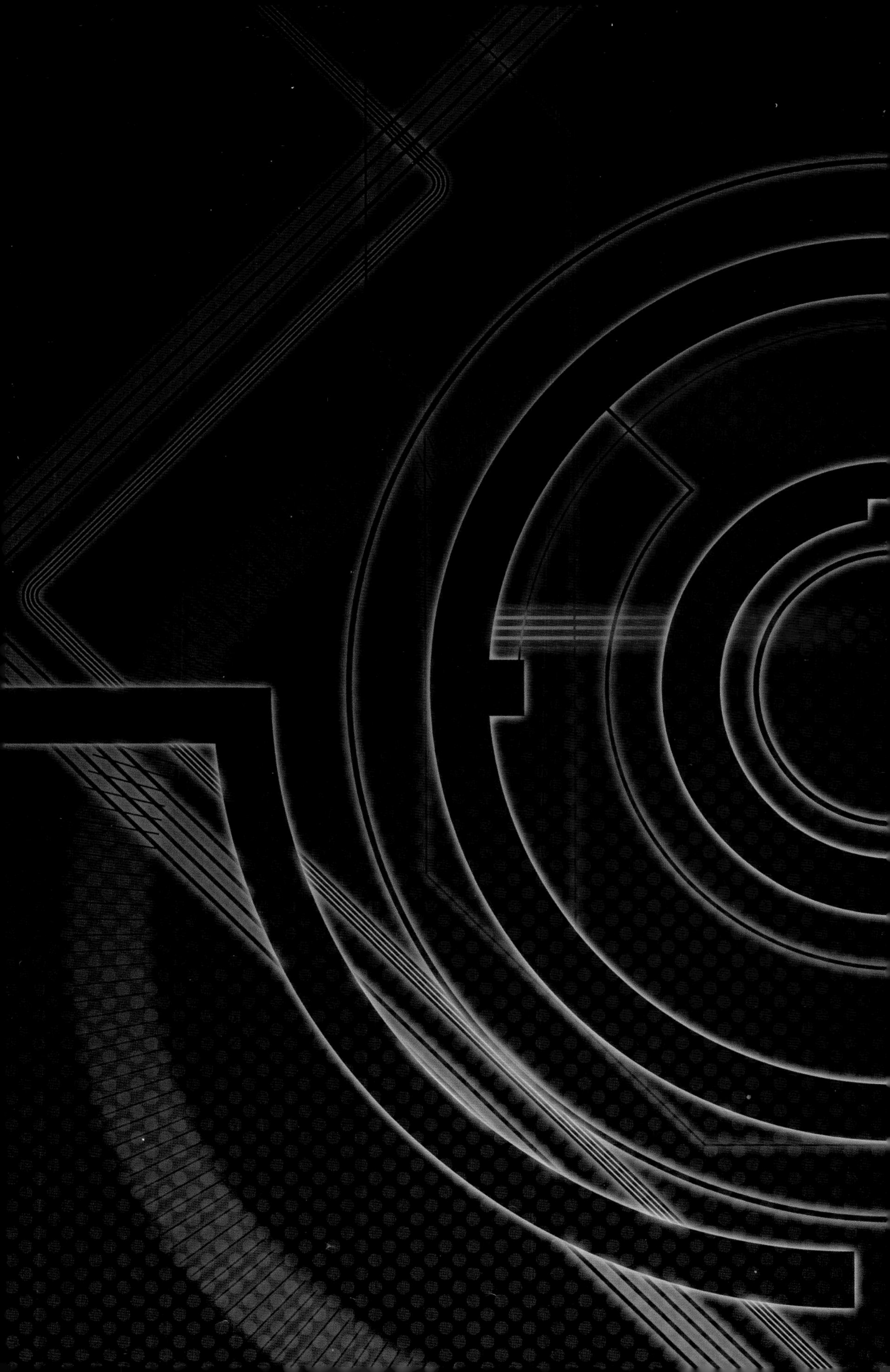

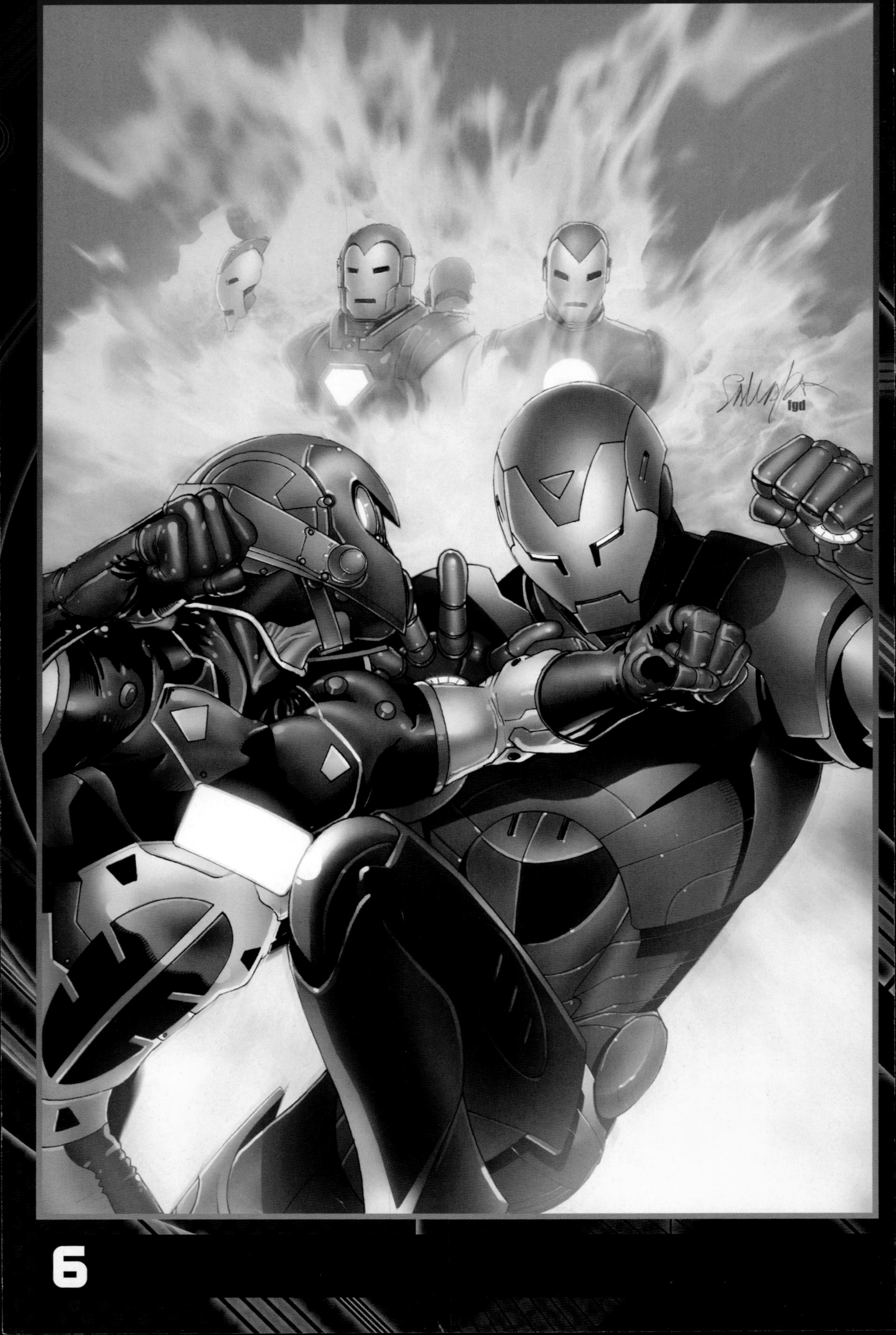

# 6

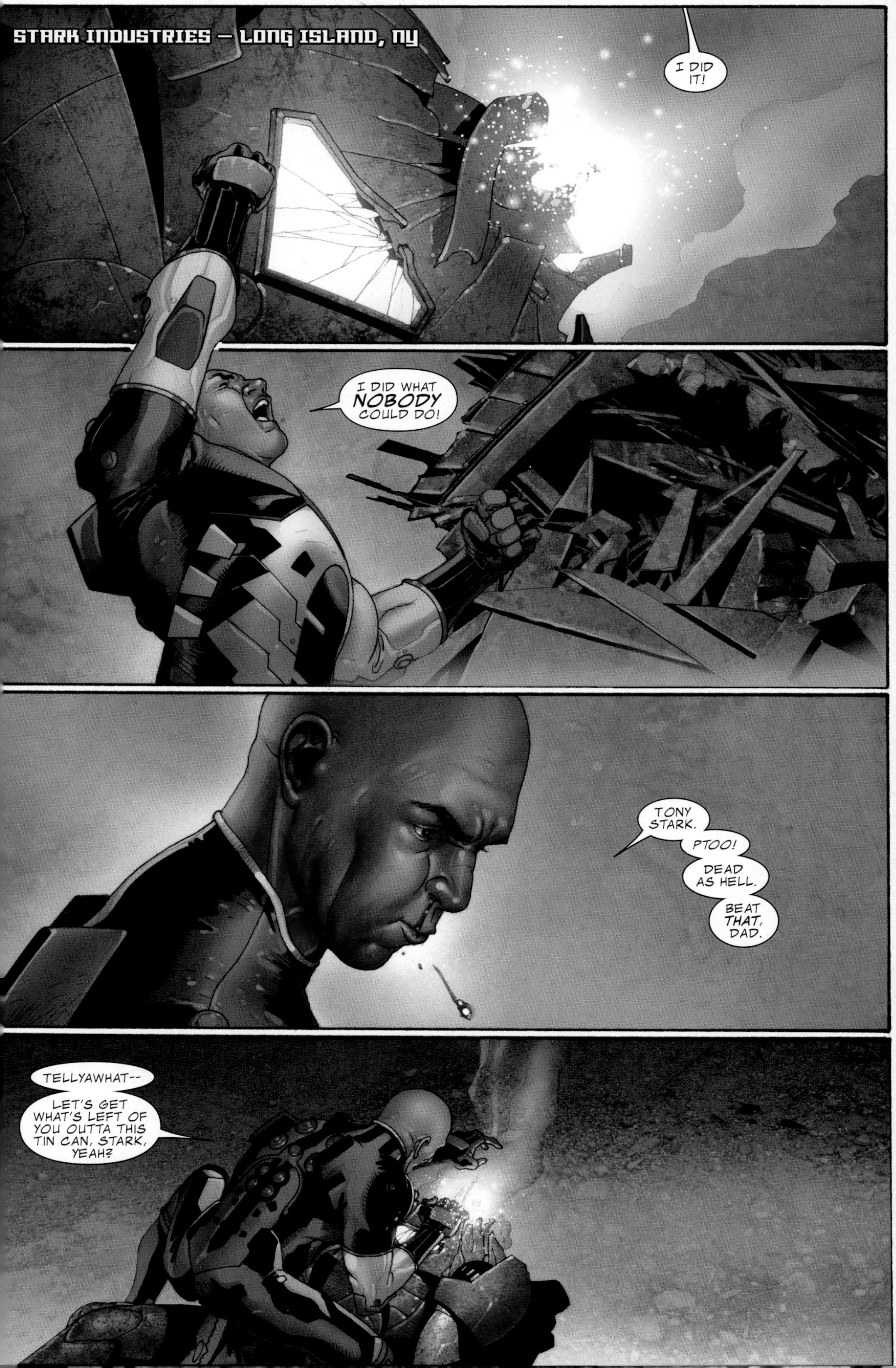
STARK INDUSTRIES — LONG ISLAND, NY
I DID IT!
I DID WHAT NOBODY COULD DO!
TONY STARK.
PTOO!
DEAD AS HELL.
BEAT THAT, DAD.
TELLYAWHAT--
LET'S GET WHAT'S LEFT OF YOU OUTTA THIS TIN CAN, STARK, YEAH?

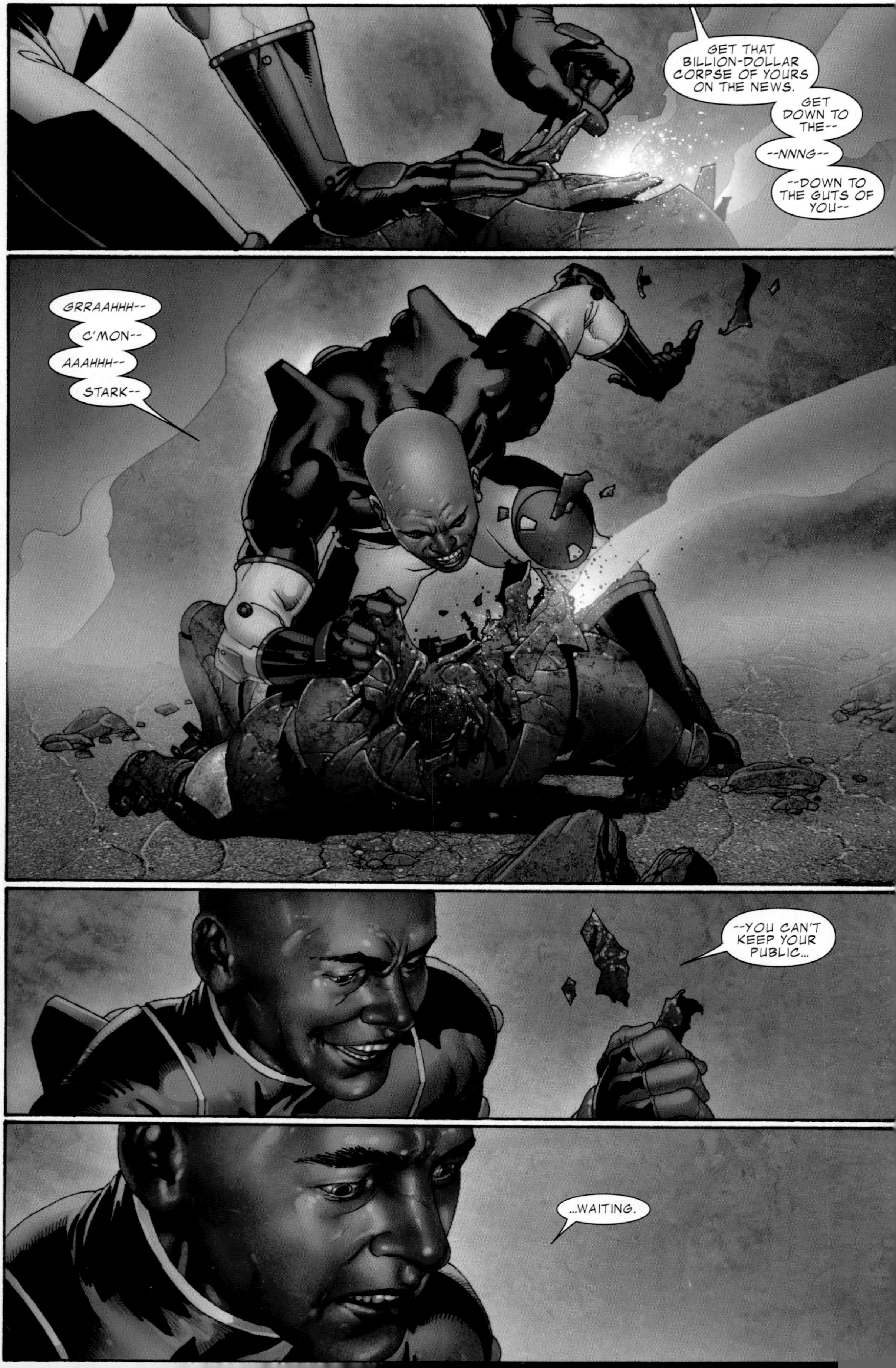
GET THAT BILLION-DOLLAR CORPSE OF YOURS ON THE NEWS.
GET DOWN TO THE--
--NNNG--
--DOWN TO THE GUTS OF YOU--
GRRAAHHH--
C'MON--
AAAHHH--
STARK--
--YOU CAN'T KEEP YOUR PUBLIC...
...WAITING.

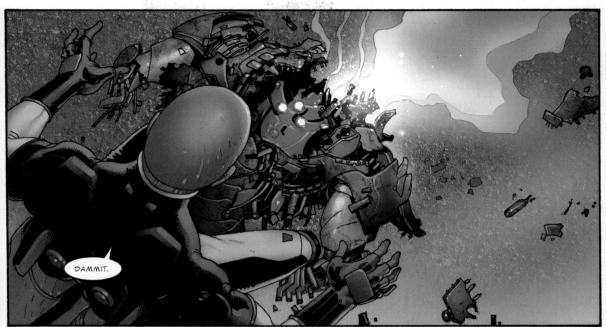

DAMMIT.

TONY STARK IS THE INVINCIBLE IRON MAN IN

# THE FIVE NIGHTMARES
## PART 6: IRRATIONAL ACTORS

I'M TWELVE MINUTES OUT FROM LONG ISLAND.

CHECKMATE, YOU LITTLE BRAT.

SASHA, GIVE THE ALL-CLEAR ORDER TO THE OTHER SQUADS-- TELL 'EM TO DETONATE AT WILL.

ZEKE, THEY'RE NOT ALL IN PLACE YET--

I DON'T CARE WHERE THE BOMB TEAMS ARE-- STARK'S SENT IRON MAN SQUADS TO STOP US. IT'S NOW OR NEVER.

ROGER THAT. POWERING UP ALL POINTS NOW.

YOU WERE THE WEIRDEST BOYFRIEND I EVER HAD, EZEKIEL STANE.

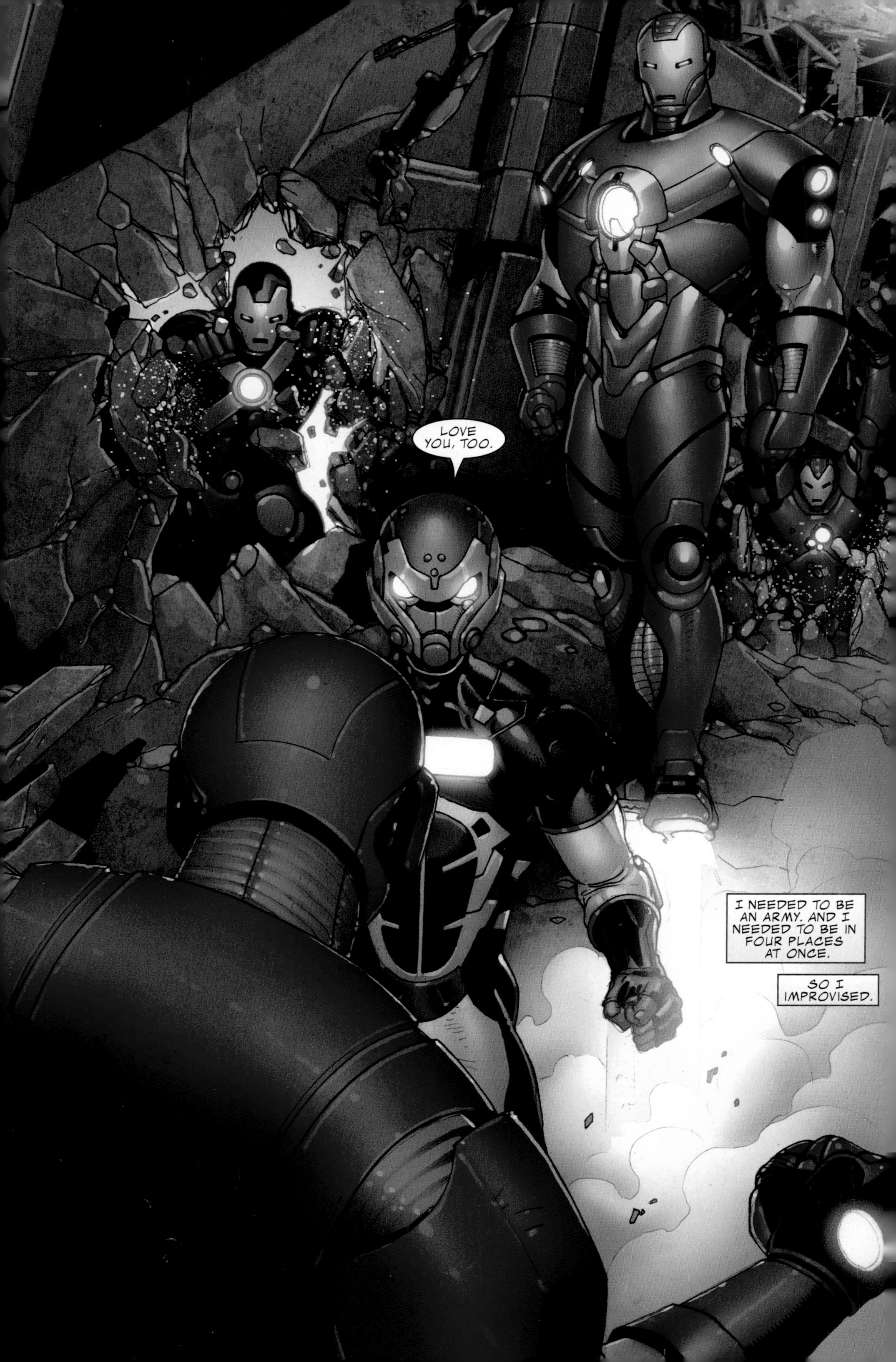
LOVE YOU, TOO.
I NEEDED TO BE AN ARMY. AND I NEEDED TO BE IN FOUR PLACES AT ONCE.
SO I IMPROVISED.

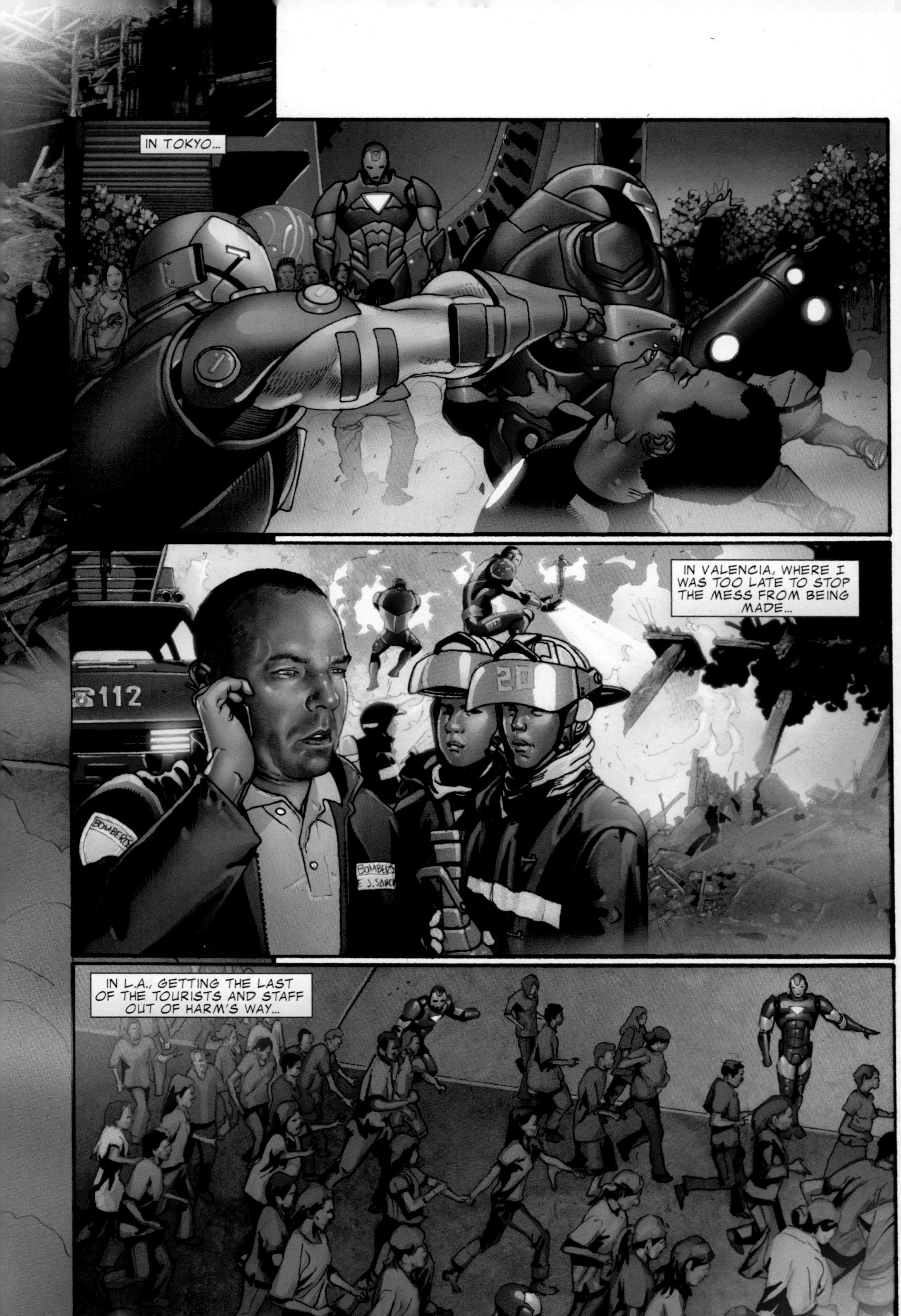
IN TOKYO...
IN VALENCIA, WHERE I WAS TOO LATE TO STOP THE MESS FROM BEING MADE...
112
BOMBEROS
IN L.A., GETTING THE LAST OF THE TOURISTS AND STAFF OUT OF HARM'S WAY...

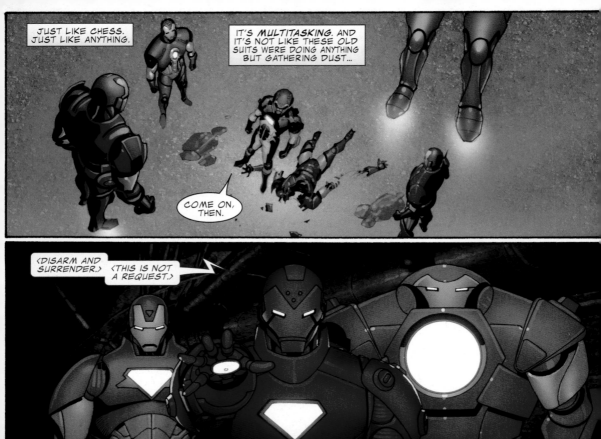

JUST LIKE CHESS. JUST LIKE ANYTHING.

IT'S *MULTITASKING*. AND IT'S NOT LIKE THESE OLD SUITS WERE DOING ANYTHING BUT GATHERING DUST...

COME ON, THEN.

〈DISARM AND SURRENDER.〉 〈THIS IS NOT A REQUEST.〉

〈WE COULDN'T STOP NOW.〉 〈NOT EVEN IF WE WANTED.〉

IRON MEN-- ALL POINTS, ALL LOCATIONS: SHUT 'EM DOWN. *NOW*.

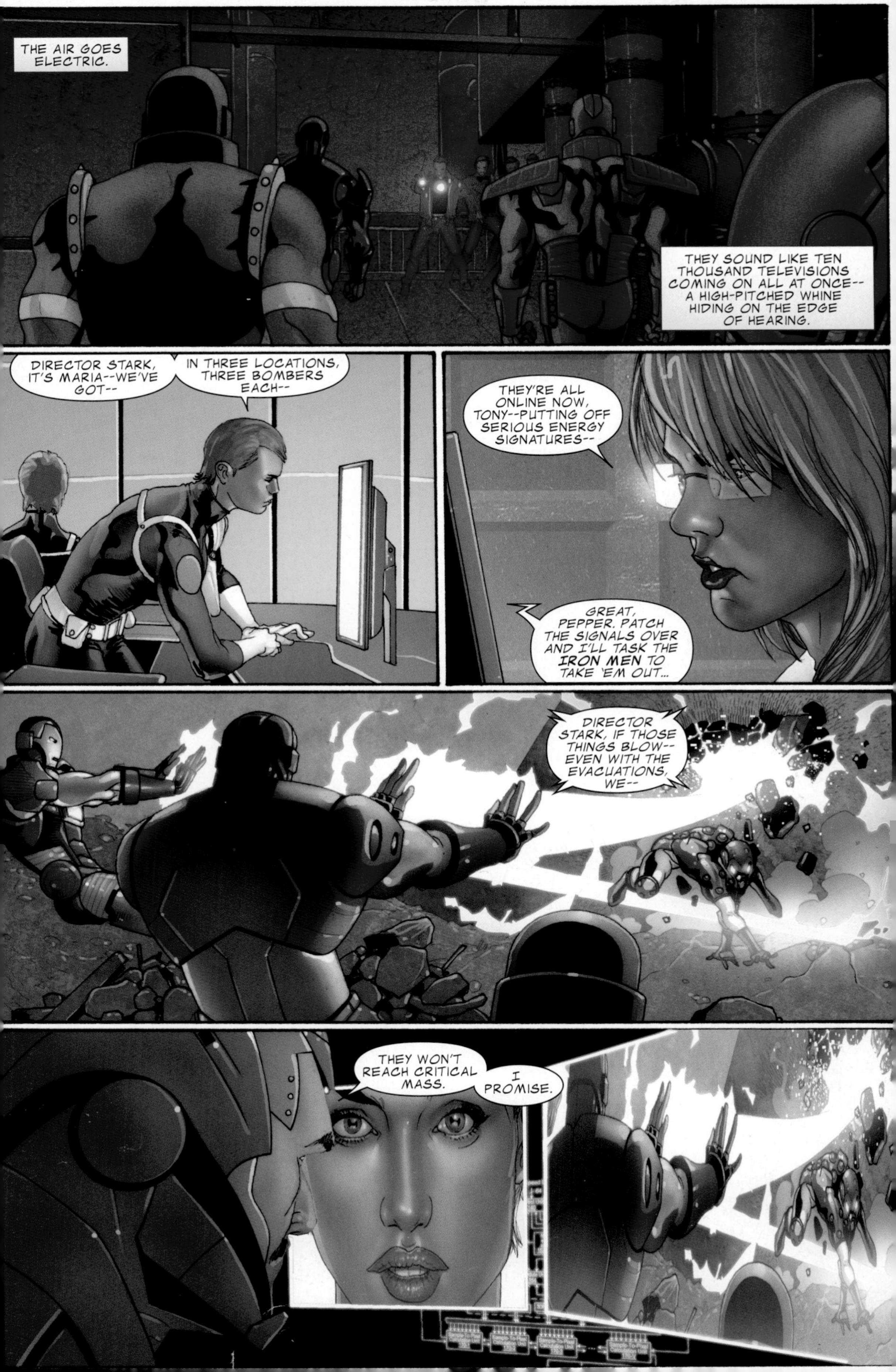

THE AIR GOES ELECTRIC.
THEY SOUND LIKE TEN THOUSAND TELEVISIONS COMING ON ALL AT ONCE-- A HIGH-PITCHED WHINE HIDING ON THE EDGE OF HEARING.
DIRECTOR STARK, IT'S MARIA--WE'VE GOT--
IN THREE LOCATIONS, THREE BOMBERS EACH--
THEY'RE ALL ONLINE NOW, TONY--PUTTING OFF SERIOUS ENERGY SIGNATURES--
GREAT, PEPPER. PATCH THE SIGNALS OVER AND I'LL TASK THE **IRON MEN** TO TAKE 'EM OUT...
DIRECTOR STARK, IF THOSE THINGS BLOW-- EVEN WITH THE EVACUATIONS, WE--
THEY WON'T REACH CRITICAL MASS.
I PROMISE.

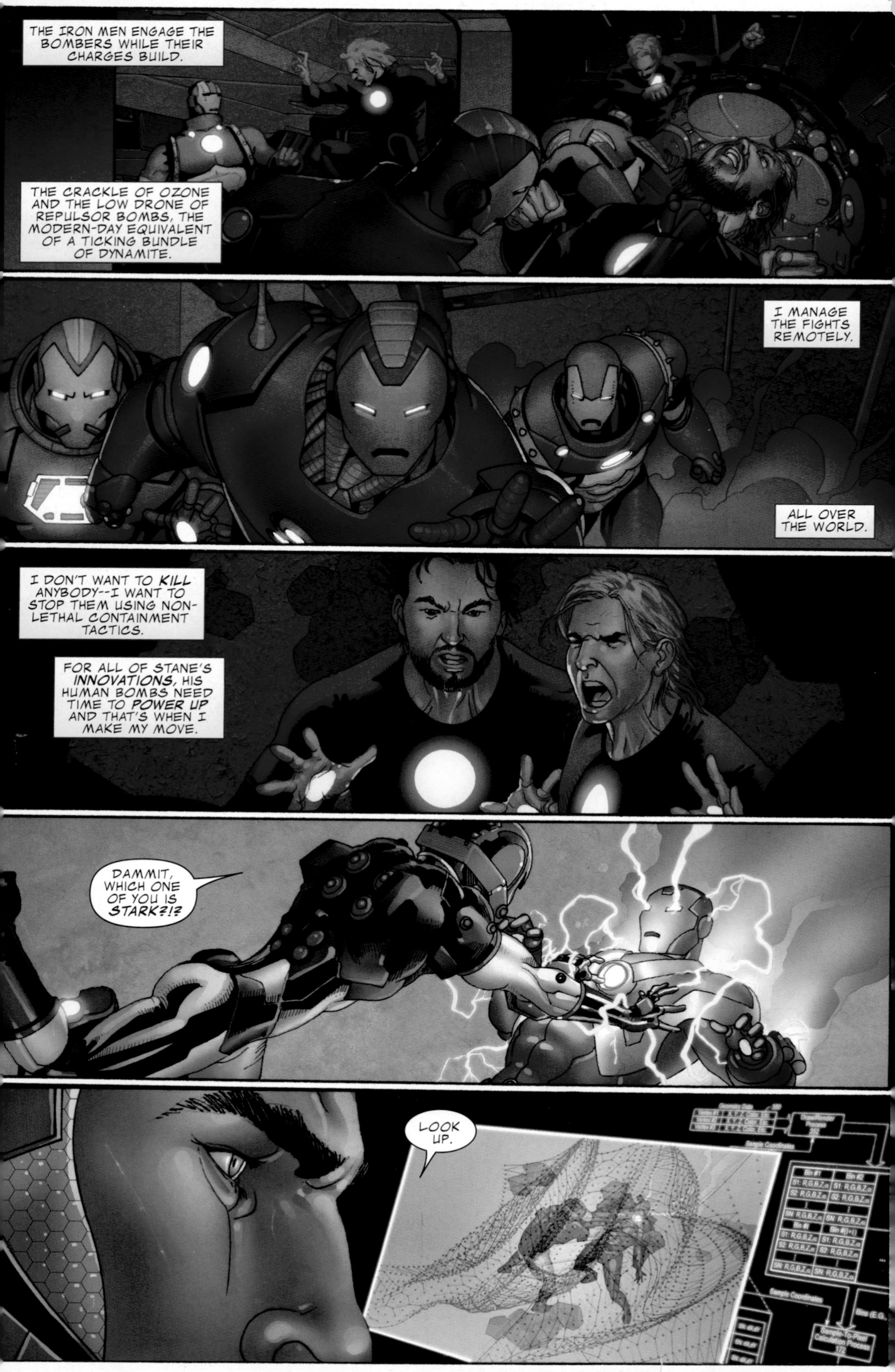
THE IRON MEN ENGAGE THE BOMBERS WHILE THEIR CHARGES BUILD.
THE CRACKLE OF OZONE AND THE LOW DRONE OF REPULSOR BOMBS, THE MODERN-DAY EQUIVALENT OF A TICKING BUNDLE OF DYNAMITE.
I MANAGE THE FIGHTS REMOTELY.
ALL OVER THE WORLD.
I DON'T WANT TO KILL ANYBODY--I WANT TO STOP THEM USING NON-LETHAL CONTAINMENT TACTICS.
FOR ALL OF STANE'S INNOVATIONS, HIS HUMAN BOMBS NEED TIME TO POWER UP AND THAT'S WHEN I MAKE MY MOVE.
DAMMIT, WHICH ONE OF YOU IS STARK?!?
LOOK UP.

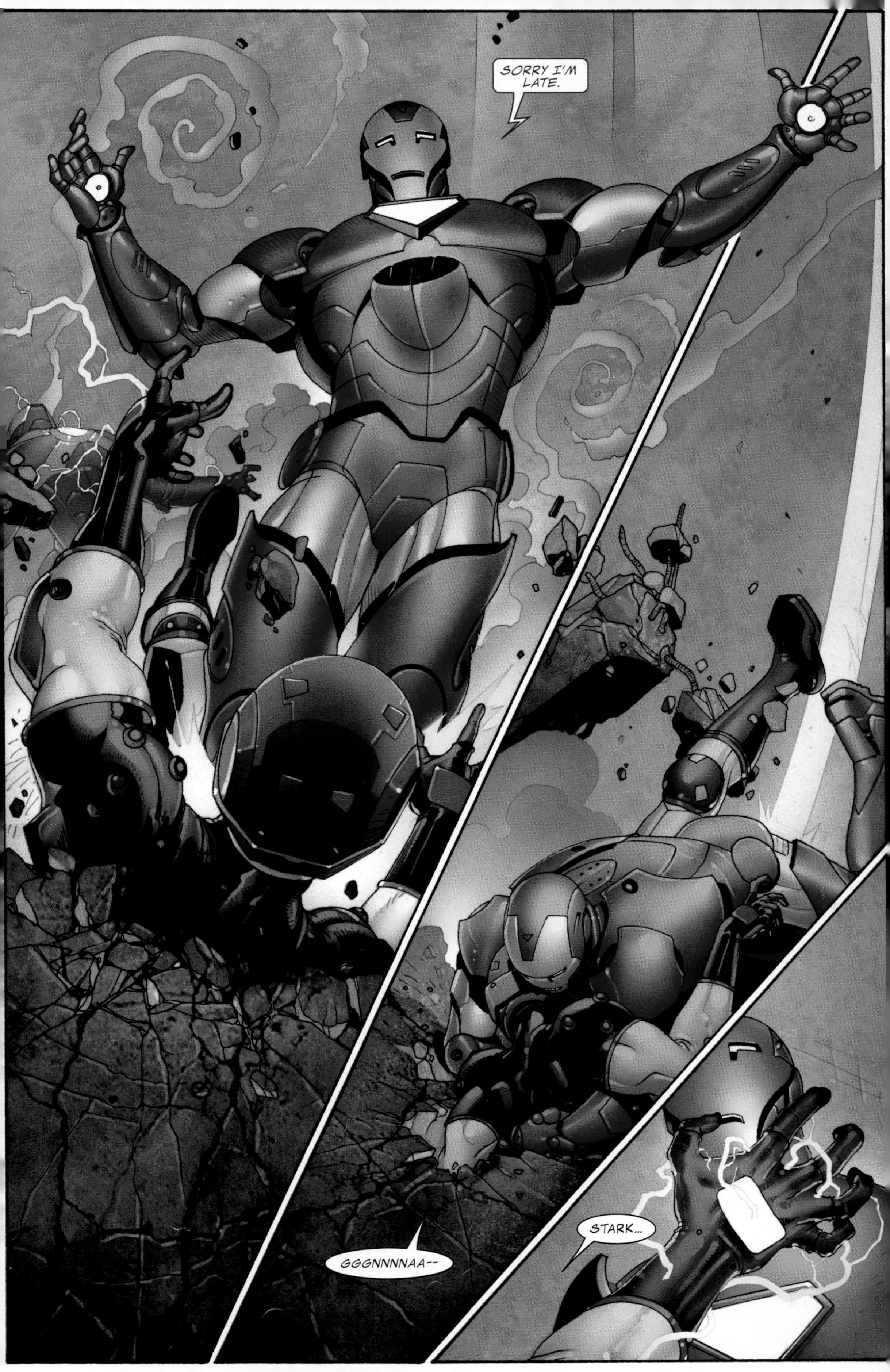
SORRY I'M LATE.
GGGNNNNAA--
STARK...

HOLD STILL.

I'M TRYING TO ARREST YOU.

ARREST ME? ;KAFF;

YOU'RE TOO LATE TO EVEN KILL ME, OLD MAN.

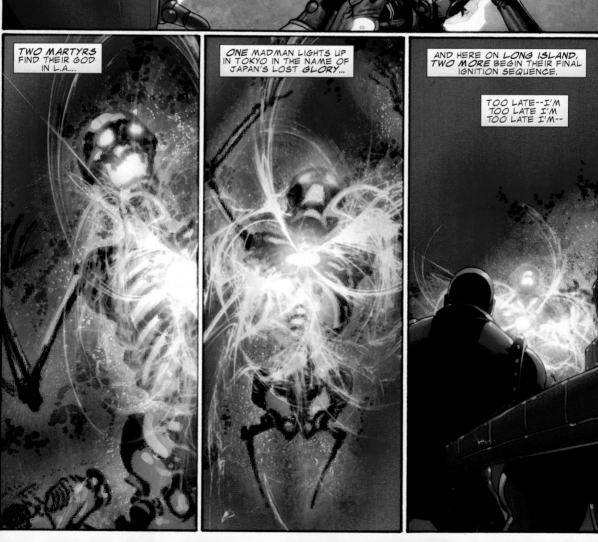

TWO MARTYRS FIND THEIR GOD IN L.A....

ONE MADMAN LIGHTS UP IN TOKYO IN THE NAME OF JAPAN'S LOST GLORY...

AND HERE ON LONG ISLAND, TWO MORE BEGIN THEIR FINAL IGNITION SEQUENCE.

TOO LATE--I'M TOO LATE I'M TOO LATE I'M--

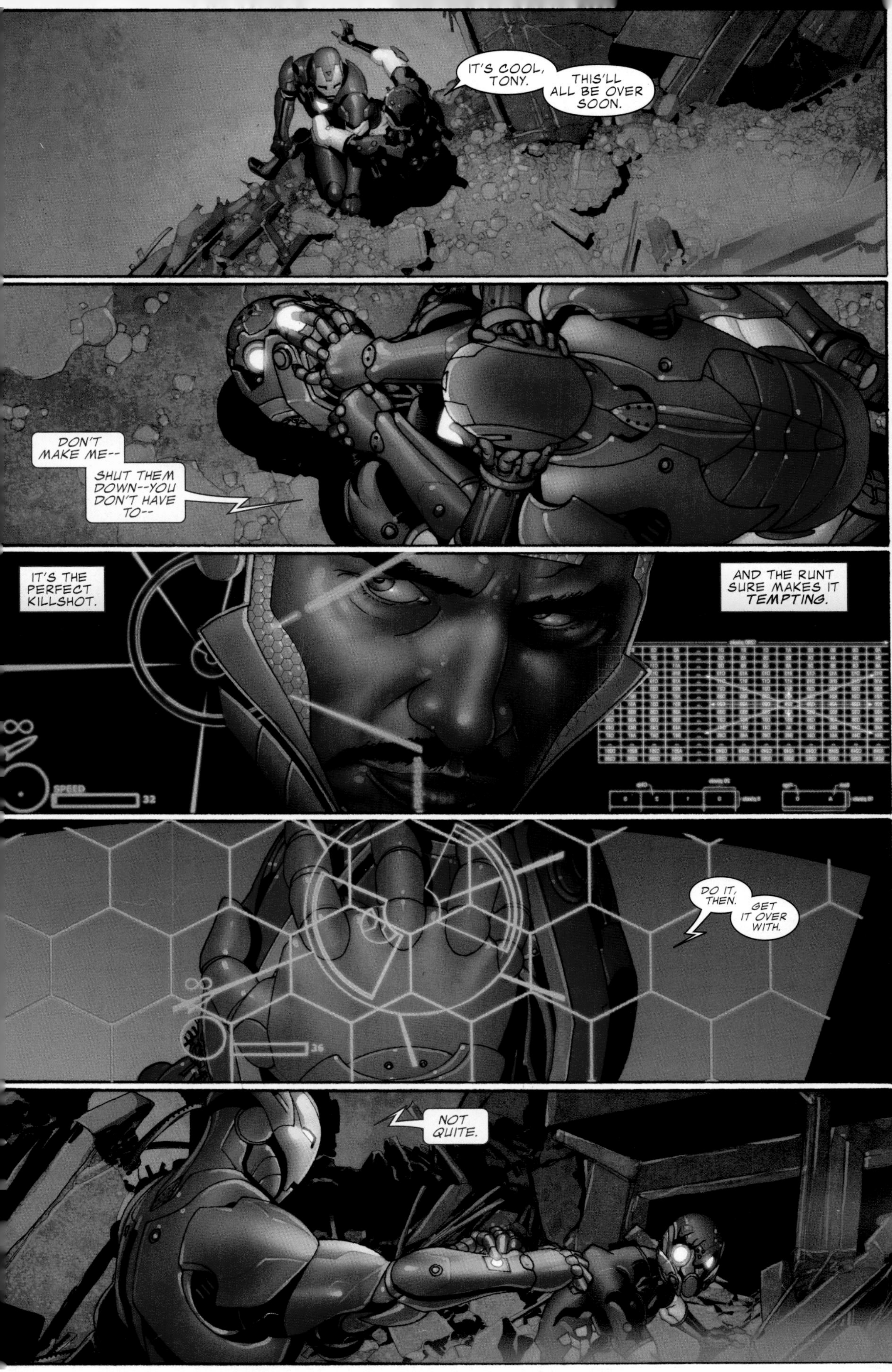
IT'S COOL, TONY.
THIS'LL ALL BE OVER SOON.
DON'T MAKE ME--
SHUT THEM DOWN--YOU DON'T HAVE TO--
IT'S THE PERFECT KILLSHOT.
AND THE RUNT SURE MAKES IT TEMPTING.
SPEED
32
DO IT, THEN.
GET IT OVER WITH.
36
NOT QUITE.

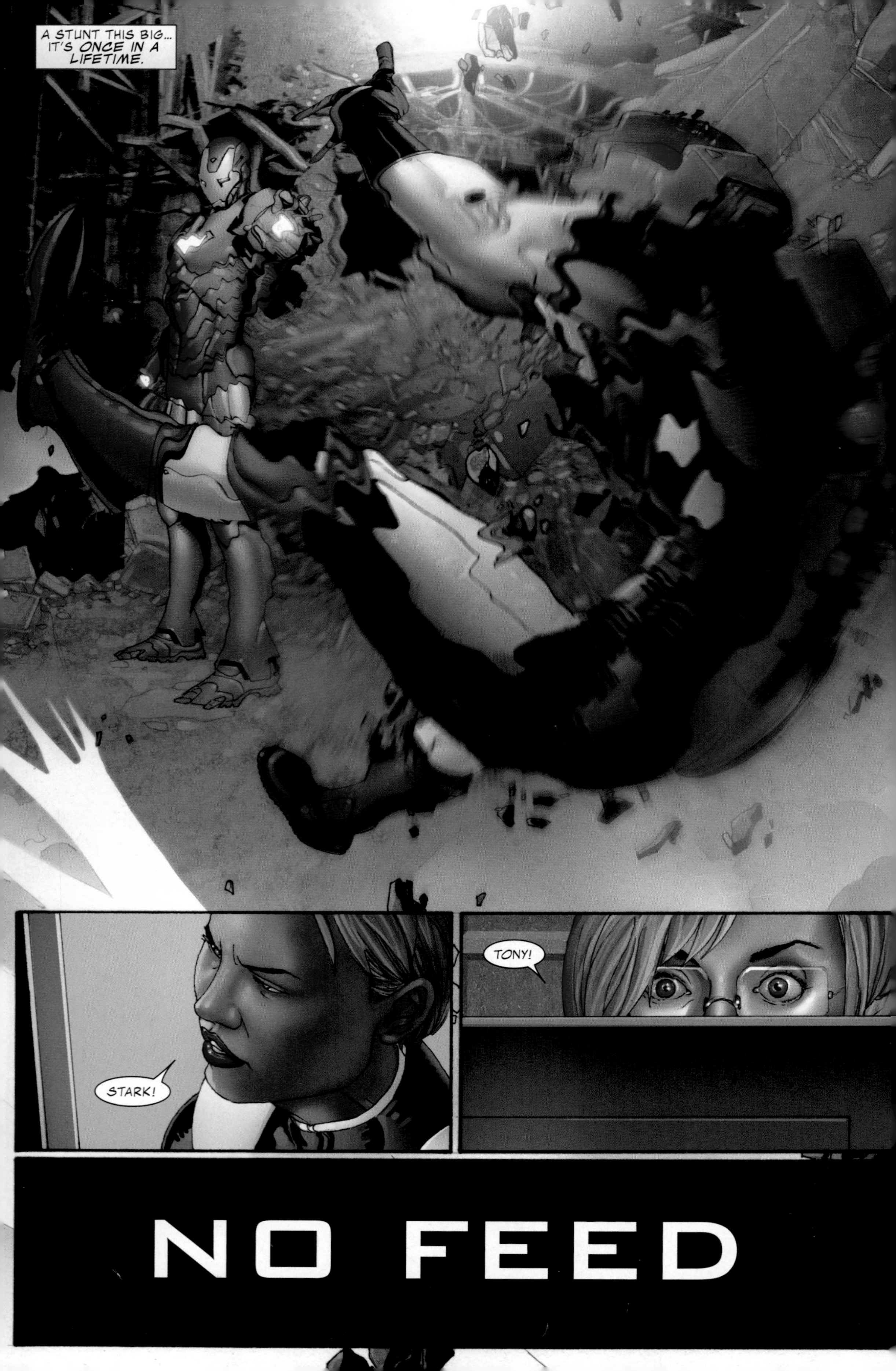
A STUNT THIS BIG... IT'S ONCE IN A LIFETIME.
STARK!
TONY!
NO FEED

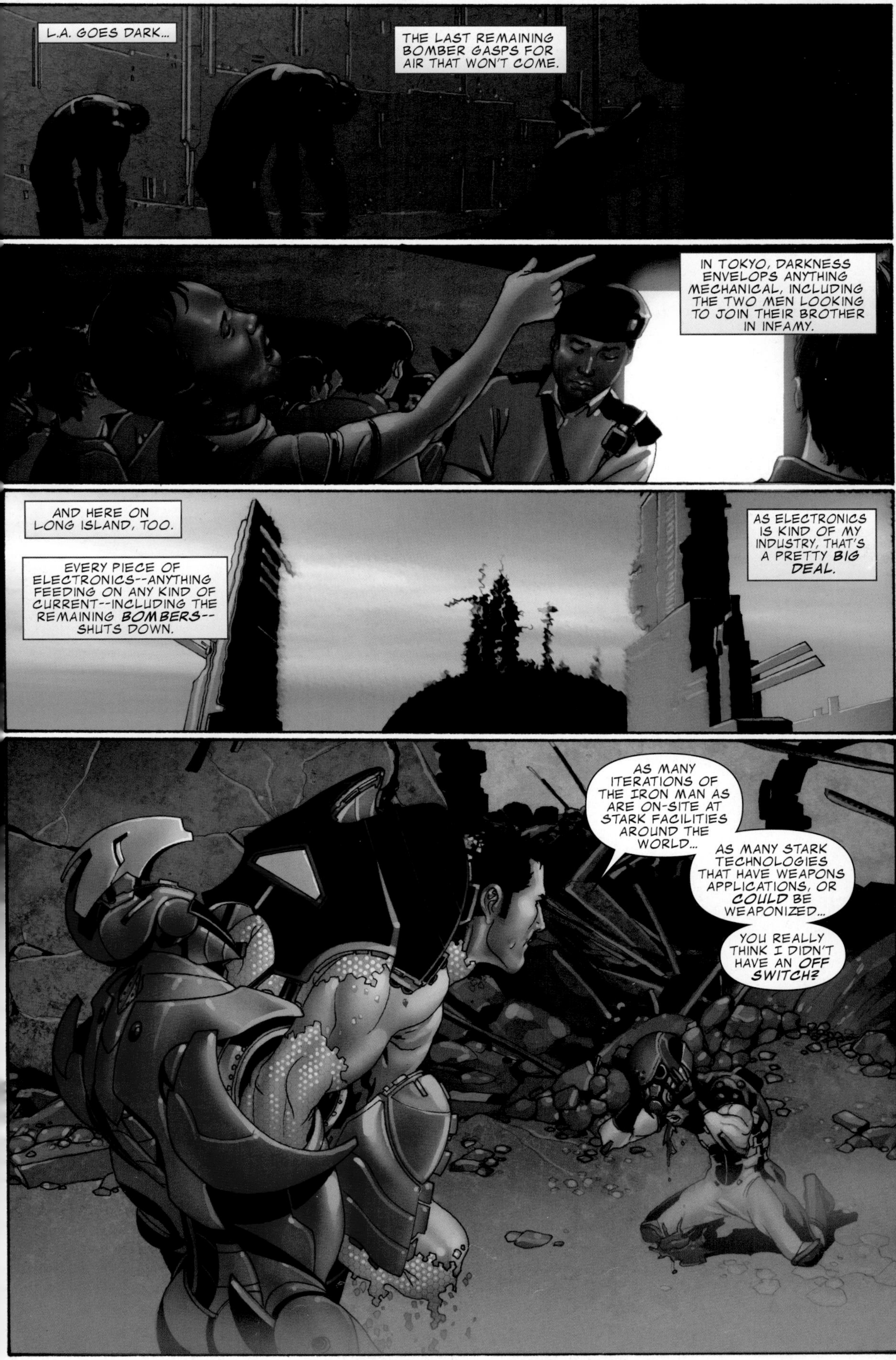
L.A. GOES DARK...
THE LAST REMAINING BOMBER GASPS FOR AIR THAT WON'T COME.
IN TOKYO, DARKNESS ENVELOPS ANYTHING MECHANICAL, INCLUDING THE TWO MEN LOOKING TO JOIN THEIR BROTHER IN INFAMY.
AND HERE ON LONG ISLAND, TOO.
EVERY PIECE OF ELECTRONICS--ANYTHING FEEDING ON ANY KIND OF CURRENT--INCLUDING THE REMAINING BOMBERS--SHUTS DOWN.
AS ELECTRONICS IS KIND OF MY INDUSTRY, THAT'S A PRETTY BIG DEAL.
AS MANY ITERATIONS OF THE IRON MAN AS ARE ON-SITE AT STARK FACILITIES AROUND THE WORLD...
AS MANY STARK TECHNOLOGIES THAT HAVE WEAPONS APPLICATIONS, OR COULD BE WEAPONIZED...
YOU REALLY THINK I DIDN'T HAVE AN OFF SWITCH?

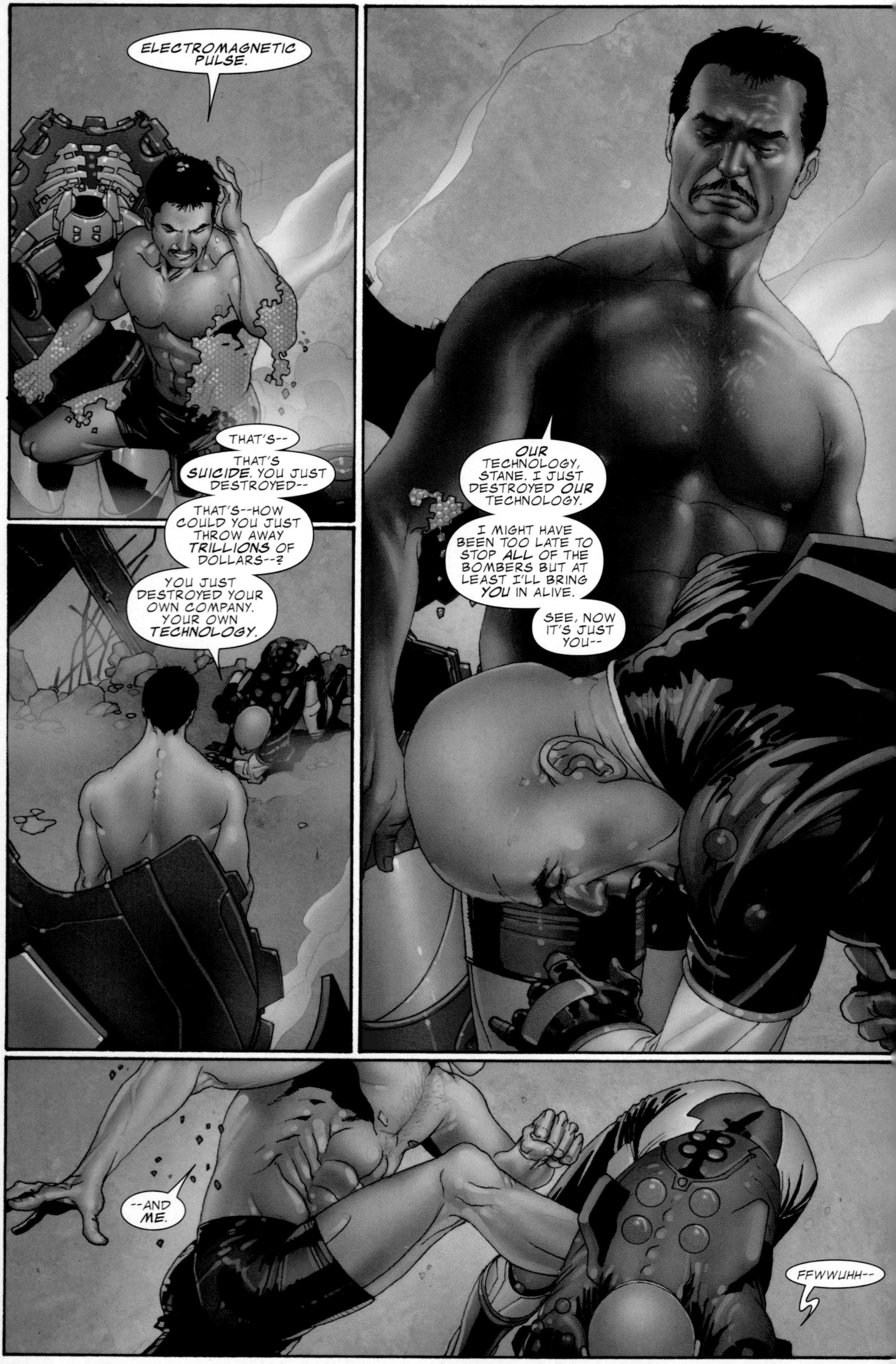
ELECTROMAGNETIC PULSE.
THAT'S--
THAT'S SUICIDE. YOU JUST DESTROYED--
THAT'S--HOW COULD YOU JUST THROW AWAY TRILLIONS OF DOLLARS--?
YOU JUST DESTROYED YOUR OWN COMPANY. YOUR OWN TECHNOLOGY.
OUR TECHNOLOGY, STANE. I JUST DESTROYED OUR TECHNOLOGY.
I MIGHT HAVE BEEN TOO LATE TO STOP ALL OF THE BOMBERS BUT AT LEAST I'LL BRING YOU IN ALIVE.
SEE, NOW IT'S JUST YOU--
--AND ME.
FFWWUHH--

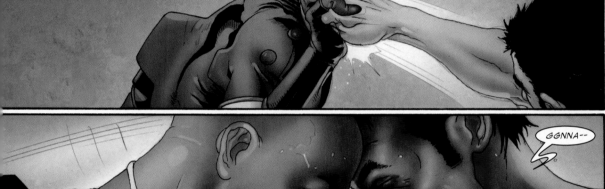

DON'T NEED-- UNNH--! --TECH TO BEAT YOU DOWN, OLD MAN.

GGNNA--

OLD MAN. OLD MAN, OLD MAN.

I'M GONNA BE THE DEATH OF YOU.

NOT YET.

WUFFF--

KRAK

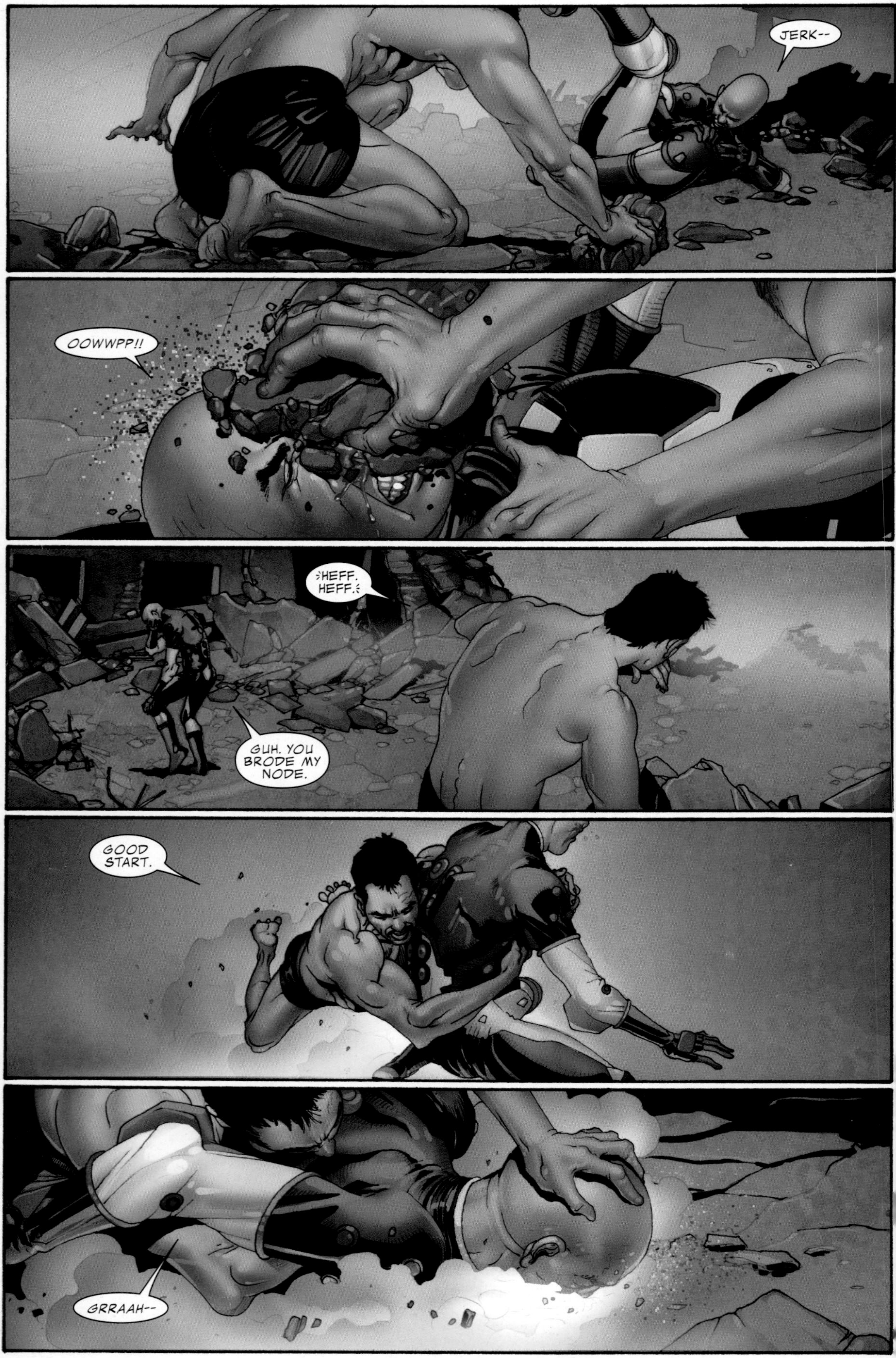
JERK--
OOWWPP!!
HEFF. HEFF.
GUH. YOU BRODE MY NODE.
GOOD START.
GRRAAH--

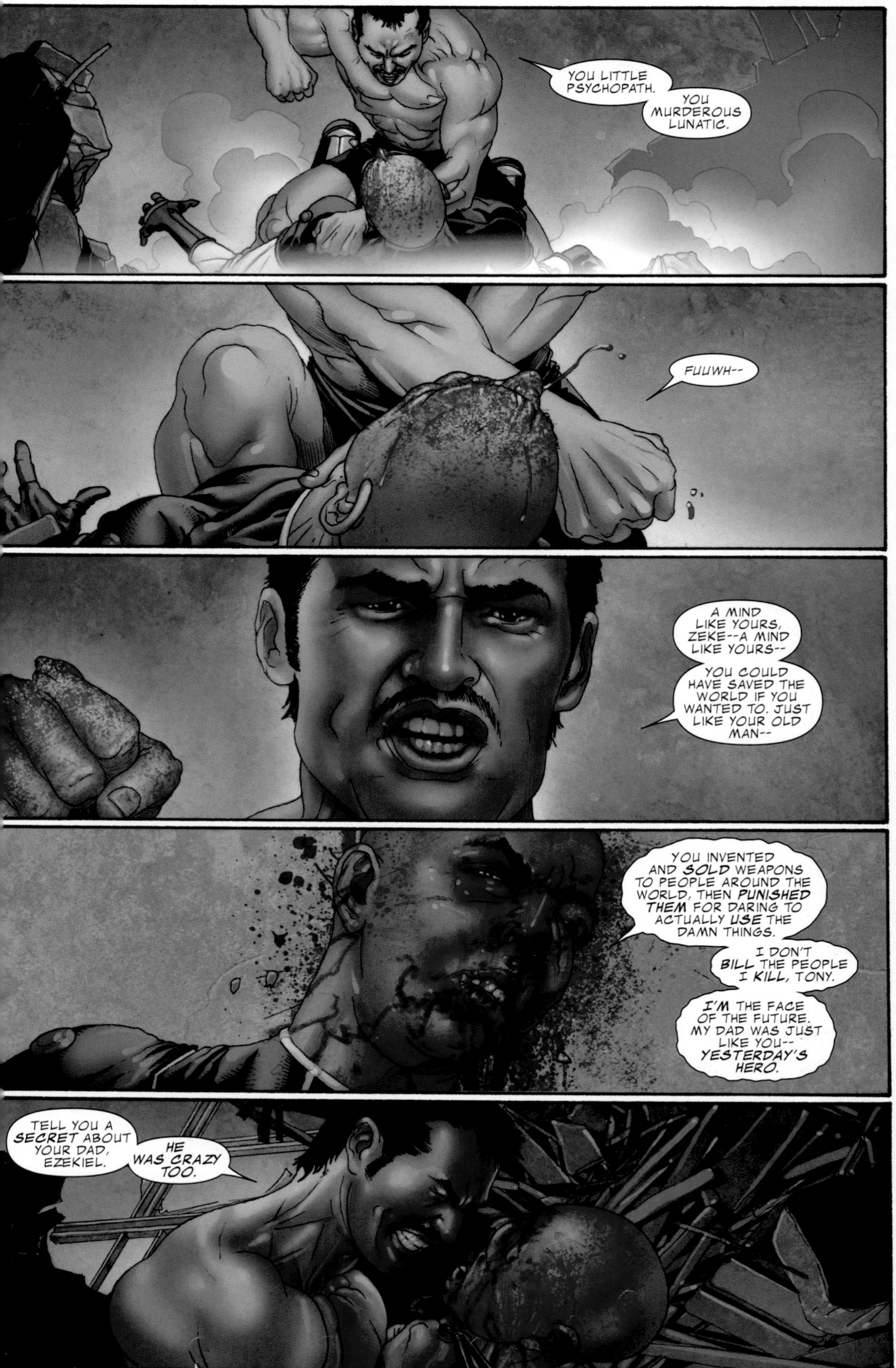
YOU LITTLE PSYCHOPATH.
YOU MURDEROUS LUNATIC.
FUUWH--
A MIND LIKE YOURS, ZEKE--A MIND LIKE YOURS--
YOU COULD HAVE SAVED THE WORLD IF YOU WANTED TO. JUST LIKE YOUR OLD MAN--
YOU INVENTED AND SOLD WEAPONS TO PEOPLE AROUND THE WORLD, THEN PUNISHED THEM FOR DARING TO ACTUALLY USE THE DAMN THINGS.
I DON'T BILL THE PEOPLE I KILL, TONY.
I'M THE FACE OF THE FUTURE. MY DAD WAS JUST LIKE YOU-- YESTERDAY'S HERO.
TELL YOU A SECRET ABOUT YOUR DAD, EZEKIEL.
HE WAS CRAZY TOO.

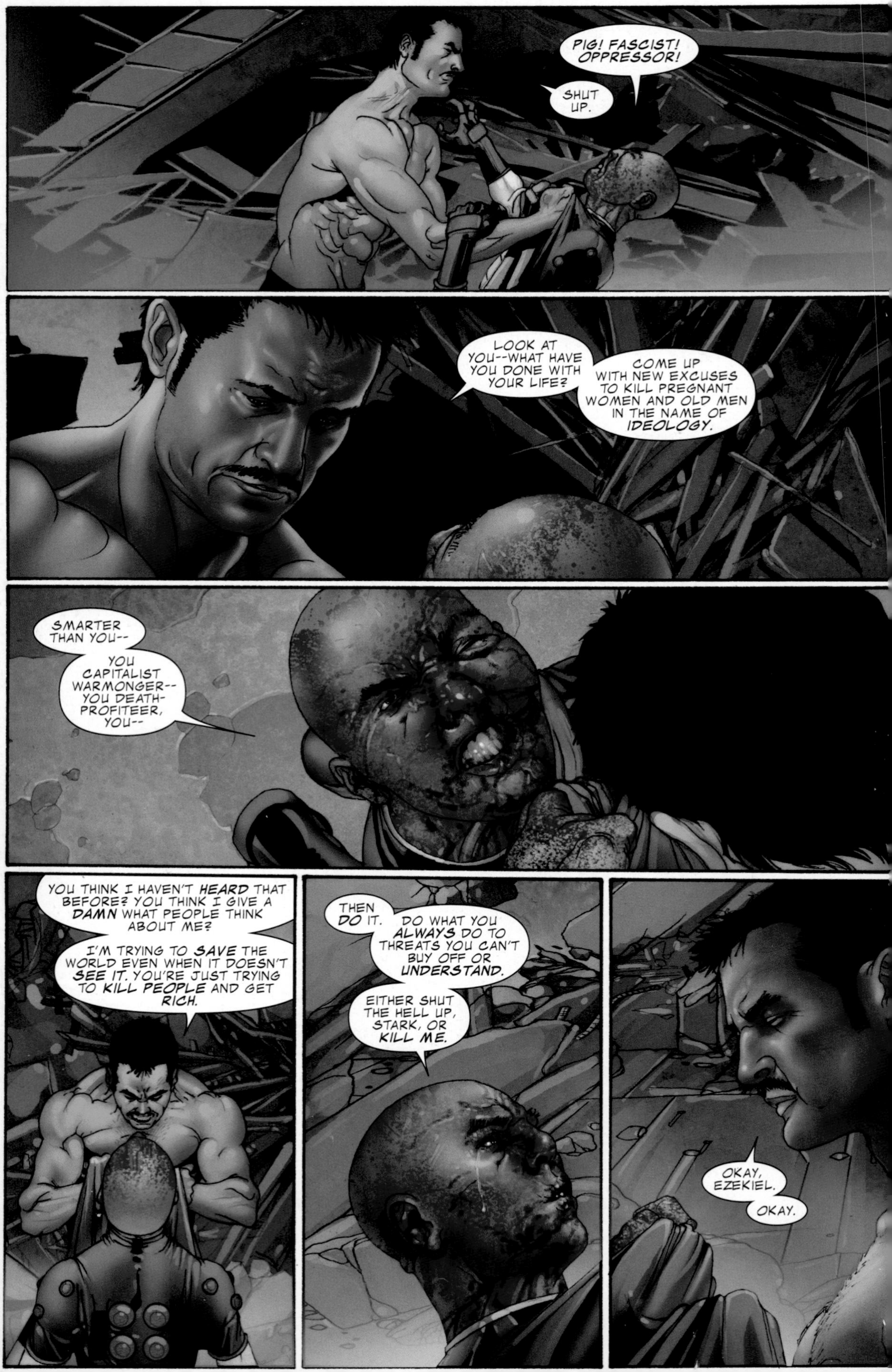
PIG! FASCIST! OPPRESSOR!
SHUT UP.
LOOK AT YOU--WHAT HAVE YOU DONE WITH YOUR LIFE?
COME UP WITH NEW EXCUSES TO KILL PREGNANT WOMEN AND OLD MEN IN THE NAME OF IDEOLOGY.
SMARTER THAN YOU--
YOU CAPITALIST WARMONGER-- YOU DEATH-PROFITEER, YOU--
YOU THINK I HAVEN'T HEARD THAT BEFORE? YOU THINK I GIVE A DAMN WHAT PEOPLE THINK ABOUT ME?
I'M TRYING TO SAVE THE WORLD EVEN WHEN IT DOESN'T SEE IT. YOU'RE JUST TRYING TO KILL PEOPLE AND GET RICH.
THEN DO IT.
DO WHAT YOU ALWAYS DO TO THREATS YOU CAN'T BUY OFF OR UNDERSTAND.
EITHER SHUT THE HELL UP, STARK, OR KILL ME.
OKAY, EZEKIEL.
OKAY.

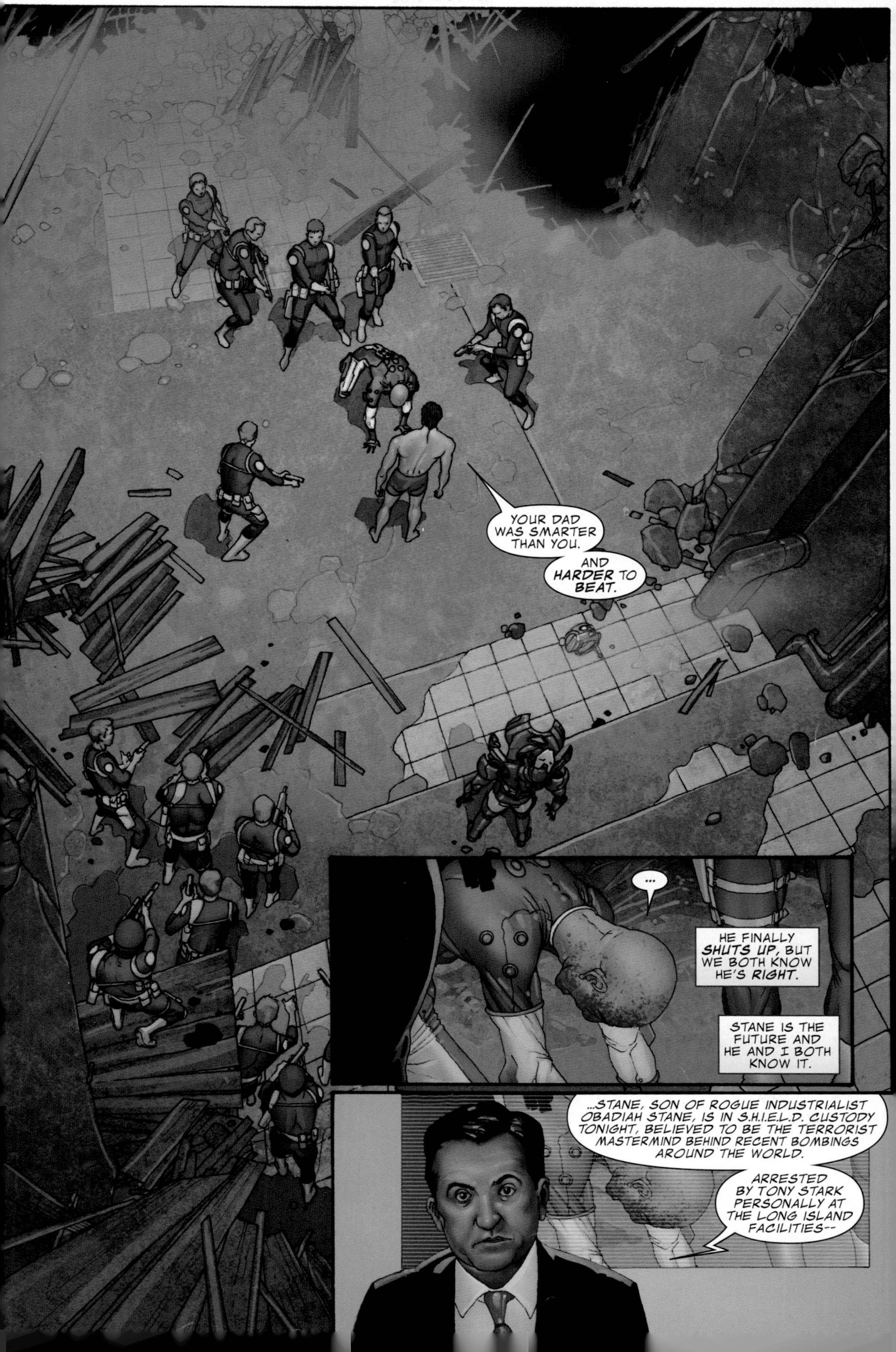
YOUR DAD WAS SMARTER THAN YOU.
AND HARDER TO BEAT.
...
HE FINALLY SHUTS UP, BUT WE BOTH KNOW HE'S RIGHT.
STANE IS THE FUTURE AND HE AND I BOTH KNOW IT.
...STANE, SON OF ROGUE INDUSTRIALIST OBADIAH STANE, IS IN S.H.I.E.L.D. CUSTODY TONIGHT, BELIEVED TO BE THE TERRORIST MASTERMIND BEHIND RECENT BOMBINGS AROUND THE WORLD.
ARRESTED BY TONY STARK PERSONALLY AT THE LONG ISLAND FACILITIES--

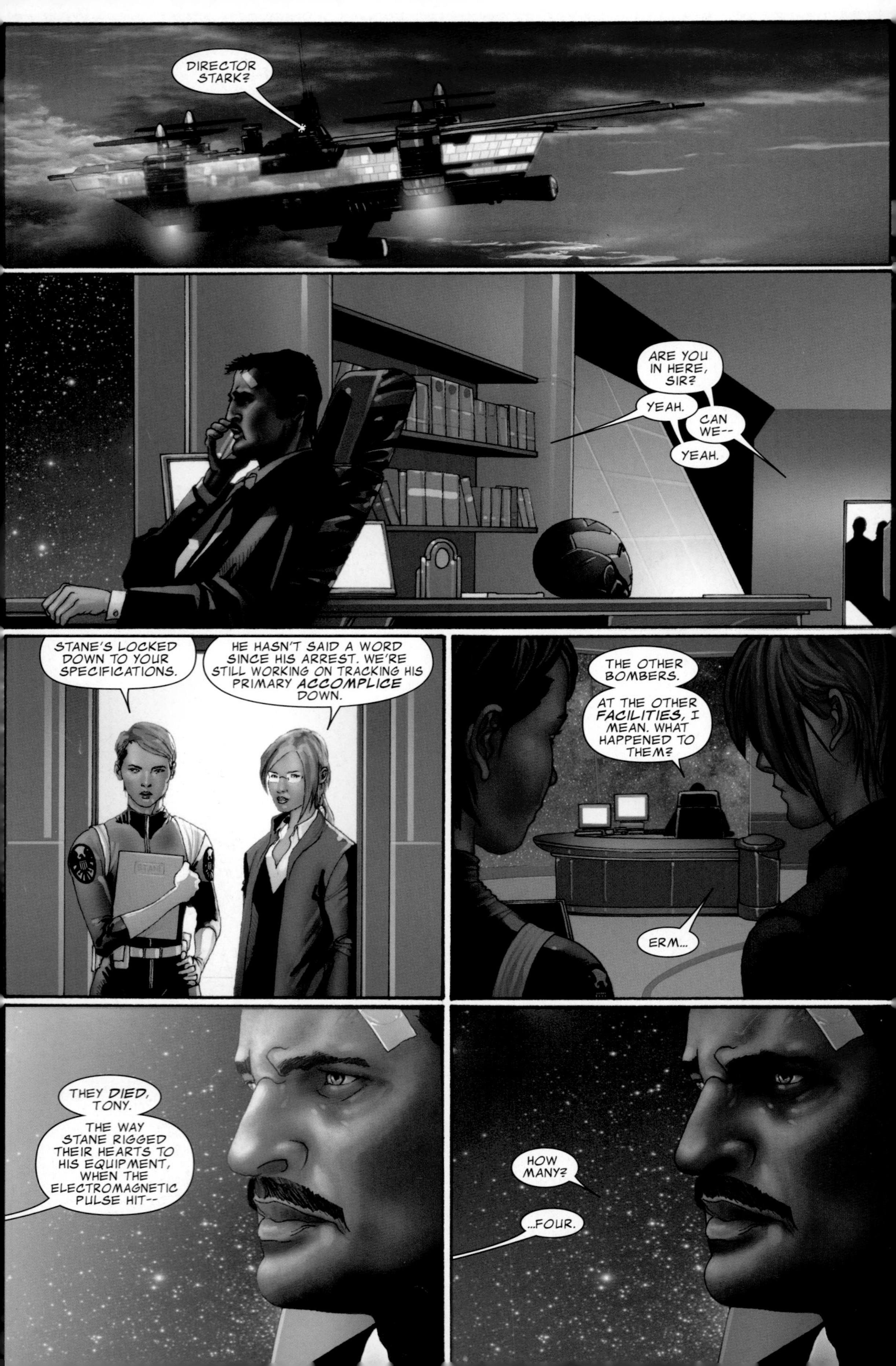

DIRECTOR STARK?
ARE YOU IN HERE, SIR?
YEAH.
CAN WE--
YEAH.
STANE'S LOCKED DOWN TO YOUR SPECIFICATIONS.
HE HASN'T SAID A WORD SINCE HIS ARREST. WE'RE STILL WORKING ON TRACKING HIS PRIMARY ACCOMPLICE DOWN.
THE OTHER BOMBERS.
AT THE OTHER FACILITIES, I MEAN. WHAT HAPPENED TO THEM?
ERM...
THEY DIED, TONY.
THE WAY STANE RIGGED THEIR HEARTS TO HIS EQUIPMENT, WHEN THE ELECTROMAGNETIC PULSE HIT--
HOW MANY?
...FOUR.

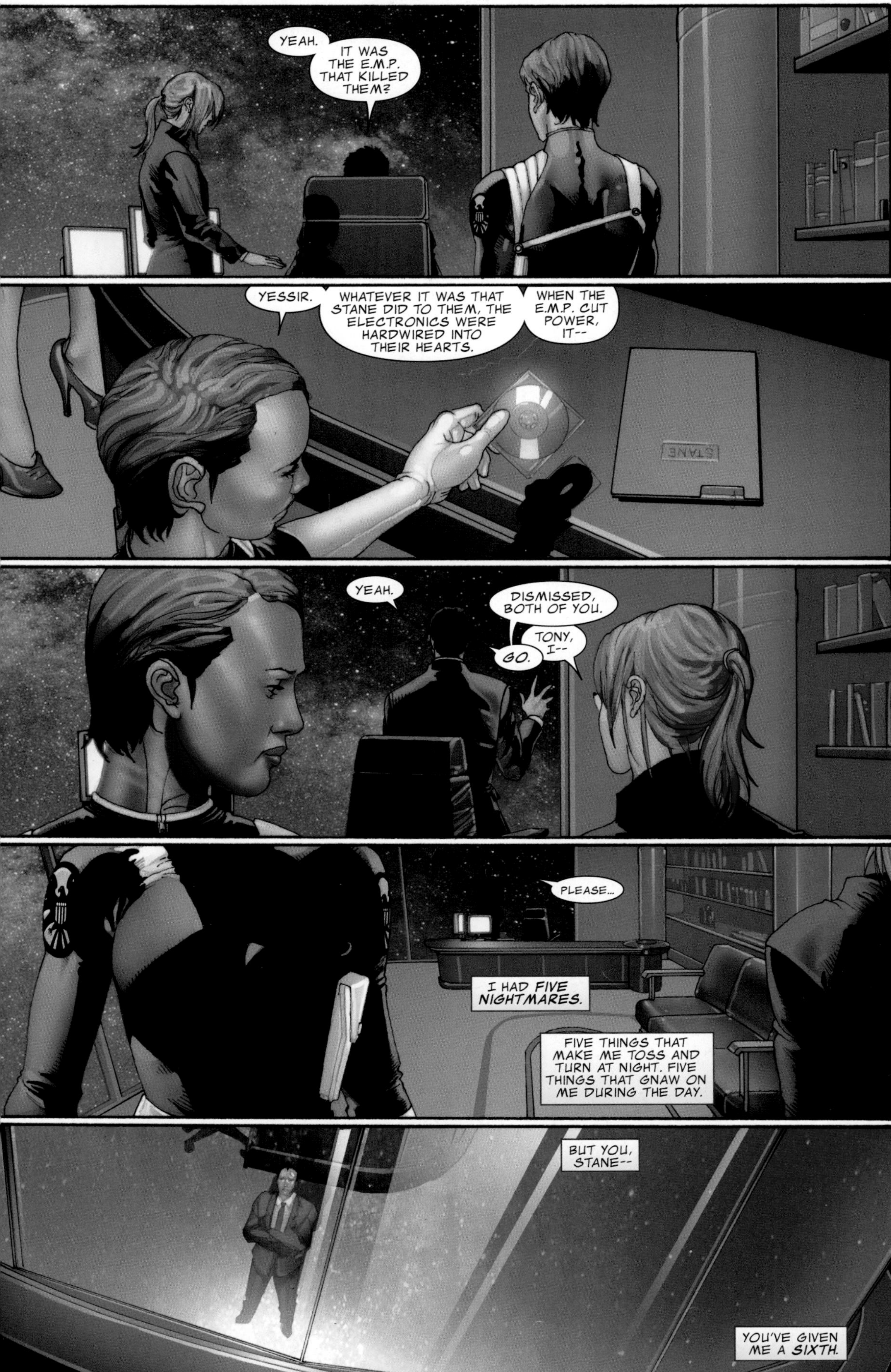

YEAH.
IT WAS THE E.M.P. THAT KILLED THEM?
YESSIR.
WHATEVER IT WAS THAT STANE DID TO THEM, THE ELECTRONICS WERE HARDWIRED INTO THEIR HEARTS.
WHEN THE E.M.P. CUT POWER, IT--
STANE
YEAH.
DISMISSED, BOTH OF YOU.
TONY, I--
GO.
PLEASE...
I HAD FIVE NIGHTMARES.
FIVE THINGS THAT MAKE ME TOSS AND TURN AT NIGHT. FIVE THINGS THAT GNAW ON ME DURING THE DAY.
BUT YOU, STANE--
YOU'VE GIVEN ME A SIXTH.

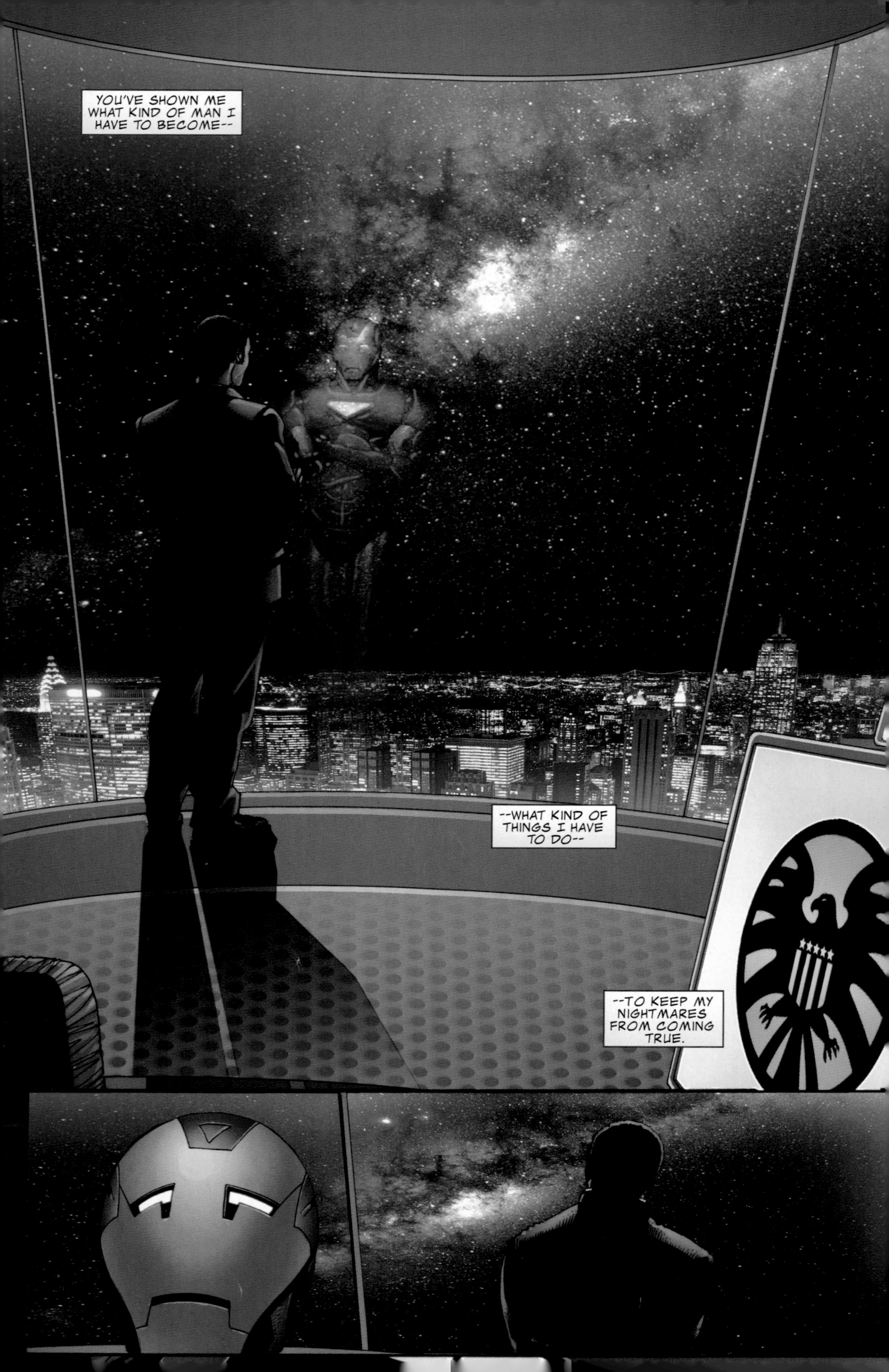
YOU'VE SHOWN ME WHAT KIND OF MAN I HAVE TO BECOME--
--WHAT KIND OF THINGS I HAVE TO DO--
--TO KEEP MY NIGHTMARES FROM COMING TRUE.

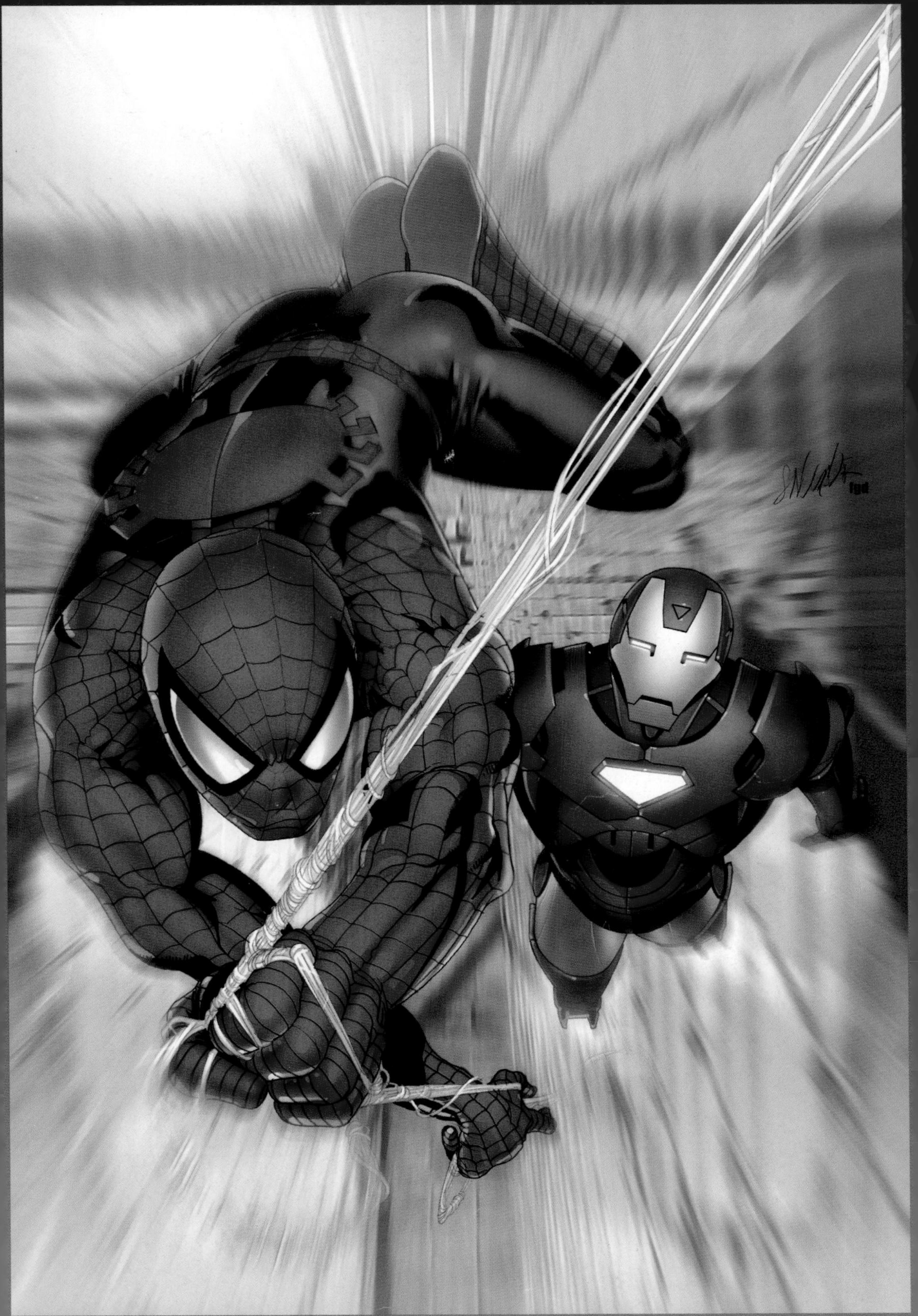

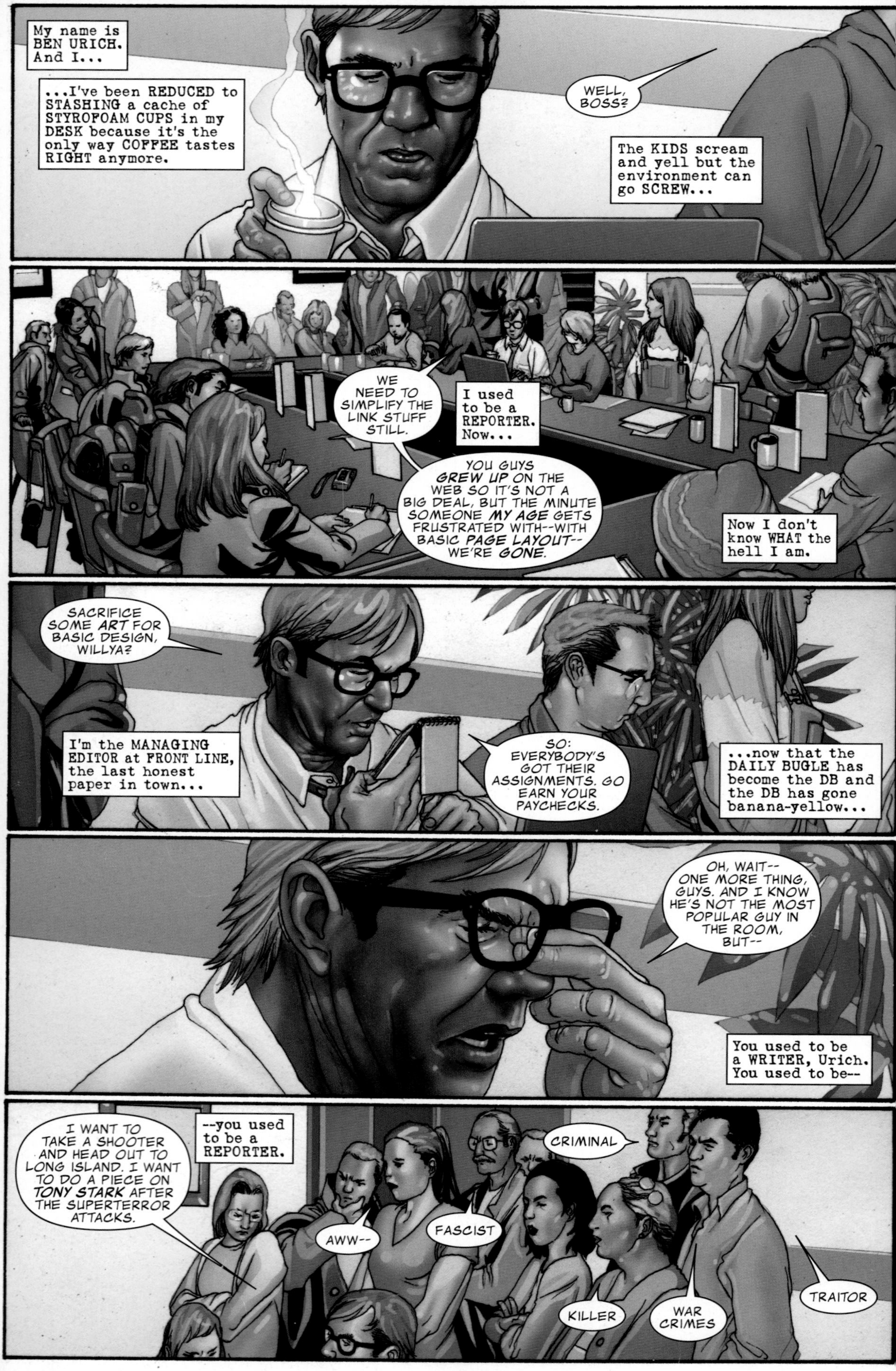
My name is BEN URICH. And I...
...I've been REDUCED to STASHING a cache of STYROFOAM CUPS in my DESK because it's the only way COFFEE tastes RIGHT anymore.
WELL, BOSS?
The KIDS scream and yell but the environment can go SCREW...
WE NEED TO SIMPLIFY THE LINK STUFF STILL.
I used to be a REPORTER. Now...
YOU GUYS GROW UP ON THE WEB SO IT'S NOT A BIG DEAL, BUT THE MINUTE SOMEONE MY AGE GETS FRUSTRATED WITH--WITH BASIC PAGE LAYOUT--WE'RE GONE.
Now I don't know WHAT the hell I am.
SACRIFICE SOME ART FOR BASIC DESIGN, WILLYA?
I'm the MANAGING EDITOR at FRONT LINE, the last honest paper in town...
SO: EVERYBODY'S GOT THEIR ASSIGNMENTS. GO EARN YOUR PAYCHECKS.
...now that the DAILY BUGLE has become the DB and the DB has gone banana-yellow...
OH, WAIT--ONE MORE THING, GUYS. AND I KNOW HE'S NOT THE MOST POPULAR GUY IN THE ROOM, BUT--
You used to be a WRITER, Urich. You used to be--
I WANT TO TAKE A SHOOTER AND HEAD OUT TO LONG ISLAND. I WANT TO DO A PIECE ON TONY STARK AFTER THE SUPERTERROR ATTACKS.
--you used to be a REPORTER.
CRIMINAL
AWW--
FASCIST
KILLER
WAR CRIMES
TRAITOR

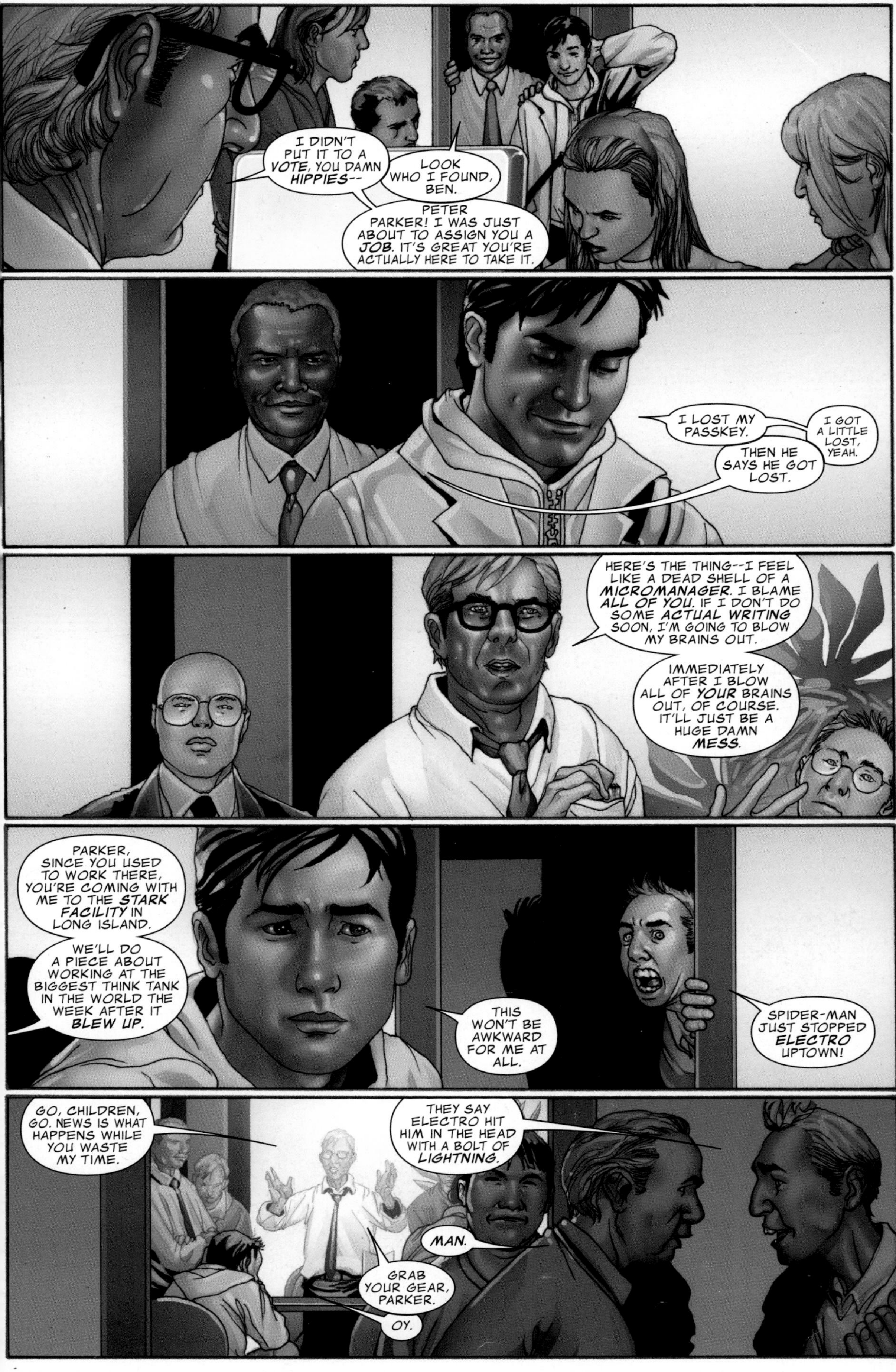
I DIDN'T PUT IT TO A VOTE, YOU DAMN HIPPIES--
LOOK WHO I FOUND, BEN.
PETER PARKER! I WAS JUST ABOUT TO ASSIGN YOU A JOB. IT'S GREAT YOU'RE ACTUALLY HERE TO TAKE IT.
I LOST MY PASSKEY.
THEN HE SAYS HE GOT LOST.
I GOT A LITTLE LOST, YEAH.
HERE'S THE THING--I FEEL LIKE A DEAD SHELL OF A MICROMANAGER. I BLAME ALL OF YOU. IF I DON'T DO SOME ACTUAL WRITING SOON, I'M GOING TO BLOW MY BRAINS OUT.
IMMEDIATELY AFTER I BLOW ALL OF YOUR BRAINS OUT, OF COURSE. IT'LL JUST BE A HUGE DAMN MESS.
PARKER, SINCE YOU USED TO WORK THERE, YOU'RE COMING WITH ME TO THE STARK FACILITY IN LONG ISLAND.
WE'LL DO A PIECE ABOUT WORKING AT THE BIGGEST THINK TANK IN THE WORLD THE WEEK AFTER IT BLEW UP.
THIS WON'T BE AWKWARD FOR ME AT ALL.
SPIDER-MAN JUST STOPPED ELECTRO UPTOWN!
GO, CHILDREN, GO. NEWS IS WHAT HAPPENS WHILE YOU WASTE MY TIME.
THEY SAY ELECTRO HIT HIM IN THE HEAD WITH A BOLT OF LIGHTNING.
MAN.
GRAB YOUR GEAR, PARKER.
OY.

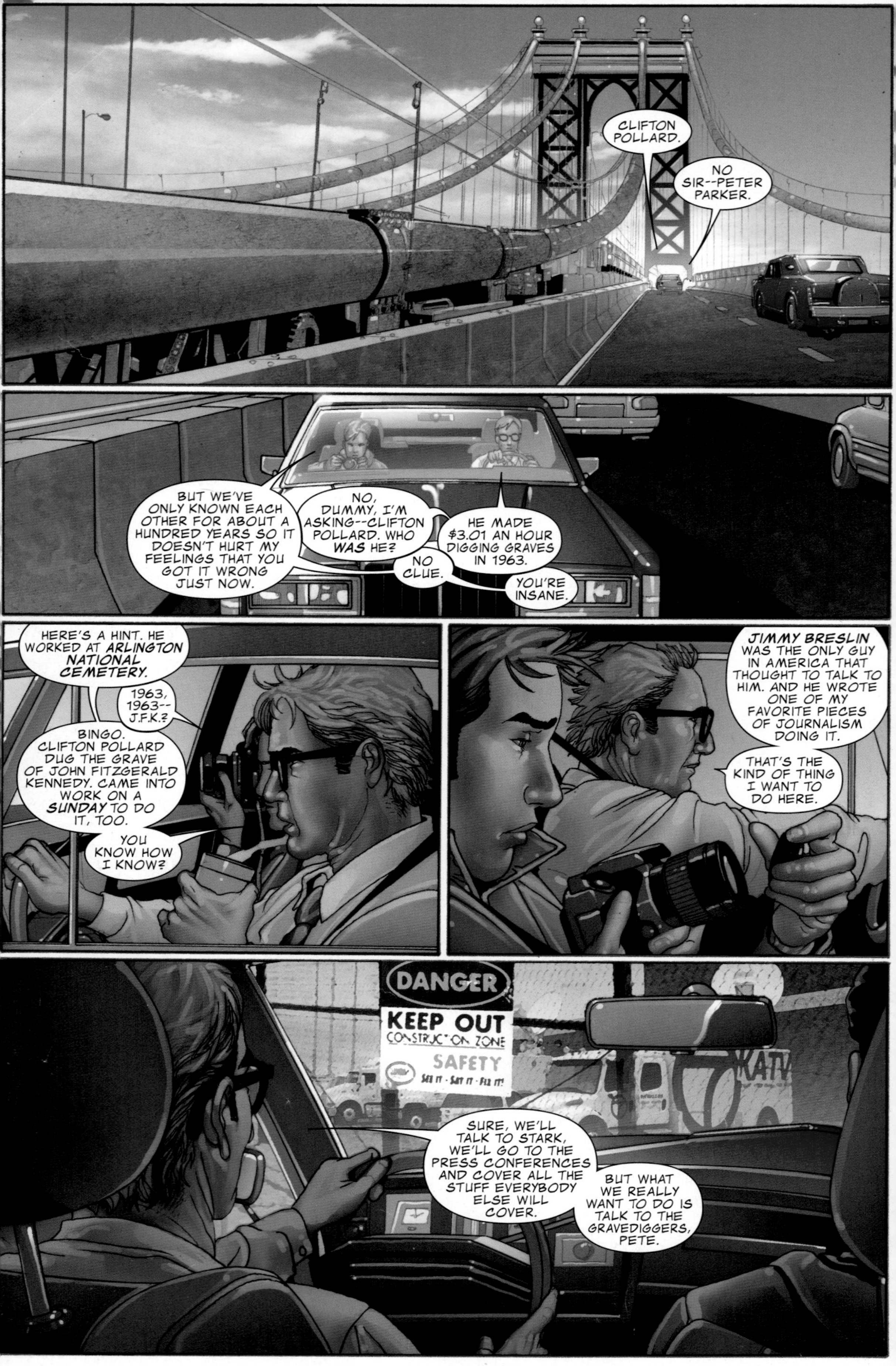
CLIFTON POLLARD.
NO SIR--PETER PARKER.
BUT WE'VE ONLY KNOWN EACH OTHER FOR ABOUT A HUNDRED YEARS SO IT DOESN'T HURT MY FEELINGS THAT YOU GOT IT WRONG JUST NOW.
NO, DUMMY, I'M ASKING--CLIFTON POLLARD. WHO WAS HE?
NO CLUE.
HE MADE $3.01 AN HOUR DIGGING GRAVES IN 1963.
YOU'RE INSANE.
HERE'S A HINT. HE WORKED AT ARLINGTON NATIONAL CEMETERY.
1963, 1963--J.F.K.?
BINGO. CLIFTON POLLARD DUG THE GRAVE OF JOHN FITZGERALD KENNEDY. CAME INTO WORK ON A SUNDAY TO DO IT, TOO.
YOU KNOW HOW I KNOW?
JIMMY BRESLIN WAS THE ONLY GUY IN AMERICA THAT THOUGHT TO TALK TO HIM. AND HE WROTE ONE OF MY FAVORITE PIECES OF JOURNALISM DOING IT.
THAT'S THE KIND OF THING I WANT TO DO HERE.
DANGER
KEEP OUT
CONSTRUCTION ZONE
SAFETY
SURE, WE'LL TALK TO STARK, WE'LL GO TO THE PRESS CONFERENCES AND COVER ALL THE STUFF EVERYBODY ELSE WILL COVER.
BUT WHAT WE REALLY WANT TO DO IS TALK TO THE GRAVEDIGGERS, PETE.

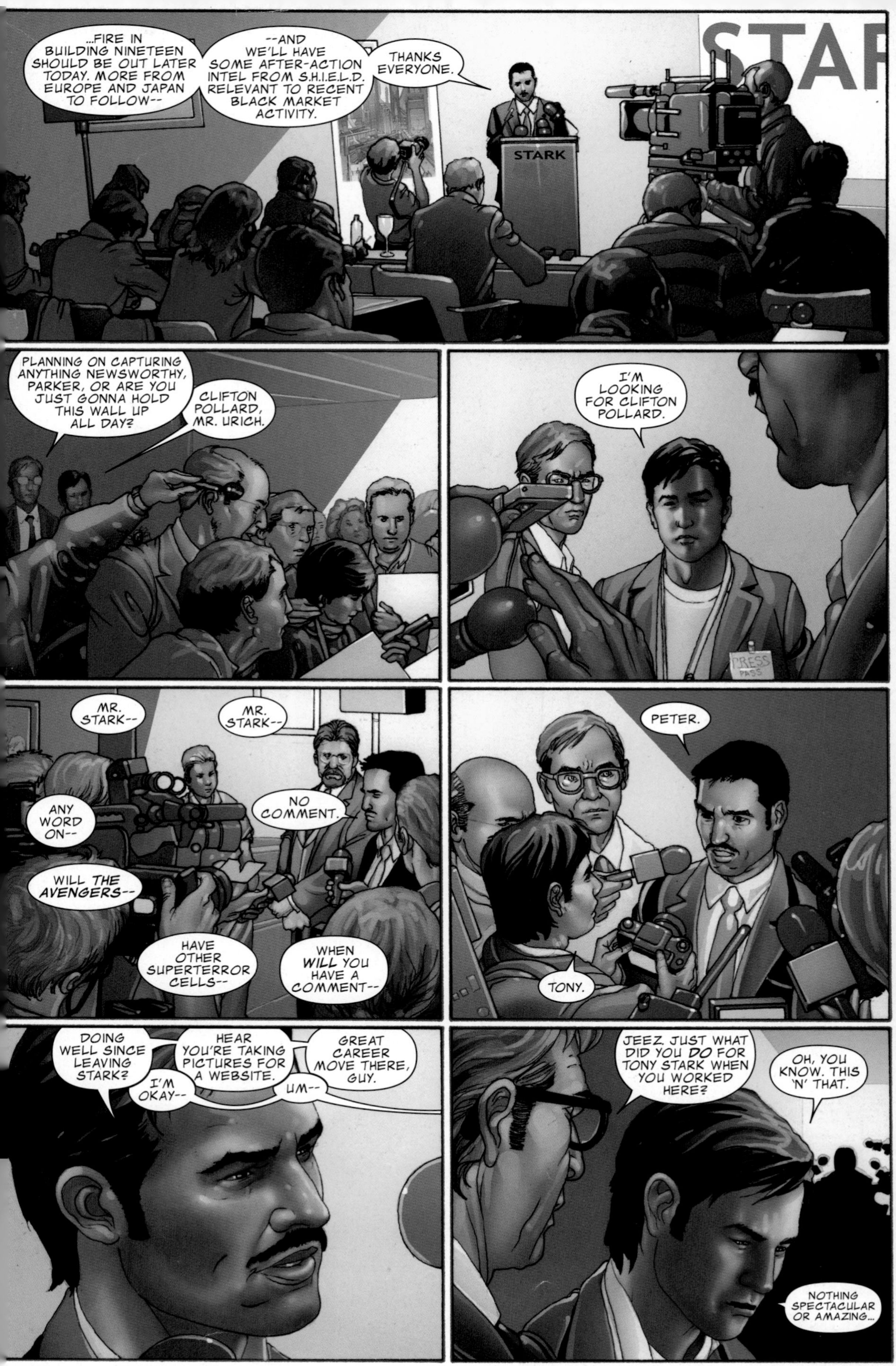

STARK
...FIRE IN BUILDING NINETEEN SHOULD BE OUT LATER TODAY. MORE FROM EUROPE AND JAPAN TO FOLLOW--
--AND WE'LL HAVE SOME AFTER-ACTION INTEL FROM S.H.I.E.L.D. RELEVANT TO RECENT BLACK MARKET ACTIVITY.
THANKS EVERYONE.
STARK
PLANNING ON CAPTURING ANYTHING NEWSWORTHY, PARKER, OR ARE YOU JUST GONNA HOLD THIS WALL UP ALL DAY?
CLIFTON POLLARD, MR. URICH.
I'M LOOKING FOR CLIFTON POLLARD.
PRESS PASS
MR. STARK--
MR. STARK--
ANY WORD ON--
NO COMMENT.
WILL THE AVENGERS--
HAVE OTHER SUPERTERROR CELLS--
WHEN WILL YOU HAVE A COMMENT--
PETER.
TONY.
DOING WELL SINCE LEAVING STARK?
I'M OKAY--
HEAR YOU'RE TAKING PICTURES FOR A WEBSITE.
UM--
GREAT CAREER MOVE THERE, GUY.
JEEZ. JUST WHAT DID YOU DO FOR TONY STARK WHEN YOU WORKED HERE?
OH, YOU KNOW. THIS 'N' THAT.
NOTHING SPECTACULAR OR AMAZING...

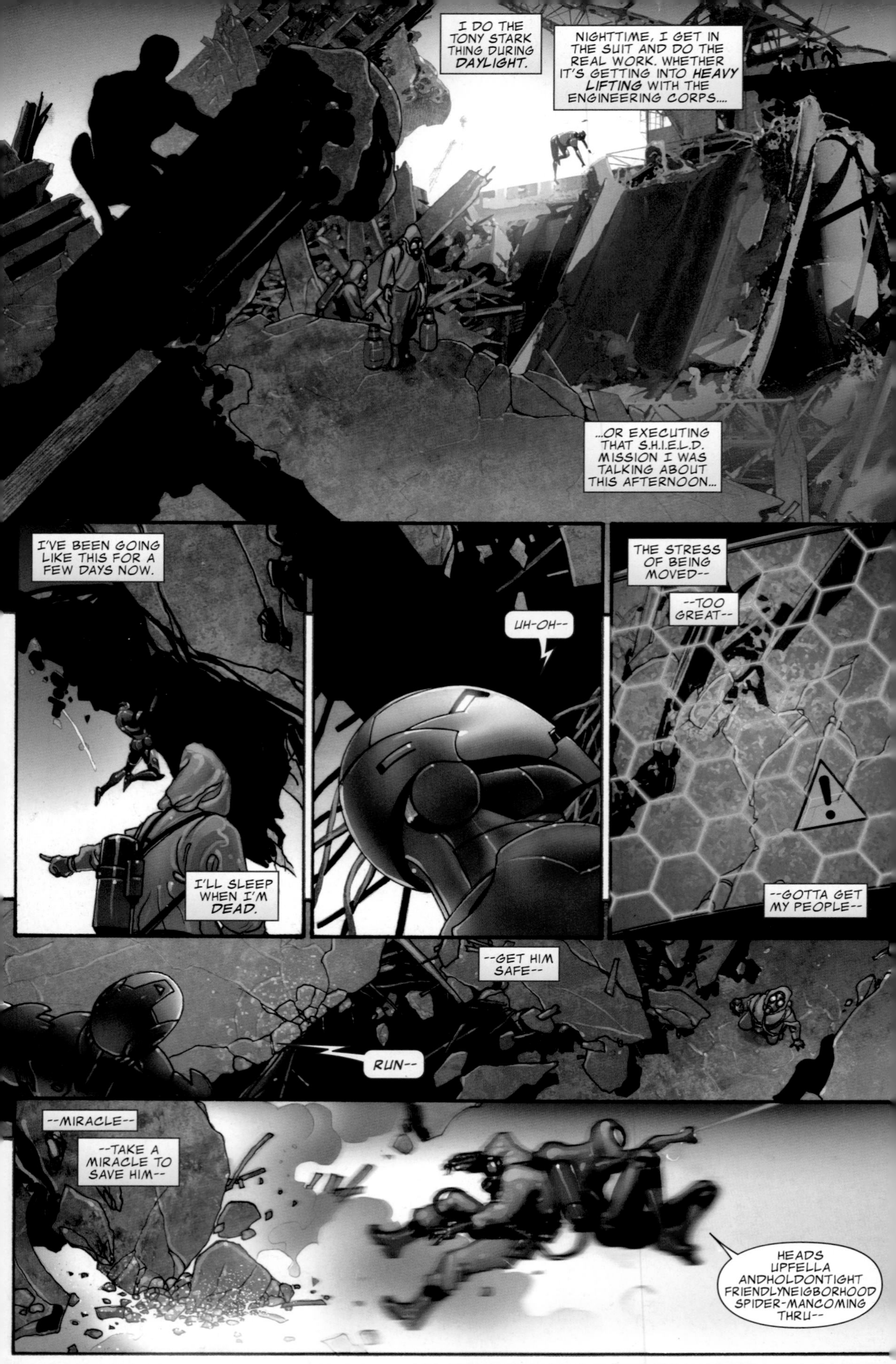
I DO THE TONY STARK THING DURING DAYLIGHT.
NIGHTTIME, I GET IN THE SUIT AND DO THE REAL WORK. WHETHER IT'S GETTING INTO HEAVY LIFTING WITH THE ENGINEERING CORPS....
...OR EXECUTING THAT S.H.I.E.L.D. MISSION I WAS TALKING ABOUT THIS AFTERNOON...
I'VE BEEN GOING LIKE THIS FOR A FEW DAYS NOW.
I'LL SLEEP WHEN I'M DEAD.
UH-OH--
THE STRESS OF BEING MOVED--
--TOO GREAT--
--GOTTA GET MY PEOPLE--
--GET HIM SAFE--
RUN--
--MIRACLE--
--TAKE A MIRACLE TO SAVE HIM--
HEADS UPFELLA ANDHOLDONTIGHT FRIENDLYNEIGBORHOOD SPIDER-MANCOMING THRU--

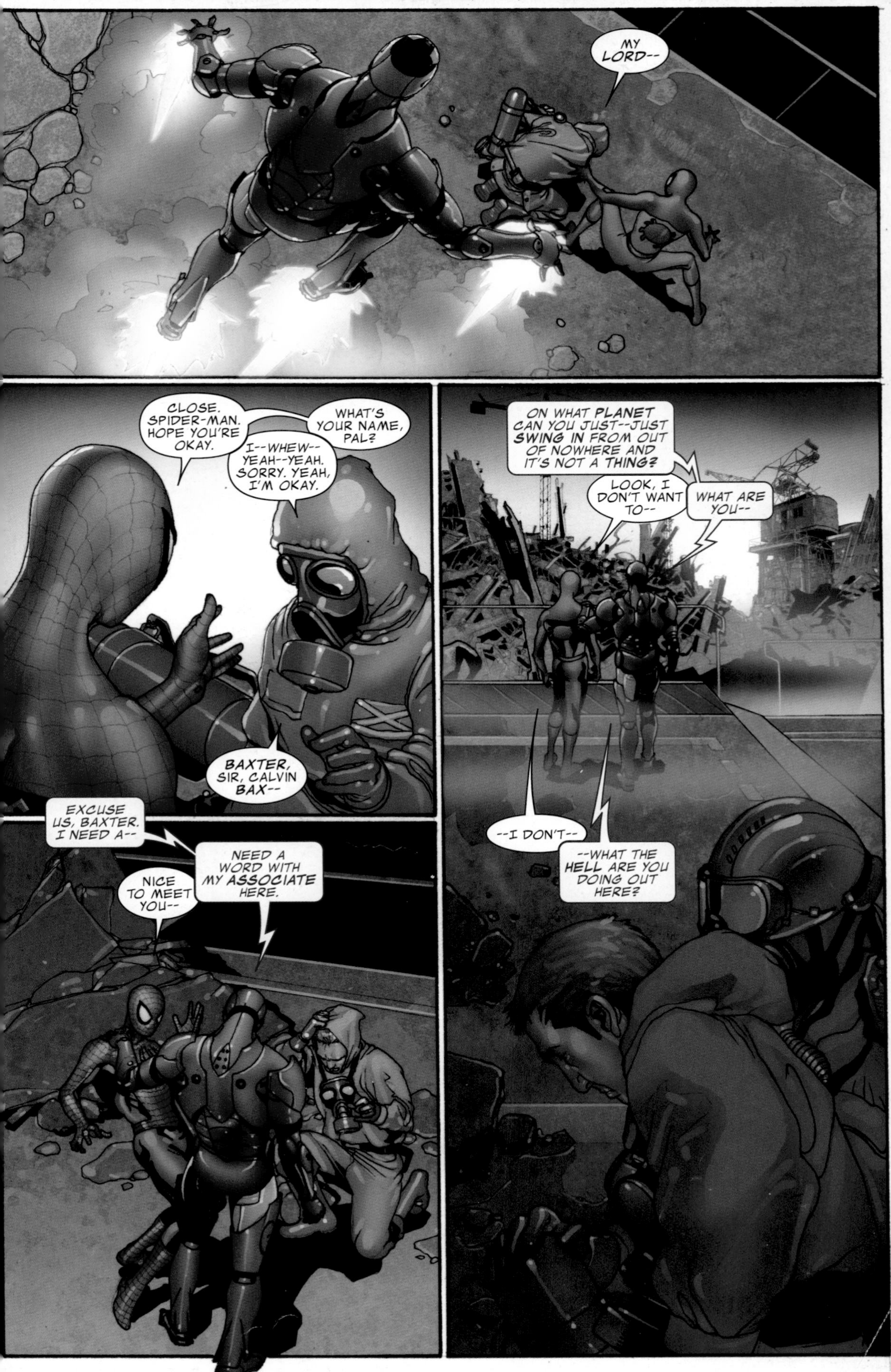
MY LORD--
CLOSE. SPIDER-MAN. HOPE YOU'RE OKAY.
WHAT'S YOUR NAME, PAL?
I--WHEW--YEAH--YEAH. SORRY. YEAH, I'M OKAY.
BAXTER, SIR, CALVIN BAX--
EXCUSE US, BAXTER. I NEED A--
NEED A WORD WITH MY ASSOCIATE HERE.
NICE TO MEET YOU--
ON WHAT PLANET CAN YOU JUST--JUST SWING IN FROM OUT OF NOWHERE AND IT'S NOT A THING?
LOOK, I DON'T WANT TO--
WHAT ARE YOU--
--I DON'T--
--WHAT THE HELL ARE YOU DOING OUT HERE?

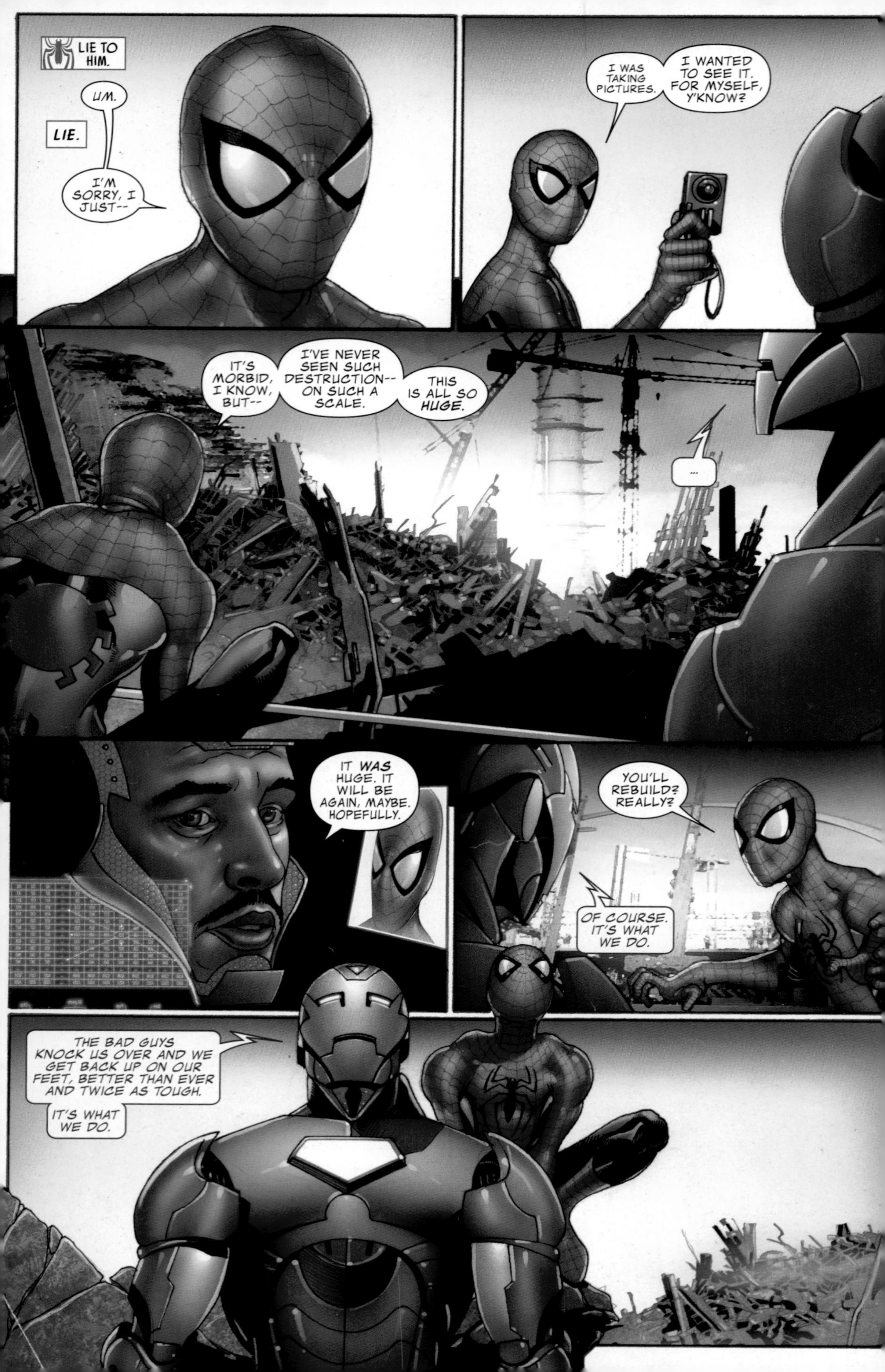
LIE TO HIM.
UM.
LIE.
I'M SORRY, I JUST--
I WAS TAKING PICTURES.
I WANTED TO SEE IT. FOR MYSELF, Y'KNOW?
IT'S MORBID, I KNOW, BUT--
I'VE NEVER SEEN SUCH DESTRUCTION-- ON SUCH A SCALE.
THIS IS ALL SO HUGE.
...
IT WAS HUGE. IT WILL BE AGAIN, MAYBE. HOPEFULLY.
YOU'LL REBUILD? REALLY?
OF COURSE. IT'S WHAT WE DO.
THE BAD GUYS KNOCK US OVER AND WE GET BACK UP ON OUR FEET, BETTER THAN EVER AND TWICE AS TOUGH.
IT'S WHAT WE DO.

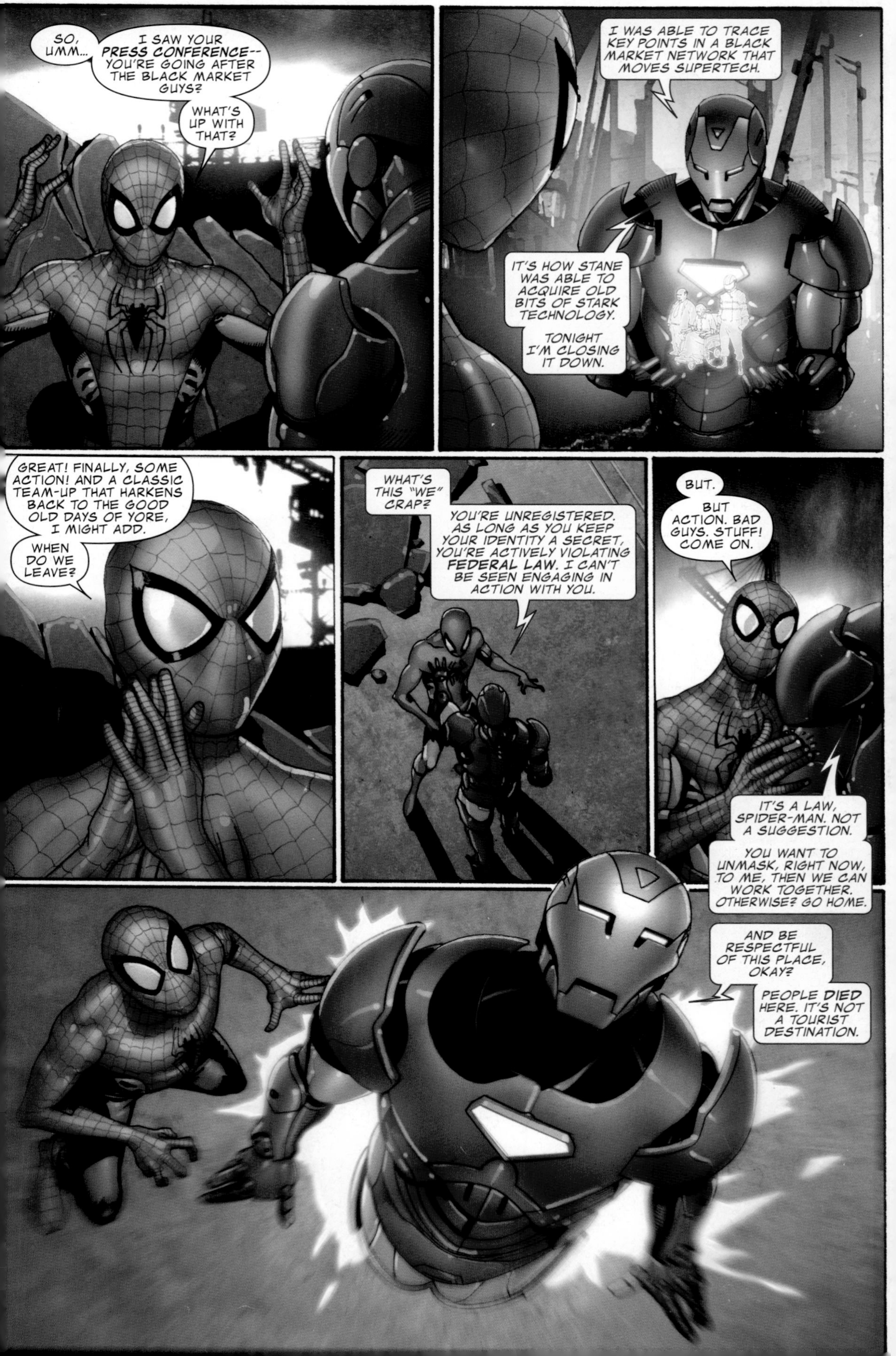
SO, UMM...
I SAW YOUR PRESS CONFERENCE-- YOU'RE GOING AFTER THE BLACK MARKET GUYS?
WHAT'S UP WITH THAT?
I WAS ABLE TO TRACE KEY POINTS IN A BLACK MARKET NETWORK THAT MOVES SUPERTECH.
IT'S HOW STANE WAS ABLE TO ACQUIRE OLD BITS OF STARK TECHNOLOGY.
TONIGHT I'M CLOSING IT DOWN.
GREAT! FINALLY, SOME ACTION! AND A CLASSIC TEAM-UP THAT HARKENS BACK TO THE GOOD OLD DAYS OF YORE, I MIGHT ADD.
WHEN DO WE LEAVE?
WHAT'S THIS "WE" CRAP?
YOU'RE UNREGISTERED. AS LONG AS YOU KEEP YOUR IDENTITY A SECRET, YOU'RE ACTIVELY VIOLATING FEDERAL LAW. I CAN'T BE SEEN ENGAGING IN ACTION WITH YOU.
BUT.
BUT ACTION. BAD GUYS. STUFF! COME ON.
IT'S A LAW, SPIDER-MAN. NOT A SUGGESTION.
YOU WANT TO UNMASK, RIGHT NOW, TO ME, THEN WE CAN WORK TOGETHER. OTHERWISE? GO HOME.
AND BE RESPECTFUL OF THIS PLACE, OKAY?
PEOPLE DIED HERE. IT'S NOT A TOURIST DESTINATION.

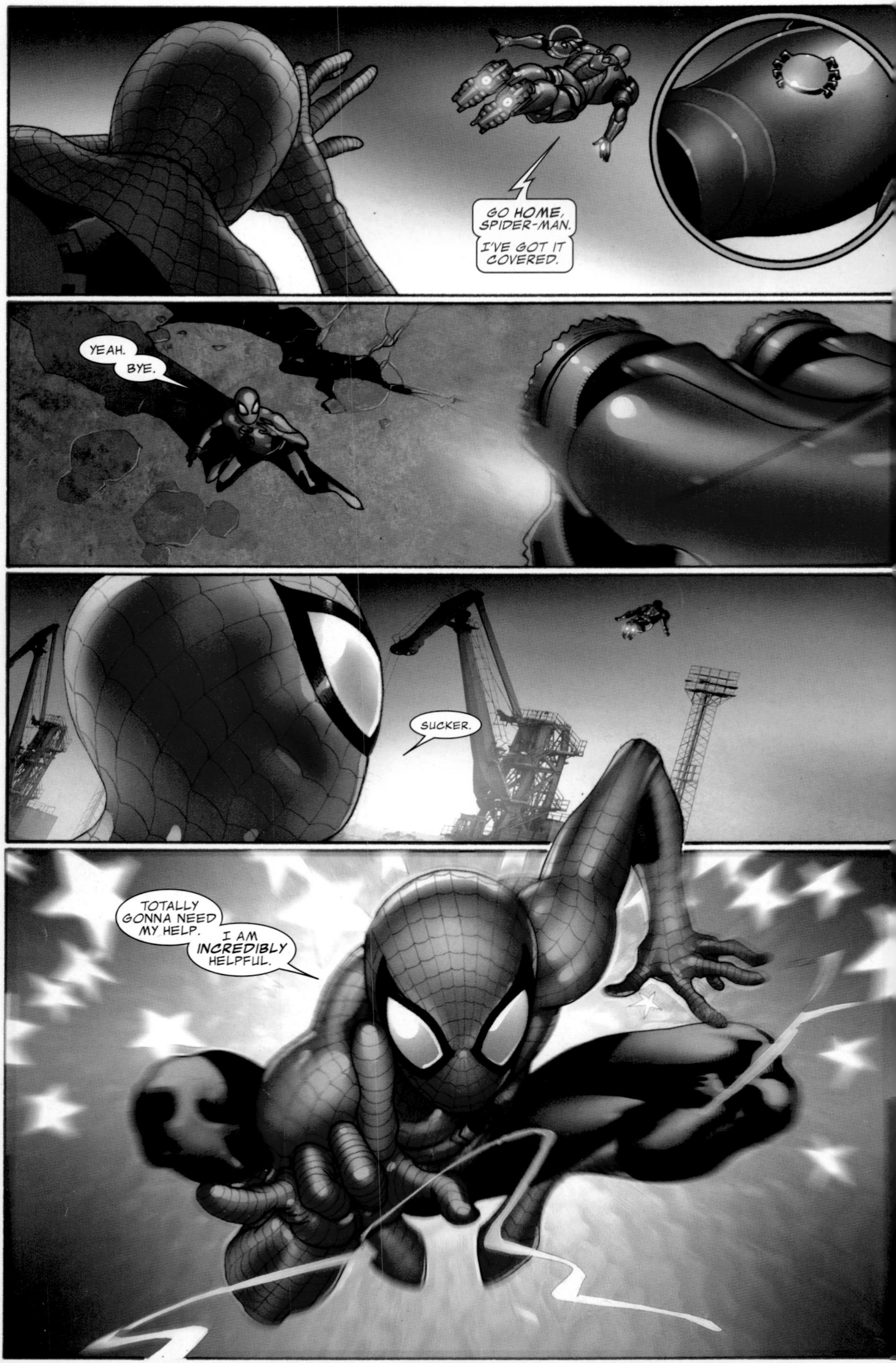
GO HOME, SPIDER-MAN.
I'VE GOT IT COVERED.
YEAH.
BYE.
SUCKER.
TOTALLY GONNA NEED MY HELP.
I AM INCREDIBLY HELPFUL.

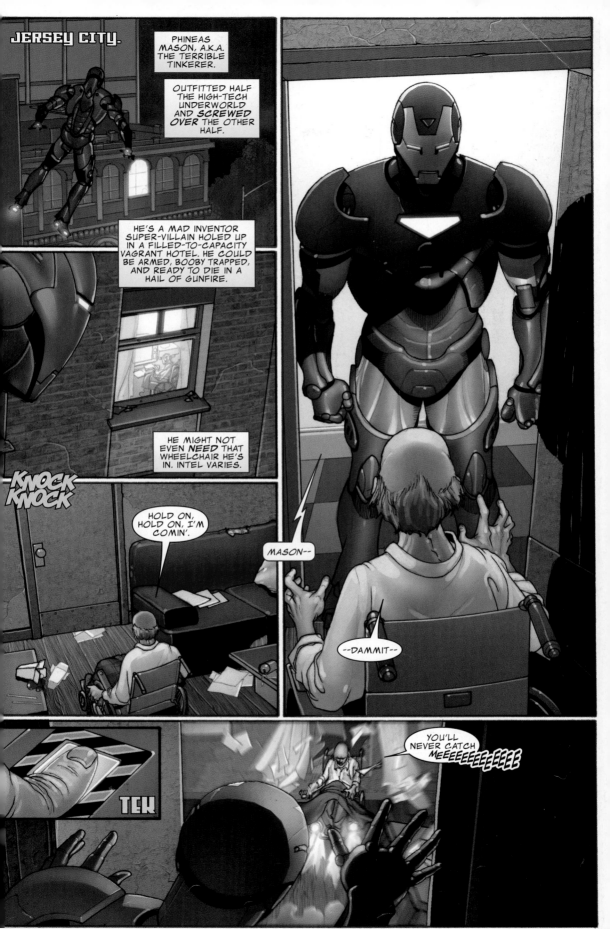

JERSEY CITY.

PHINEAS MASON, A.K.A. THE TERRIBLE TINKERER.

OUTFITTED HALF THE HIGH-TECH UNDERWORLD AND *SCREWED OVER* THE OTHER HALF.

HE'S A MAD INVENTOR SUPER-VILLAIN HOLED UP IN A FILLED-TO-CAPACITY VAGRANT HOTEL. HE COULD BE ARMED, BOOBY TRAPPED, AND READY TO DIE IN A HAIL OF GUNFIRE.

HE MIGHT NOT EVEN *NEED* THAT WHEELCHAIR HE'S IN. INTEL VARIES.

KNOCK KNOCK

HOLD ON, HOLD ON, I'M COMIN'.

MASON--

--DAMMIT--

TEK

YOU'LL NEVER CATCH MEEEEEEEEEEEEE

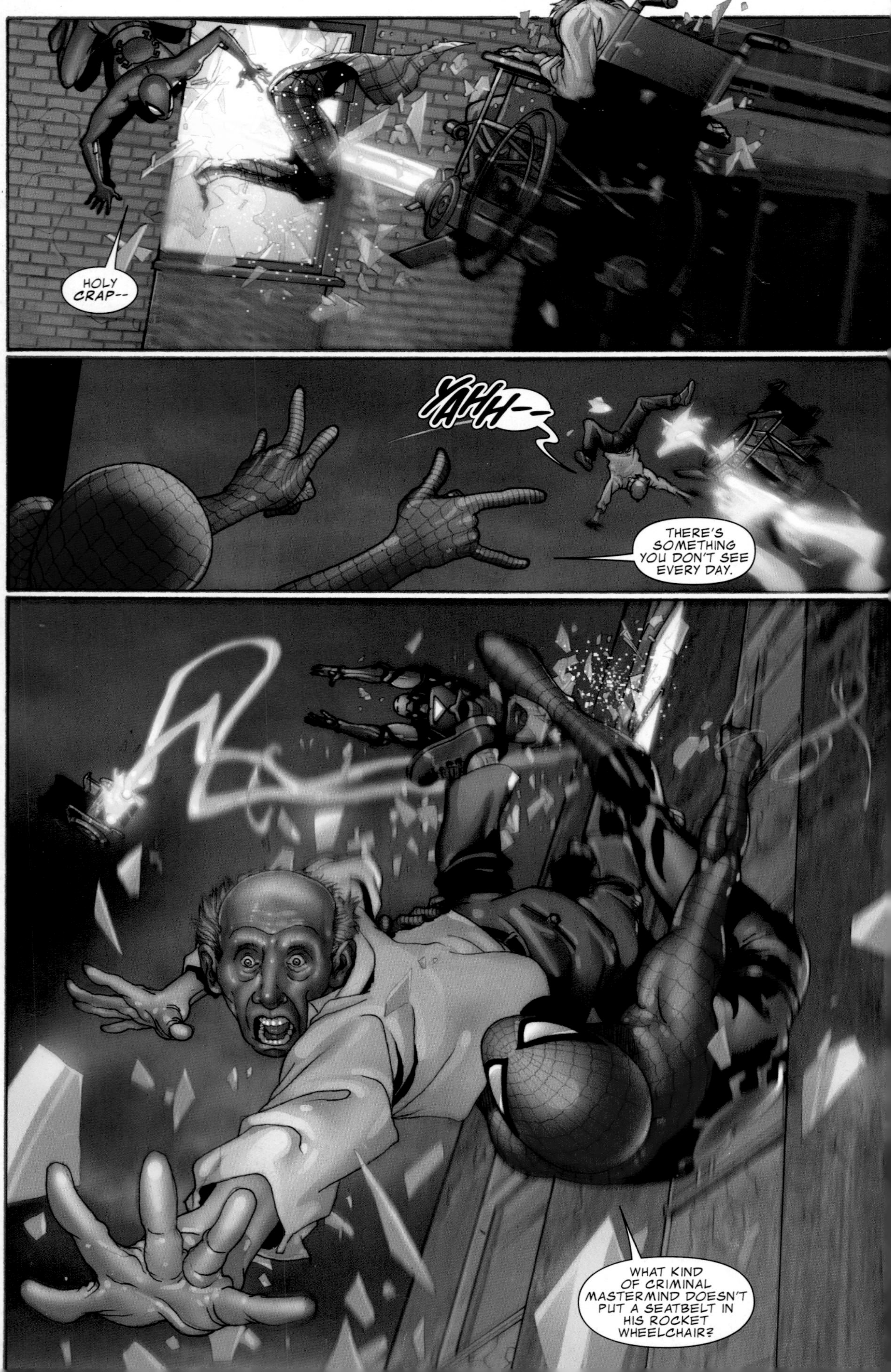
HOLY CRAP--
YAHH--
THERE'S SOMETHING YOU DON'T SEE EVERY DAY.
WHAT KIND OF CRIMINAL MASTERMIND DOESN'T PUT A SEATBELT IN HIS ROCKET WHEELCHAIR?

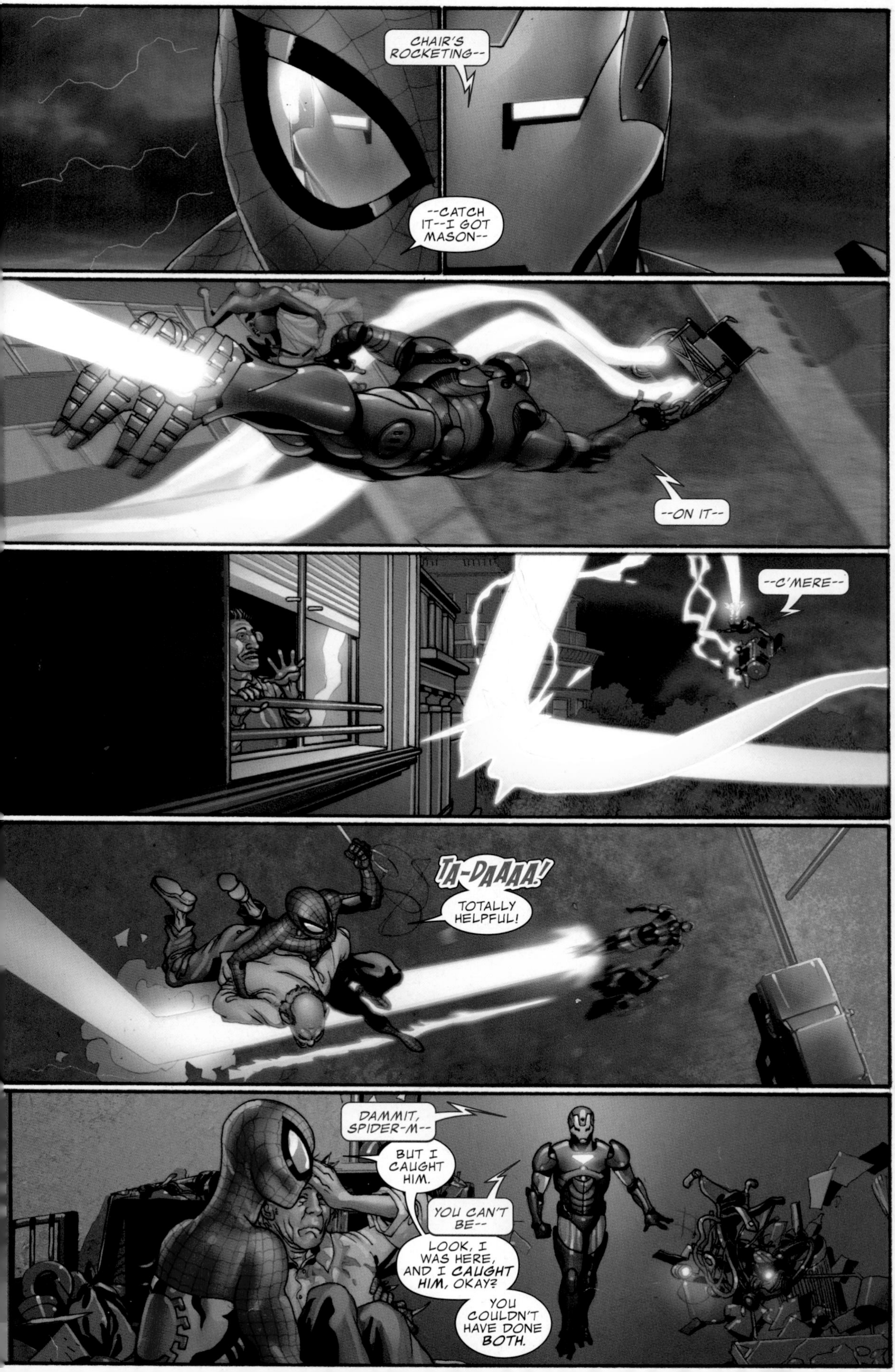
CHAIR'S ROCKETING--
--CATCH IT--I GOT MASON--
--ON IT--
--C'MERE--
TA-DAAAA!
TOTALLY HELPFUL!
DAMMIT, SPIDER-M--
BUT I CAUGHT HIM.
YOU CAN'T BE--
LOOK, I WAS HERE, AND I CAUGHT HIM, OKAY?
YOU COULDN'T HAVE DONE BOTH.

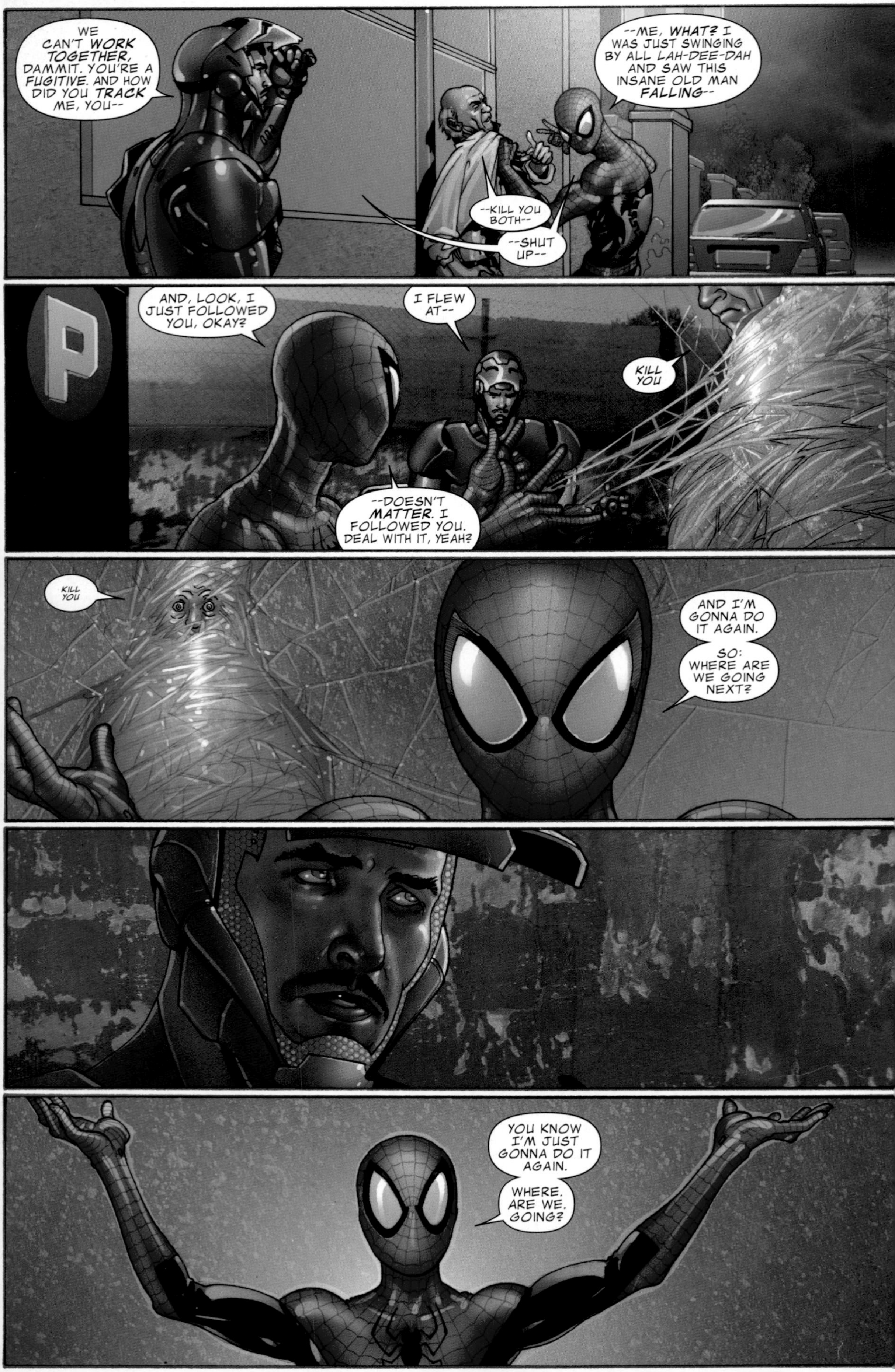

WE CAN'T WORK TOGETHER, DAMMIT. YOU'RE A FUGITIVE. AND HOW DID YOU TRACK ME, YOU--
--ME, WHAT? I WAS JUST SWINGING BY ALL LAH-DEE-DAH AND SAW THIS INSANE OLD MAN FALLING--
--KILL YOU BOTH--
--SHUT UP--
AND, LOOK, I JUST FOLLOWED YOU, OKAY?
I FLEW AT--
KILL YOU
--DOESN'T MATTER. I FOLLOWED YOU. DEAL WITH IT, YEAH?
KILL YOU
AND I'M GONNA DO IT AGAIN.
SO: WHERE ARE WE GOING NEXT?
YOU KNOW I'M JUST GONNA DO IT AGAIN.
WHERE. ARE WE. GOING?

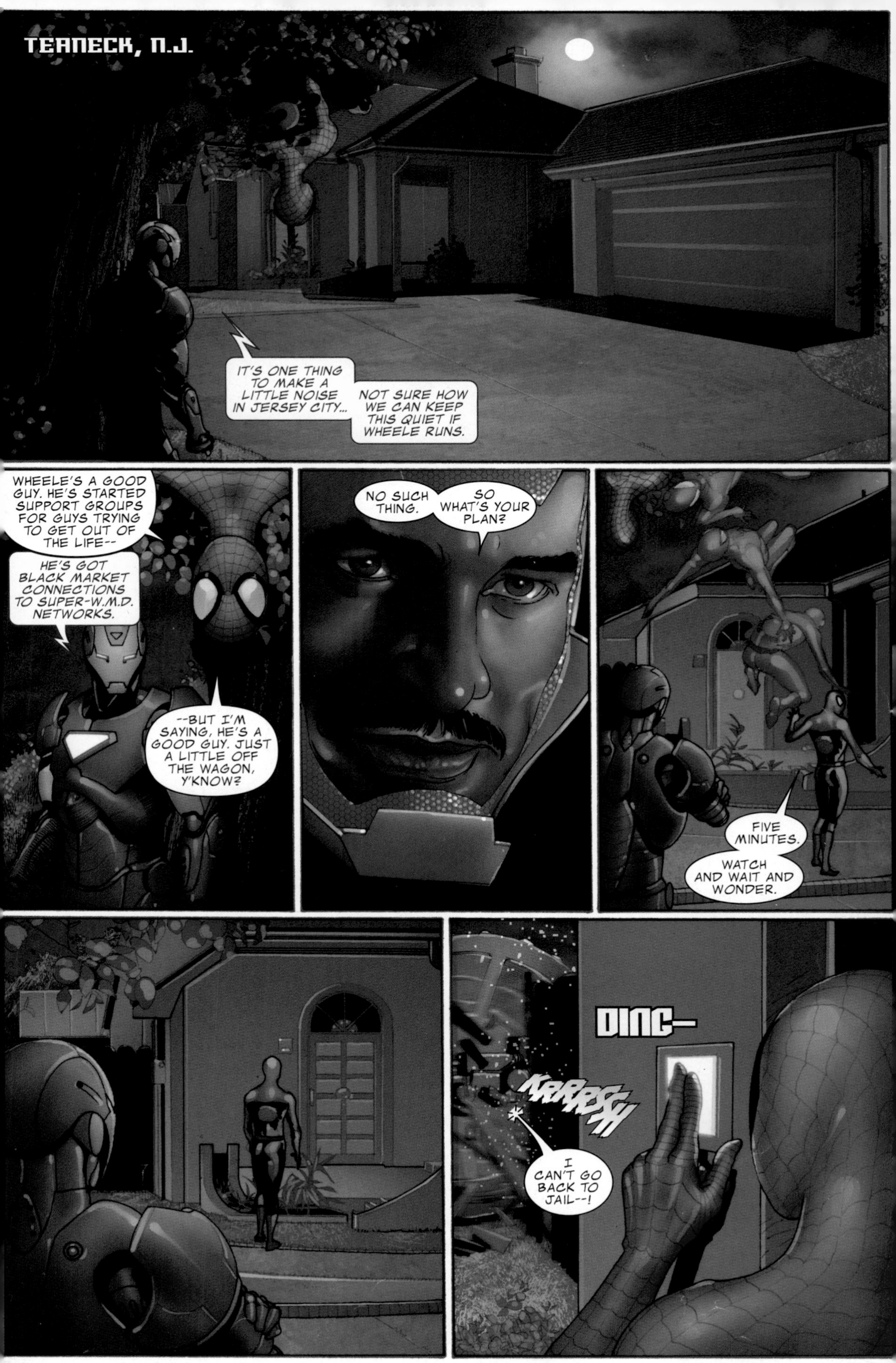
TEANECK, N.J.
IT'S ONE THING TO MAKE A LITTLE NOISE IN JERSEY CITY...
NOT SURE HOW WE CAN KEEP THIS QUIET IF WHEELE RUNS.
WHEELE'S A GOOD GUY. HE'S STARTED SUPPORT GROUPS FOR GUYS TRYING TO GET OUT OF THE LIFE--
HE'S GOT BLACK MARKET CONNECTIONS TO SUPER-W.M.D. NETWORKS.
--BUT I'M SAYING, HE'S A GOOD GUY. JUST A LITTLE OFF THE WAGON, Y'KNOW?
NO SUCH THING.
SO WHAT'S YOUR PLAN?
FIVE MINUTES.
WATCH AND WAIT AND WONDER.
DING-
KRRRSSH
I CAN'T GO BACK TO JAIL--!

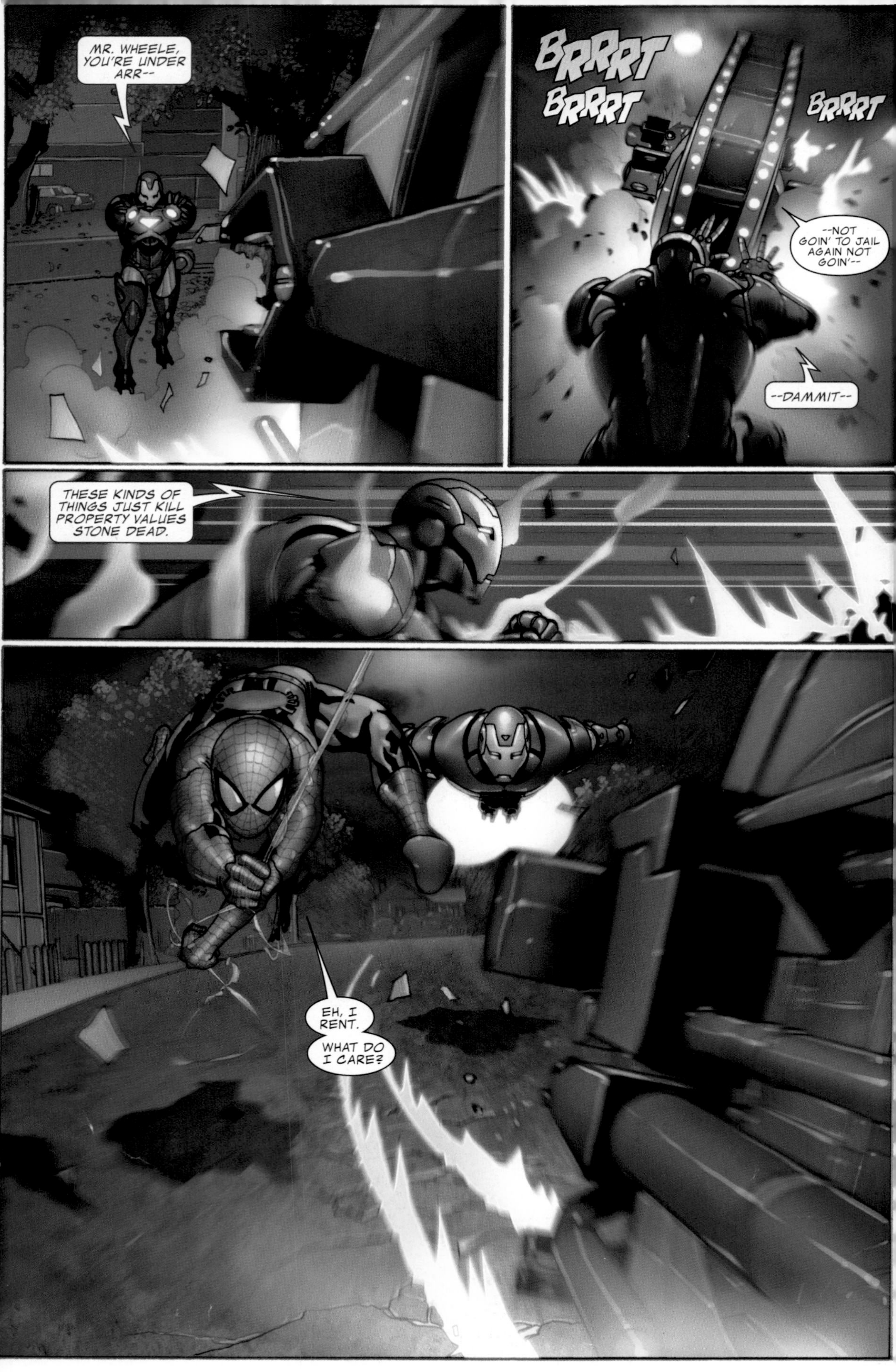
MR. WHEELE, YOU'RE UNDER ARR--
BRRRT
BRRRT
BRRRT
--NOT GOIN' TO JAIL AGAIN NOT GOIN'--
--DAMMIT--
THESE KINDS OF THINGS JUST KILL PROPERTY VALUES STONE DEAD.
EH, I RENT.
WHAT DO I CARE?

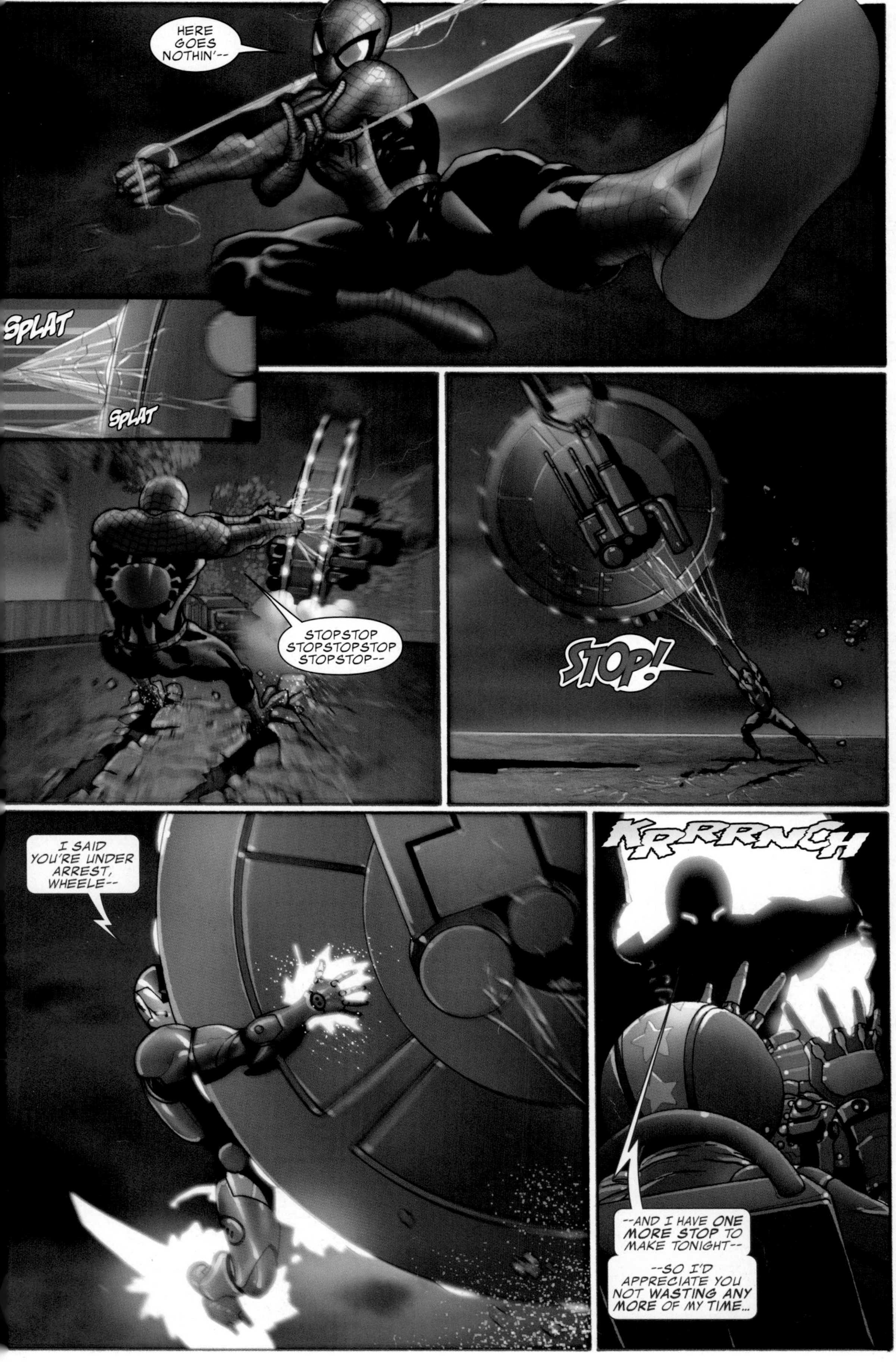
HERE GOES NOTHIN'--
SPLAT
SPLAT
STOPSTOP STOPSTOPSTOP STOPSTOP--
STOP!
I SAID YOU'RE UNDER ARREST, WHEELE--
KRRRNCH
--AND I HAVE ONE MORE STOP TO MAKE TONIGHT--
--SO I'D APPRECIATE YOU NOT WASTING ANY MORE OF MY TIME...

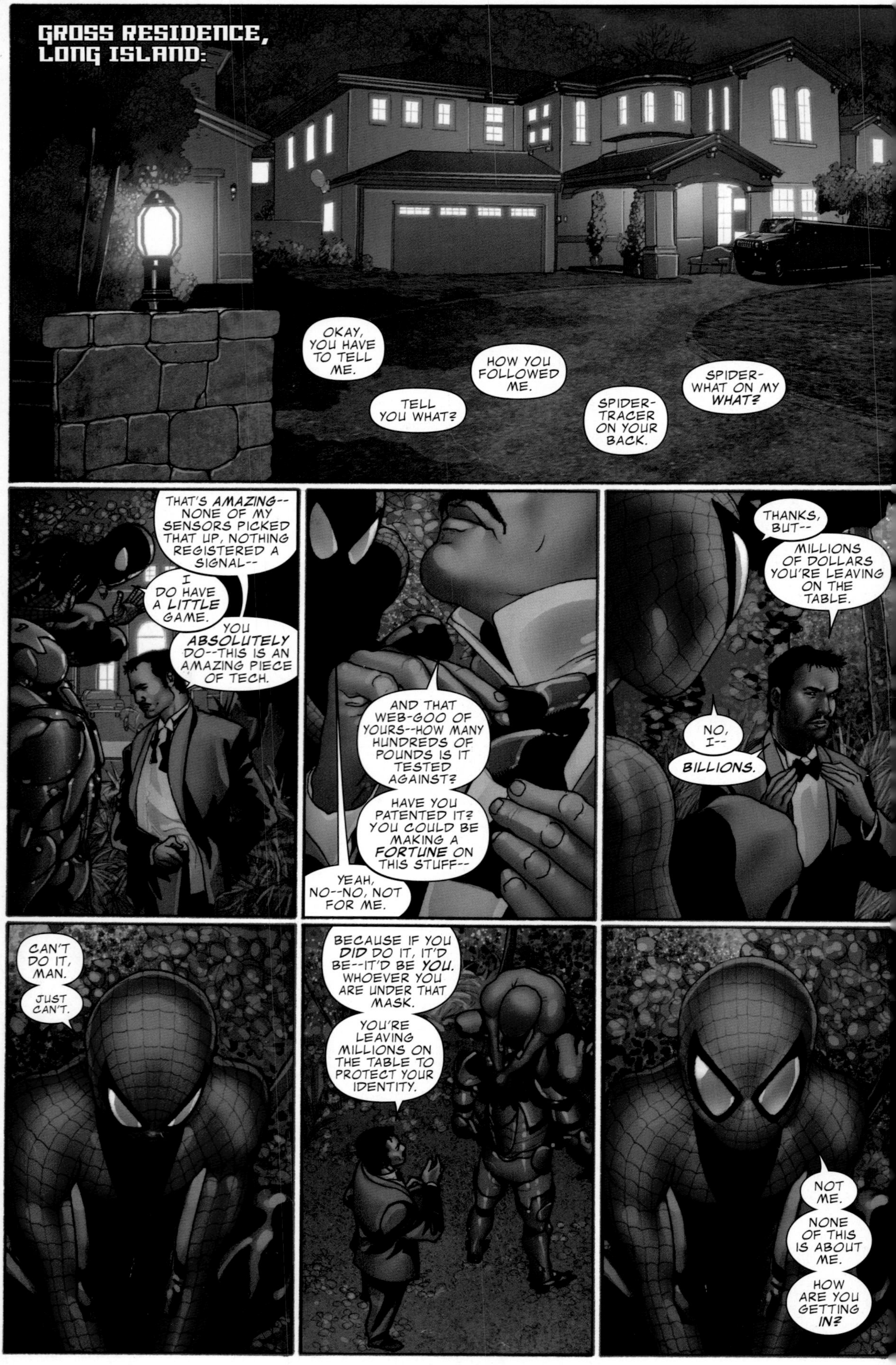
GROSS RESIDENCE, LONG ISLAND:
OKAY, YOU HAVE TO TELL ME.
TELL YOU WHAT?
HOW YOU FOLLOWED ME.
SPIDER-TRACER ON YOUR BACK.
SPIDER-WHAT ON MY WHAT?
THAT'S AMAZING--NONE OF MY SENSORS PICKED THAT UP, NOTHING REGISTERED A SIGNAL--
I DO HAVE A LITTLE GAME.
YOU ABSOLUTELY DO--THIS IS AN AMAZING PIECE OF TECH.
AND THAT WEB-GOO OF YOURS--HOW MANY HUNDREDS OF POUNDS IS IT TESTED AGAINST?
HAVE YOU PATENTED IT? YOU COULD BE MAKING A FORTUNE ON THIS STUFF--
YEAH, NO--NO, NOT FOR ME.
THANKS, BUT--
MILLIONS OF DOLLARS YOU'RE LEAVING ON THE TABLE.
NO, I--
BILLIONS.
CAN'T DO IT, MAN.
JUST CAN'T.
BECAUSE IF YOU DID DO IT, IT'D BE--IT'D BE YOU. WHOEVER YOU ARE UNDER THAT MASK.
YOU'RE LEAVING MILLIONS ON THE TABLE TO PROTECT YOUR IDENTITY.
NOT ME.
NONE OF THIS IS ABOUT ME.
HOW ARE YOU GETTING IN?

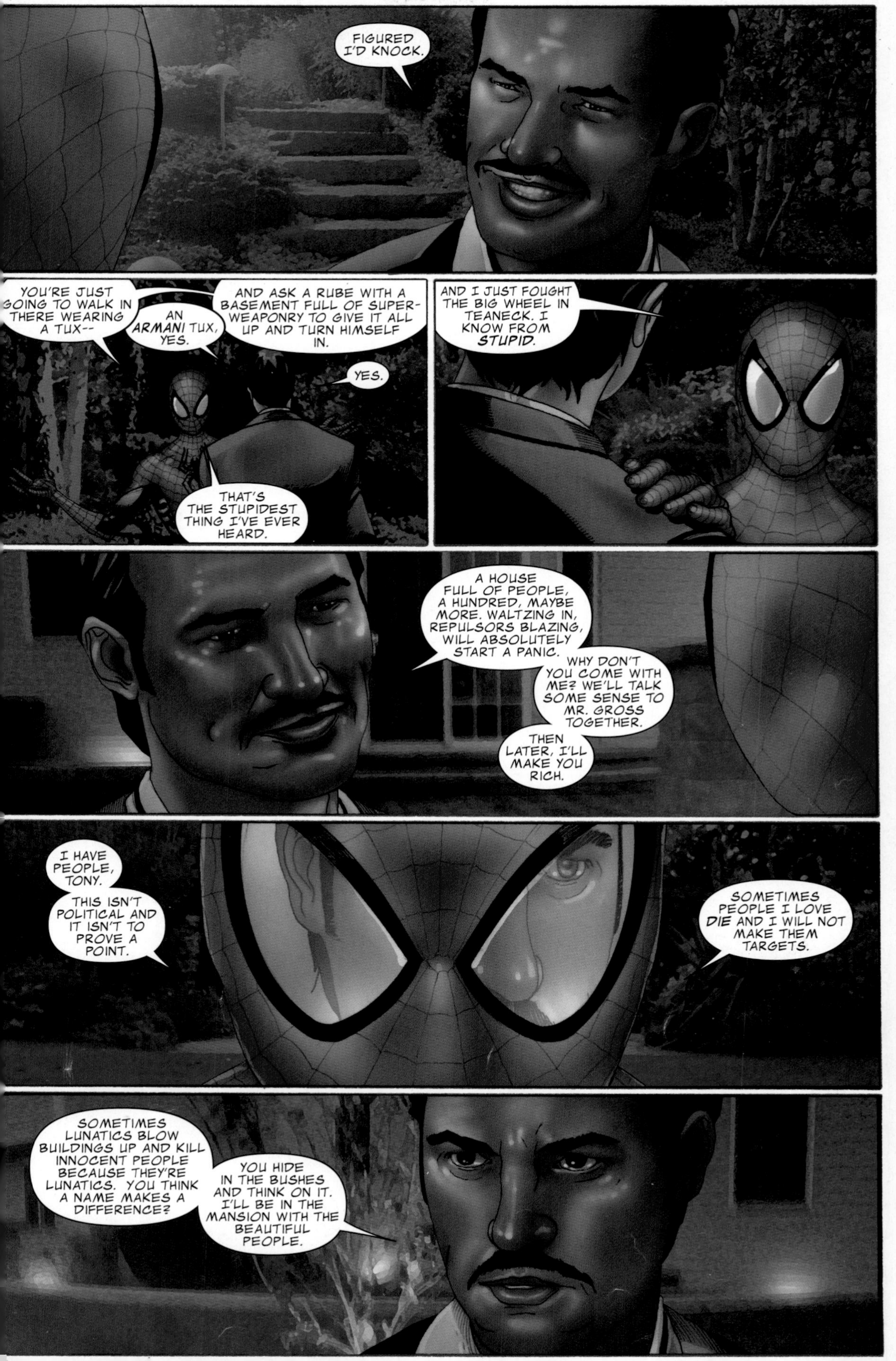
FIGURED I'D KNOCK.
YOU'RE JUST GOING TO WALK IN THERE WEARING A TUX--
AN ARMANI TUX, YES.
AND ASK A RUBE WITH A BASEMENT FULL OF SUPER-WEAPONRY TO GIVE IT ALL UP AND TURN HIMSELF IN.
YES.
THAT'S THE STUPIDEST THING I'VE EVER HEARD.
AND I JUST FOUGHT THE BIG WHEEL IN TEANECK. I KNOW FROM STUPID.
A HOUSE FULL OF PEOPLE, A HUNDRED, MAYBE MORE. WALTZING IN, REPULSORS BLAZING, WILL ABSOLUTELY START A PANIC.
WHY DON'T YOU COME WITH ME? WE'LL TALK SOME SENSE TO MR. GROSS TOGETHER.
THEN LATER, I'LL MAKE YOU RICH.
I HAVE PEOPLE, TONY.
THIS ISN'T POLITICAL AND IT ISN'T TO PROVE A POINT.
SOMETIMES PEOPLE I LOVE DIE AND I WILL NOT MAKE THEM TARGETS.
SOMETIMES LUNATICS BLOW BUILDINGS UP AND KILL INNOCENT PEOPLE BECAUSE THEY'RE LUNATICS. YOU THINK A NAME MAKES A DIFFERENCE?
YOU HIDE IN THE BUSHES AND THINK ON IT. I'LL BE IN THE MANSION WITH THE BEAUTIFUL PEOPLE.

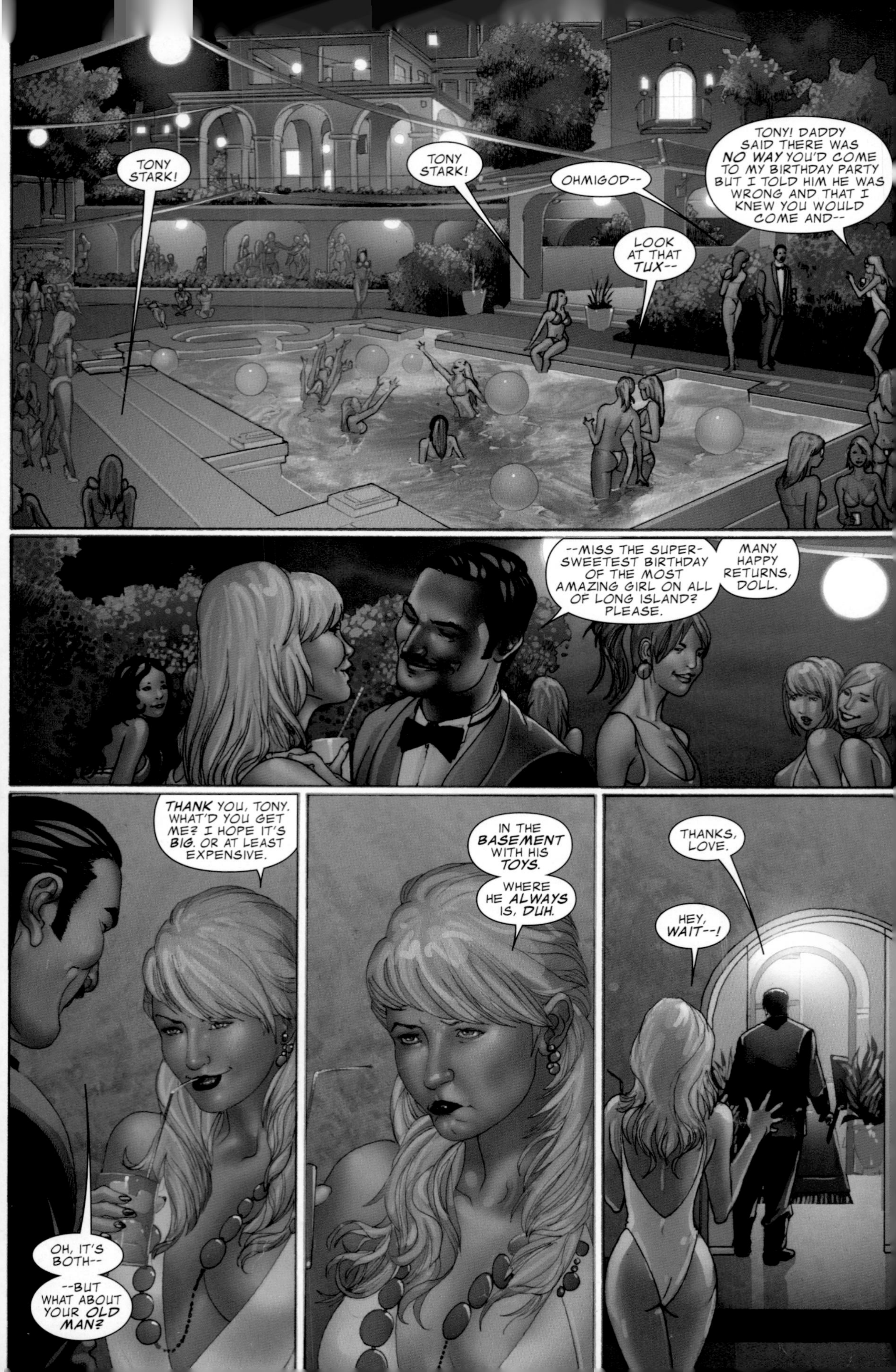
TONY STARK!
TONY STARK!
OHMIGOD--
LOOK AT THAT TUX--
TONY! DADDY SAID THERE WAS NO WAY YOU'D COME TO MY BIRTHDAY PARTY BUT I TOLD HIM HE WAS WRONG AND THAT I KNEW YOU WOULD COME AND--
--MISS THE SUPER-SWEETEST BIRTHDAY OF THE MOST AMAZING GIRL ON ALL OF LONG ISLAND? PLEASE.
MANY HAPPY RETURNS, DOLL.
THANK YOU, TONY. WHAT'D YOU GET ME? I HOPE IT'S BIG. OR AT LEAST EXPENSIVE.
OH, IT'S BOTH--
--BUT WHAT ABOUT YOUR OLD MAN?
IN THE BASEMENT WITH HIS TOYS.
WHERE HE ALWAYS IS, DUH.
THANKS, LOVE.
HEY, WAIT--!

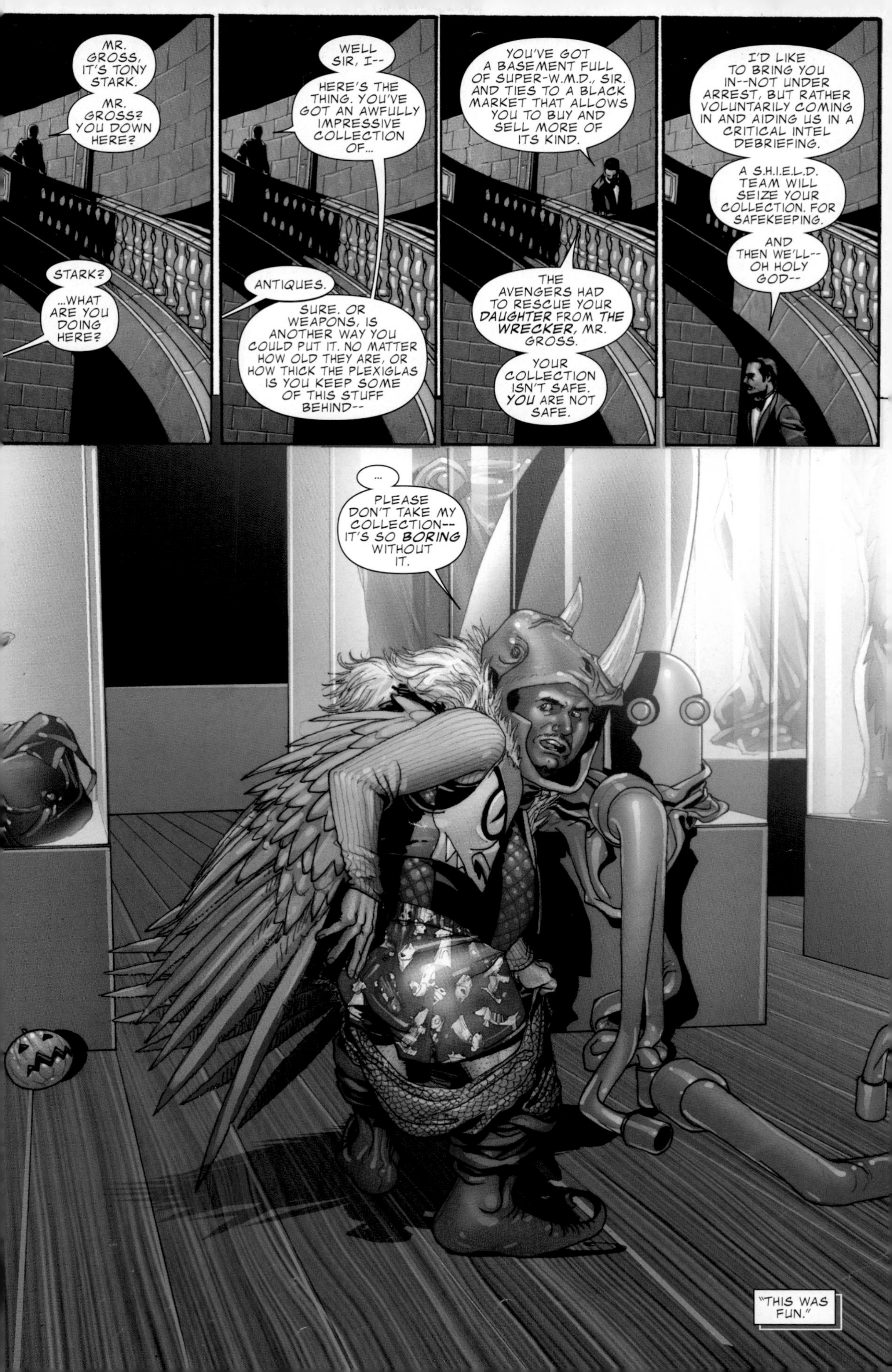

MR. GROSS, IT'S TONY STARK.
MR. GROSS? YOU DOWN HERE?
STARK?
...WHAT ARE YOU DOING HERE?
WELL SIR, I--
HERE'S THE THING. YOU'VE GOT AN AWFULLY IMPRESSIVE COLLECTION OF...
ANTIQUES.
SURE. OR WEAPONS, IS ANOTHER WAY YOU COULD PUT IT. NO MATTER HOW OLD THEY ARE, OR HOW THICK THE PLEXIGLAS IS YOU KEEP SOME OF THIS STUFF BEHIND--
YOU'VE GOT A BASEMENT FULL OF SUPER-W.M.D., SIR. AND TIES TO A BLACK MARKET THAT ALLOWS YOU TO BUY AND SELL MORE OF ITS KIND.
THE AVENGERS HAD TO RESCUE YOUR DAUGHTER FROM THE WRECKER, MR. GROSS.
YOUR COLLECTION ISN'T SAFE. YOU ARE NOT SAFE.
I'D LIKE TO BRING YOU IN--NOT UNDER ARREST, BUT RATHER VOLUNTARILY COMING IN AND AIDING US IN A CRITICAL INTEL DEBRIEFING.
A S.H.I.E.L.D. TEAM WILL SEIZE YOUR COLLECTION. FOR SAFEKEEPING.
AND THEN WE'LL-- OH HOLY GOD--
...
PLEASE DON'T TAKE MY COLLECTION-- IT'S SO BORING WITHOUT IT.
"THIS WAS FUN."

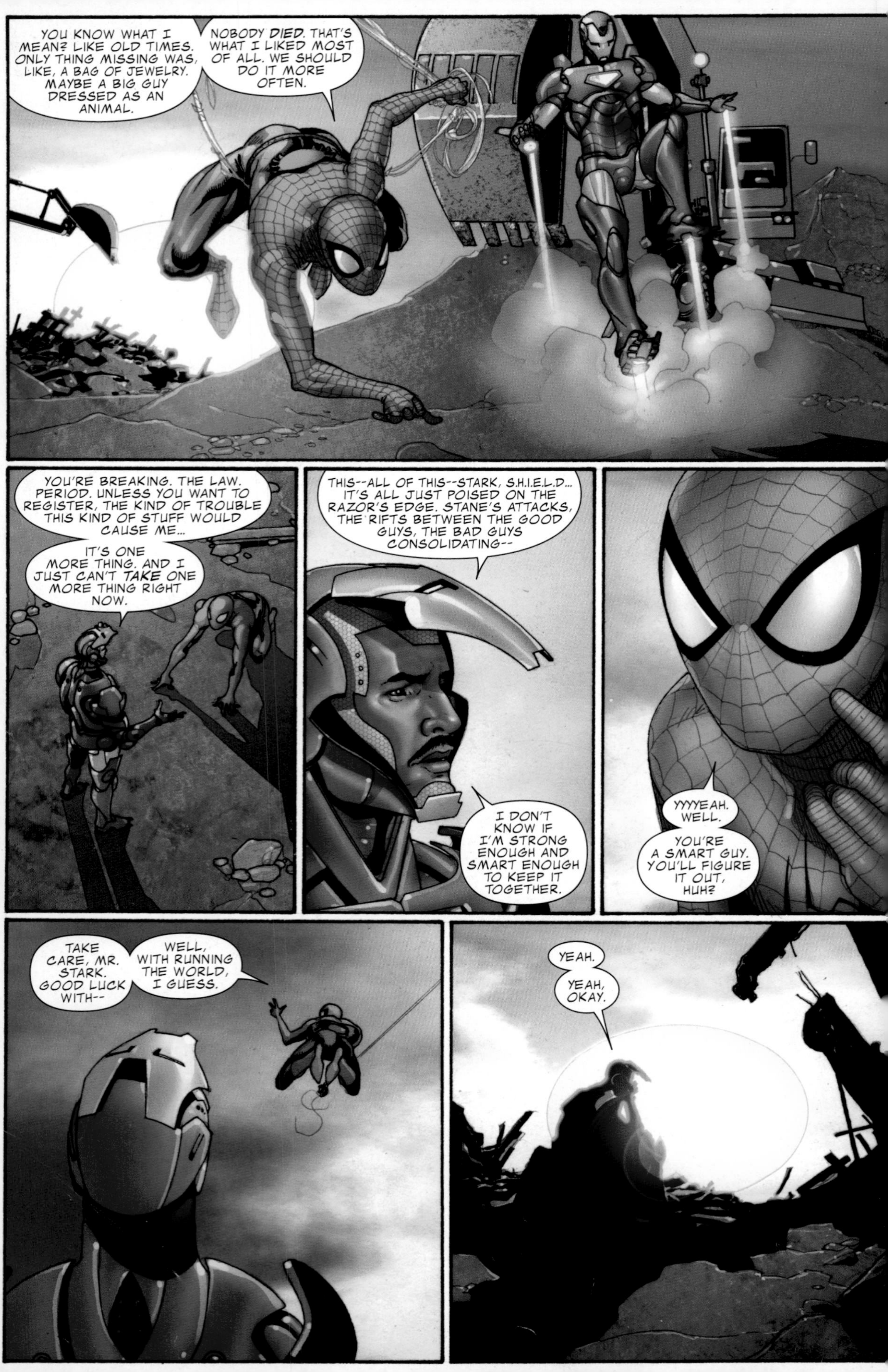
YOU KNOW WHAT I MEAN? LIKE OLD TIMES. ONLY THING MISSING WAS, LIKE, A BAG OF JEWELRY. MAYBE A BIG GUY DRESSED AS AN ANIMAL.
NOBODY DIED. THAT'S WHAT I LIKED MOST OF ALL. WE SHOULD DO IT MORE OFTEN.
YOU'RE BREAKING. THE LAW. PERIOD. UNLESS YOU WANT TO REGISTER, THE KIND OF TROUBLE THIS KIND OF STUFF WOULD CAUSE ME...
IT'S ONE MORE THING. AND I JUST CAN'T TAKE ONE MORE THING RIGHT NOW.
THIS--ALL OF THIS--STARK, S.H.I.E.L.D... IT'S ALL JUST POISED ON THE RAZOR'S EDGE. STANE'S ATTACKS, THE RIFTS BETWEEN THE GOOD GUYS, THE BAD GUYS CONSOLIDATING--
I DON'T KNOW IF I'M STRONG ENOUGH AND SMART ENOUGH TO KEEP IT TOGETHER.
YYYYEAH. WELL.
YOU'RE A SMART GUY. YOU'LL FIGURE IT OUT, HUH?
TAKE CARE, MR. STARK. GOOD LUCK WITH--
WELL, WITH RUNNING THE WORLD, I GUESS.
YEAH.
YEAH, OKAY.

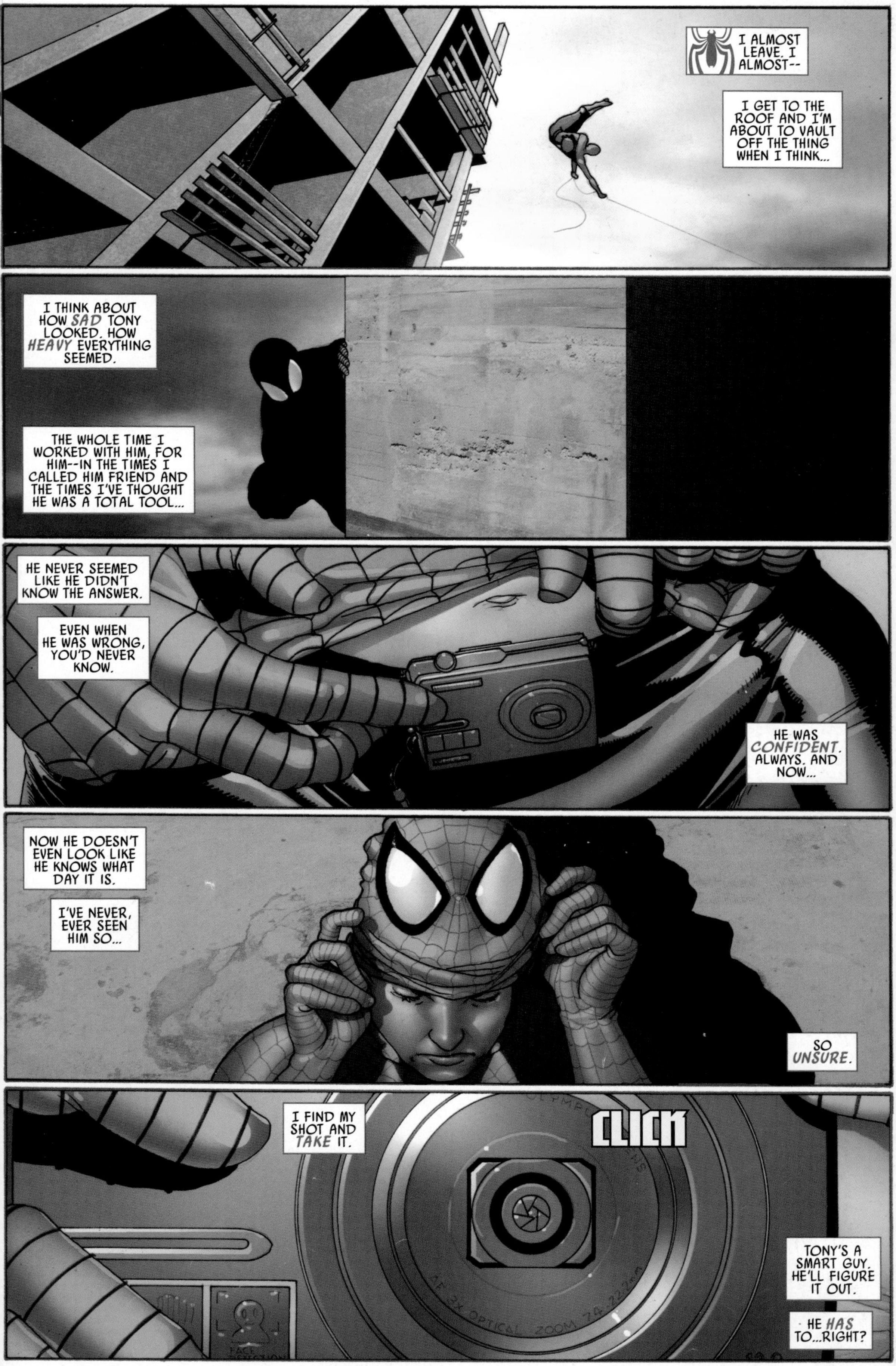

I ALMOST LEAVE. I ALMOST--
I GET TO THE ROOF AND I'M ABOUT TO VAULT OFF THE THING WHEN I THINK...
I THINK ABOUT HOW SAD TONY LOOKED. HOW HEAVY EVERYTHING SEEMED.
THE WHOLE TIME I WORKED WITH HIM, FOR HIM--IN THE TIMES I CALLED HIM FRIEND AND THE TIMES I'VE THOUGHT HE WAS A TOTAL TOOL...
HE NEVER SEEMED LIKE HE DIDN'T KNOW THE ANSWER.
EVEN WHEN HE WAS WRONG, YOU'D NEVER KNOW.
HE WAS CONFIDENT. ALWAYS. AND NOW...
NOW HE DOESN'T EVEN LOOK LIKE HE KNOWS WHAT DAY IT IS.
I'VE NEVER, EVER SEEN HIM SO...
SO UNSURE.
I FIND MY SHOT AND TAKE IT.
CLICK
TONY'S A SMART GUY. HE'LL FIGURE IT OUT.
HE HAS TO...RIGHT?

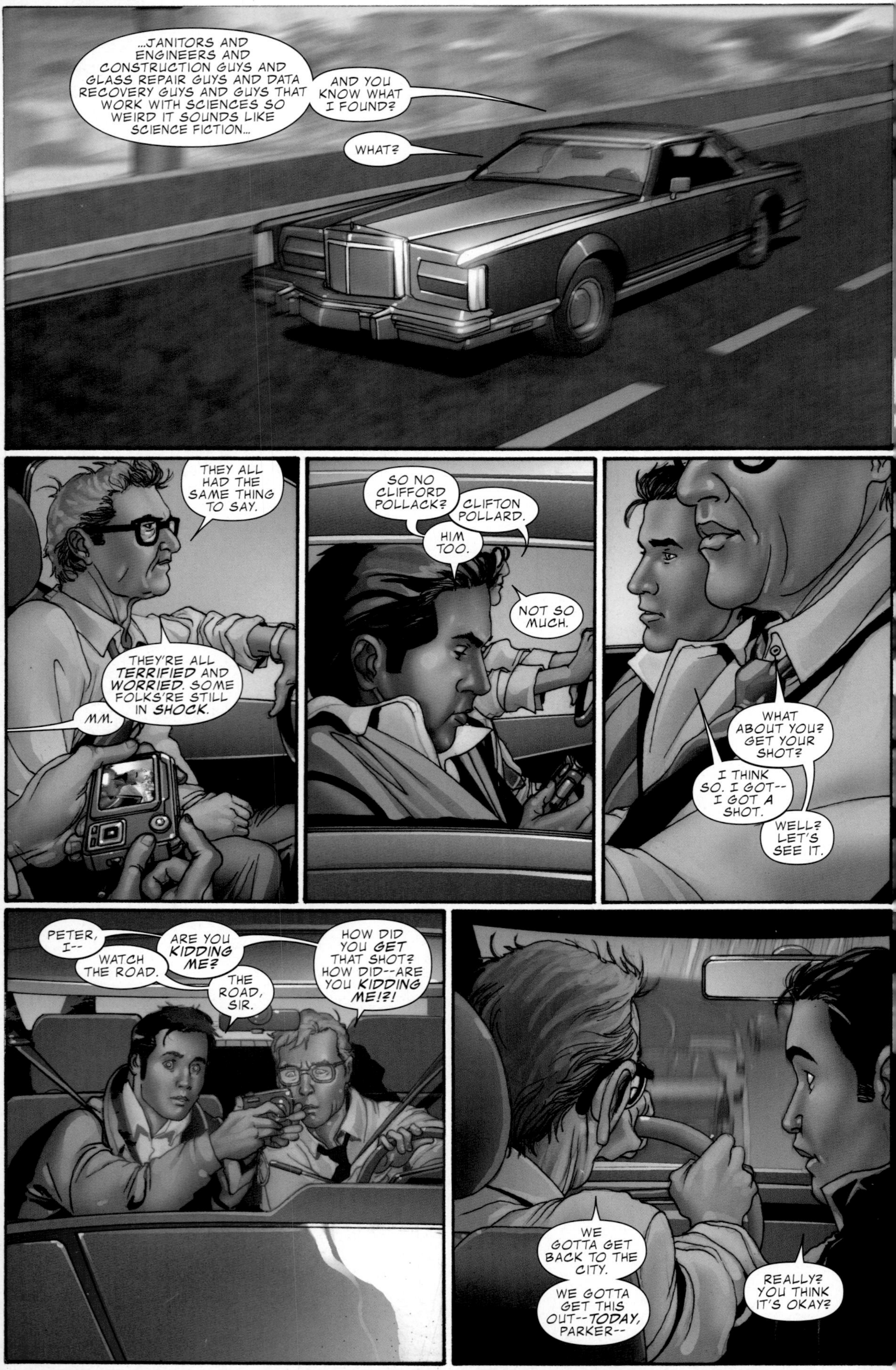
...JANITORS AND ENGINEERS AND CONSTRUCTION GUYS AND GLASS REPAIR GUYS AND DATA RECOVERY GUYS AND GUYS THAT WORK WITH SCIENCES SO WEIRD IT SOUNDS LIKE SCIENCE FICTION...
AND YOU KNOW WHAT I FOUND?
WHAT?
THEY ALL HAD THE SAME THING TO SAY.
THEY'RE ALL TERRIFIED AND WORRIED. SOME FOLKS'RE STILL IN SHOCK.
MM.
SO NO CLIFFORD POLLACK?
CLIFTON POLLARD.
HIM TOO.
NOT SO MUCH.
WHAT ABOUT YOU? GET YOUR SHOT?
I THINK SO. I GOT-- I GOT A SHOT.
WELL? LET'S SEE IT.
PETER, I--
ARE YOU KIDDING ME?
WATCH THE ROAD.
THE ROAD, SIR.
HOW DID YOU GET THAT SHOT? HOW DID--ARE YOU KIDDING ME!?!
WE GOTTA GET BACK TO THE CITY.
WE GOTTA GET THIS OUT--TODAY, PARKER--
REALLY? YOU THINK IT'S OKAY?

# FRONT LINE

MORNING EDITION - 50 CENTS                    WEDNESDAY, NOVEMBER 5, 2008

## THE HEAD THAT WEARS THE CROWN

*FEATURE ARTICLE*
*BY BEN URICH*

*PHOTOGRAPH BY PETER PARKER*

LONG ISLAND–The fires at Stark Industries have been burning for a week now. It smells like burnt fish and hot dust. They tell you it's all the wiring that melted when a high-tech lunatic named Ezekiel Stane tried to wipe Tony Stark, and Stark Industries, off the face of the earth.

And Stark, as anyone with a television can tell you, hasn't slept since the fires started.

The mood at Stark Industries, or what's left of it, is that of a bereaved family, only instead of mourning the passing of a beloved patriarch or doddering old aunt, this is a family dozens of lives smaller, stolen in an instant by an inhuman monster, in an inhumanly monstrous moment of cruelty. There are not words to adequately explain the loss.

Stark employees, as they'll tell you if you give them half a second, tend to work for Stark as long as possible. Every employee I spoke with--from the janitors to the particle physicists-- would introduce themselves to me, then rattle off their tenure at Stark like it was their last name.

"I can't imagine a world without Stark Industries."

*Continued on pg. 19*

**TONY STARK AT THE LONG ISLAND FACILITY**

## MORE HEADLINES

# "CLIFTON POLLARD"
## THE FIVE NIGHTMARES: EPILOGUE

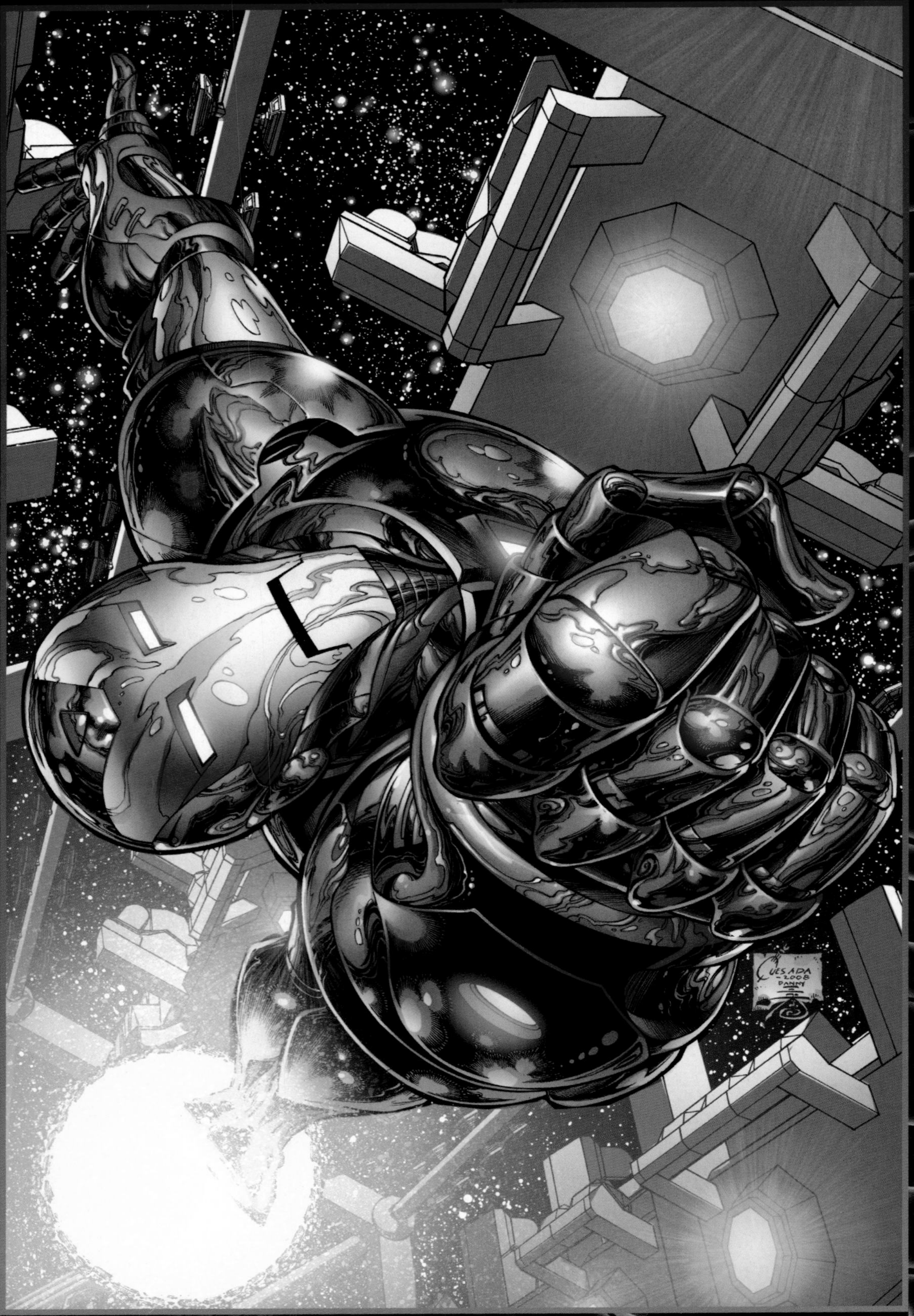
QUESADA
2008
DANNY

#1 VARIANT BY JOE QUESADA

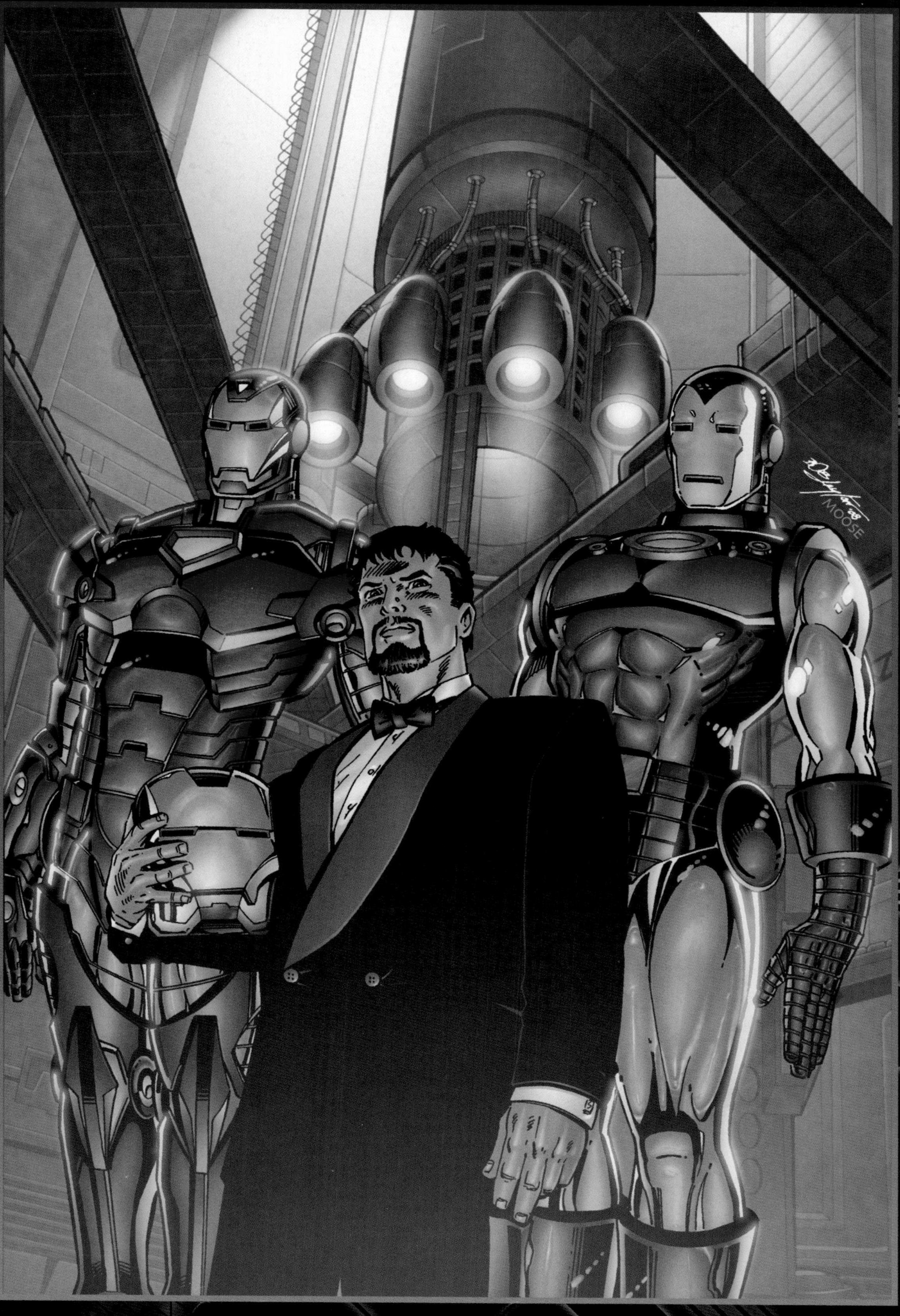
MOOSE

**#1 VARIANT** BY BOB LAYTON

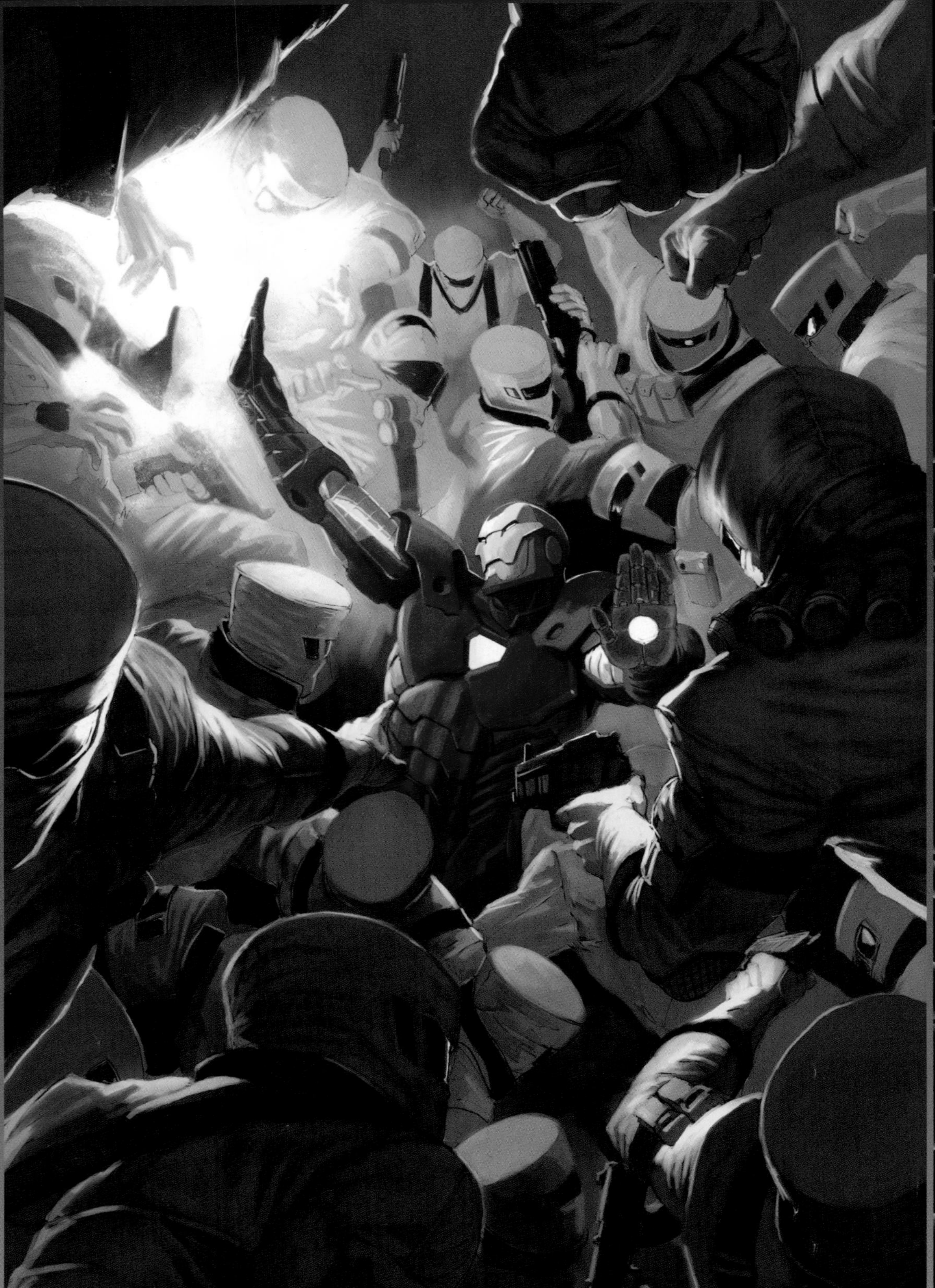

#1 VARIANT BY MARKO DJURDJEVIC

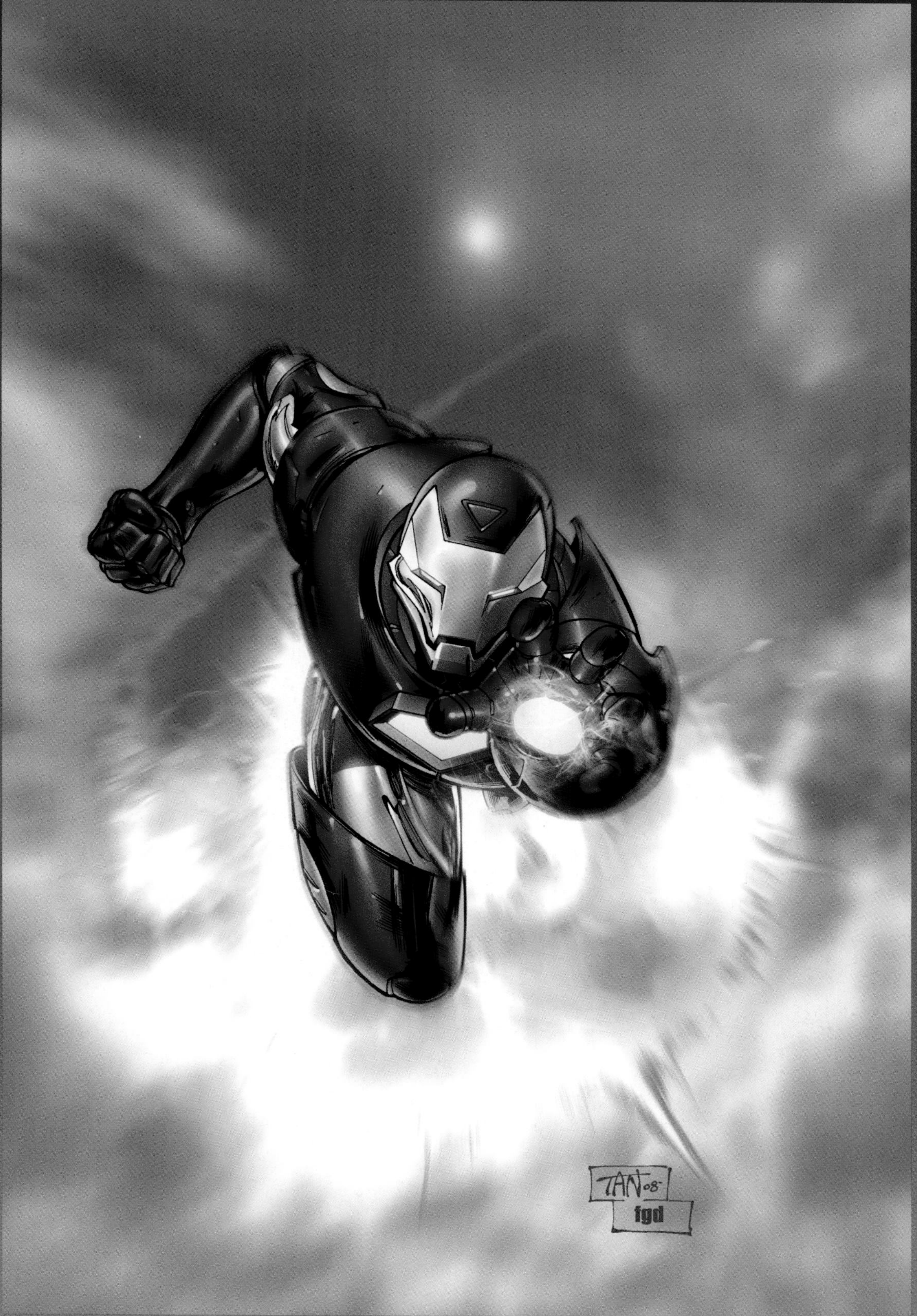
TAN 08
fgd

#1 VARIANT BY BILLY TAN

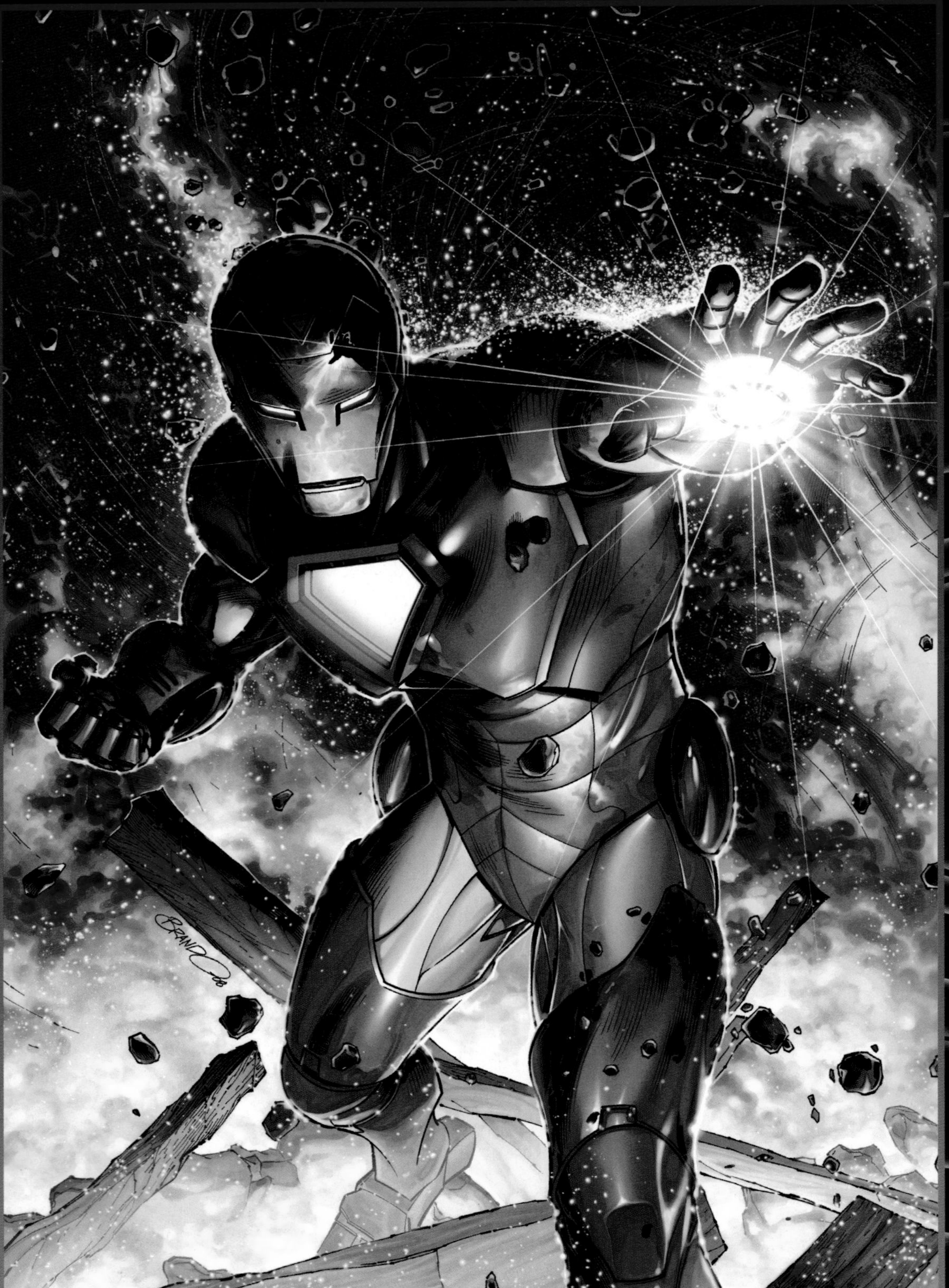

**#2 VARIANT** BY BRANDON PETERSON

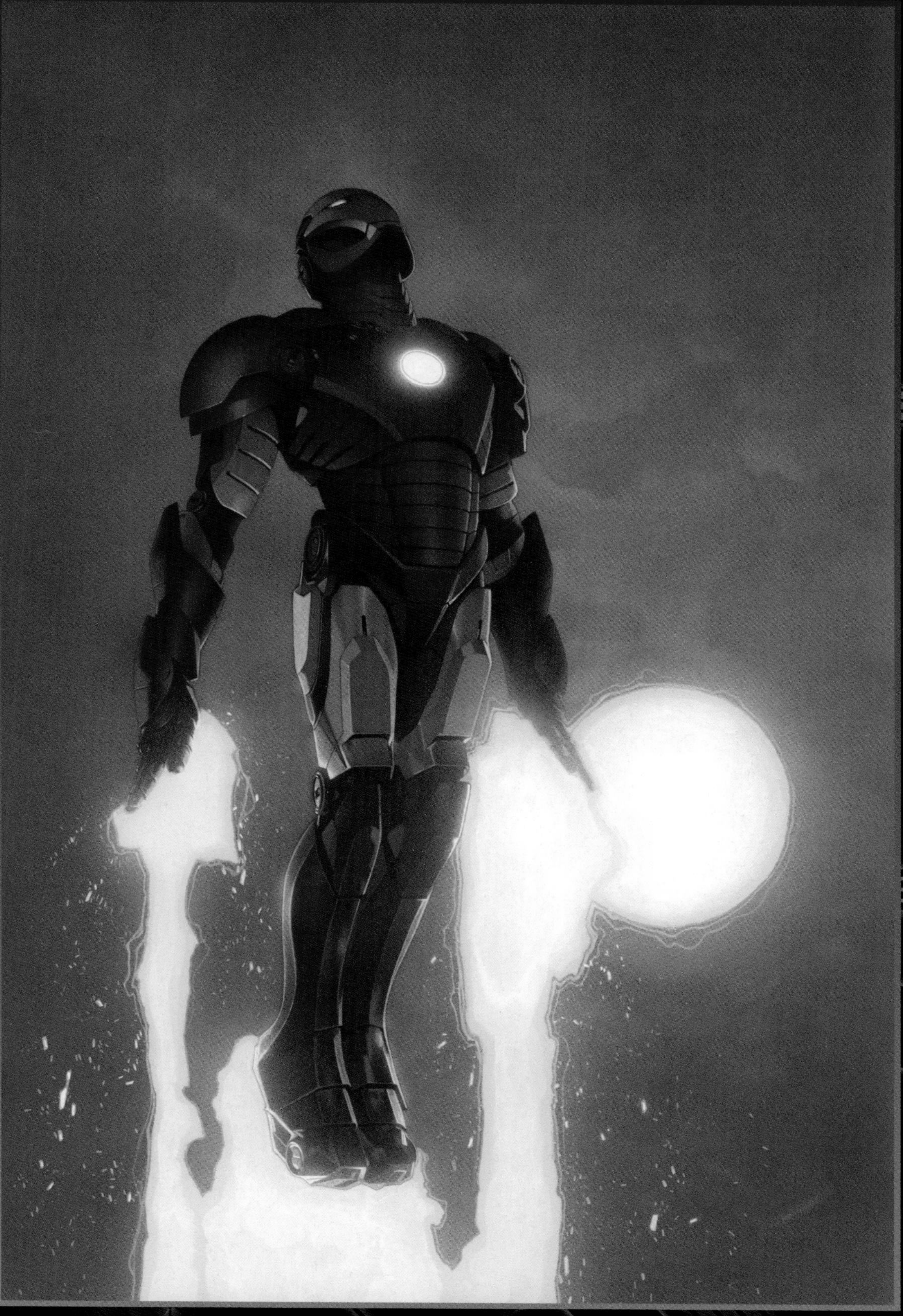

#3 VARIANT BY TRAVIS CHAREST

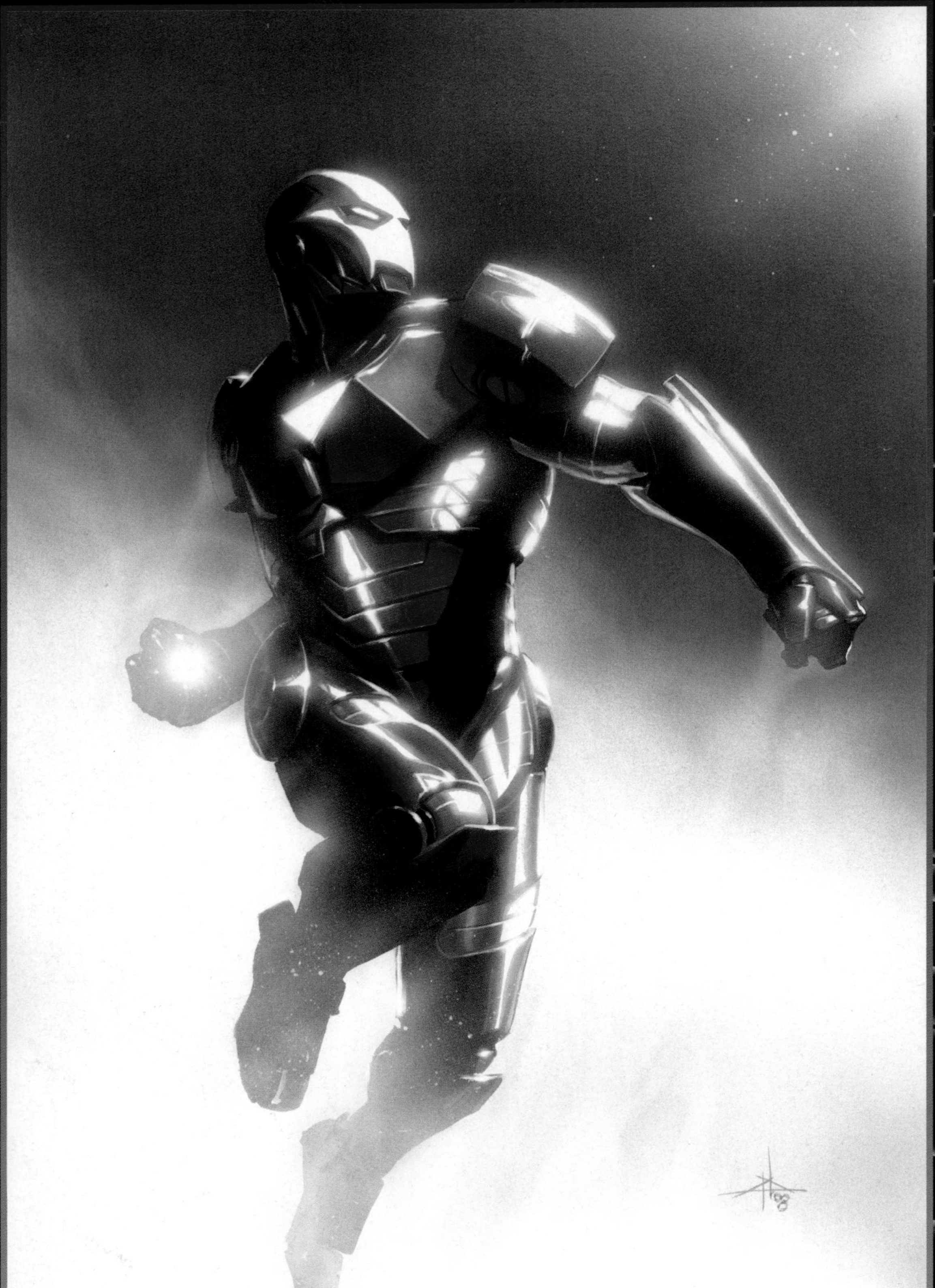

**#4 VARIANT** BY GABRIELE DELL'OTTO

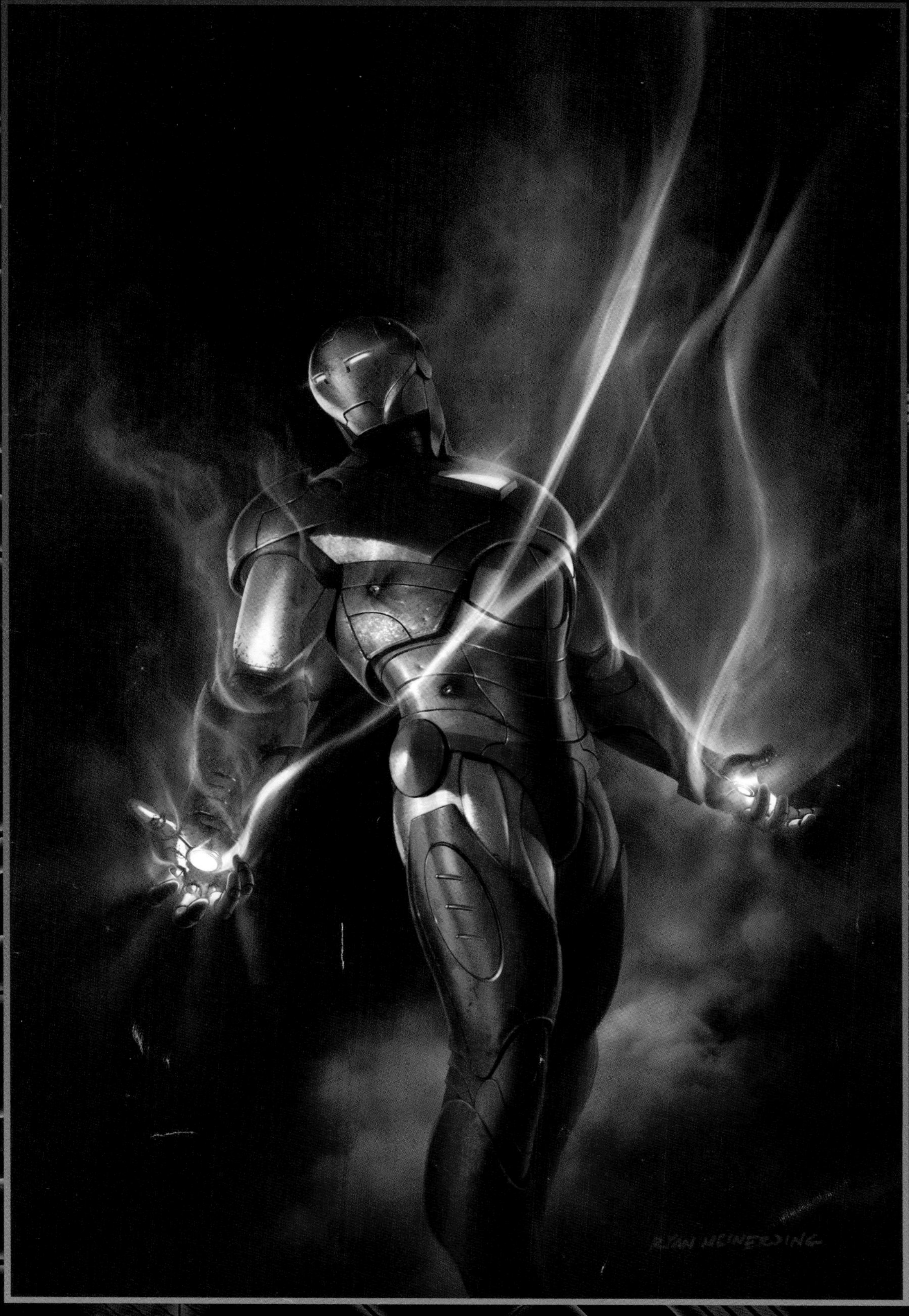
RYAN MEINERDING

**#5 VARIANT** BY RYAN MEINERDING

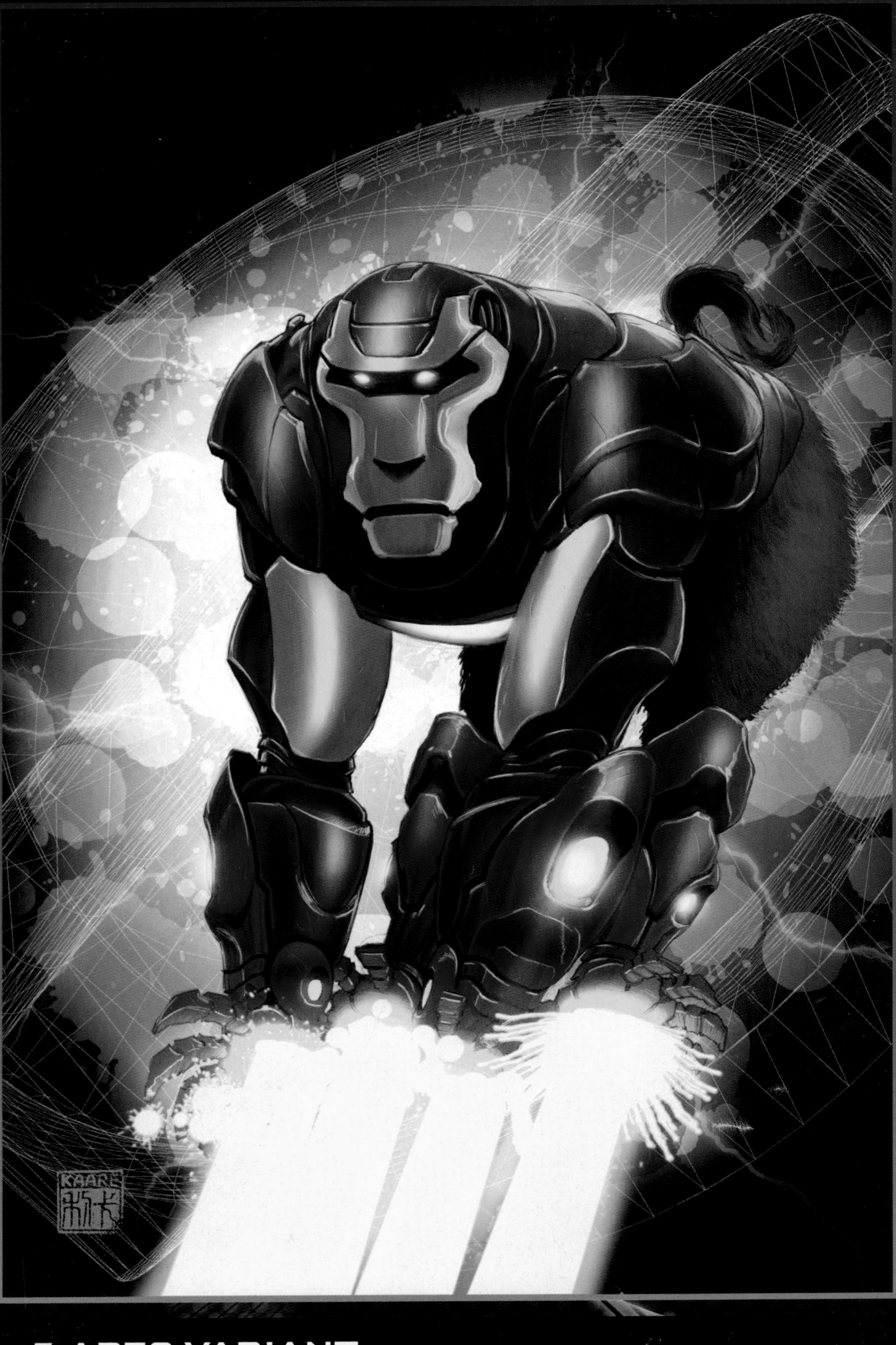
KAARE

#5 APES VARIANT BY KAARE ANDREWS

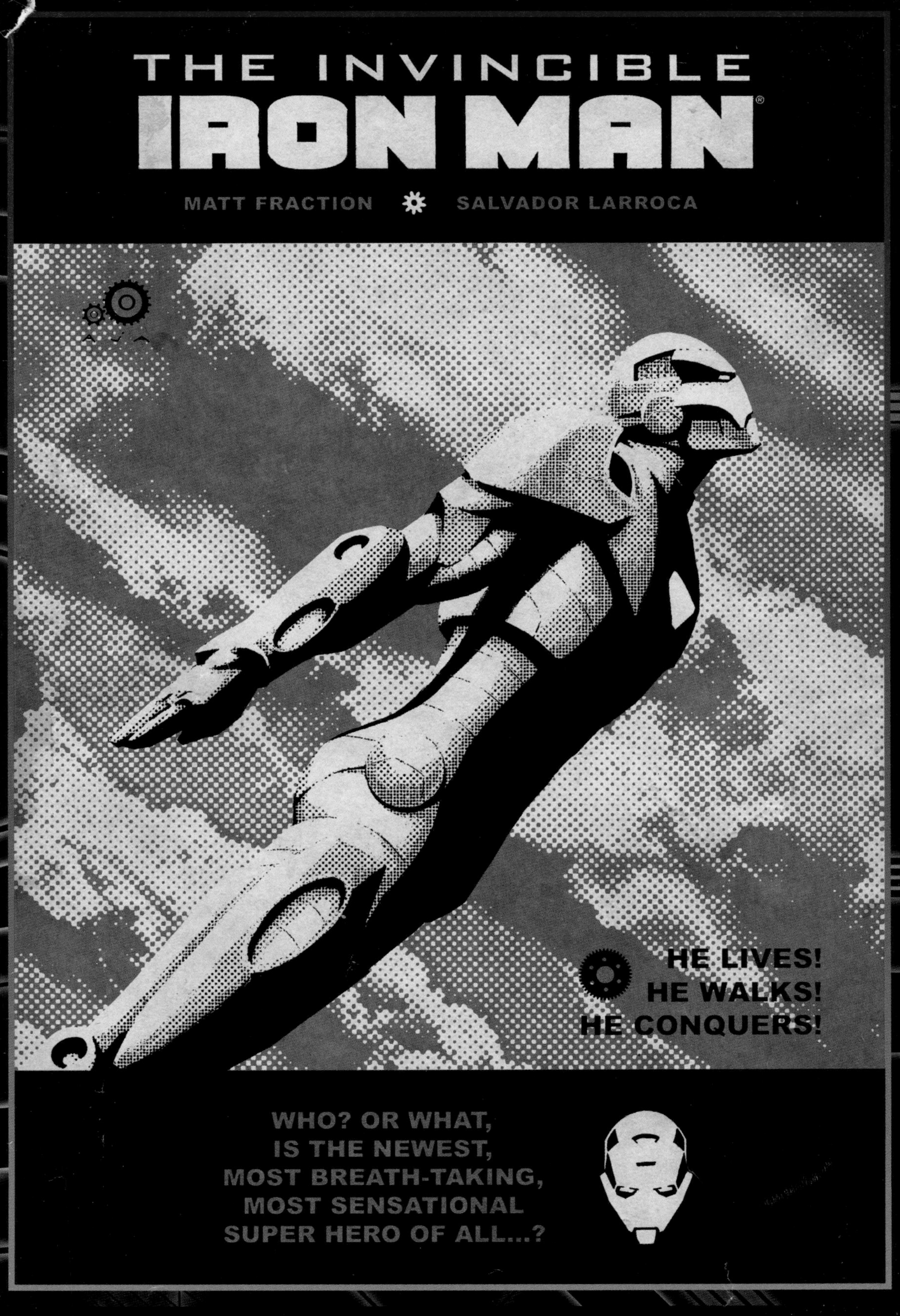
THE INVINCIBLE
IRON MAN
MATT FRACTION
SALVADOR LARROCA
HE LIVES!
HE WALKS!
HE CONQUERS!
WHO? OR WHAT,
IS THE NEWEST,
MOST BREATH-TAKING,
MOST SENSATIONAL
SUPER HERO OF ALL...?

#6 VARIANT BY DAVID AJA

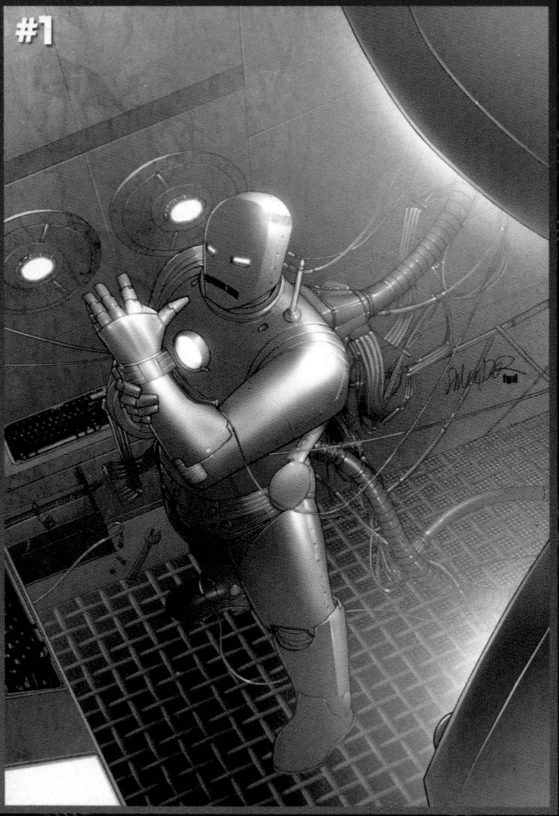
#1

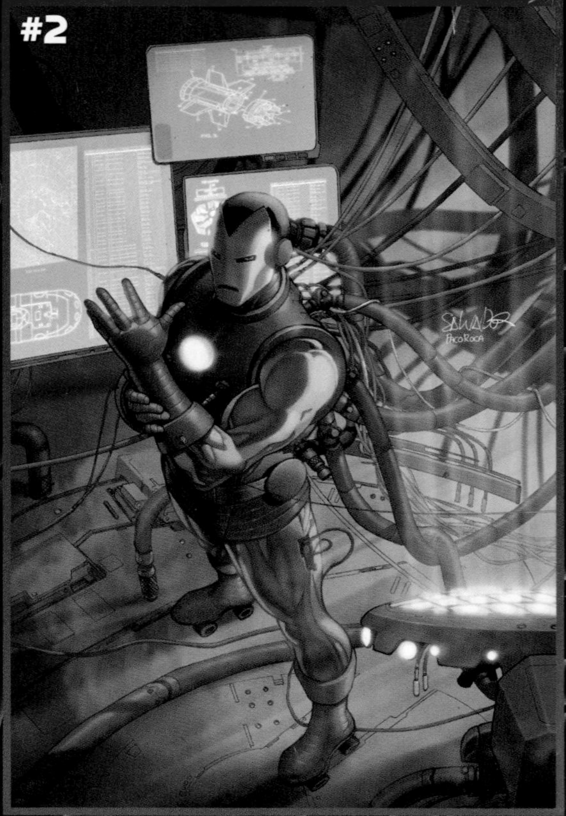
#2

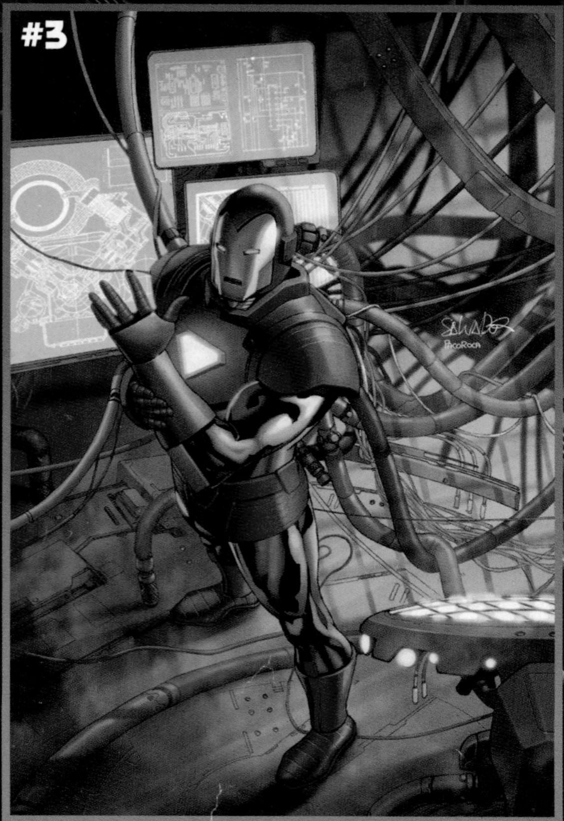
#3

## 2ND-PRINTING VARIANTS
BY SALVADOR LARROCA